Implementing Splunk: Big Data Reporting and Development for Operational Intelligence

Learn to transform your machine data into valuable
IT and business insights with this comprehensive
and practical tutorial

Vincent Bumgarner

PUBLISHING

BIRMINGHAM - MUMBAI

Implementing Splunk: Big Data Reporting and Development for Operational Intelligence

First published: January 2013

Production Reference: 1140113

Published by Packt Publishing Ltd.
Livery Place
35 Livery Street
Birmingham B3 2PB, UK.

ISBN 978-1-84969-328-8

www.packtpub.com

Cover Image by Vincent Bumgarner (vincent.bumgarner@gmail.com)

Credits

Author
Vincent Bumgarner

Reviewers
Mathieu Dessus
Cindy McCririe
Nick Mealy

Acquisition Editor
Kartikey Pandey

Lead Technical Editor
Azharuddin Sheikh

Technical Editors
Charmaine Pereira
Varun Pius Rodrigues

Copy Editors
Brandt D'Mello
Aditya Nair
Alfida Paiva
Laxmi Subramanian
Ruta Waghmare

Project Coordinator
Anish Ramchandani

Proofreader
Martin Diver

Indexer
Tejal Soni

Graphics
Aditi Gajjar

Production Coordinator
Nitesh Thakur

Cover Work
Nitesh Thakur

About the Author

Vincent Bumgarner has been designing software for nearly 20 years, working in many languages on nearly as many platforms. He started using Splunk in 2007 and has enjoyed watching the product evolve over the years.

While working for Splunk, he helped many companies, training dozens of users to drive, extend, and administer this extremely flexible product. At least one person at every company he worked with asked for a book on Splunk, and he hopes his effort helps fill their shelves.

I would like to thank my wife and kids as this book could not have happened without their support. A big thank you to all of the reviewers for contributing their time and expertise, and special thanks to SplunkNinja for the recommendation.

About the Reviewers

Mathieu Dessus is a security consultant for Verizon in France and acts as the SIEM leader for EMEA. With more than 12 years of experience in the security area, he has acquired a deep technical background in the management, design, assessment, and systems integration of information security technologies. He specializes in web security, Unix, SIEM, and security architecture design.

Cindy McCririe is a client architect at Splunk. In this role, she has worked with several of Splunk's enterprise customers, ensuring successful deployment of the technology. Many of these customers are using Splunk in unique ways. Sample use cases include PCI compliance, security, operations management, business intelligence, Dev/Ops, and transaction profiling.

Nick Mealy was an early employee at Splunk and worked as the Mad Scientist / Principal User Interface Developer at Splunk from March 2005 to September 2010. He led the technical design and development of the systems that power Splunk's search and reporting interfaces as well as on the general systems that power Splunk's configurable views and dashboards. In 2010, he left Splunk to found his current company, Sideview, which is creating new Splunk apps and new products on top of the Splunk platform. The most widely known of these products is the Sideview Utils app, which has become very widely deployed (and will be discussed in *Chapter 8, Building Advanced Dashboards*). Sideview Utils provides new UI modules and new techniques that make it easier for Splunk app developers and dashboard creators to create and maintain their custom views and dashboards.

www.PacktPub.com

Support files, eBooks, discount offers and more

You might want to visit `www.PacktPub.com` for support files and downloads related to your book.

Did you know that Packt offers eBook versions of every book published, with PDF and ePub files available? You can upgrade to the eBook version at `www.PacktPub.com` and as a print book customer, you are entitled to a discount on the eBook copy. Get in touch with us at `service@packtpub.com` for more details.

At `www.PacktPub.com`, you can also read a collection of free technical articles, sign up for a range of free newsletters and receive exclusive discounts and offers on Packt books and eBooks.

`http://PacktLib.PacktPub.com`

Do you need instant solutions to your IT questions? PacktLib is Packt's online digital book library. Here, you can access, read and search across Packt's entire library of books.

Why Subscribe?
- Fully searchable across every book published by Packt
- Copy and paste, print and bookmark content
- On demand and accessible via web browser

Free Access for Packt account holders

If you have an account with Packt at `www.PacktPub.com`, you can use this to access PacktLib today and view nine entirely free books. Simply use your login credentials for immediate access.

Table of Contents

Preface

Splunk is a powerful tool for collecting, storing, alerting, reporting, and studying machine data. This machine data usually comes from server logs, but it could also be collected from other sources. Splunk is by far the most flexible and scalable solution available to tackle the huge problem of making machine data useful.

The goal of this book is to serve as an organized and curated guide to Splunk 4.3. As the documentation and community resources available for Splunk are vast, finding the important pieces of knowledge can be daunting at times. My goal is to present what is needed for an effective implementation of Splunk in as concise and useful a manner as possible.

What this book covers

Chapter 1, The Splunk Interface, walks the reader through the user interface elements.

Chapter 2, Understanding Search, covers the basics of the search language, paying particular attention to writing efficient queries.

Chapter 3, Tables, Charts, and Fields, shows how to use fields for reporting, then covers the process of building our own fields.

Chapter 4, Simple XML Dashboards, first uses the Splunk web interface to build our first dashboards. It then examines how to build forms and more efficient dashboards.

Chapter 5, Advanced Search Examples, walks the reader through examples of using Splunk's powerful search language in interesting ways.

Chapter 6, Extending Search, exposes a number of features in Splunk to help you categorize events and act upon search results in powerful ways.

Chapter 7, Working with Apps, covers the concepts of an app, helps you install a couple of popular apps, and then helps you build your own app.

Chapter 8, Building Advanced Dashboards, explains the concepts of advanced XML dashboards, and covers practical ways to transition from simple XML to advanced XML dashboards.

Chapter 9, Summary Indexes and CSV Files, introduces the concept of summary indexes, and how they can be used to increase performance. It also discusses how CSV files can be used in interesting ways.

Chapter 10, Configuring Splunk, explains the structure and meaning of common configurations in Splunk. It also explains the process of merging configurations in great detail.

Chapter 11, Advanced Deployments, covers common questions about multimachine Splunk deployments, including data inputs, syslog, configuration management, and scaling up.

Chapter 12, Extending Splunk, demonstrates ways in which code can be used to extend Splunk for data input, external querying, rendering, custom commands, and custom actions.

What you need for this book

To work through the examples in this book, you will need an installation of Splunk, preferably a non-production instance. If you are already working with Splunk, then the concepts introduced by the examples should be applicable to your own data.

Splunk can be downloaded for free from `http://www.splunk.com/download`, for most popular platforms.

The sample code was developed on a Unix system, so you will probably have better luck using an installation of Splunk that is running on a Unix operating system. Knowledge of Python is necessary to follow some of the examples in the later chapters.

Who this book is for

This book should be useful for new users, seasoned users, dashboard designers, and system administrators alike. This book does not try to act as a replacement for the official Splunk documentation, but should serve as a shortcut for many concepts.

For some sections, a good understanding of regular expressions would be helpful. For some sections, the ability to read Python would be helpful.

Conventions

In this book, you will find a number of styles of text that distinguish between different kinds of information. Here are some examples of these styles, and an explanation of their meaning.

Code words in text are shown as follows: "If a field value looks like `key=value` in the text of an event, you will want to use one of the field widgets."

A block of code is set as follows:

```
index=myapplicationindex
(
  sourcetype=security
  AND
  (
    (bob NOT error)
    OR
    (mary AND warn)
  )
)
```

When we wish to draw your attention to a particular part of a code block, the relevant lines or items are set in bold:

```
<searchPostProcess>
  timechart span=1h sum(count) as "Error count" by network
</searchPostProcess>
<title>Dashboard - Errors - errors by network timechart</title>
```

Any command-line input or output is written as follows:

```
ERROR LogoutClass error, ERROR, Error! [user=mary, ip=3.2.4.5]
WARN AuthClass error, ERROR, Error! [user=mary, ip=1.2.3.3]
```

New terms and **important words** are shown in bold. Words that you see on the screen, in menus or dialog boxes for example, appear in the text like this: "Quickly create a simple dashboard using the wizard interface that we used before, by selecting **Create | Dashboard Panel**."

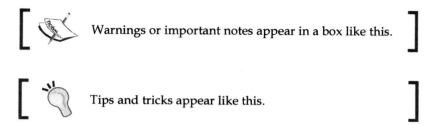

Warnings or important notes appear in a box like this.

Tips and tricks appear like this.

Reader feedback

Feedback from our readers is always welcome. Let us know what you think about this book—what you liked or may have disliked. Reader feedback is important for us to develop titles that you really get the most out of.

To send us general feedback, simply send an e-mail to feedback@packtpub.com, and mention the book title via the subject of your message.

If there is a topic that you have expertise in and you are interested in either writing or contributing to a book, see our author guide on www.packtpub.com/authors.

Customer support

Now that you are the proud owner of a Packt book, we have a number of things to help you to get the most from your purchase.

Downloading the example code

You can download the example code files for all Packt books you have purchased from your account at http://www.PacktPub.com. If you purchased this book elsewhere, you can visit http://www.PacktPub.com/support and register to have the files e-mailed directly to you.

Errata

Although we have taken every care to ensure the accuracy of our content, mistakes do happen. If you find a mistake in one of our books—maybe a mistake in the text or the code—we would be grateful if you would report this to us. By doing so, you can save other readers from frustration and help us improve subsequent versions of this book. If you find any errata, please report them by visiting http://www.packtpub.com/support, selecting your book, clicking on the **errata submission form** link, and entering the details of your errata. Once your errata are verified, your submission will be accepted and the errata will be uploaded on our website, or added to any list of existing errata, under the Errata section of that title. Any existing errata can be viewed by selecting your title from http://www.packtpub.com/support.

Piracy

Piracy of copyright material on the Internet is an ongoing problem across all media. At Packt, we take the protection of our copyright and licenses very seriously. If you come across any illegal copies of our works, in any form, on the Internet, please provide us with the location address or website name immediately so that we can pursue a remedy.

Please contact us at copyright@packtpub.com with a link to the suspected pirated material.

We appreciate your help in protecting our authors, and our ability to bring you valuable content.

Questions

You can contact us at questions@packtpub.com if you are having a problem with any aspect of the book, and we will do our best to address it.

The Splunk Interface

1

This chapter will walk you through the most common elements in the Splunk interface, and will touch upon concepts that are covered in greater detail in later chapters. You may want to dive right into search, but an overview of the user interface elements might save you some frustration later. We will walk through:

- Logging in and app selection
- A detailed explanation of the search interface widgets
- A quick overview of the admin interface

Logging in to Splunk

The Splunk interface is web-based, which means that no client needs to be installed. Newer browsers with fast Javascript engines, such as Chrome, Firefox, and Safari, work better with the interface.

As of Splunk Version 4.3, no browser extensions are required. Splunk Versions 4.2 and earlier require Flash to render graphs. Flash can still be used by older browsers, or for older apps that reference Flash explicitly.

The default port for a Splunk installation is 8000. The address will look like `http://mysplunkserver:8000` or `http://mysplunkserver.mycompany.com:8000`. If you have installed Splunk on your local machine, the address can be some variant of `http://localhost:8000`, `http://127.0.0.1:8000`, `http://machinename:8000`, or `http://machinename.local:8000`.

Once you determine the address, the first page you will see is the login screen.

The default username is *admin* with the password *changeme*. The first time you log in, you will be prompted to change the password for the admin user. It is a good idea to change this password to prevent unwanted changes to your deployment.

By default, accounts are configured and stored within Splunk. Authentication can be configured to use another system, for instance LDAP.

The Home app

After logging in, the default app is **Home**. This app is a launching pad for apps and tutorials.

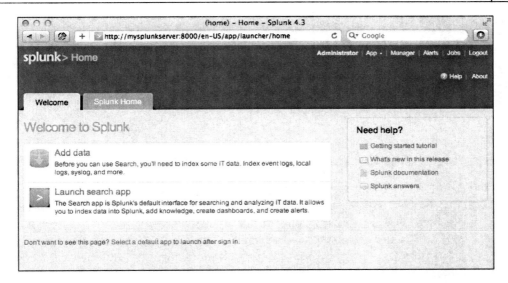

The **Welcome** tab provides two important shortcuts, **Add data** and **Launch search app**. These links appear again on the second tab, **Splunk Home**.

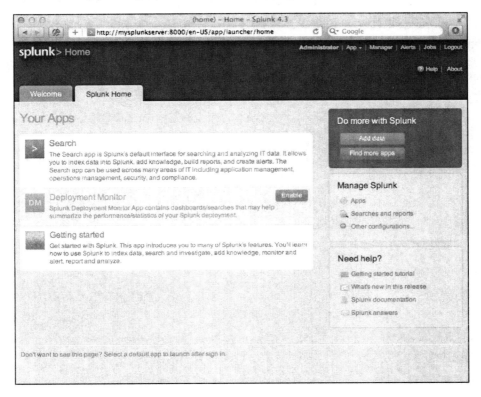

The **Your Apps** section shows the apps that have GUI elements on your instance of Splunk.

 App is an overloaded term in Splunk. An app doesn't necessarily have a GUI at all; it is simply a collection of configurations wrapped into a directory structure that means something to Splunk. We will discuss apps in a more detailed manner in *Chapter 7, Working with Apps*.

Under **Do more with Splunk**, we find:

- **Add data**: This links to the **Add Data to Splunk** page. This interface is a great start for getting local data flowing into Splunk. The new **Preview data** interface takes an enormous amount of complexity out of configuring dates and line breaking. We won't go through those interfaces here, but we will go through the configuration files that these wizards produce in *Chapter 10, Configuring Splunk*.

- **Find more apps**: This allows you to find and install more apps from **Splunkbase**. Splunkbase (http://splunk-base.splunk.com/) is a very useful community-driven resource where Splunk users and Splunk employees post questions, answers, code snippets, and apps.

Manage Splunk takes the user to the **Manager** section of Splunk. The **Manager** section is used to configure most aspects of Splunk. The options provided change depending on the capabilities of the user. We will use the **Manager** section throughout the book as we learn about different objects.

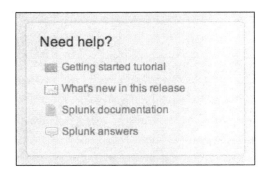

Getting started tutorial provides a quick but thorough overview of the major functionality of Splunk.

Splunk documentation takes you to the official Splunk documentation. The documentation, hosted at splunk.com, is truly vast.

Two quick notes about the Splunk documentation:

To get to documentation for search and reporting commands, quick help is provided while searching, and a link to the documentation for that command is provided through the interface.

When working directly with configuration files, the fastest route to the documentation for that file is to search for splunk name.conf using your favorite search engine. The documentation is almost always the first link.

Splunk answers goes to the Splunkbase site we just mentioned. Splunkbase and Splunk Answers used to be different sites but were merged into one site.

The top bar

The bar across the top of the window contains information about where you are as well as quick links to preferences, other apps, and administration.

The current app is specified in the upper-left corner.

Clicking on the Splunk logo or the text takes you to the default page for that app. In most apps, the text next to the logo is simply changed, but the whole block can be customized with logos and alternate text by modifying the app's CSS. We will cover this in *Chapter 7, Working with Apps*.

The upper-right corner of the window contains action links that are almost always available:

- The name of the user that is currently logged in appears first. In this case, the user is **Administrator**. Clicking on the username takes you to the **Your account** page.

- The **App** menu provides quick links to installed apps and to app administration. Only apps with GUI components that the current user has permissions to see will be listed in this menu.

- The **Manager** link is always available at the top of the window. The availability of options on the **Manager** page is controlled by the role of the user.

- The **Jobs** link pops up the **Jobs** window. The **Jobs** window provides a listing of current and past search jobs that have been run on this Splunk instance. It is useful for retrieving past results as well as determining what searches are using resources. We will discuss this interface in detail in *Chapter 2, Understanding Search*.

- **Logout** ends the session and forces the user to log in again.

The following screenshot shows what the **Your account** page looks like:

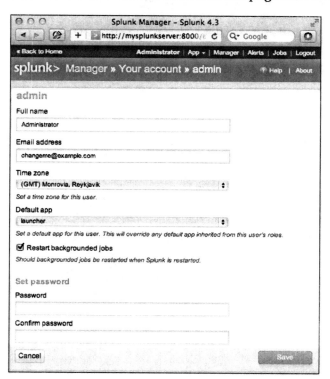

This form presents the global preferences that a user is allowed to change. Other settings that affect users are configured through permissions on objects and settings on roles.

- **Full name** and **Email address** are stored for the administrator's convenience.

- **Time zone** can be changed for each user. This is a new feature in Splunk 4.3.

 Setting the time zone only affects the time zone used to display the data. It is very important that the date is parsed properly when events are indexed. We will discuss this in detail in *Chapter 2, Understanding Search*.

- **Default app** controls where you first land after login. Most users will want to change this to **search**.

- **Restart backgrounded jobs** controls whether unfinished queries should run again if Splunk is restarted.

- **Set password** allows you to change your password. This is only relevant if Splunk is configured to use internal authentication. For instance, if the system is configured to use Windows Active Directory via LDAP (a very common configuration), users must change their password in Windows.

Search app

The search app is where most actions in Splunk start.

Data generator

If you want to follow the examples that appear in the next few chapters, install the *ImplementingSplunkDataGenerator* demo app by following these steps:

1. Download *ImplementingSplunkDataGenerator.tar.gz* from the code bundle available on the site `http://www.packtpub.com/support`.

2. Choose **Manage apps...** from the **Apps** menu.

3. Click on the button labeled **Install app from file**.

4. Click on **Choose File**, select the file, and then click on **Upload**.

This data generator app will produce about 16 megabytes of output per day. The app can be disabled so that it stops producing data by using **Manage apps...**, under the **App** menu.

The Summary view

The user is initially presented with the **Summary** view, which contains information about what data that user searches by default. This is an important distinction—in a mature Splunk installation, not all users will always search all data by default.

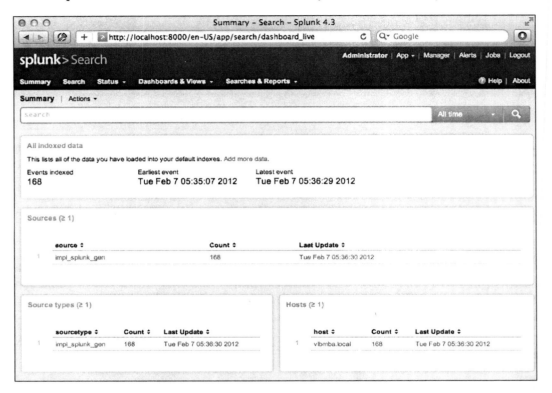

Let's start below the app name and discuss all the new widgets. The first widget is the navigation bar.

On most pages we encounter from now on, you will see this navigation bar. Items with downward triangles are menus. Items without a downward triangle are links. We will cover customizing the navigation bar in *Chapter 7, Working with Apps*.

Next we find the search bar. This is where the magic starts. We'll go into great detail shortly.

The **All indexed data** panel shows statistics for all indexed data. Remember that this only reflects indexes that this particular user searches by default. There are other events that are indexed by Splunk, including events Splunk indexes about itself. We will discuss indexes in *Chapter 9, Building Advanced Dashboards*.

The next three panels give a breakdown of your data using three important pieces of metadata—**source**, **sourcetype**, and **host**.

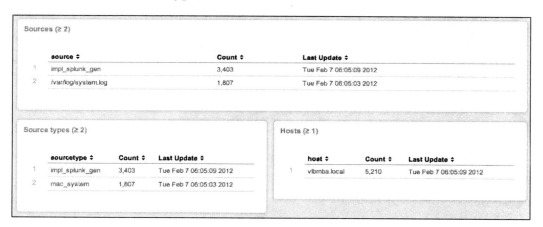

A **source** in Splunk is a unique path or name. In a large installation, there may be thousands of machines submitting data, but all data at the same path across these machines counts as one source. When the data source is not a file, the value of the source can be arbitrary, for instance the name of a script or network port.

A **source type** is an arbitrary categorization of events. There may be many sources across many hosts in the same source type. For instance, given the sources `/var/log/access.2012-03-01.log` and `/var/log/access.2012-03-02.log` on the hosts `fred` and `wilma`, you could reference all of these logs with source type access or any other name you like.

A **host** is a captured hostname for an event. In majority of the cases, the **host** field is set to the name of the machine where the data originated. There are cases where this is not known, so the host can also be configured arbitrarily.

Search

We've finally made it to search. This is where the real power of Splunk lies.

For our first search, we will search for the word error. Click in the search bar, type the word error, and then either press *Enter* or click on the magnifying glass on the right of the bar.

Upon initiating the search, we are taken to the search results page.

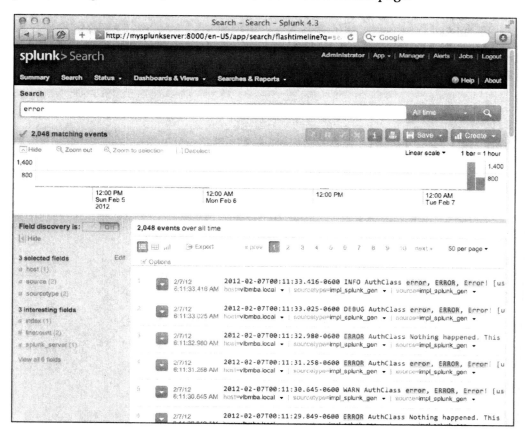

Note that the URL in the browser has changed to **flashtimeline**. You may see references to flashtimeline from time to time. It is simply another name for the search interface.

See the *Using the time picker* section for details on changing the time frame of your search.

Actions

Let's inspect the elements on this page. Below the search bar itself, we have the event count, actions icons, and menus.

Starting at the left, we have:

- The number of events matched by the base search. Technically, this may not be the number of results pulled from disk, depending on your search. Also, if your query uses commands, this number may not match what is shown in the event listing.
- **Send to background** ( ), which sends the currently running search to the background, where it will continue to run. Jobs sent to the background and past jobs can be restored from the **Jobs** window.
- **Pause** ( ), which causes the current search to stop locating events but keeps the job open. This is useful if you want to inspect the current results to determine whether you want to continue a long running search.
- **Finalize** ( ), which stops the execution of the current search but keeps the results generated so far. This is useful when you have found enough and want to inspect or share the results found so far.
- **Cancel** ( ), which stops the execution of the current search and immediately deletes the results.
- **Job Inspector** ( ), which opens the **Search job inspector** window, which provides very detailed information about the query that was run.
- **Print** ( ), which formats the page for printing and instructs the browser to print.

- **Save**, which provides different options for saving the search or the results. We will discuss this later in this chapter.
- **Create**, which provides wizard-like interfaces for building different objects from this search. We will discuss these options in *Chapter 4, Simple XML Dashboards*.

Timeline

Below the actions icons, we have the timeline.

Along with providing a quick overview of the event distribution over a period of time, the timeline is also a very useful tool for selecting sections of time. Placing the pointer over the timeline displays a pop up for the number of events in that slice of time. Clicking on the timeline selects the events for a particular slice of time.

Clicking and dragging selects a range of time.

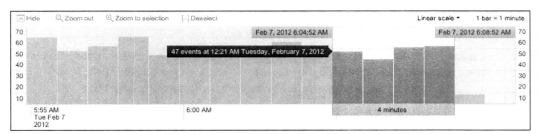

Once you have selected a period of time, clicking on **Zoom to selection** changes the time frame and re-runs the search for that specific slice of time. Repeating this process is an effective way to drill down to specific events.

Deselect shows all events for the time range selected in the time picker.

Zoom out changes the timeframe to a larger timeframe around the events in the current timeframe.

The field picker

To the left of the search results, we find the field picker. This is a great tool for discovering patterns and filtering search results.

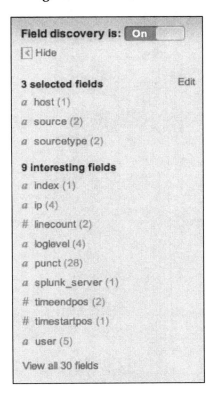

Fields

The fields list contains two lists:

- Selected fields, which have their values displayed under the search event in the search results
- Interesting fields, which are other fields that Splunk has picked out for you

The **Edit** link next to selected fields and the **View all 30 fields** link at the bottom of the field picker both take you to the **Fields** window.

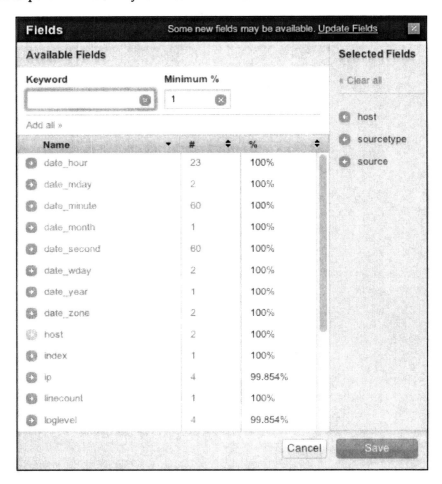

Search results

We are almost through all of the widgets on the page. We still have a number of items to cover in the search results section though, just to be thorough.

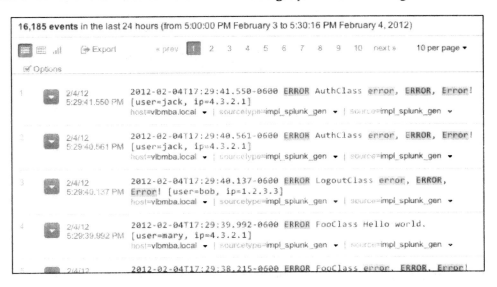

Starting at the top of this section, we have the number of events displayed. When viewing all results in their raw form, this number will match the number above the timeline. This value can be changed either by making a selection on the timeline or by using other search commands.

Next, we have actions that affect these particular results. Starting at the left we have:

- **Events List** ( ), which will show the raw events. This is the default view when running a simple search, as we have done so far.

- **Table** ( ), which shows a table view of the results. This is the default view when any reporting commands are used. When looking at raw events, this view will show a table with the time of the event, any selected fields, and finally the raw event.

- **Results Chart** ( ), which shows a chart, if the data allows. For simple searches, charts don't make sense, but they are very useful for reporting.

- **Export**, which allows you to export these particular results to CSV, Raw events, XML, or JSON. New to Splunk 4.3 is the ability to export an unlimited number of results from the web interface.

- **Options** presents display options for the event viewer. See the following section for a discussion about these options.

- To the right, you can choose a page of results and change the number of events per page.

Options

The items presented in the options pop up deserve a short discussion.

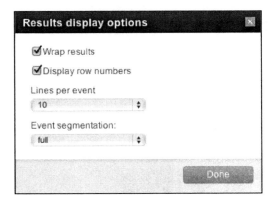

- **Wrap results** controls whether events are wrapped at the right edge of the browser window.

- **Display row numbers** toggles the display of the row number to the left of each event.

- **Lines per event** changes the maximum number of lines of an event displayed in the browser per event. There are a few things to note here:

    ° All lines of the event are indexed and searchable

    ° If the value for this setting is too large, and if a search returns many large messages, your browser may have trouble rendering what it is told to display

    ° Events with many lines will have a link at the bottom to see more lines in the event

- The most interesting option here is **Event segmentation**. This setting changes what text is highlighted as you mouse over events. We will discuss this further in *Chapter 2, Understanding Search*.

Events viewer

Finally, we make it to the actual events. Let's examine a single event.

Starting at the left, we have:

- The event number: Raw search results are always returned in the order "most recent first".

- The event options menu (): This menu contains workflow actions, a few of which are always available.

    ° **Build Eventtype**: Event types are a way to name events that match a certain query. We will dive into event types in *Chapter 6, Extending Search*.

    ° **Extract Fields**: This launches an interface for creating custom field extractions. We will cover field extraction in *Chapter 3, Tables, Charts, and Fields*.

    ° **Show Source**: This pops up a window with a simulated view of the original source.

- Next appear any workflow actions that have been configured. Workflow actions let you create new searches or links to other sites using data from an event. We will discuss workflow actions in *Chapter 6, Extending Search*.

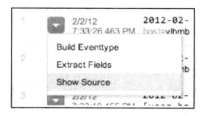

- Next comes the parsed date from this event, displayed in the time zone selected by the user. This is an important and often confusing distinction. In most installations, everything is in one time zone—the servers, the user, and the events. When one of these three things is not in the same time zone as the others, things can get confusing. We will discuss time in great detail in *Chapter 2, Understanding Search*.

- Next, we see the raw event itself. This is what Splunk saw as an event. With no help, Splunk can do a good job finding the date and breaking lines appropriately, but as we will see later, with a little help, event parsing can be more reliable and more efficient.

- Below the event are the fields that were selected in the field picker. Clicking on the value adds the field value to the search. Each field value also has a menu:

  - `Tag fieldname=value` allows you to create a tag that can be used for classification of events. We will discuss tags in *Chapter 6, Extending Search*.

  - **Report on field** launches a wizard showingv the values of this field over time.

  - Workflow actions can also appear in these field menus, allowing you to create actions that link to new searches or external sites by using a particular field value.

Using the time picker

Now that we've looked through all of the widgets, let's use them to modify our search. First we will change our time. The default setting of **All time** is fine when there are few events, but when Splunk has been gathering events for weeks or months, this is less than optimal. Let's change our search time to one hour.

The search will run again, and now we only see results for the last hour. Let's try a custom time. **Date** is the first option.

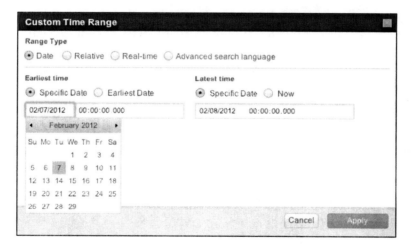

If you know specifically when an event happened, you can drill down to whatever time range you want here. We will examine the other options in *Chapter 2, Understanding Search*.

 The time zone used in **Custom Time Range** is the time zone selected in the user's preferences, which is by default the time zone of the Splunk server.

Using the field picker

The field picker is very useful for investigating and navigating data. Clicking on any field in the field picker pops open a panel with a wealth of information about that field in the results of your search.

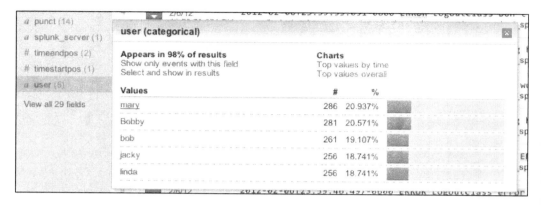

Looking through the information, we observe:

- *Appears in X% of results* tells you how many events contain a value for this field.

- **Show only events with this field** will modify the query to only show events that have this field defined.

- **Select and show in results** is a shortcut for adding a field to your selected fields.

- **Top values by time** and **Top values overall** present graphs about the data in this search. This is a great way to dive into reporting and graphing. We will use this as a launching point later.

- The chart below the links is actually a quick representation of the top values overall. Clicking on a value adds that value to the query. Let's click on **mary**.

This will rerun the search, now looking for errors that affect only the user mary. Going back to the field picker and clicking on other fields will filter the results even more. You can also click on words in the results, or values of fields displayed underneath events.

Using Manager

The **Manager** section, in a nutshell, is an interface for managing configuration files. The number of files and options in these configuration files is truly daunting, so the web interface concentrates on the most commonly used options across the different configuration types.

> Splunk is controlled exclusively by plain text configuration files. Feel free to take a look at the configuration files that are being modified as you make changes in the admin interface. You will find them in $SPLUNK_HOME/etc/system/local/ and $SPLUNK_HOME/etc/apps/.
>
> You may notice configuration files with the same name in different locations. We will cover, in detail, the different configuration files, their purposes, and how these configurations merge together, in *Chapter 10, Configuring Splunk*. Don't start modifying the configurations directly until you understand what they do and how they merge.

Clicking on **Manager**, on the top bar, takes you to the **Manager** page.

The options are organized into logical groupings, as follows:

- **Apps**: This interface allows you to easily add new apps and manage apps that are currently installed. If you installed the *ImplementingSplunkDataGenerator* app, you have already seen this interface.

- **Knowledge**: Each of the links under **Knowledge** allows you to control one of the many object types that are used at search time. The following screenshot shows an example of one object type, workflow actions.

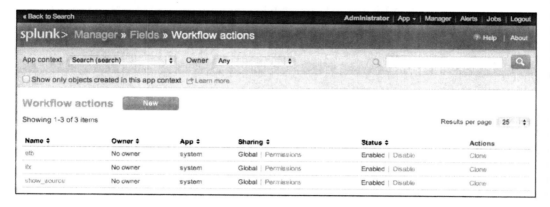

Let's cover the administration of each object type that we will cover in later chapters:

- **System**: The options under this section control system-wide settings.
    - ○ **System settings** covers network settings, the default location to store indexes, outbound e-mail server settings, and how much data Splunk logs about itself
    - ○ **Server controls** contains a single page that lets you restart Splunk from the web interface
    - ○ **Licensing** lets you add license files or configure Splunk as a slave to a Splunk license server

- **Data**: This section is where you manage data flow.
    - ○ **Data Inputs**: Splunk can receive data by reading files (either in batch mode or in real time), listening to network ports, or running scripts

- **Forwarding and receiving**: Splunk instances don't typically stand alone. Most installations consist of at least one Splunk indexer and many Splunk forwarders. Using this interface, you can configure each side of this relationship and more complicated setups (we will discuss this in a more detail in *Chapter 11, Advanced Deployments*):

- ◦ **Indexes**: An Index is essentially a datastore. Under the covers, it is simply a set of directories, created and managed by Splunk. For small installations, a single index is usually acceptable. For larger installations, using multiple indexes allows flexibility in security, retention, and performance tuning, and better use of hardware. We will discuss this further in *Chapter 10, Configuring Splunk*.

- **Deployment**: The two options here relate to distributed deployments. (we will cover these options in detail in *Chapter 11, Advanced Deployments*):

  - ◦ **Distributed Search**: Any Splunk instance running searches can utilize itself and other Splunk instances to retrieve results. This interface allows you to configure access to other Splunk instances.

  - ◦ **Deployment**: Splunk includes a deployment server component to aid in distributing configurations to the many instances that can be involved in a distributed installation. There is no need to use the deployment server, particularly if you already have something to manage configurations.

- **Users and authentication**: This section provides authentication controls and an account link.

  - ◦ **Access controls**: This section is for controlling how Splunk authenticates users and what users are allowed to see and do. We will discuss this further in *Chapter 10, Configuring Splunk*.

  - ◦ **Your account**: We saw this earlier when we clicked on the name of the user currently logged in on the top bar.

Summary

As you have seen in this chapter, the Splunk GUI provides a rich interface for working with search results. We have really only scratched the surface and will cover more elements as we use them in later chapters.

In the next chapter, we will dive into the nuts and bolts of how search works, so that you can make efficient searches to populate the cool reports we will make in *Chapter 3, Tables, Charts, and Fields*, and beyond.

2

Understanding Search

To successfully use Splunk, it is vital that you write effective searches. Using the index efficiently will make your initial discoveries faster, and the reports you create will run faster for you and others. In this chapter, we will cover:

- How to write effective searches
- How to search using fields
- Understanding time
- Saving and sharing searches

Using search terms effectively

The key to creating an effective search is to take advantage of the index. Splunk's index is effectively a huge word index, sliced by time. The single most important factor for the performance of your searches is how many events are pulled from disk. The following few key points should be committed to memory:

- **Search terms are case insensitive**: Searches for error, Error, ERROR, and ErRoR are all the same thing.

- **Search terms are additive**: Given the search item mary error, only events that contain *both* words will be found. There are Boolean and grouping operators to change this behavior; we will discuss these later.

- **Only the time frame specified is queried**: This may seem obvious, but it's a big difference from a database, which would always have a single index across all events in a table. Since each index is sliced into new buckets over time, only the buckets that contain events for the time frame in question need to be queried.

- **Search terms are words, not parts of words**: A search for foo will not match foobar.

With just these concepts, you can write fairly effective searches. Let's dig a little deeper, though:

- **A word is anything surrounded by whitespace or punctuation**: For instance, given the log line 2012-02-07T01:03:31.104-0600 INFO AuthClass Hello world. [user=Bobby, ip=1.2.3.3], the "words" indexed are 2012, 02, 07T01, 03, 31, 104, 0600, INFO, AuthClass, Hello, world, user, Bobby, ip, 1, 2, 3, and 3. This may seem strange, and possibly a bit wasteful, but this is what Splunk's index is really *really* good at—dealing with huge numbers of words across huge numbers of events.

- **Splunk is not grep with an interface**: One of the most common questions is whether Splunk uses regular expressions for search. Technically, the answer is no, but most of what you would do with regular expressions is available in other ways. Using the index as it is designed is the best way to build fast searches. Regular expressions can then be used to further filter results or extract fields.

- **Numbers are not numbers until after they have been parsed at search time**: This means that searching for foo>5 will not use the index as the value of foo is not known until it has been parsed out of the event at search time. There are different ways to deal with this behavior, depending on the question you're trying to answer.

- **Field names are case sensitive**: When searching for host=myhost, host must be lowercase. Likewise, any extracted or configured fields have case sensitive field names, but the values are case insensitive.
  - Host=myhost will not work
  - host=myhost will work
  - host=MyHost will work

- **Fields do not have to be defined before indexing data**: An **indexed field** is a field that is added to the metadata of an event at index time. There are legitimate reasons to define indexed fields, but in the vast majority of cases it is unnecessary and is actually wasteful. We will discuss this in *Chapter 3, Tables, Charts, and Fields*.

Boolean and grouping operators

There are a few operators that you can use to refine your searches (note that these operators *must* be in uppercase to not be considered search terms):

- **AND** is implied between terms. error mary is the same as error AND mary.

- **OR** allows you to specify multiple values. `error OR mary` means "find any event that contains either word".

- **NOT** applies to the next term or group. `error NOT mary` would find events that contain `error` but do not contain `mary`.

- **""** identifies a phrase. `"Out of this world"` will find this exact sequence of words. `Out of this world` would find any event that contains *all* of these words, but not necessarily in that order.

- **( )** is used for grouping terms. Parentheses can help avoid confusion in logic. For instance, these two statements are equivalent:

  ° `bob error OR warn NOT debug`

  ° `(bob AND (error OR warn)) AND NOT debug`

- **=** is reserved for specifying fields. Searching for an equal sign can be accomplished by wrapping it in quotes.

- **[ ]** is used to perform a subsearch. We will discuss this in *Chapter 5, Advanced Search Examples*.

You can use these operators in fairly complicated ways, if you want to be very specific, or even to find multiple sets of events in a single query. The following are a few examples:

- `error mary NOT jacky`

- `error NOT (mary warn) NOT (jacky error)`

- `index=myapplicationindex ( sourcetype=sourcetype1 AND ( (bob NOT error) OR (mary AND warn) ) ) OR ( sourcetype=sourcetype2 (jacky info) )`

This can also be written with some whitespace for clarity:

```
index=myapplicationindex
(
  sourcetype=security
  AND
  (
    (bob NOT error)
    OR
    (mary AND warn)
  )
)
OR
(
  sourcetype=application
  (jacky info)
)
```

Downloading the example code

You can download the example code files for all Packt books you have purchased from your account at `http://www.PacktPub.com`. If you purchased this book elsewhere, you can visit `http://www.PacktPub.com/support` and register to have the files e-mailed directly to you.t

Clicking to modify your search

Though you can probably figure it out by just clicking around, it is worth discussing the behavior of the GUI when moving your mouse around and clicking.

- Clicking on any word or field value will add that term to the search.
- Clicking on a word or field value that is already in the query will remove it from the query.
- Clicking on any word or field value while holding down *Alt* (option on the Mac) will append that search term to the query, preceded by NOT. This is a very handy way to remove irrelevant results from query results.

Event segmentation

In *Chapter 1, The Splunk Interface*, we touched upon this setting in the **Options** dialog. The different options change what is highlighted as you mouse over the text in the search results, and therefore what is added to your query when clicked on. Let's see what happens to the phrase `ip=10.20.30.40` with each setting:

- **inner** highlights individual words between punctuation. Highlighted items would be **ip, 10, 20, 30**, and **40**.
- **outer** highlights everything between whitespace. The entire phrase **ip=10.20.30.40** would be highlighted.
- **full** will highlight everything from the beginning of the block of text as you move your mouse. Rolling from left to right would highlight **ip**, then **ip=10**, then **ip=10.20**, then **ip=10.20.30**, and finally **ip=10.20.30.40**. This is the default setting and works well for most data.
- **raw** disables highlighting completely, allowing the user to simply select the text at will. Some users will prefer this setting as it takes away any unexpected behavior. It is also slightly faster as the browser is doing less work.

Field widgets

Clicking on values in the field picker or in the field value widgets underneath an event will append the field value to a query. For instance, if **ip=10.20.30.40** appears under your event, clicking on the value will append **ip=10.20.30.40** to your query.

If a field value looks like key=value in the text of an event, you will want to use one of the field widgets instead of clicking on the raw text of the event. Depending on your event segmentation setting, clicking on the word will either add value or "key=value". The former will not take advantage of the field definition; instead, it will simply search for the word. The latter will work for events that contain the exact quoted text but not for other events that actually contain the same field value extracted in a different way.

Time

Clicking on the time next to an event will change the search to only find events that happened in that second.

 To zoom in to a short time frame, one convenient approach is to click on the time of an event to search only that second, then click on **Zoom out** above the timeline until the appropriate time frame is reached.

Using fields to search

When we explored the GUI in *Chapter 1*, *The Splunk Interface*, you probably noticed fields everywhere. Fields appear in the field picker on the left and under every event. Where fields actually come from is transparent to the user, who simply searches for key=value. We will discuss adding new fields in *Chapter 3*, *Tables, Charts, and Fields*, and in *Chapter 10*, *Configuring Splunk*.

Using the field picker

The field picker gives us easy access to the fields currently defined for the results of our query. Clicking on any field presents us with details about that field in our current search results.

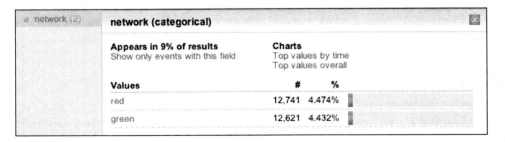

As we go through the following items in this widget, we see a wealth of information right away:

- *Appears in X% of results* is a good indication of whether we are getting the results we think we're getting. If every event in your results should contain this field, and this is not 100 percent, either your search can be made more specific or a field definition needs to be modified.
- **Show only events with this field** adds `fieldname="*"` to your existing search to make sure you only get events that have this field.

> If the events you are searching for always contain the name of the field, in this case `network`, your query will be more efficient if you also add the field name to the query. In this case, the query would look like this: `sourcetype="impl_splunk_gen" network="*" network`.

- **Select and show in results** adds the field to the **selected fields** list at the top of the field picker and displays the field value under each event.
- **Charts** contains the following links, which we will use as starting points for examples in *Chapter 3, Tables, Charts, and Fields*:
  1. **Top values by time** shows a graph of the most common values occurring in the time frame searched.
  2. **Top values overall** shows a table of the most common values for this field for the time frame searched.
- **Values** shows a very useful snapshot of the top ten most common values.

Using wildcards efficiently

Though the index is based on words, it is possible to use wildcards when needed, although some care must be taken.

Only trailing wildcards are efficient

Stated simply, `bob*` will find events containing `Bobby` efficiently, but `*by` or `*ob*` will not. The latter cases will scan all events in the time frame specified.

Wildcards are tested last

Wildcards are tested *after* all other terms. Given the search: `authclass *ob* hello world`, all other terms besides `*ob*` will be searched *first*. The more you can limit the results using full words and fields, the better your search will perform.

Supplementing wildcards in fields

Given the following events, a search for `world` would return both events:

```
2012-02-07T01:04:31.102-0600 INFO AuthClass Hello world. [user=Bobby,
ip=1.2.3.3]
2012-02-07T01:23:34.204-0600 INFO BarClass Goodbye. [user=Bobby,
ip=1.2.3.3, message="Out of this world"]
```

What if you only wanted the second event, but all you know is that the event contains `world` somewhere in the field `message`? The query `message="*world*"` would work but is very inefficient because Splunk must scan every event looking for `*world*` and then determine whether `world` is in the field `message`.

You can take advantage of the behavior mentioned before — wildcards are tested last. Rewriting the query as `world message="*world*"` gives Splunk a chance to find all records with `world`, then inspect those events for the more specific wildcard condition.

All about time

Time is an important and confusing topic in Splunk. If you want to skip this section, absorb one concept — time *must* be parsed properly on the way into the index as it cannot be changed later without indexing the raw data again.

How Splunk parses time

Given the date `11-03-04`, how would you interpret this date? Your answer probably depends on where you live. In the United States, you would probably read this as November 3, 2004. In Europe, you would probably read this as March 11, 2004. It would also be reasonable to read this as March 4, 2011.

Luckily, most dates are not this ambiguous, and Splunk makes a good effort. It is absolutely worth the trouble to give Splunk a little help by configuring the time format. We'll discuss the relevant configurations in *Chapter 10, Configuring Splunk*.

How Splunk stores time

Once the date is parsed, the date stored in Splunk is always stored as GMT epoch. **Epoch time** is the number of seconds since January 1, 1970, the birthday of Unix. By storing all events using a single time zone, there is never a problem lining up events that happen in different time zones. This, of course, only works properly if the time zone of the event can be determined when it is indexed. This numeric value is stored in the field `_time`.

How Splunk displays time

The text of the original event, and the date it contains, is never modified. It is always displayed as it was received. The date displayed to the left of the event is determined by the time zone of the Splunk instance or the user's preference as specified in **Your account**.

How time zones are determined and why it matters

Since all events are stored according to their GMT time, the time zone of an event only matters at parse time, but it is vital to get it right. Once the event is written into the index, it cannot be changed without re-indexing the raw data.

The time zone can come from a number of places, in this order of precedence:

*   The time zone specified in the log. For instance, the date `2012-02-07T01:03:23.575-0600`, `-0600` indicates that the zone is 6 hours behind GMT. Likewise, `Tue 02 Feb, 01:03:23 CST 2012` represents the same date.

*   The configuration associated with a source, host, or source type, in that order. This is specified in `props.conf`. This can actually be used to override the time zone listed in the log itself, if needed. We will discuss this in *Chapter 10, Configuring Splunk.*

*   The time zone of the Splunk instance forwarding the events. The time zone is relayed along with the events, just in case it is not specified elsewhere. This is usually an acceptable default. The exception is when different logs are written with different time zones on the same host, without the time zone in the logs. In that case, it needs to be specified in `props.conf`.

*   The time zone of the Splunk instance parsing the events. This is sometimes acceptable and can be used in interesting ways in distributed environments.

The important takeaway, again, is that the time zone needs to be known at the time of parsing and indexing the event.

Different ways to search against time

Now that we have our time indexed properly, how do we search against time?
The time picker provides a neat set of defaults for relative time.

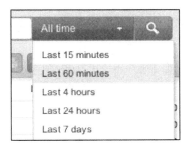

These options search back from the present to a relative point in time,
but sometimes, you need to search over a specific period of time.

The last option, **Custom time...**, provides an interface that helps specify
specific times.

- **Date** is the first option.

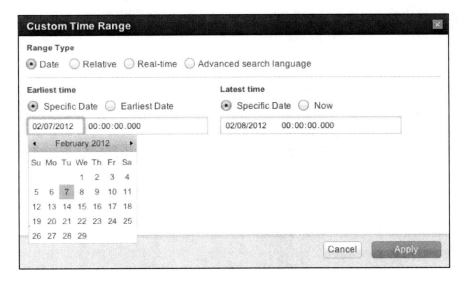

If you know specifically when an event happened, you can drill down to
whatever time range you want here. The time zone here is what you have
chosen in **Your account**, or the system default if you didn't change it. This
may not be the time zone of the events you are looking for.

- **Relative** lets you choose a time in the past.

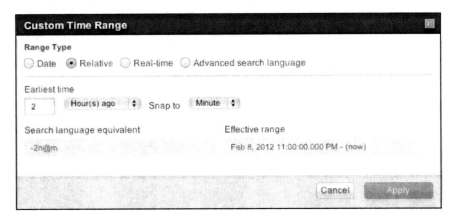

The end of the search will always be the current time. The **Snap to** option lets you choose a unit to round down to. For instance, if the current time is 4:32 and you choose 2 for the **Hour(s) ago** option, and **Hour** for the **Snap to** option, the earliest time for the search will be 2:00. **Effective range** will tell you what time range is being searched.

Note the text under **Search language equivalent**. This is the way you express relative times in Splunk. We will see this often as we move forward.

- Like **Relative** time, **Real-time** lets you choose a time in the past and shows you the search language equivalent. A real-time search is different in that it continues to run, continuously updating your query results, but only keeps the events with a parsed date that is newer than the time frame specified.

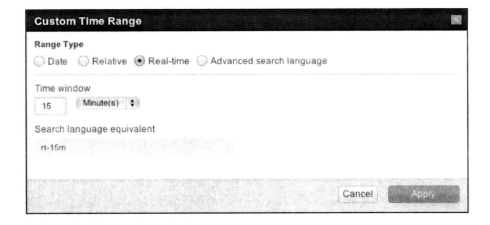

- Lastly, we have **Advanced search language**.

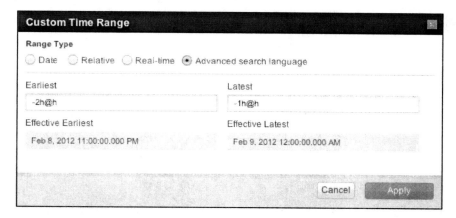

If you noticed, we have selected the **2** for the **Hour(s) ago** option, and **Minute** for the **Snap to** option in the **Relative** tab. The search language equivalent for this selection is **-2h@m**, which means "go back 2 hours (7,200 seconds) from this moment, and then snap to the beginning of the minute that second falls in". So, given the time 15:11:23, the relative time would 13:11:00. The language is very powerful and can be used whenever a search is specified.

Specifying time in-line in your search

You can also directly use relative and exact times in your searches. For instance, given the search item bob error, you can specify directly in the search the time frame you want to use, using the fields **earliest** and **latest**.

- To search for errors affecting bob in the last 60 minutes, use earliest=-60m bob error

- To search for errors affecting bob in the last 3 hours, snap to the beginning of the hour using earliest=-3h@h bob error

- To search for errors affecting bob yesterday, use earliest=-1d@d latest=-0d@d bob error

- To search for errors affecting bob since Monday at midnight, use earliest=-0@w1 bob error

You cannot use different time ranges in the same query; for instance, in a Boolean search, (earliest=-1d@d latest=-0d@d bob error) OR (earliest=-2d@d latest=-1d@d mary error) will not work. The append command provides a way of accomplishing this.

_indextime versus _time

It is important to note that events are generally not received at the same time as stated in the event. In most installations, the discrepancy is usually of a few seconds, but if logs arrive in batches, the latency can be much larger. The time at which an event is actually written in the Splunk index is kept in the internal field _indextime. The time that is parsed out of the event is stored in _time.

You will probably never search against _indextime, but you should understand that the time you are searching against is the time parsed from the event, not the time at which the event was indexed.

Making searches faster

We have talked about using the index to make searches faster. When starting a new investigation, following a few steps will help you get results faster:

1. Set the time to the minimum time that you believe will be required to locate relevant events. For a chatty log, this may be as little as a minute. If you don't know when the events occurred, you might search a larger time frame and then zoom in by clicking on the timeline while the search is running.

2. Specify the index if you have multiple indexes. It's good to get into the habit of starting your queries with the index name, for example, index=myapplicationindex error bob.

3. Specify other fields that are relevant. The most common fields to specify are sourcetype and host, for example, index=myapplicationindex sourcetype="impl_splunk_gen" error bob.

 If you find yourself specifying the field source on a regular basis, you could probably benefit from defining more source types. Avoid using the sourcetype field to capture other information, for instance datacenter or environment. You would be better off using a lookup against host or creating another indexed field for those cases.

4. Add more words from the relevant messages as and when you find them. This can be done simply be clicking on words or field values in events or field values in the field picker, for example, `index=myapplicationindex sourcetype="impl_splunk_gen" error bob authclass OR fooclass`.

5. Expand your time range once you have found the events that you need, and then refine the search further.

6. Disable **Field discovery** (at the top of the field picker). This can greatly improve speed, particularly if your query retrieves a lot of events. Extracting all of the fields from events simply takes a lot of computing time, and disabling this option prevents Splunk from doing all of that work when not needed.

> If the query you are running is taking a long time to run, and you will be running this query on a regular basis — perhaps for an alert or dashboard — using a summary index may be appropriate. We will discuss this in *Chapter 9, Summary Indexes and CSV Files*.

Sharing results with others

It is often convenient to share a specific set of results with another user. You could always export the results to a CSV file and share it, but this is cumbersome. Instead, to use a URL for sharing, start by choosing **Save & share results...** from the **Save** menu.

This opens the **Save and Share Results** panel.

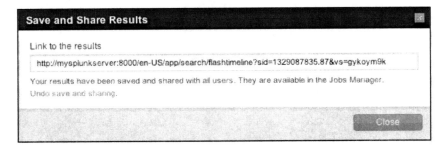

The URL under **Link to the results** can be copied and sent to other users. A user visiting this URL will see exactly the same results you did, assuming the job has not expired.

The results are also available in the **Jobs** window. Clicking on the **Jobs** link in the top bar opens the **Jobs** window.

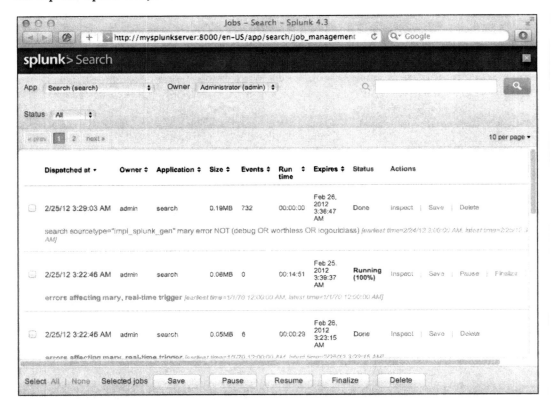

The **App** menu, **Owner** menu, **Status** menu, and search bar let you filter what jobs are displayed.

The table has the following columns:

- **Dispatched at** is the time at which the search started.
- **Owner** is the user that started the job. Sometimes jobs will appear with **system** as the user if the saved search is configured in an application but not owned by a particular user.
- **Application** specifies the application in which the search was started. This is useful for locating your searches as well as unfamiliar searches being fired off by other apps.
- **Size** is the amount of disk space being used to store the results of this query.
- **Events** shows the number of events that were matched by the search. In a complicated search or report, the results returned may be different from this number.
- **Run time** is how long a search took to run or the elapsed time if the search is still running.
- **Expires** is the time at which the results will be removed from disk.
- **Status** lets you see and sort searches based on whether they are still running.

 One simple way to find running jobs is to change the **Status** menu to **Running** and click the magnifying glass.

- **Actions** provides the following links to affect a search or its results:
    - **Inspect** shows detailed information about the query. We will cover the search job inspector in *Chapter 5, Advanced Search Examples*.
    - **Save** keeps the search results indefinitely.
    - **Pause** pauses the execution of a job.
    - **Finalize** stops the execution but keeps the results located up to this point.
    - **Delete** removes the results from the disk immediately. It is generally not necessary to delete search results as they will expire on their own.
- The search bar at the top of this window is useful for finding present and past jobs.

Saving searches for reuse

Let's build a query, save it, and make an alert out of it.

First, let's find errors that affect `mary`, one of our most important users. This can simply be the query `mary error`. Looking at some sample log messages that match this query, we see that some of these events probably don't matter (the dates have been removed to shorten the lines).

```
ERROR LogoutClass error, ERROR, Error! [user=mary, ip=3.2.4.5]

WARN AuthClass error, ERROR, Error! [user=mary, ip=1.2.3.3]

ERROR BarCLass Hello world. [user=mary, ip=4.3.2.1]

WARN LogoutClass error, ERROR, Error! [user=mary, ip=1.2.3.4]

DEBUG FooClass error, ERROR, Error! [user=mary, ip=3.2.4.5]

ERROR AuthClass Nothing happened. This is worthless. Don't log this.
[user=mary, ip=1.2.3.3]
```

We can probably skip the DEBUG messages; the LogoutClass messages look harmless; and the last message actually *says* that it's worthless.

`mary error NOT debug NOT worthless NOT logoutclass` limits the results to:

```
WARN AuthClass error, ERROR, Error! [user=mary, ip=1.2.3.3]

ERROR BarCLass Hello world. [user=mary, ip=4.3.2.1]
```

For good measure, let's add the `sourcetype` field and some parentheses.

```
sourcetype="impl_splunk_gen" (mary AND error) NOT debug NOT worthless
NOT logoutclass
```

Another way of writing the same thing is as follows:

```
sourcetype="impl_splunk_gen" mary error NOT (debug OR worthless OR
logoutclass)
```

So that we don't have to type our query every time, we can save this search for quick retrieval.

First, choose **Save search...** from the **Save** menu.

The **Save Search** window appears.

Enter a value for **Search name,** in our case, errors affecting mary. The time range is filled in based on what was selected in the time picker. **Share** lets you specify whether other users should be able to see this search in their menus. Standard users will not have the ability to share their searches with others.

The search is then available in the **Searches & Reports** menu under **Errors**.

Selecting the search from the menu runs the search using the latest data available.

 Note the small square next to **errors affecting mary**. This indicates that this search is not shared and is only viewable by its owner.

Creating alerts from searches

Any saved search can also be run on a schedule. One use for scheduled searches is firing alerts. To get started, choose **Alert...** from the **Create** menu.

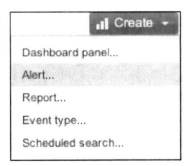

A wizard interface is presented, covering three steps.

Schedule

The **Schedule** step provides the following options:

- **Trigger in real-time whenever a result matches**: This option will leave a real-time search running *all the time* and will *immediately* fire an alert whenever an event is seen.

This option will create an alert *every time* an event that matches your search occurs. There is an important throttling option in the next step.

- **Run on a schedule once every...**: New options now appear below the menu.

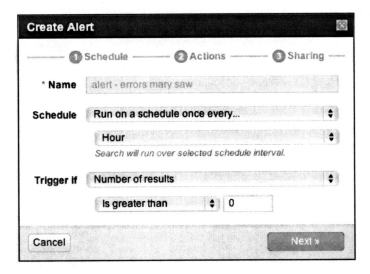

○ **Schedule**: You can choose to either run your search on a set schedule or run your alert according to a cron schedule. Keep in mind that the time frame selected in the time picker will be used each time the query runs—you probably don't want to run a query looking at 24 hours of data every minute.

○ **Trigger if** lets you choose when to trigger the alert.

- **Number of results** lets you build a rule based on the count. **Is greater than 0** is the most commonly used option.

- **A custom condition is met** lets you use a bit of search language to decide whether to fire the alert. If any events pass the search language test then the rule passes and the alert is fired. For example, `search authclass` would test each event for the word `authclass`, which in our example would pass one event. In most cases, you would use a threshold value. The purpose is to test the search results without affecting the search results that are handed along to the defined action.

- **Monitor in real-time over a rolling window of...**: This is a very useful option for generating alerts as soon as some threshold is passed. For instance, you could watch the access logs for a web server, and if the number of events seen in the last minute falls below 100, send an alert.

Working with our example data, let's set an alert to fire any time more than five errors affecting the user `mary` are matched in the last **5** minutes.

Actions

Once we've set all of our options, we can click on **Next >>** to proceed to **Actions**.

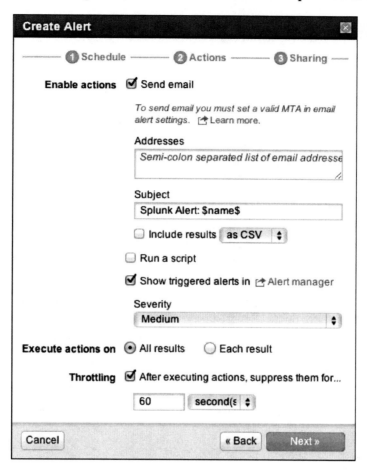

The **Actions** pane is where you decide what you want to do with the results of your alert. There are several options under **Enable actions**, as follows:

- **Send email**: This is the most common action. Simply fill out the list of e-mail addresses. The resulting e-mail will always contain a link back to this Splunk server, directly to the search results. You can customize the **Subject** string and optionally include the results of the search in the e-mail.

- **Run a script**: This will run a script with the results of the search. Any script must be installed by the administrator at `$SPLUNK_HOME/bin/scripts/`. This is covered in *Chapter 12, Extending Splunk*.

- **Show triggered alerts in Alert manager**: The alert manager is a listing of alerts populated by saved searches. The alerts window is a convenient way to group all alerts without filling your mailbox. Use the **Alerts** link at the top of the window.

The next two options determine how many alerts to issue:

- **Execute actions on**: Your options are **All results** and **Each result**. In most cases, you will only want one alert per search (**All results**), but you could treat each event independently and issue an alert per event, in special cases. You should be cautious with **Each result**, making sure to limit the number of results returned, most likely by using reporting commands.

- **Throttling**: This allows you to determine how often the same alert will be fired. You may want to search for a particular event every minute, but you probably don't want an e-mail every minute. With throttling, you can tell Splunk to only send you an e-mail every half hour even if the error continues to happen every minute.

If you choose **Execute actions on each result**, another input box appears to let you throttle against specific fields. For instance, if host A has an error, you may not want to know about any other host A errors for another 30 minutes, but if host B has an error in those 30 minutes, you would like to know immediately. Simply entering host in this field will compare the values of the host field.

The third screen simply lets you choose whether this search is available to other users. Not all users will have permissions to make searches public.

Summary

In this chapter, we covered searching in Splunk and doing a few useful things with those search results. There are lots of little tricks that we will touch upon as we go forward.

In the next chapter, we will start using fields for more than searches; we'll build tables and graphs, and then, we'll learn how to make our own fields.

3
Tables, Charts, and Fields

Up to this point, we have learned how to search for and retrieve raw events, but you will most likely want to create tables and charts to expose useful patterns. Thankfully, the reporting commands in Splunk make short work of most reporting tasks. We will step through a few common use cases in this chapter. Later in the chapter, we will learn how to create custom fields for even more custom reports.

About the pipe symbol

Before we dive into the actual commands, it is important to understand what the pipe symbol (|) is used for in Splunk. In a command line, the pipe symbol is used to represent the sending of data from one process to another. For example, in a Unix-style operating system, you might say:

```
grep foo access.log | grep bar
```

The first command finds, in the file access.log, lines that contain foo. Its output is taken and piped to the input of the next grep command, which finds lines that contain bar. The final output goes wherever it was destined, usually the terminal window.

The pipe symbol is different in Splunk in a few important ways:

1. Unlike the command line, events are not simply text, but rather each is a set of key/value pairs. You can think of each event as a database row, a Python dictionary, a Javascript object, a Java map, or a Perl associative array. Some fields are hidden from the user but are available for use. Many of these hidden fields are prefixed with an underscore, for instance _raw, which contains the original event text, and _time, which contains the parsed time in UTC epoch form. Unlike a database, events do not adhere to a schema, and fields are created dynamically.

_time

2. Commands can do anything to the events they are handed. Usually, a command does one of the following:

   ○ Modifies or creates fields — for example, `eval`, `rex`

   ○ Filters events — for example, `head`, `where`

   ○ Replaces events with a report — for example, `top`, `stats`

3. Some commands can act as generators, which produce what you might call "synthetic" events, such as `|metadata` and `|inputcsv`.

We will get to know the pipe symbol very well through examples.

Using top to show common field values

A very common question to answer is, "What values are most common?" When looking for errors, you are probably interested in what piece of code has the most errors. The `top` command provides a very simple way to answer this question. Let's step through a few examples.

First, run a search for errors:

```
source="impl_splunk_gen" error
```

Using our sample data, we find events containing the word `error`, a sampling of which is listed here:

```
2012-03-03T19:36:23.138-0600 ERROR Don't worry, be happy.
[logger=AuthClass, user=mary, ip=1.2.3.4]

2012-03-03T19:36:22.244-0600 ERROR error, ERROR, Error!
[logger=LogoutClass, user=mary, ip=3.2.4.5, network=green]

2012-03-03T19:36:21.158-0600 WARN error, ERROR, Error!
[logger=LogoutClass, user=bob, ip=3.2.4.5, network=red]

2012-03-03T19:36:21.103-0600 ERROR Hello world. [logger=AuthClass,
user=jacky, ip=4.3.2.1]

2012-03-03T19:36:19.832-0600 ERROR Nothing happened. This is worthless.
Don't log this. [logger=AuthClass, user=bob, ip=4.3.2.1]

2012-03-03T19:36:18.933-0600 ERROR Hello world. [logger=FooClass,
user=Bobby, ip=1.2.3.4]

2012-03-03T19:36:16.631-0600 ERROR error, ERROR, Error!
[logger=LogoutClass, user=bob, ip=1.2.3.3]

2012-03-03T19:36:13.380-0600 WARN error, ERROR, Error! [logger=FooClass,
user=jacky, ip=4.3.2.1, network=red]

2012-03-03T19:36:12.399-0600 ERROR error, ERROR, Error!
[logger=LogoutClass, user=linda, ip=3.2.4.5, network=green]
```

```
2012-03-03T19:36:11.615-0600 WARN error, ERROR, Error! [logger=FooClass,
user=mary, ip=1.2.3.4]
```

```
2012-03-03T19:36:10.860-0600 ERROR Don't worry, be happy.
[logger=BarCLass, user=linda, ip=4.3.2.1, network=green]
```

To find the most common values of `logger`, simply add | `top logger` to our search, like so:

```
source="impl_splunk_gen" error | top logger
```

The results are transformed by `top` into a table like the following one:

	logger ⇕	count ⇕	percent ⇕
1	BarClass	242	63.185379
2	FooClass	49	12.793734
3	AuthClass	47	12.271540
4	LogoutClass	45	11.749347

From these results, we see that **BarClass** is logging significantly more errors than any other logger. We should probably contact the developer of that code.

Next, let's determine whom those errors are happening to. Adding another field name to the end of the command instructs `top` to slice the data again. For example, let's add `user` to the end of our previous query, like so:

```
sourcetype="impl_splunk_gen" error | top logger user
```

The results might look like the following screenshot:

	logger ⇕	user ⇕	count ⇕	percent ⇕
1	BarClass	mary	114	14.709677
2	BarClass	Bobby	101	13.032258
3	BarClass	linda	98	12.645161
4	BarClass	jacky	89	11.483871
5	BarClass	bob	83	10.709677
6	FooClass	mary	28	3.612903
7	FooClass	jacky	25	3.225806
8	FooClass	linda	24	3.096774
9	LogoutClass	Bobby	23	2.967742
10	LogoutClass	bob	22	2.838710

In these results, we see that mary is logging the most errors from the logger BarClass. If we simply wanted to see the distribution of errors by user, you could specify only the user field, like so:

```
sourcetype="impl_splunk_gen" error | top user
```

Controlling the output of top

The default behavior for top is to show the 10 largest counts. The possible row count is the product of all fields specified, in this case logger and user. In this case, there are 25 possible combinations. If you would like to see more than 10 rows, add the argument limit, like so:

```
sourcetype="impl_splunk_gen" error | top limit=100 logger user
```

ORDER DOESN'T MATTER

Arguments change the behavior of a command; they take the form of name=value. Many commands require the arguments to immediately follow the command name, so it's a good idea to always follow this structure.

Each command has different arguments, as appropriate. As you type in the search bar, a help drop-down box will appear for the last command in your search, as shown in the following figure:

```
top | Help | More »
Displays the most common values of a field.

Examples

Return the 20 most common values of the "url" field.
    ... | top limit=20 url

Return top "user" values for each "host".
    ... | top user by host

Return top URL values.
    ... | top url
```

Help takes you to the documentation for that command at splunk.com. **More >>** provides concise documentation in-line.

Let's use a few arguments to make a shorter list but also roll all other results into another line:

```
sourcetype="impl_splunk_gen" error
   | top
       limit=5
       useother=true
       otherstr="everything else"
       logger user
```

This produces results like those shown in the following screenshot:

	logger ⇕	user ⇕	count ⇕	percent ⇕
1	BarClass	mary	162	19.565217
2	BarClass	linda	102	12.318841
3	BarClass	jacky	97	11.714976
4	BarClass	Bobby	89	10.748792
5	BarClass	bob	72	8.695652
6	everything else	everything else	306	36.956522

The last line represents everything that didn't fit into the top five. useother enables this last row, while otherstr controls the value printed instead of the default value "other".

For the opposite of top, see the rare command.

Using stats to aggregate values

While top is very convenient, stats is extremely versatile. The basic structure of a stats statement is:

```
stats functions by fields
```

Many of the functions available in stats mimic similar functions in SQL or Excel, but there are many functions unique to Splunk. The simplest stats function is count. Given the following query, the results will contain exactly one row, with a value for the field count:

```
sourcetype="impl_splunk_gen" error | stats count
```

Using the by clause, stats will produce a row per unique value for each field listed, which is similar to the behavior of top. Run the following query:

```
sourcetype="impl_splunk_gen" error | stats count by logger user
```

It will produce a table like that shown in the following screenshot:

	logger ⇕	user ⇕	count ⇕
1	AuthClass	Bobby	877
2	AuthClass	bob	939
3	AuthClass	jacky	851
4	AuthClass	linda	890
5	AuthClass	mary	1809
6	BarClass	Bobby	4470
7	BarClass	bob	4340
8	BarClass	jacky	4558
9	BarClass	linda	4513
10	BarClass	mary	8799
11	FooClass	Bobby	933
12	FooClass	bob	877
13	FooClass	jacky	934
14	FooClass	linda	940
15	FooClass	mary	1737
16	LogoutClass	Bobby	885
17	LogoutClass	bob	834
18	LogoutClass	jacky	944
19	LogoutClass	linda	860
20	LogoutClass	mary	1720

There are a few things to notice about these results:

1. The results are sorted against the values of the "by" fields, in this case `logger` followed by `user`. Unlike `top`, the largest value will not necessarily be at the top of the list. You can sort in the GUI simply by clicking on the field names at the top of the table, or by using the `sort` command.

2. There is no limit to the number of rows produced. The number of rows will equal the possible combinations of field values.

3. The function results are displayed last. In the next example, we will add a few more functions, and this will become more obvious.

Using `stats`, you can add as many "by" fields or functions as you want into a single statement. Let's run this query:

```
sourcetype="impl_splunk_gen" error
    | stats
        count avg(req_time) max(req_time) as "Slowest time"
        by logger user
```

The results look like those in the following screenshot:

	logger ⇕	user ⇕	count ⇕	avg(req_time) ⇕	Slowest time ⇕
1	AuthClass	Bobby	9	7568.000000	10875
2	AuthClass	bob	15	6799.600000	11749
3	AuthClass	jacky	17	4726.714286	9051
4	AuthClass	linda	13	5927.142857	10764
5	AuthClass	mary	39	6029.200000	12108
6	BarClass	Bobby	79	6462.081081	11969
7	BarClass	bob	86	5579.666667	11163
8	BarClass	jacky	99	5647.111111	11688
9	BarClass	linda	100	7122.333333	12071
10	BarClass	mary	142	6100.516667	12187
11	FooClass	Bobby	16	6468.200000	12164
12	FooClass	bob	15	3890.125000	9388
13	FooClass	jacky	20	4502.444444	12128
14	FooClass	linda	19	7087.200000	12151
15	FooClass	mary	36	6375.166667	11421
16	LogoutClass	Bobby	19	6110.666667	11170
17	LogoutClass	bob	25	5784.100000	12169
18	LogoutClass	jacky	17	4448.428571	10820
19	LogoutClass	linda	14	5731.428571	10709
20	LogoutClass	mary	28	5938.600000	10957

Let's step through every part of this query, just to be clear:

- `sourcetype="impl_splunk_gen" error` is the query itself.
- `| stats` starts the `stats` command.
- `count` will return the number of events.

- `avg(req_time)` produces an average value of the `req_time` field.

- `max(req_time) as "Slowest time"` finds the maximum value of the `req_time` field and places the value in a field called `Slowest time`. The quotes are necessary because the field name contains a space.

- `by` indicates that we are done listing functions and want to list the fields to slice the data by. If the data does not need to be sliced, `by` and the fields following it can be omitted.

- `logger` and `user` are our fields for slicing the data. All functions are actually run against each set of data produced per possible combination of `logger` and `user`.

> If an event is missing a field that is referenced in a `stats` command, you may not see the results you are expecting. For instance, when computing an average, you may wish for events missing a field to count as zeroes in the average. Also, for events that do not contain a field listed in the `by` fields, the event will simply be ignored.
>
> To deal with both of these cases, you can use the `fillnull` command to make sure that the fields you want exist. We will cover this in *Chapter 5, Advanced Search Examples*.

Let's look at another example, using a time-based function and a little trick. Let's say we wanted to know the most recent time at which each user saw a particular error. We can use the following query:

```
sourcetype="impl_splunk_gen" error logger="FooClass"
    | stats count first(ip) max(_time) as _time by user
```

This query produces the following table:

_time ‡	user ‡	count ‡	first(ip) ‡
3/20/12 5:50:00.335 PM	Bobby	115	1.2.3.4
3/20/12 5:47:50.467 PM	bob	116	1.2.3.
3/20/12 5:48:29.899 PM	extrauser	56	1.2.3.
3/20/12 5:49:10.541 PM	jacky	113	1.2.3.4
3/20/12 5:44:20.408 PM	linda	120	1.2.3.4
3/20/12 5:49:36.602 PM	mary	221	3.2.4.5

Let's step through this example:

- `sourcetype="impl_splunk_gen" error logger="FooClass"` is the query that will find all errors logged by the class `FooClass`.
- `| stats` is our command.
- `count` shows how many times each user saw this error.
- `first(ip)` gives us the IP address that was most recently logged for this user. This will be the most recent event, since results are returned in the order of the most recent first.
- `max(_time) as _time` returns the time at which each user most recently saw this error. This takes advantage of three aspects of time in Splunk:
    - `_time` is always present in raw events. As discussed in *Chapter 2, Understanding Search,* the value is the number of seconds since 1970, UTC.
    - `_time` is stored as a number and can be treated as such.
    - If there is a field called `_time` in the results, Splunk will always display the value as the first column of a table in the time zone selected by the user.
- `by user` is our field to split results against.

We have only seen a few functions in `stats`. There are dozens of functions and some advanced syntax that we will touch upon in later chapters. The simplest way to find the full listing is to search with your favorite search engine for `splunk stats functions`.

Using chart to turn data

The `chart` command is useful for "turning" data across two dimensions. It is useful for both tables and charts. Let's start with one of our examples from `stats`:

```
sourcetype="impl_splunk_gen" error | chart count over logger by user
```

The resulting table looks like this:

logger ‡	Bobby ‡	NULL ‡	bob ‡	extrauser ‡	jacky ‡	linda ‡	mary ‡
AuthClass	106	197	114	49	116	119	254
BarClass	615	1027	597	238	592	605	1235
FooClass	126	164	119	57	131	132	226
LogoutClass	123	200	119	49	119	127	261

If you look back at the results from `stats`, the data is presented as one row per combination. Instead of a row per combination, `chart` generates the intersection of the two fields. You can specify multiple functions, but you may only specify one field each for `over` and `by`.

Switching the fields turns the data the other way.

	user ⬍	AuthClass ⬍	BarClass ⬍	FooClass ⬍	LogoutClass ⬍	NULL ⬍
1	Bobby	106	615	126	123	298
2	bob	114	597	119	119	316
3	extrauser	49	238	57	49	0
4	jacky	116	592	131	119	315
5	linda	119	605	132	127	295
6	mary	254	1235	226	261	638

By simply clicking on the chart icon above the table, we can see these results in a chart:

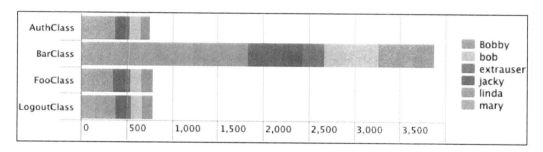

This is a bar chart, with **Stack mode** set to **Stacked**, and `usenull` set to `false`, like so:

```
sourcetype="impl_splunk_gen" error
  | chart usenull=false count over logger by user
```

`chart` can also be used to simply turn data, even if the data is non-numerical. For example, say we enter this query:

```
sourcetype="impl_splunk_gen" error
  | chart usenull=false values(network) over logger by user
```

It will create a table like this:

	logger ⇕	Bobby ⇕	bob ⇕	jacky ⇕	linda ⇕	mary ⇕
1	AuthClass		red	red	red	green
2	BarClass	red	green red	green	green red	green red
3	FooClass			green red	red	
4	LogoutClass		red			green red

Since there are no numbers, this cannot be directly made into an image, but it is still a very useful representation of the data.

Using timechart to show values over time

timechart lets us show numerical values over time. It is similar to the chart command, except that time is always plotted on the x axis. Here are a couple of things to note:

- The events must have an _time field. If you are simply sending the results of a search to timechart, this will always be true. If you are using interim commands, you will need to be mindful of this requirement.

- Time is always "bucketed", meaning that there is no way to draw a point per event.

Let's see how many errors have been occurring:

```
sourcetype="impl_splunk_gen" error | timechart count
```

The default chart will look something like this:

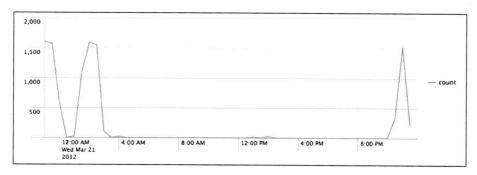

Now let's see how many errors have occurred per user over the same time period. We simply need to add by user to the query:

```
sourcetype="impl_splunk_gen" error | timechart count by user
```

This produces the following chart:

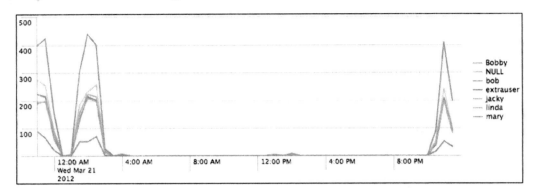

As we stated before, the x axis is always time. The y axis can be:

- One or more functions
- A single function with a by clause
- Multiple functions with a by clause (a new feature in Splunk 4.3)

An example of a timechart with multiple functions might be:

```
sourcetype="impl_splunk_gen" error
   | timechart
       count as "Error count"
       max(req_time) as "Max request time"
```

This would produce a graph like this:

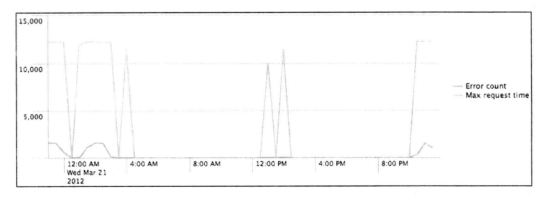

timechart options

`timechart` has many arguments and formatting options. We'll touch upon a few examples of formatting, but they are too numerous to cover in detail. We will use other chart types in later chapters. Let's throw a few options in and see what they do.

```
timechart bins=100 limit=3 useother=false usenull=false
    count as "Error count" by user
```

Let's step through each of these arguments:

- `bins` defines how many "bins" to slice time into. The number of bins will probably not be exactly 100 as the time will be sliced into logical units. In our example, this comes to 10 minutes per bin. To be more exact, you can use `span` (for example, `span=1h`) for hourly slices, but note that if your span value creates too many time slices, the chart will be truncated.

- `limit` changes the number of series returned. The series with the largest values are returned, much like in `top`. In this case, the most common values of `user` will be returned.

- `useother` instructs `timechart` whether to group all series beyond the limit into an "other" bucket. The default value is `true`.

- `usenull` instructs `timechart` whether to bucket, into the group NULL, events that do not have a value for the fields in the `by` clause. The default value is `true`.

This combination of arguments produces a graph similar to this:

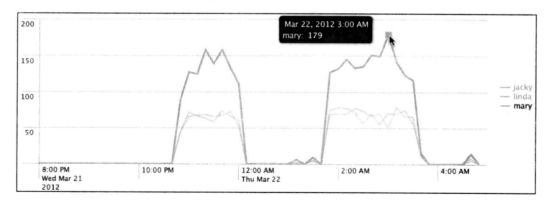

Clicking on **Formatting options** above the graph gives us quite a few options to work with.

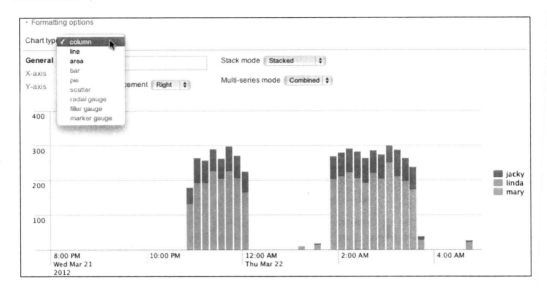

This graph shows one of my personal favorite chart styles, the stacked column. This graph is useful for showing how many events of a certain kind occurred, but with colors to give us an idea of distribution. splunk.com has great examples of all of the available chart styles, and we will touch upon more styles in future chapters.

Working with fields

All of the fields we have used so far were either indexed fields (such as host, sourcetype, and _time) or fields that were automatically extracted from key=value pairs. Unfortunately, most logs don't follow this format, especially for the first few values in each event. New fields can be created either inline, by using commands, or through configuration.

A regular expression primer

Most of the ways to create new fields in Splunk involve regular expressions. There are many books and sites dedicated to regular expressions, so we will only touch upon the subject here.

Given the log snippet `ip=1.2.3.4`, let's pull out the subnet (`1.2.3`) into a new field called `subnet`. The simplest pattern would be the literal string:

```
ip=(?P<subnet>1.2.3).4
```

This is not terribly useful as it will only find the subnet of that one IP address. Let's try a slightly more complicated example:

```
ip=(?P<subnet>\d+\.\d+\.\d+)\.\d+
```

Let's step through this pattern:

- `ip=` simply looks for the raw string `ip=`.
- `(` starts a "capture buffer". Everything until the closing parentheses is part of this capture buffer.
- `?P<subnet>` immediately inside a parentheses, says "create a field called subnet from the results of this capture buffer".
- `\d` matches any single digit, from 0 to 9.
- `+` says "one or more of the item immediately before".
- `\.` matches a literal period. A period without the backslash matches any character.
- `\d+\.\d+` matches the next two parts of the IP address.
- `)` ends our capture buffer.
- `\.\d+` matches the last part of the IP address. Since it is outside of the capture buffer, it will be discarded.

Now let's step through an overly complicated pattern to illustrate a few more concepts:

```
ip=(?P<subnet>\d+.\d*\.[01234-9]+)\.\d+
```

Let's step through this pattern:

- `ip=` simply looks for the raw string `ip=`.
- `(?P<subnet>` starts our capture buffer and defines our field name.
- `\d` means digit. This is one of the many backslash character combinations that represent some sets of characters.
- `+` says "one or more of what came before", in this case `\d`.
- `.` matches a single character. This will match the period after the first set of digits, though it would match any single character.

- \d* means zero or more digits.

- \. matches a literal period. The backslash negates the special meaning of any special punctuation character. Not all punctuation marks have a special meaning, but so many do that there is no harm adding a backslash before a punctuation mark that you want to literally match.

- [starts a character set. Anything inside the brackets will match a single character in the character set.

- 01234-9 means the characters 0, 1, 2, 3, and the range 4-9.

-] closes the character set.

- + says "one or more of what came before", in this case the character set.

-) ends our capture buffer.

- \.\d+ is the final part of the IP address that we are throwing away. It is not actually necessary to include this, but it ensures that we only match if there were in fact four sets of numbers.

There are a number of different ways to accomplish the task at hand. Here are a few examples that will work:

```
ip=(?P<subnet>\d+\.\d+\.\d+)\.\d+
ip=(?P<subnet>(\d+\.){2}\d+)\.\d+
ip=(?P<subnet>[\d\.]+)\.\d
ip=(?P<subnet>.*?\..*?\..*?)\.
ip=(?P<subnet>\S+)\.
```

For more information about regular expressions, consult the man pages for **Perl Compatible Regular Expressions (PCRE)**, which can be found online at http://www.pcre.org/pcre.txt, or one of the many regular expression books or websites dedicated to the subject. We will build more expressions as we work through different configurations and searches, but it's definitely worthwhile to have a reference handy.

Commands that create fields

There are a number of commands that create new fields, but the most commonly used are eval and rex.

eval

eval allows you to use functions to build new fields, much as you would build a formula column in Excel, for example:

NOT PERSISTED

```
sourcetype="impl_splunk_gen"
  | eval req_time_seconds=req_time/1000
  | stats avg(req_time_seconds)
```

This creates a new field called req_time_seconds on every event that has a value for req_time. Commands after this statement see the field as if it were part of the original event. stats then creates a table of the average value of our newly created field.

avg(req_time_seconds) ⬍
6.175161

There are a huge number of functions available for use with eval. The simplest way to find the full listing is to search google.com for splunk eval functions. I would suggest bookmarking this page as you will find yourself referring to it often.

rex

rex lets you use regular expressions to create fields. It can work against any existing field but, by default, will use the field _raw. Let's try one of the patterns we wrote in our short regular expression primer:

```
sourcetype="impl_splunk_gen"
  | rex "ip=(?P<subnet>\d+\.\d+\.\d+)\.\d+"
  | chart values(subnet) by user network
```

This would create a table like this:

user ⬍	green ⬍	red ⬍
bob	1.2.3 3.2.4	1.2.3
jacky	1.2.3 3.2.4	1.2.3
linda	1.2.3	1.2.3 3.2.4
mary	1.2.3 4.3.2	1.2.3

With the addition of the `field` argument, we can work against the `ip` field that is already being created automatically from the `name=value` pair in the event.

```
sourcetype="impl_splunk_gen"
  | rex field=ip "(?P<subnet>.*)\."
  | chart values(subnet) by user network
```

This will create exactly the same result as the previous example.

Extracting loglevel

In our examples, we searched for the raw word `error`. You may have noticed that many of the events weren't actually errors, but simply contained the word `error` somewhere in the message. For example, given the following events, we probably only care about the second event:

```
2012-03-21T18:59:55.472-0500 INFO This is not an error
2012-03-21T18:59:42.907-0500 ERROR Something bad happened
```

Using an extracted field, we can easily create fields in our data, without re-indexing, that allow you to search for values that occur in a specific location in your events.

Using the Extract Fields interface

There are several ways to define a field. Let's start by using the **Extract Fields** interface. To access this interface, choose **Extract Fields** from the workflow actions menu next to any event:

PERSISTED FIELDS

This menu launches the **Extract fields** view:

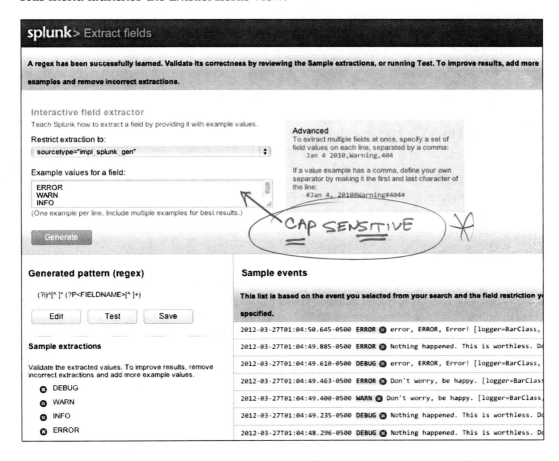

In this view, you simply provide example values, and Splunk will attempt to build a regular expression that matches. In this case, we specify **ERROR**, **WARN**, and **INFO**.

Under **Sample extractions**, we see that the values **DEBUG**, **WARN**, **INFO**, and **ERROR** were matched. Notice that there are more values than we listed—the pattern is looking for placement, not our sample values.

Under **Sample events**, we get a preview of what data was matched, in context.

$(?i).*?$

Finally, under **Generated pattern**, we see the regular expression that Splunk generated, which is as follows:

```
(?i)^[^ ]* (?P<FIELDNAME>[^ ]+)
```

Let's step through the pattern:

- `(?i)` says that this pattern is case insensitive. By default, regular expressions are case sensitive.
- `^` says that this pattern must match at the beginning of the line.
- `[^ ]*` says "any character but a space, zero or more times".
- The space is literal.
- `(?P<FIELDNAME>[^ ]+)` says to match anything that is not a space, and capture it in the field `FIELDNAME`. You will have the opportunity to name the field when you click on **Save**.

Edit presents a dialog to let you modify the pattern manually:

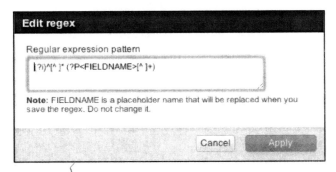

Test will launch a new search window with the pattern loaded into a very useful query that shows the most common values extracted. In this case, it is the following query:

```
index=main sourcetype="impl_splunk_gen"
  | head 10000
  | rex "(?i)^[^ ]* (?P<FIELDNAME>[^ ]+)"
  | top 50 FIELDNAME
```

Save prompts you for a name for your new field. Let's call this field `loglevel` and save it:

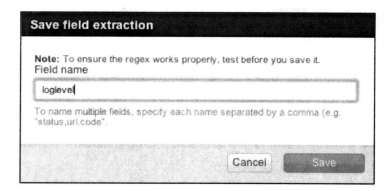

Now that we've defined our field, we can use it in a number of ways, as follows:

- We can search for the value using the fieldname, for instance,
  `loglevel=error`

 When searching for values by fieldname, the fieldname *is* case sensitive, but the value *is not* case sensitive. In this case `loglevel=Error` would work just fine, but `LogLevel=error` would not.

- We can report on the field, whether we searched for it or not. For instance:
  `sourcetype="impl_splunk_gen" user=mary | top loglevel`

- We can search for only events that contain our field:

  `sourcetype="impl_splunk_gen" user=mary loglevel="*"`

Using rex to prototype a field

When defining fields, it is often convenient to build the pattern directly in the query and then copy the pattern into configuration. You might have noticed that the test in the Extract fields workflow used `rex`.

Let's turn the subnet pattern we built earlier into a field. First, we build the query with the `rex` statement:

```
sourcetype="impl_splunk_gen" ip="*"
  | rex "ip=(?P<subnet>\d\.\d\.\d+)\.\d+"
  | table ip subnet
```

Since we know there will be an `ip` field in the events we care about, we can use `ip="*"` to limit the results to events that have a value for that field.

`table` takes a list of fields and displays a table, one row per event:

	ip ⇕	subnet ⇕
1	1.2.3.4	1.2.3
2	1.2.3.4	1.2.3
3	4.31.2.1	
4	4.31.2.1	
5	4.31.2.1	
6	4.31.2.1	
7	1.22.3.3	
8	1.2.3.4	1.2.3
9	1.22.3.3	
10	1.22.3.3	
11	1.22.3.3	

As we can see, the `rex` statement doesn't always work. Looking at the pattern again, you may notice that the first two instances of `\d` are now missing their trailing +. Without the plus sign, only addresses with a single digit in both their first and second sections will match. After adding the missing plus signs to our pattern, all rows will have a subnet.

```
sourcetype="impl_splunk_gen" ip="*"
  | rex "ip=(?P<subnet>\d+\.\d+\.\d+)\.\d+"
  | table ip subnet
```

We can now take the pattern from the `rex` statement and use it to build a configuration.

Using the admin interface to build a field

Taking our pattern from the previous example, we can build the configuration to "wire up" this extract.

First, click on **Manager** in the upper-right corner. The **Fields** section contains everything, funnily enough, about fields.

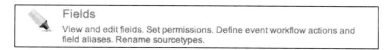

Fields

View and edit fields. Set permissions. Define event workflow actions and field aliases. Rename sourcetypes.

There are a number of different things you can do with fields via configuration, but for now, we're interested in **Field extractions**.

Field extractions

View and edit all field extractions. Add new field extractions and update permissions.

After clicking on **Add new** to the right of **Field extractions**, or on the **New** button after clicking on **Field extractions**, we are presented with the interface for creating a new field.

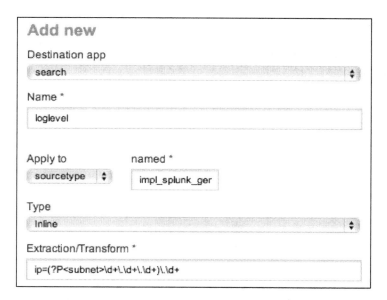

Now, we step through the fields:

- **Destination app** lets us choose the app where this extraction will live and by default, where it will take effect. We will discuss the scope of configurations in *Chapter 10, Configuring Splunk*.
- **Name** is simply a display name for the extraction. Make it as descriptive as you like.
- **Apply to** lets you choose what to bind this extraction to. Your choices are **sourcetype**, **source**, and **host**. The usual choice is **sourcetype**.
- **named** is the name of the item we are binding our extraction to.
- **Type** lets you choose **Inline**, which means specifying the regular expression here, or **Uses transform**, which means we will specify a named transform that exists already in configuration.
- **Extraction/Transform** is where we place either our pattern, if we chose a **Type** option of **Inline**, or the name of a **Transform** object.

Once you click on **Save**, you will return to the listing of extractions. By default, your extraction will be private to you and will only function in the application it was created in. If you have rights to do so, you can share the extraction with other users and change the scope of where it runs. Click on **Permissions** in the listing to see the permissions page, which most objects in Splunk use.

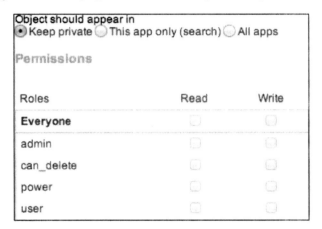

The top section controls the context in which this extraction will run. Think about when the field would be useful, and limit the extractions accordingly. An excessive number of extractions can affect performance, so it is a good idea to limit the extracts to a specific app when appropriate. We will talk more about creating apps in *Chapter 7, Working with Apps*.

The second section controls what roles can read or write this configuration. The usual selections are the **Read** option for the **Everyone** parameter and the **Write** option for the **admin** parameter. As you build objects going forward, you will become very familiar with this dialog.

Indexed fields versus extracted fields

When an event is written to an index, the raw text of the event is captured along with a set of indexed fields. The default indexed fields include host, sourcetype, source, and _time. There are distinct advantages and a few serious disadvantages to using indexed fields.

First, let's look at the advantages of an indexed field (we will actually discuss configuring indexed fields in *Chapter 10, Configuring Splunk*):

- As an indexed field is stored in the index with the event itself, it is only calculated at index time, and in fact, can only be calculated once at index time.
- It can make finding specific instances of common terms efficient. See use case 1 in the following section, as an example.
- You can create new words to search against that simply don't exist in the raw text or are embedded inside a word. See use cases 2–4 in the following sections.
- You can efficiently search for words in other indexed fields. See the *Indexed field case 3 – application from source* section.

Now for the disadvantages of an indexed field:

- It is not retroactive. This is different from extracted fields, where all events, past and present, will gain the newly defined field if the pattern matches. This is the biggest disadvantage of indexed fields and has a few implications, as follows:
    - Only newly indexed events will gain a newly defined indexed field
    - If the pattern is wrong in certain cases, there is no practical way to apply the field to already indexed events
    - Likewise, if the log format changes, the indexed field may not be generated (or generated incorrectly)
- It adds to the size of your index on disk.
- It counts against your license.

- Any changes usually require a restart to be applied.
- In most cases, the value of the field is already an indexed word, in which case creating an indexed field will likely have no benefit, except in the rare cases where that value is very common.

With the disadvantages out of the way, let's look at a few cases where an indexed field would improve search performance and then at one case where it would probably make no difference.

Indexed field case 1 – rare instances of a common term

Let's say your log captures process exit codes. If a 1 represents a failure, you probably want to be able to search for this efficiently. Consider a log that looks something like this:

```
4/1/12 6:35:50.000 PM process=important_process.sh, exitcode=1
```

It would be easy to search for this log entry using exitcode=1. The problem is that, when working with extracted fields, the search is effectively reduced to this:

```
1 | search exitcode="1"
```

Since the date contains a 1, this search would find every event for the entire day and then filter the events to the few that we are looking for. In contrast, if exitcode were defined as an indexed field, the query would immediately find the events, only retrieving the appropriate events from the disk.

Indexed field case 2 – splitting words

In some log formats, multiple pieces of information may be encoded into a single word without whitespace or punctuation to separate the useful pieces of information. For instance, consider a log message such as this:

```
4/2/12 6:35:50.000 PM kernel: abc5s2: 0xc014 (UNDEFINED).
```

Let's pretend that 5s2 is an important piece of information that we need to be able to search for efficiently. The query *5s2 would find the events but would be a very inefficient search (in essence, a full table scan). By defining an indexed field, you can very efficiently search for this instance of the string 5s2, because in essence, we create a new "word" in the metadata of this event.

Defining an indexed field only makes sense if you know the format of the logs before indexing, if you believe the filed will actually make the query more efficient (see previous section), and if you will be searching for the field value. If you will only be reporting on the values of this field, an extracted field will be sufficient, except in the most extreme performance cases.

Indexed field case 3 – application from source

A common requirement is to be able to search for events from a particular web application. Often, the only easy way to determine the application that created the logs is by inspecting the path to the logs, which Splunk stores in the indexed field `source`. For example, given the following path, the application name is `app_one`:

```
/opt/instance19/apps/app_one/logs/important.log
```

You could search for this instance using `source="*/app_one/*"`, but this effectively initiates a full table scan. You could define an extracted field and then search for `app="app_one"`, but unfortunately, this approach will be no more efficient because the word we're looking for is not contained in the field `_raw`. If we define this field as an indexed field, `app="app_one"` will be an efficient search.

Once again, if you only need this field for reporting, the extracted field is just fine.

Indexed field case 4 – slow requests

Consider a web access log with a trailing request time in microseconds:

```
[31/Jan/2012:18:18:07 +0000] "GET / HTTP/1.1" 200 7918 ""
"Mozilla/5.0..." 11/11033255
```

Let's say we want to find all requests that took longer than 10 seconds. We can easily extract the value into a field, perhaps `request_ms`. We could then run the search `request_ms>10000000`. This query will work, but it requires scanning every event in the given time frame. Whether the field is extracted or indexed, we would face the same problem as Splunk has to convert the field value to a number before it can test the value.

What if we could define a field and instead search for `slow_request=1`? To do this, we can take advantage of the fact that, when defining an indexed field, the value can be a static value. This could be accomplished with a transform, like so:

```
REGEX = .*/(\d{7,})$
FORMAT = slow_request::1
```

We will cover transforms, and the configurations involved, in *Chapter 10, Configuring Splunk.*

Once again, this is only worth the trouble if you need to efficiently search for these events and not simply report on the value of request_ms.

Indexed field case 5 – unneeded work

Once you learn to make indexed fields, it may be tempting to convert all of your important fields into indexed fields. In most cases it is essentially a wasted effort and ends up using extra disk space, wasting license, and adding no performance boost.

For example, consider this log message:

```
4/2/12 6:35:50.000 PM [vincentbumgarner] [893783] sudo bash
```

Assuming the layout of this message is as follows, it might be tempting to put both userid and pid into indexed fields:

```
date [userid] [pid] action
```

Since the values are uncommon, and are unlikely to occur in unrelated locations, defining these fields as indexed fields is most likely wasteful. It is much simpler to define these fields as extracted fields and shield ourselves from the disadvantages of indexed fields.

Summary

This has been a very dense chapter, but we have really just scratched the surface on a number of important topics. In future chapters, we will use these commands and techniques in more and more interesting ways. The possibilities can be a bit dizzying, so we will step through a multitude of examples to illustrate as many scenarios as possible.

In the next chapter, we will build a few dashboards using the wizard-style interfaces provided by Splunk.

Simple XML Dashboards

4

Dashboards are a way for you to capture, group, and automate tables and charts into useful and informative views. We will quickly cover the wizards provided in Splunk 4.3 and then dig into the underlying XML. With that XML, you can easily build interactive forms, further customize panels, and use the same query for multiple panels, among other things. We will also cover how and when to schedule the generation of dashboards to reduce both the wait time for users and the load on the server.

The purpose of dashboards

Any search, table, or chart you create can be saved and made to appear in the menus for other users to see. With that power, why would you bother creating a dashboard? Here are a few reasons:

- A dashboard can contain multiple panels, each running a different query.
- Every dashboard has a unique URL, which is easy to share.
- Dashboards are more customizable than an individual query.
- The search bar is removed, making it less intimidating to many users.
- Forms allow you to present the user with a custom search interface that only requires specific values.
- Dashboards look great. Many organizations place dashboards on projectors and monitors for at-a-glance information about their environment.
- Dashboards can be scheduled for PDF delivery by e-mail. This feature is not the most robust, but with some consideration, it can be used effectively.

With all of this said, if a saved search is working the way it is, there is no strong reason to turn it into a dashboard.

Using wizards to build dashboards

Using some of the queries from previous chapters, let's make an operational dashboard for errors occurring in our infrastructure. We will start by making a query (note that this query relies on the `loglevel` fields we created in *Chapter 3, Tables, Charts, and Fields*):

```
sourcetype="impl_splunk_gen" loglevel=error | timechart count as
"Error count" by network
```

This will produce a graph like this one:

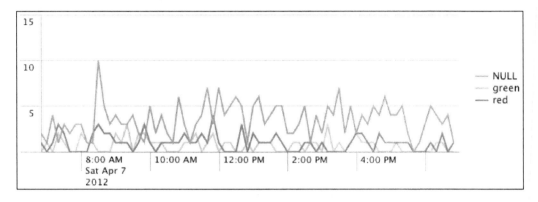

To add this to a dashboard, we perform the following steps:

1. Choose **Create | Dashboard panel....**

2. This opens a wizard interface that guides you through saving the query, adding it to a dashboard, and then scheduling the search. First, we name the search.

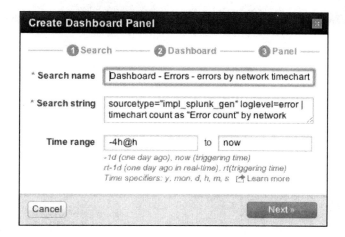

As you create more dashboards, you will end up creating a lot of searches. A naming convention will help you keep track of what search belongs to what dashboard. Here is one possible approach: `Dashboard - [dashboard name] - [search name and panel type]`. When the number of dashboards and searches becomes large, apps can be used to group dashboards and searches together, providing yet another way to organize and share assets.

3. The next step is to create or choose an existing dashboard.

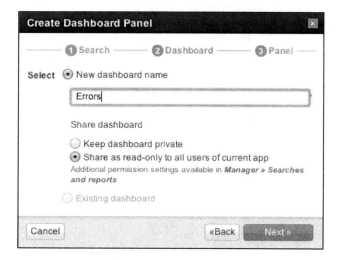

4. Let's create a new dashboard called `Errors`. The next step is to add our new saved search to our new dashboard in a new panel.

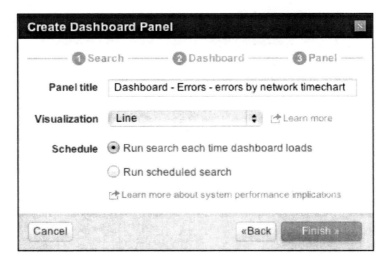

5. **Panel title** is the text that will appear above your new panel in the dashboard. **Visualization** lets you choose a chart type and will default to the type of chart you started with. We will discuss **Schedule** in the next section.

6. After clicking on **Finish** and saving our dashboard, it will now be available in the **Dashboards & Views** menu.

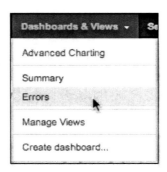

7. The dashboard with our first panel looks as follows:

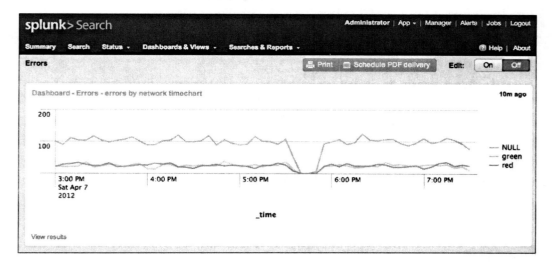

Following the same steps, let's add a few pie charts showing this information broken down in a few ways.

```
sourcetype="impl_splunk_gen" loglevel=error | stats count by user
```

This query produces the following chart:

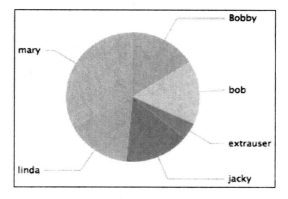

This gives us a breakdown of errors by user. Next, let's add a breakdown by logger.

```
sourcetype="impl_splunk_gen" loglevel=error | stats count by logger
```

This query produces the following chart:

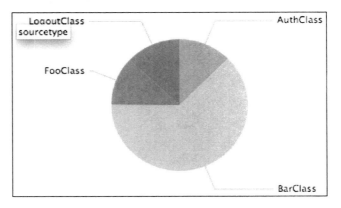

With this breakdown, we can see that the main producer of errors is the logger **BarClass**.

Let's learn another command, bucket. The bucket command is used to group sets of numeric values and has special capabilities with the _time field. This example will group the values of the field req_time in up to 10 evenly distributed bins. bucket has some other cool tricks we will use later. The following query will group req_time:

```
sourcetype="impl_splunk_gen" loglevel=error
    | bucket bins=10 req_time | stats count by req_time
```

The results produce the following pie chart:

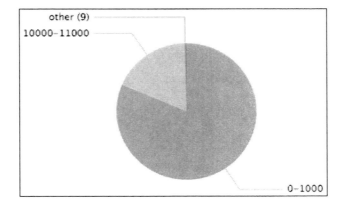

Using the wizard interface, step through the same actions to add these pie charts to our dashboard, this time choosing **Existing dashboard** in step 2.

By default, each new panel is added to the bottom of the dashboard. Dashboards allow you to have up to three panels distributed horizontally, which is a great way to show pie charts.

After clicking on the **On** button for **Edit**, near the top of the dashboard, you can drag the panels around the page, like so:

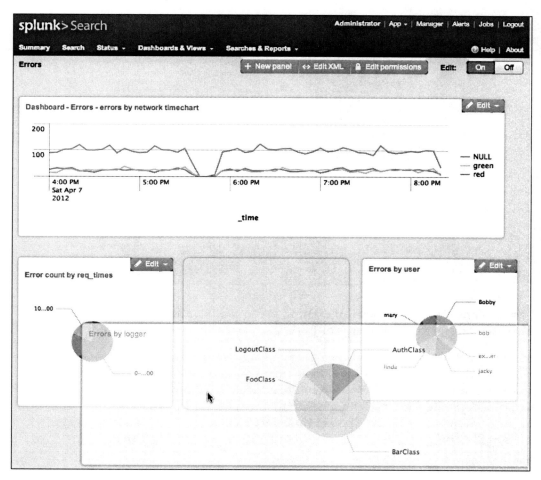

You may have noticed the three new buttons that appeared at the top of the dashboard after we clicked on the **On** button:

- **Edit XML** allows you to directly edit the XML underlying this dashboard. We will use this later in the chapter.

- **Edit permissions** takes you to the standard permissions panel that we have seen before.

- Clicking on **New panel** opens the following dialog to allow us to add new panels directly:

Saved search lets you choose an existing saved search. This allows you to reuse queries on different dashboards or build queries without a dashboard in mind.

Inline search string lets us build a query directly in the dashboard. This is often convenient as many searches will have no purpose but for a particular dashboard, so there is no reason for these searches to appear in the menus. This also reduces external dependencies, making it easier to move the dashboard to another app. Be sure to either specify an **Earliest time** value, or append | head to your query to limit the number of results, or the query will be run over **All time**.

In this case, we want to create an event listing. After clicking on **Save**, this panel is added to our dashboard.

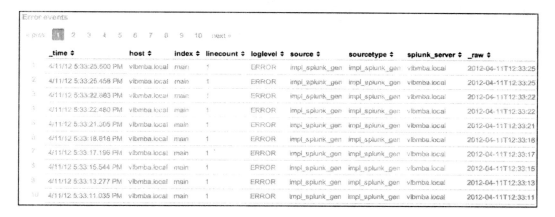

The default visualization type is **Table**, which is not what we want in this case. To change this, choose **Edit visualization** on the panel.

This presents us with an editor window where we can change the visualization type.

After saving and disabling the **Edit** mode, we see our event listing.

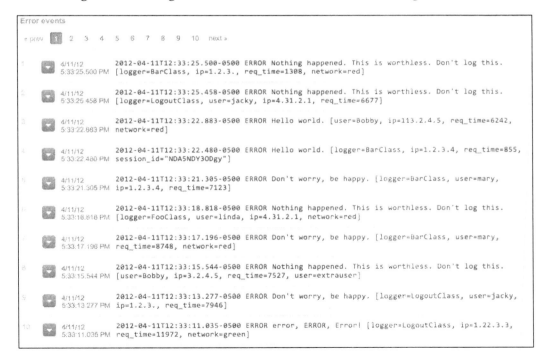

This panel is added to the bottom of the dashboard, which is just right in this case.

Scheduling the generation of dashboards

As we stepped through the wizard interface to create panels, we accepted the default value of **Run search each time dashboard loads**. If we instead select **Run scheduled search**, we are given a time picker.

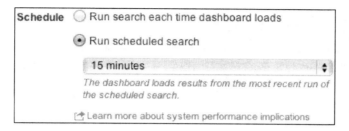

When the dashboard is loaded, the results from the last scheduled run will be used. The dashboard will draw as quickly as the browser can draw the panels. This is particularly useful when multiple users use a dashboard, perhaps in an operations group. If there are no saved results available, the query will simply be run normally.

Be sure to ask yourself just how fresh the data on a dashboard needs to be. If you are looking at a week's worth of data, is up to one-hour-old data acceptable? What about four hours old? 24 hours old? The less often the search is run, the fewer resources you will use, and the more responsive the system will be for everyone else. As your data volume increases, the searches will take more time to complete. If you notice your installation becoming less responsive, check the performance of your scheduled searches in the **Jobs** or the **Status** dashboards in the **Search** app.

For a dashboard that will be constantly monitored, real-time queries are probably more efficient, particularly if multiple people will be using the dashboard. New in Splunk 4.3, real-time queries are first backfilled. For instance, a real-time query watching 24 hours will first run a query against the previous 24 hours and then add new events to the results as they appear. This feature makes real-time queries over fairly long periods practical and useful.

Editing the XML directly

First let me take a moment to tip my hat to Splunk for the new dashboard editor in Splunk 4.3. There are only of a couple of reasons why you would still need to edit simplified XML dashboards: forms and post-processing data. I predict that these reasons will go away in the future as more features are added to the dashboard editor.

The documentation for simplified XML panels can be found by searching `splunk.com` for **Panel reference for simple XML**.

UI Examples app

Before digging into the XML behind dashboards, it's a very good idea to install the app *Splunk UI examples app for 4.1+*, available from Splunkbase (see *Chapter 7, Working with Apps*, for information about Splunkbase). The examples provided in this app give a good overview of the features available in both simplified XML and advanced XML dashboards.

The simplest way to find this app is by searching for `examples` in **App | Find more apps...**.

Building forms

Forms allow you to make a template that needs one or more pieces of information supplied to run. You can build these directly using raw XML, but I find it simpler to build a simple dashboard and then modify the XML accordingly. The other option is to copy an example, like those found in the *UI Examples* app (see the *UI Examples app* section, earlier in this chapter). We will touch on a simple use case in the following section.

Creating a form from a dashboard

First, let's think of a use case. How about a form that tells us about errors for a particular user? Let's start with a report for a particular user, our friend `mary`:

```
sourcetype="impl_splunk_gen" error user="mary"
  | stats count by logger
```

Now let's create a simple dashboard using this query:

1. Quickly create a simple dashboard using the wizard interface that we used before, by selecting **Create | Dashboard Panel**.

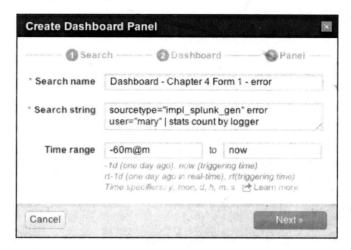

2. Select a destination for our new panel. In this case, we are making a new dashboard.

3. Select **Table** and give our panel a title.

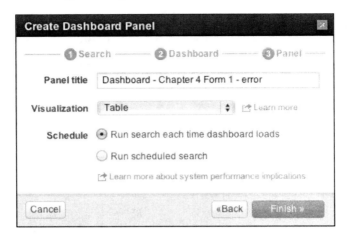

4. On the final window, click on the title next to **View dashboard**.

Let's look at the XML for our new dashboard. Click on the **On** button near the **Edit** label, then on **Edit XML**. The XML for our dashboard looks like this:

```
<?xml version='1.0' encoding='utf-8'?>
<dashboard>
  <label>Chapter 4 Form 1</label>
  <row>
    <table>
      <searchName>Dashboard - Chapter 4 Form 1 - error</searchName>
      <title>Dashboard - Chapter 4 Form 1 - error</title>
    </table>
  </row>
</dashboard>
```

That's pretty simple. To convert this dashboard into a form, we have to do the following things:

1. Searches need to be defined directly in the XML so that we can insert variables into the searches. We can use the editor itself to change the XML for us. Choose **Edit search** from the **Edit** menu on our table panel.

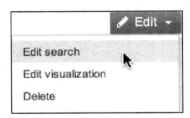

2. Then, click on **Edit as an inline search** followed by **Save**. This will convert the XML defining the query for us. The changes are highlighted.

```xml
<?xml version='1.0' encoding='utf-8'?>
<dashboard>
  <label>Chapter 4 Form 1</label>
  <row>
    <table>
      <searchString>
        sourcetype="impl_splunk_gen" error user="mary"
        | stats count by logger
      </searchString>
      <title>Dashboard - Chapter 4 Form 1 - error</title>
      <earliestTime>-60m@m</earliestTime>
      <latestTime>now</latestTime>
    </table>
  </row>
</dashboard>
```

3. Change `<dashboard>` to `<form>`. Don't forget the closing tag.

```xml
<form>
  <label>Chapter 4 Form 1</label>
...
  </row>
</form>
```

4. Create a `<fieldset>` tag with any form elements.

```
<form>
  <label>Chapter 4 Form 1</label>
  <fieldset>
    <input type="text" token="user">
      <label>User</label>
    </input>
  </fieldset>
  <row>
```

5. Add appropriate variables in `<searchString>` to reflect the form values.

```
<searchString>
  sourcetype="impl_splunk_gen" error user="$user$"
  | stats count by logger
</searchString>
```

When we're through, our XML looks like this:

```
<?xml version='1.0' encoding='utf-8'?>
<form>

  <label>Chapter 4 Form 1</label>

  <fieldset>
    <input type="text" token="user">
      <label>User</label>
    </input>
  </fieldset>

  <row>
    <table>
      <searchString>
        sourcetype="impl_splunk_gen" error user="$user$"
        | stats count by logger</searchString>
      <title>Dashboard - Chapter 4 Form 1 - error</title>
      <earliestTime>-60m@m</earliestTime>
      <latestTime>now</latestTime>
    </table>
  </row>

</form>
```

Let's click on **Save** and then search for bobby.

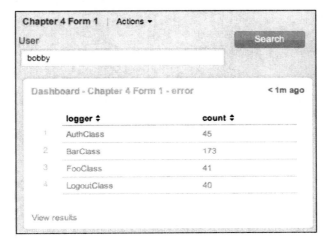

We now have a useful form for seeing errors by logger for a particular user.

Driving multiple panels from one form

A single form can also be used to drive multiple panels at once. Let's convert a copy of the **Errors** dashboard that we created earlier in the chapter into a form:

1. Choose **Manage Views** from **Dashboards & Views**, or select **Manager |
   User interface | Views**.

2. To make a copy, click on **Clone** on the same row as **errors**.

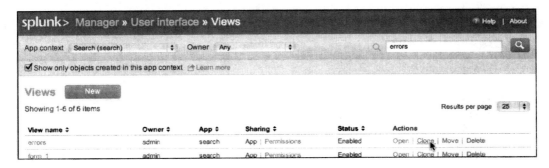

3. In the editor that appears next, the value of **View name** will actually be used as the filename and URL, so it must not contain spaces or special characters. Let's call it `errors_user_form`.

4. The name in the menu comes from the `label` tag inside the dashboard's XML. Let's change that to `Errors User Form`:

```
<label>Errors User Form</label>
```

5. Save the new dashboard and click on **Open** next to the dashboard.

6. Next, convert all of the searches to inline using **Edit | Edit search | Edit as inline search**, as we did in the previous example.

7. Change `<dashboard>` to `<form>` and add the same `<fieldset>` block as before.

8. Insert `user="$user$"` into each `<searchString>` tag appropriately.

The XML in the end will be much larger than what we saw before, but hopefully still understandable. Lines changed manually are highlighted in the following code snippet:

```
<?xml version='1.0' encoding='utf-8'?>
<form>

  <label>Errors User Form</label>

  <fieldset>
    <input type="text" token="user">
      <label>User</label>
    </input>
  </fieldset>

<row>
    <chart>
      <searchString>
        sourcetype="impl_splunk_gen" loglevel=error user="$user$"
        | timechart count as "Error count" by network
```

```
      </searchString>
      <title>Dashboard - Errors - errors by network timechart</title>
      <earliestTime>-4h@h</earliestTime>
      <latestTime>now</latestTime>
      <option name="charting.chart">line</option>
    </chart>
  </row>

  <row>
    <chart>
      <searchString>
        sourcetype="impl_splunk_gen" loglevel=error user="$user$"
        | bucket bins=10 req_time | stats count by req_time
      </searchString>
      <title>Error count by req_times</title>
      <earliestTime>-4h@h</earliestTime>
      <latestTime>now</latestTime>
      <option name="charting.chart">pie</option>
    </chart>
    <chart>
      <searchString>
        sourcetype="impl_splunk_gen" loglevel=error user="$user$"
        | stats count by logger
      </searchString>
      <title>Errors by logger</title>
      <earliestTime>-4h@h</earliestTime>
      <latestTime>now</latestTime>
      <option name="charting.chart">pie</option>
    </chart>
    <chart>
      <searchString>
        sourcetype="impl_splunk_gen" loglevel=error user="$user$"
        | stats count by user
      </searchString>
      <title>Errors by user</title>
      <earliestTime>-4h@h</earliestTime>
      <latestTime>now</latestTime>
      <option name="charting.chart">pie</option>
    </chart>
  </row>

  <row>
    <event>
      <searchString>
        sourcetype="impl_splunk_gen" loglevel=error user="$user$"
      </searchString>
      <title>Error events</title>
      <earliestTime>-4h@h</earliestTime>
      <latestTime>now</latestTime>
      <option name="count">10</option>
```

```
        <option name="displayRowNumbers">true</option>
        <option name="maxLines">10</option>
        <option name="segmentation">outer</option>
        <option name="softWrap">true</option>
      </event>
    </row>

  </form>
```

After clicking on **Save**, we should be back at the dashboard, which is now a form. Searching for bobby renders this:

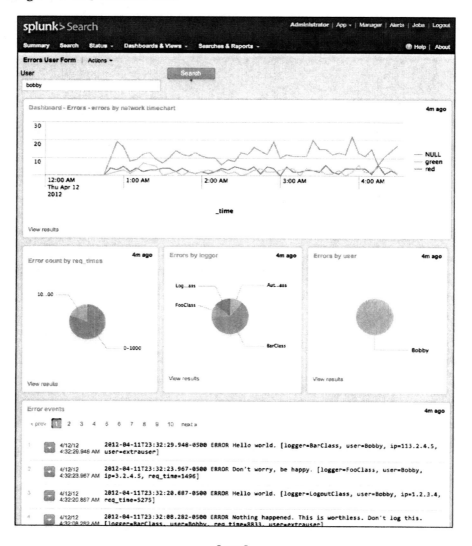

Let's make a few more changes:

1. Remove the **Errors by user** pie chart.

2. Add a `time` input to `<fieldset>`.

3. Remove the earliest and latest times from the queries. If a panel has time specified, it will always take precedence over the time field specified in `<fieldset>`.

Our XML now looks like this:

```
<?xml version='1.0' encoding='utf-8'?>
<form>

  <label>Errors User Form</label>

  <fieldset>
    <input type="text" token="user">
      <label>User</label>
    </input>
    <input type="time" />
  </fieldset>

  <row>
    <chart>
      <searchString>
        sourcetype="impl_splunk_gen" loglevel=error user="$user$"
        | timechart count as "Error count" by network
      </searchString>
      <title>Dashboard - Errors - errors by network timechart</title>
      <!-- remove time specifier -->
      <option name="charting.chart">line</option>
  </chart>
  </row>

  <row>
    <chart>
      <searchString>
        sourcetype="impl_splunk_gen" loglevel=error user="$user$"
        | bucket bins=10 req_time | stats count by req_time
      </searchString>
      <title>Error count by req_times</title>
      <!-- remove time specifier -->
      <option name="charting.chart">pie</option>
    </chart>
```

```
    <chart>
      <searchString>
        sourcetype="impl_splunk_gen" loglevel=error user="$user$"
        | stats count by logger
      </searchString>
      <title>Errors by logger</title>
    <!-- remove time specifier -->
      <option name="charting.chart">pie</option>
    </chart>
    <!-- errors by user removed -->
  </row>

  <row>
    <event>
      <searchString>
        sourcetype="impl_splunk_gen" loglevel=error user="$user$"
      </searchString>
      <title>Error events</title>
    <!-- remove time specifier -->
      <option name="count">10</option>
      <option name="displayRowNumbers">true</option>
      <option name="maxLines">10</option>
      <option name="segmentation">outer</option>
      <option name="softWrap">true</option>
    </event>
  </row>

</form>
```

Our dashboard now looks like this:

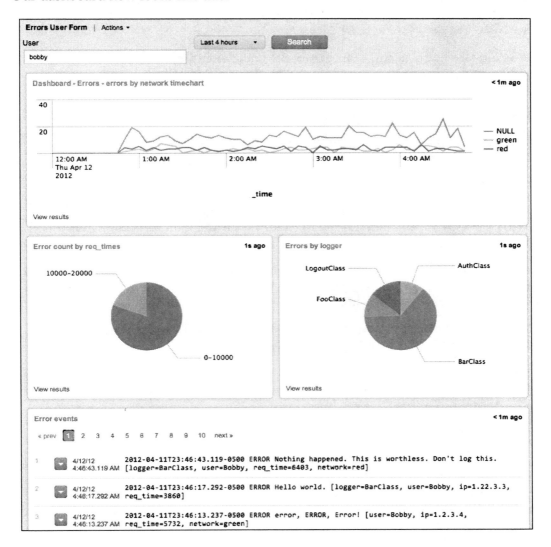

There are several other form elements available, with many options to customize their behavior. To find the official documentation, search `splunk.com` for `Build and edit forms with simple XML`.

There are also many useful examples in the documentation and in the *UI Examples* app (see the *UI Examples app* section, earlier in this chapter).

Post-processing search results

You may have noticed that, in our previous example, all of our queries started with the same actual query:

```
sourcetype="impl_splunk_gen" loglevel=error user="$user$"
```

It is of course wasteful to run the same query four times. Using `<searchPostProcess>`, we can run the query once and then run commands on the results for each panel.

The first step is to move the initial query out of the panel to the top level of the XML. The results from `<searchTemplate>` will be used by a panel if it has no query of its own or will be used as the source for `<searchPostProcess>`.

One additional piece of information is needed—the fields that are needed by the panels. We can get this by using `table`, like so:

```
<?xml version='1.0' encoding='utf-8'?>
<form>
  <searchTemplate>
    sourcetype="impl_splunk_gen" loglevel=error user="$user$"
    | table _time _raw network req_time logger
  </searchTemplate>
```

`table` mandates what fields will be passed from this query. `_time` is needed by the `timechart` command. `_raw` is used by the events listing panel at the bottom. `network`, `req_time`, and `logger` are used in the `by` clauses of each panel, respectively.

Let's edit our dashboard XML accordingly.

```
<?xml version='1.0' encoding='utf-8'?>
<form>

  <label>Errors User Form PostProcess</label>

  <searchTemplate>
```

```
    sourcetype="impl_splunk_gen" loglevel=error user="$user$"
    | table _time _raw network req_time logger
  </searchTemplate>

  <fieldset>
    <input type="text" token="user">
      <label>User</label>
    </input>
    <input type="time" />
  </fieldset>

  <row>
    <chart>
      <searchPostProcess>
        timechart count as "Error count" by network
      </searchPostProcess>
      <title>Dashboard - Errors - errors by network timechart</title>
      <option name="charting.chart">line</option>
    </chart>
  </row>

  <row>
    <chart>
      <searchPostProcess>
        bucket bins=10 req_time | stats count by req_time
      </searchPostProcess>
      <title>Error count by req_times</title>
      <option name="charting.chart">pie</option>
    </chart>
    <chart>
      <searchPostProcess>
        stats count by logger
      </searchPostProcess>
      <title>Errors by logger</title>
      <option name="charting.chart">pie</option>
    </chart>
  </row>

  <row>
    <event>
      <!-- remove searchString and use the events from searchTemplate
-->
      <title>Error events</title>
      <option name="count">10</option>
```

```
        <option name="displayRowNumbers">true</option>
        <option name="maxLines">10</option>
        <option name="segmentation">outer</option>
        <option name="softWrap">true</option>
      </event>
    </row>

  </form>
```

This will work exactly like our previous example but will only run the query once, drawing more quickly, and saving resources for everyone.

Post-processing limitations

When using `<searchPostProcess>`, there is one big limitation and several smaller limitations that often mandate a little extra work:

1. Only the first 10,000 results are passed from a raw query. To deal with this, it is necessary to run events through `stats`, `timechart`, or `table`. Transforming commands such as `stats` will reduce the number of rows produced by the initial query, increasing the performance.

2. Only fields referenced specifically are passed from the original events. This can be dealt with by using `table` (as we did in the previous example) or by aggregating results into fewer rows with `stats`.

3. `<searchPostProcess>` elements cannot use form values. If you need the values of form elements, you need to hand them along from the initial query.

4. Panels cannot use form values in a `<searchString>` element if they are referenced in the top level `<searchTemplate>` element. This can be accomplished in advanced XML, which we will cover in *Chapter 8, Building Advanced Dashboards*.

The first limitation is the most common item to affect users. The usual solution is to pre-aggregate the events into a superset of what is needed by the panels. To accomplish this, our first task is to look at the queries and figure out what fields need to be handed along for all queries to work.

Panel 1

Our first chart applies this post-processing:

```
timechart count as "Error count" by network
```

For this query to work, we need `_time`, `count` and `network`. Since `_time` is the actual time of the event, we need to group the times to reduce the number of rows produced by `stats`. We can use `bucket` for this task. Our initial query will now look like this:

```
sourcetype="impl_splunk_gen" loglevel=error user="$user$"
    | bucket span=1h _time
    | stats count by network _time
```

This query will produce results such as those shown in the following screenshot:

	_time ‡	network ‡	count ‡
1	4/16/12 2:00:00.000 AM	green	68
2	4/16/12 3:00:00.000 AM	green	55
3	4/16/12 4:00:00.000 AM	green	60
4	4/16/12 5:00:00.000 AM	green	77
5	4/16/12 6:00:00.000 AM	green	54
6	4/16/12 7:00:00.000 AM	green	72
7	4/16/12 8:00:00.000 AM	green	70
8	4/16/12 9:00:00.000 AM	green	69
9	4/16/12 10:00:00.000 AM	green	62
10	4/16/12 11:00:00.000 AM	green	69

To actually use these results in our panel, we need to modify the contents of `<searchPostProcess>` slightly. Since `count` expects to see raw events, the count will not be what we expect. We need instead to apply the `sum` function to the `count` field. We will also set the `span` value to match the span we used in the initial query:

```
timechart span=1h sum(count) as "Error count" by network
```

Panel 2

In the next panel, we currently have:

```
bucket bins=10 req_time | stats count by req_time
```

Since the `bucket` command needs to run against the raw events, we will add the command to the original query and also add `req_time` to `stats`:

```
sourcetype="impl_splunk_gen" loglevel=error user="$user$"
    | bucket span=1h _time
    | bucket bins=10 req_time
    | stats count by network _time req_time
```

Our results will then look like this:

	_time ‡	network ‡	req_time ‡	count ‡
1	4/16/12 3:00:00.000 AM	green	0-10000	29
2	4/16/12 3:00:00.000 AM	green	10000-20000	8
3	4/16/12 4:00:00.000 AM	green	0-10000	32
4	4/16/12 4:00:00.000 AM	green	10000-20000	7
5	4/16/12 5:00:00.000 AM	green	0-10000	50
6	4/16/12 5:00:00.000 AM	green	10000-20000	6
7	4/16/12 6:00:00.000 AM	green	0-10000	26
8	4/16/12 6:00:00.000 AM	green	10000-20000	5
9	4/16/12 7:00:00.000 AM	green	0-10000	34
10	4/16/12 7:00:00.000 AM	green	10000-20000	10

The panel query then becomes:

```
stats sum(count) by req_time
```

Panel 3

The last panel that we can add is the simplest yet.

```
stats count by logger
```

We simply need to add `logger` to the end of our initial query.

```
sourcetype="impl_splunk_gen" loglevel=error user="$user$"
  | bucket span=1h _time
  | bucket bins=10 req_time
  | stats count by network _time req_time logger
```

We will also need to replace count with sum(count), thus:

```
stats sum(count) by logger
```

Final XML

What we have built is a query that produces a row for every combination of fields. You can avoid this work by using `table`, but doing this extra work to reduce the rows produced by the initial query can increase performance considerably.

After all of these changes, here is our final XML. The changed lines are highlighted:

```xml
<?xml version='1.0' encoding='utf-8'?>
<form>

  <label>Errors User Form PostProcess</label>

  <searchTemplate>
    sourcetype="impl_splunk_gen" loglevel=error user="$user$"
      | bucket span=1h _time
      | bucket bins=10 req_time
      | stats count by network _time req_time logger
  </searchTemplate>

  <fieldset>
    <input type="text" token="user">
      <label>User</label>
    </input>
    <input type="time" />
  </fieldset>

  <row>
    <chart>
      <searchPostProcess>
        timechart span=1h sum(count) as "Error count" by network
      </searchPostProcess>
      <title>Dashboard - Errors - errors by network timechart</title>
      <option name="charting.chart">line</option>
    </chart>
  </row>

  <row>
    <chart>
      <searchPostProcess>
        stats sum(count) by req_time
      </searchPostProcess>
      <title>Error count by req_times</title>
      <option name="charting.chart">pie</option>
    </chart>
    <chart>
      <searchPostProcess>
        stats sum(count) by logger
      </searchPostProcess>
      <title>Errors by logger</title>
      <option name="charting.chart">pie</option>
    </chart>
  </row>

  <!-- remove the event listing, as per limitation #4 -->
</form>
```

Summary

Once again, we have really only scratched the surface of what is possible, using simplified XML dashboards. I encourage you to dig into the examples in the *UI Examples* app (see the *UI Examples app* section, earlier in this chapter).

When you are ready to make additional customizations or use some of the cool modules available from Splunk and the community, you can use advanced XML features, which we will look at in *Chapter 8, Building Advanced Dashboards*.

In *Chapter 5, Advanced Search Examples*, we will dive into advanced search examples, which can be a lot of fun. We'll expose some really powerful features of the search language and go over a few tricks that I've learned over the years.

Advanced Search Examples

In this chapter, we will work through a few advanced search examples in great detail. The examples and data shown are fictitious, but hopefully will spark some ideas that you can apply to your own data. For a huge collection of examples and help topics, check out Splunk answers at http://answers.splunk.com.

Using subsearches to find loosely related events

The number of use cases for subsearches in the real world might be small, but for those situations where they can be applied, subsearches can be a magic bullet. Let's look at an example and then talk about some rules.

Subsearch

Let's start with these events:

```
2012-04-20 13:07:03 msgid=123456 from=mary@companyx.com
2012-04-20 13:07:04 msgid=654321 from=bobby@companyx.com
2012-04-20 13:07:05 msgid=123456 to=bob@vendor1.co.uk
2012-04-20 13:07:06 msgid=234567 from=mary@companyx.com
2012-04-20 13:07:07 msgid=234567 to=larry@vender3.org
2012-04-20 13:07:08 msgid=654321 to=bob@vendor2.co.uk
```

From these events, let's find out who mary has sent messages to. In these events, we see that the from and to values are in different entries. We could use stats to pull these events together, and then filter the resulting rows, like this:

```
sourcetype=mail to OR from
   | stats values(from) as from values(to) as to by msgid
   | search from=mary@companyx.com
```

The problem is that on a busy mail server, this search might retrieve millions of events and then throw most of the work away. We want to actually use the index efficiently, and a subsearch can help us do that.

Here is how we could tackle this with a subsearch:

```
[search sourcetype=mail from=mary@companyx.com | fields msgid]
    sourcetype=mail to
```

Let's step through everything that's happening here:

1. The search inside the brackets is run:

    ```
    sourcetype=mail from=mary@companyx.com
    ```

    Given our sample events, this will locate two events:

    ```
    2012-04-20 13:07:03 msgid=123456 from=mary@companyx.com
    2012-04-20 13:07:06 msgid=234567 from=mary@companyx.com
    ```

2. `| fields msgid` then instructs the subsearch to only return the field `msgid`. Behind the scenes, the subsearch results are essentially added to the outer search as an OR statement, producing this search:

    ```
    ( (msgid=123456) OR (msgid=234567) ) sourcetype=mail to
    ```

    This will be a much more efficient search, using the index effectively.

3. This new search returns the answer we're looking for:

    ```
    2012-04-20 13:07:05 msgid=123456 to=bob@vendor1.co.uk
    2012-04-20 13:07:07 msgid=234567 to=larry@vender3.org
    ```

Subsearch caveats

To prevent a subsearch from being too expensive, they are limited by a time and event count:

*   The default time limit for the subsearch to complete is 60 seconds. If the subsearch is still running at that point, the subsearch is finalized, and only the events located up to that point are added to the outer search.

*   Likewise, the default event limit for the subsearch is 1,000. After this point, any further events will be truncated.

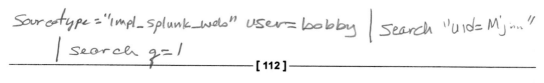

If either of these limits is reached, there is probably a better way to accomplish the task at hand.

Another consideration is that the fields returned from the subsearch must be searchable. There is a magical field called "search" that will be added to the query as a raw search term, but you have to do a little more work. See "search context" later in this chapter for an example.

Nested subsearches

Subsearches can also be nested, if needed. With mail server logs, it is sometimes necessary to find all the events related to a particular message. Some fictitious log entries are given, such as:

```
... in=123 msgid=123456 from=mary@companyx.com
... msgid=123456 out=987 subject=Important
... out=987 to=bob@vendor1.co.uk
```

We can see that the first event has the value of `from`, but there is no longer anything in common with the event that contains the `to` field. Luckily, there is an interim event that does contain `out`, and contains `msgid`, which we *do* have in the first event.

We can write a query like this to find our events:

```
[search sourcetype=mail out
  [search sourcetype=mail from=mary@companyx.com | fields msgid]
  | fields out]
  sourcetype=mail to
```

Here are the parts of the search, numbered according to the order of execution:

1. `[search sourcetype=mail from=mary@companyx.com | fields msgid]`

2. `[search sourcetype=mail out`

   `| fields out]`

3. `sourcetype=mail to`

Let's step through this example:

1. The innermost nested search (1) is run:

   ```
   sourcetype=mail from=mary@companyx.com | fields msgid
   ```

2. This is attached to the next innermost search (2), like this:

```
sourcetype=mail out
   (msgid=123456)
   | fields out
```

3. The results of this search are attached to the outermost search (3), like this:

```
(out=987)
   sourcetype=mail to
```

This is the final query, which returns the answer we are looking for:

```
... out=987 to=bob@vendor1.co.uk
```

Using transaction

The `transaction` command lets you group events based on their proximity to other events. This proximity is determined either by ranges of time, or by specifying the text contained in the first and/or last event in a transaction. This is an expensive process, but is sometimes the best way to group certain events. Unlike other transforming commands, when using `transaction`, the original events are maintained and instead are grouped together into multivalued events.

Some rules of thumb for the usage of `transaction` are as follows:

- If the question can be answered using `stats`, it will almost always be more efficient.
- All of the events needed for the transaction have to be found in one search.
- When grouping is based on field values, and all of the events need at least one field in common with at least one other event, then it can be considered as part of the transaction. This doesn't mean that every event must have the same field, but that all events should have some field from the list of fields specified.
- When grouping is based solely on `startswith` and `endswith`, it is important that transactions do not interleave in the search results.
- Every effort should be made to reduce the number of open transactions, as an inefficient query can use a lot of resources. This is controlled by limiting the scope of time with `maxspan` and `maxpause`, and/or by using `startswith` and `endswith`.

Let's step through a few possible examples of the `transaction` command in use.

Using transaction to determine the session length

Some fictitious events are given as follows. Assuming this is a busy server, there might be a huge number of events occurring between requests from this particular session:

```
2012-04-27T03:14:31 user=mary GET /foo?q=1 uid=abcdefg
```

...hundreds of events...

```
2012-04-27T03:14:46 user=mary GET /bar?q=2 uid=abcdefg
```

...hundreds of thousands of events...

```
2012-04-27T06:40:45 user=mary GET /foo?q=3 uid=abcdefg
```

...hundreds of events...

```
2012-04-27T06:41:49 user=mary GET /bar?q=4 uid=abcdefg
```

> The definition of "huge" depends on the infrastructure that you have dedicated to Splunk. See *Chapter 11, Advanced Deployments*, for more information about sizing your installation, or contact Splunk support.

Let's build a query to see the transactions belonging to `mary`. We will consider a session complete when there have been no events for five minutes:

```
sourcetype="impl_splunk_web" user=mary
  | transaction maxpause=5m user
```

Let's step through everything that's happening here:

1. The initial query is run, simply returning all events for the user `mary`:

   ```
   sourcetype="impl_splunk_web" user=mary
   ```

2. `| transaction` starts the command.

3. `maxpause=5m` indicates that any transaction that has not seen an event for five minutes will be closed. On a large dataset, this time frame might be too expensive, leaving a huge number of transactions open longer than necessary.

4. `user` is the field to use to link events together. If events have different values of user, a new transaction will start with the new value of user.

Given our events, we will end up with two groupings of events:

Each of these groupings can then be treated like a single event.

A `transaction` command has some interesting properties as follows:

- The field `_time` is assigned the value of `_time` from the first event in the transaction.
- The field `duration` contains the time difference between the first and last event in the transaction.
- The field `eventcount` contains the number of events in the transaction.
- All fields are merged into unique sets. In this case, the field `user` would only ever contain `mary`, but the field `q` would contain the values `[1,2]`, and `[3,4]` respectively.

With these extra fields, we can render a nice table of transactions belonging to `mary` like this:

```
sourcetype="impl_splunk_web" user=mary
    | transaction maxpause=5m user
    | table _time duration eventcount q
```

This will produce a table like this:

_time ‡	duration ‡	eventcount ‡	q ‡
4/30/12 5:39:49.000 PM	58	2	3 4
4/30/12 2:13:43.000 PM	2	2	1 2

Combining `transaction` with `stats` or `timechart`, we can generate statistics about the transactions themselves:

```
sourcetype="impl_splunk_web" user=mary
  | transaction maxpause=5m user
  | stats avg(duration) avg(eventcount)
```

This would give us a table, as shown in the following screenshot:

avg(duration) ⇕	avg(eventcount) ⇕
30.000000	2.000000

Calculating the aggregate of transaction statistics

Using the values added by `transaction`, we can somewhat naively answer the questions of how long the users spend on a site and how many pages they view per session.

Let's create sessions based on the `uid` field for all events. Using `stats`, we will then calculate the average `duration` value, the average `eventcount` value, and while we're at it, we will determine the distinct number of users and session IDs.

```
sourcetype="impl_splunk_web"
  | transaction maxpause=5m uid
  | stats avg(duration) avg(eventcount) dc(user) dc(uid)
```

This will give us a table as shown in the following screenshot:

avg(duration) ⇕	avg(eventcount) ⇕	dc(user) ⇕	dc(uid) ⇕
892.857143	227.553571	5	55

Transactions have an average length of 892 seconds, and 227 events.

For large amounts of web traffic, you will want to calculate transactions over small slices of time into a summary index. We will cover summary indexes in *Chapter 9, Using Summary Indexes*.

Combining subsearches with transaction

Let's put what we learned about subsearches together with transactions. Let's imagine that q=1 represents a particular entry point into our site, perhaps a link from an advertisement. We can use subsearch to find users that clicked on the advertisement, then use `transaction` to determine how long these users stayed on our site.

To do this, first we need to locate the sessions initiated from this link. The search can be as simple as:

```
sourcetype="impl_splunk_web" q=1
```

This will return events like:

```
2012-04-27T07:13:19 user=user1 GET /foo?q=1 uid=NDQ5NjIzNw
```

In our fictitious logs, the field `uid` represents a session ID. Let's use `stats` to return one row per unique `uid`:

```
sourcetype="impl_splunk_web" q=1
  | stats count by uid
```

This will render a table like this (the first 10 rows are shown):

	uid ⬍	count ⬍
1	MTA4NDI5Nw	2
2	MTAxNzE4NA	10
3	MTE3MDE0NQ	3
4	MTExMjM5NQ	1
5	MTI4OTc0Ng	1
6	MTM3NTIyNg	2
7	MTM3NjA1Ng	2
8	MTQ4MTEzNQ	3
9	MTY4NzYwMQ	3
10	MTcwNzIyNw	1

We need to add one more command, `fields`, to limit the fields that come out of our subsearch:

```
sourcetype="impl_splunk_web" q=1
  | stats count by uid
  | fields uid
```

Now we feed this back to our outer search:

```
[search
  sourcetype="impl_splunk_web" q=1
  | stats count by uid
  | fields uid
]
  sourcetype="impl_splunk_web"
```

After the subsearch runs, the combined query is essentially as follows:

```
( (uid=MTAyMjQ2OA) OR (uid=MTI2NzEzNg) OR (uid=MTM0MjQ3NA) )
  sourcetype="impl_splunk_web"
```

From this combined query, we now have every event from every `uid` that clicked a link that contained q=1 in our time frame. We can now add `transaction` as we saw earlier to combine these sessions into groups:

```
[search sourcetype="impl_splunk_web" q=1
  | stats count by uid
  | fields uid]
    sourcetype="impl_splunk_web"
    | transaction maxpause=5m uid
```

This gives us the following transactions:

Notice that not all of our transactions start with `q=1`. This means that this transaction did not start when the user clicked the advertisement. Let's make sure our transactions start from the desired entry point of `q=1`:

```
[search sourcetype="impl_splunk_web" q=1
 | stats count by uid
 | fields uid]
   sourcetype="impl_splunk_web"
   | transaction maxpause=5m
   startswith="q=1"
   uid
```

`startswith` indicates that a new transaction should start at the time the search term `q=1` is found in an event.

 `startswith` only works on the field `_raw` (the actual event text). In this case, `startswith="q=1"`, is looking for the literal phrase `"q=1"`, *not* the field q.

This will cause any occurrence of `q=1` to start a new transaction. We still have a few transactions that do not contain `q=1`, which we will eliminate next.

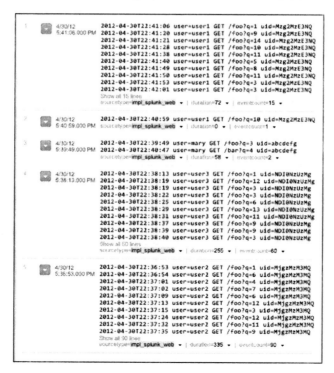

To discard the transactions that do not contain `q=1`, add a `search` command:

```
[search sourcetype="impl_splunk_web" q=1
  | stats count by uid
  | fields uid]
    sourcetype="impl_splunk_web"
    | transaction maxpause=5m startswith="q=1" uid
    | search q=1
```

Finally, let's add `stats` to count the number of transactions, the distinct values of `uid`, the average duration of each transaction, and the average number of clicks per transaction:

```
[search sourcetype="impl_splunk_web" q=1
  | stats count by uid
  | fields uid]
    sourcetype="impl_splunk_web"
    | transaction maxpause=5m startswith="q=1" uid
    | search q=1
    | stats count dc(uid) avg(duration) avg(eventcount)
```

This gives us a table as shown in the following screenshot:

count ⬍	dc(uid) ⬍	avg(duration) ⬍	avg(eventcount) ⬍
118	54	409.254237	103.440678

We can swap `timechart` with `stats` to see how these statistics change over time:

```
[search sourcetype="impl_splunk_web" q=1
  | stats count by uid
  | fields uid]
    sourcetype="impl_splunk_web"
    | transaction maxpause=5m startswith="q=1" uid
    | search q=1
    | timechart bins=500 avg(duration) avg(eventcount)
```

This produces a graph as shown in the following screenshot:

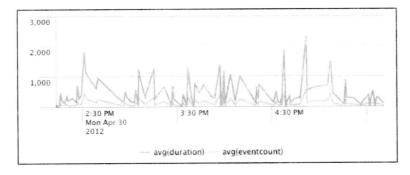

Determining concurrency

Determining the number of users currently using a system is difficult, particularly if the log does not contain events for both the beginning and end of a transaction. With web server logs in particular, it is not quite possible to know when a user has left a site. Let's investigate a couple of strategies for answering this question.

Using transaction with concurrency

If the question you are trying to answer is "how many transactions were happening at a time?", you can use `transaction` to combine related events and calculate the duration of each transaction. We will then use the `concurrency` command to increase a counter when the events start, and decrease when the time has expired for each transaction. Let's start with our searches from the previous section:

```
sourcetype="impl_splunk_web"
  | transaction maxpause=5m uid
```

This will return a transaction for every `uid`, assuming that if no requests were made for five minutes, the session is complete. This provides results as shown in the following screenshot:

By simply adding the `concurrency` command, we can determine the overlap of these transactions, and find out how many transactions were occurring at a time. Let's also add the `table` and `sort` commands to create a table:

```
sourcetype="impl_splunk_web"
  | transaction maxpause=5m uid
```

```
| concurrency duration=duration
| table _time concurrency duration eventcount
| sort _time
```

This produces a table as follows:

_time ⬍	concurrency ⬍	duration ⬍	eventcount ⬍
11/11/12 10:00:24.000 AM	1	1524	360
11/11/12 10:00:24.000 AM	2	130	60
11/11/12 10:00:24.000 AM	3	507	148
11/11/12 10:00:25.000 AM	4	690	187
11/11/12 10:00:25.000 AM	5	2033	439
11/11/12 10:00:27.000 AM	6	0	2
11/11/12 10:02:33.000 AM	6	966	194
11/11/12 10:08:56.000 AM	5	1768	365
11/11/12 10:11:54.000 AM	6	649	140
11/11/12 10:18:38.000 AM	6	1229	243
11/11/12 10:22:52.000 AM	5	163	39

From these results, we can see that as transactions begin, concurrency increases and then levels off as transactions expire. In our sample data, the highest value of **concurrency** we see is **6**.

Using concurrency to estimate server load

In the previous example, the number of concurrent sessions was quite low, since each transaction is counted as one event, no matter how many events make up that transaction. While this provides an accurate picture of the number of concurrent transactions, it doesn't necessarily provide a clear picture of server load.

Looking at the timeline of our events, we see a large spike of events at the beginning of our log. This did not affect the previous example, because most of these events belong to a single user session.

Some web logs provide the time it took to serve a request. Our log does not have this duration, so we'll use `eval` to simulate a value for `duration` per request:

```
sourcetype="impl_splunk_web"
  | eval duration=2
  | concurrency duration=duration
  | timechart max(concurrency)
```

Here we have set the duration of each request to 2 seconds. `concurrency` will use the value of `duration`, treating each event as if it were a 2-second long transaction. The timechart looks like this:

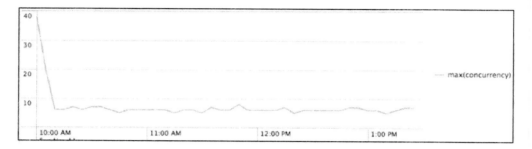

As we can see, in our sample data, the large spike of requests at the beginning of our log translates to high concurrency.

Later in this chapter, we will calculate events per some period of time, which will provide a very similar answer more efficiently, but it's not quite the same answer, as the count will be by fixed slices of time instead of a running total that changes with each event.

Calculating concurrency with a by clause

One limitation of the `concurrency` command is that there is no way to simultaneously calculate concurrency for multiple sets of data. For instance, what if you wanted to know the concurrency *per host*, as opposed to concurrency across your entire environment?

In our sample set of data, we only have one `host`, but we have multiple values for the `network` field. Let's use that field for our exercise.

Our fake concurrency example from the previous example looks like this:

```
sourcetype=impl_splunk_gen network="*"
   | eval d=2
   | concurrency duration=d
   | timechart max(concurrency)
```

First, let's rebuild this search using the `streamstats` command. This command will calculate rolling statistics and attach the calculated values to the events themselves.

To accommodate `streamstats`, we will need an event representing the start and end of each transaction. We can accomplish this by creating a multivalued field, essentially an array, and then duplicate our events based on the values in this field.

First, let's create our end time. Remember that `_time` is simply the UTC epoch time at which this event happened, so we can treat it as a number.

```
sourcetype=impl_splunk_gen network="*"
 | eval endtime=_time+2
```

Piping that through `table _time network endtime`, we see:

	_time ⬍	network ⬍	endtime ⬍
1	11/30/12 1:23:28.046 PM	qa	1354303410.046
2	11/30/12 1:23:25.869 PM	qa	1354303407.869
3	11/30/12 1:23:25.057 PM	qa	1354303407.057
4	11/30/12 1:23:22.736 PM	qa	1354303404.736
5	11/30/12 1:23:20.944 PM	prod	1354303402.944
6	11/30/12 1:23:19.729 PM	prod	1354303401.729
7	11/30/12 1:23:16.351 PM	qa	1354303398.351
8	11/30/12 1:23:15.544 PM	qa	1354303397.544
9	11/30/12 1:23:13.553 PM	prod	1354303395.553
10	11/30/12 1:23:11.155 PM	prod	1354303393.155

Next, we want to combine `_time` and our `endtime` into a multivalued field, which we will call `t`:

```
sourcetype=impl_splunk_gen network="*"
   | eval endtime=_time+2
   | eval t=mvappend(_time,endtime)
```

Piping that through `table _time network t`, we see:

_time ⬍	network ⬍	t ⬍
1	11/30/12 1:23:28.046 PM	qa	1354303408.046 1354303410.046
2	11/30/12 1:23:25.869 PM	qa	1354303405.869 1354303407.869
3	11/30/12 1:23:25.057 PM	qa	1354303405.057 1354303407.057
4	11/30/12 1:23:22.736 PM	qa	1354303402.736 1354303404.736
5	11/30/12 1:23:20.944 PM	prod	1354303400.944 1354303402.944
6	11/30/12 1:23:19.729 PM	prod	1354303399.729 1354303401.729
7	11/30/12 1:23:16.351 PM	qa	1354303396.351 1354303398.351
8	11/30/12 1:23:15.544 PM	qa	1354303395.544 1354303397.544
9	11/30/12 1:23:13.553 PM	prod	1354303393.553 1354303395.553
10	11/30/12 1:23:11.155 PM	prod	1354303391.155 1354303393.155

As you can see, we have our actual `_time`, which Splunk always draws according to the user's preferences, then our `network` value, and then the two values for `t` created using `mvappend`. Now we can expand each event into two events, so that we have a start and end event:

```
sourcetype=impl_splunk_gen network="*"
    | eval endtime=_time+2
    | eval t=mvappend(_time,endtime)
    | mvexpand t
```

`mvexpand` replicates each event for each value in the field specified. In our case, each event will create two events, as `t` always contains two values. All other fields are copied into the new event. With the addition of `table _time network t`, our events now look like this:

_time ⬍	network ⬍	t ⬍
1	11/30/12 1:23:28.046 PM	qa	1354303408.046
2	11/30/12 1:23:28.046 PM	qa	1354303410.046
3	11/30/12 1:23:25.869 PM	qa	1354303405.869
4	11/30/12 1:23:25.869 PM	qa	1354303407.869
5	11/30/12 1:23:25.057 PM	qa	1354303405.057
6	11/30/12 1:23:25.057 PM	qa	1354303407.057
7	11/30/12 1:23:22.736 PM	qa	1354303402.736
8	11/30/12 1:23:22.736 PM	qa	1354303404.736
9	11/30/12 1:23:20.944 PM	prod	1354303400.944
10	11/30/12 1:23:20.944 PM	prod	1354303402.944

Now that we have a start and end event, we need to mark the events as such. We will create a field named `increment` that we can use to create a running total. Start events will be positive, while end events will be negative. As the events stream through `streamstats`, the positive value will increment our counter, and the negative value will decrement our counter.

Our start events will have the value of `_time` replicated in `t`, so we will use `eval` to test this and set the value of `increment` accordingly. After setting `increment`, we will reset the value of `_time` to the value of `t`, so that our end events appear to have happened in the future.

```
sourcetype=impl_splunk_gen network="*"
  | eval endtime=_time+2
  | eval t=mvappend(_time,endtime)
  | mvexpand t
  | eval increment=if(_time=t,1,-1)
  | eval _time=t
```

With the addition of `table _time network increment`, this gives us results as shown in the following screenshot:

	_time ‡	network ‡	increment ‡
1	11/30/12 1:23:28.046 PM	qa	1
2	11/30/12 1:23:30.046 PM	qa	-1
3	11/30/12 1:23:25.869 PM	qa	1
4	11/30/12 1:23:27.869 PM	qa	-1
5	11/30/12 1:23:25.057 PM	qa	1
6	11/30/12 1:23:27.057 PM	qa	-1
7	11/30/12 1:23:22.736 PM	qa	1
8	11/30/12 1:23:24.736 PM	qa	-1
9	11/30/12 1:23:20.944 PM	prod	1
10	11/30/12 1:23:22.944 PM	prod	-1

`streamstats` expects events to be in the order that you want to calculate your statistics. Currently, our fictitious end events are sitting right next to the start events, but we want to calculate a running total of `increment`, based on the order of `_time`. The `sort` command will take care of this for us. The `0` value before the field list defeats the default limit of 10,000 rows.

```
sourcetype=impl_splunk_gen network="*"
  | eval endtime=_time+2
  | eval t=mvappend(_time,endtime)
  | mvexpand t
```

```
| eval increment=if(_time=t,1,-1)
| eval _time=t
| sort 0 _time network increment
```

 One thing to note at this point is that we have reset several values in this query using commands. We have changed _time, and now we have changed increment. A field can be changed as many times as is needed, and the last assignment in the chain wins.

Now that our events are sorted by _time, we are finally ready for streamstats. This command calculates statistics over a rolling set of events, in the order the events are seen. In combination with our increment field, this command will act just like concurrency, but will keep separate running totals for each of the fields listed after by:

```
sourcetype=impl_splunk_gen network="*"
| eval endtime=_time+2
| eval t=mvappend(_time,endtime)
| mvexpand t
| eval increment=if(_time=t,1,-1)
| eval _time=t
| sort 0 _time network increment
| streamstats sum(increment) as concurrency by network
| search increment="1"
```

The last search statement will eliminate our synthetic end events.

Piping the results through table _time network increment concurrency, we get these results:

	_time ‡	network ‡	increment ‡	concurrency ‡
1	11/29/12 12:00:00.788 AM	qa	1	1
2	11/29/12 12:00:01.005 AM	prod	1	1
3	11/29/12 12:00:03.551 AM	qa	1	1
4	11/29/12 12:00:03.981 AM	qa	1	2
5	11/29/12 12:00:04.671 AM	qa	1	3
6	11/29/12 12:00:05.573 AM	qa	1	3
7	11/29/12 12:00:06.013 AM	qa	1	3
8	11/29/12 12:00:07.694 AM	qa	1	2
9	11/29/12 12:00:08.212 AM	qa	1	2
10	11/29/12 12:00:10.714 AM	prod	1	1

With the addition of `timechart max(concurrency) by network`, we see:

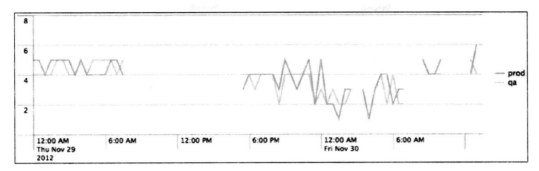

While this has been an interesting exercise, in the real world, you probably wouldn't calculate web server utilization in such a manner. The number of events is often quite large, and the time each event takes is normally negligible. This approach would be more interesting for longer running processes, such as batch or database processes.

The more common approach for web logs is to simply count events over time. We'll look at several ways to accomplish this next.

Calculating events per slice of time

There are a number of ways to calculate events per some period of time. All of these techniques rely on rounding `_time` down to some period of time, and then grouping the results by the rounded "buckets" of `_time`.

Using timechart

The simplest approach to count events over time is simply to use `timechart`, like this:

```
sourcetype=impl_splunk_gen
  | timechart span=1m count
```

In table view, we see:

_time ⬍	count ⬍
1	5/3/12 12:00:00.000 AM	109
2	5/3/12 12:01:00.000 AM	122
3	5/3/12 12:02:00.000 AM	122
4	5/3/12 12:03:00.000 AM	119
5	5/3/12 12:04:00.000 AM	125
6	5/3/12 12:05:00.000 AM	126
7	5/3/12 12:06:00.000 AM	119
8	5/3/12 12:07:00.000 AM	126
9	5/3/12 12:08:00.000 AM	120
10	5/3/12 12:09:00.000 AM	129
11	5/3/12 12:10:00.000 AM	114
12	5/3/12 12:11:00.000 AM	126
13	5/3/12 12:12:00.000 AM	120

Looking at a 24-hour period, we are presented with 1,440 rows, one per minute.

Charts in Splunk do not attempt to show more points than the pixels present on the screen. The user is instead expected to change the number of points to graph, using the bins or span attributes. *Calculating average events per minute, per hour shows another way of dealing with this behavior.*

If we only wanted to know about minutes that actually had events, instead of every minute of the day, we could use bucket and stats, like this:

```
sourcetype=impl_splunk_gen
   | bucket span=1m _time
   | stats count by _time
```

bucket rounds the _time field of each event *down* to the minute in which it occurred, which is exactly what timechart does internally. This data will look the same, but any minutes with out events will not be included. Another way to accomplish the same thing would be as follows:

```
sourcetype=impl_splunk_gen
   | timechart span=1m count
   | where count>0
```

Calculating average requests per minute

If we take our previous queries and send the results through `stats`, we can calculate the average events per minute, like this:

```
sourcetype=impl_splunk_gen
    | timechart span=1m count
    | stats avg(count) as "Average events per minute"
```

This gives us exactly one row:

Average events per minute ⬍
1   61.240972

Alternatively, we can use `bucket` to group events by minute, and `stats` to count by each minute that has values, as shown in the following code:

```
sourcetype=impl_splunk_gen
    | bucket span=1m _time
    | stats count by _time
    | stats avg(count) as "Average events per minute"
```

We are now presented with a much higher number:

Average events per minute ⬍
1   118.690444

Why? In this case, our fictitious server was down for about 10 hours. In our second example, only minutes that actually had events were included in the results, because `stats` does not produce an event for every slice of time, as `timechart` does. To illustrate this difference, look at the results of two queries:

```
sourcetype=impl_splunk_gen
    | timechart span=1h count
```

This query produces the following table:

	_time ⬍	count ⬍
1	5/8/12 7:00:00.000 AM	3362
2	5/8/12 8:00:00.000 AM	498
3	5/8/12 9:00:00.000 AM	0
4	5/8/12 10:00:00.000 AM	38

Using `bucket` and `stats`, like this:

```
sourcetype=impl_splunk_gen
   | bucket span=1h _time
   | stats count by _time
```

We then get this table:

	_time ‡	count ‡
1	5/8/12 7:00:00.000 AM	3362
2	5/8/12 8:00:00.000 AM	498
3	5/8/12 10:00:00.000 AM	38

In this case, there are no results for the 9:00 AM to 10:00 AM time slot.

Calculating average events per minute, per hour

One limitation of graphing in Splunk is that only a certain number of events can be drawn, as there are only so many pixels available to draw. When counting or adding values over varying periods of time, it can be difficult to know what timescale is being represented. For example, given the following query:

```
earliest=-1h sourcetype=impl_splunk_gen
   | timechart count
```

Splunk will produce this graph:

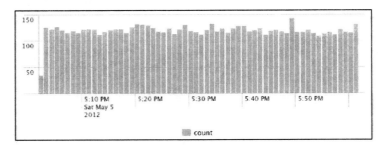

Each of these bars represent one minute. If we change the time frame to 24 hours:

```
earliest=-24h sourcetype=impl_splunk_gen
   | timechart count
```

We are presented with this graph:

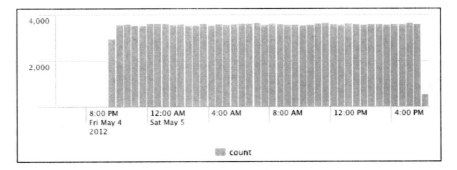

There is no indication of what period of time is represented by each bar unless you roll over the chart. In this case, each bar represents 30 minutes. This makes the significance of the y axis difficult to judge. In both cases, we can add span=1m to timechart, and we would know that each bar represents one minute. This would be fine for a chart representing one hour, but a query for 24 hours would produce too many points, and we would see a truncated chart.

Another approach would be to calculate the average events per minute, and then calculate that value over whatever time frame we are looking at. timechart provides a convenient function to accomplish this, but we have to do a little extra work.

```
earliest=-24h sourcetype=impl_splunk_gen
  | eval eventcount=1
  | timechart span=1h per_minute(eventcount)
```

per_minute calculates the sum of eventcount per minute, then finds the average value for the slice of time each bar represents. In this case, we are seeing the average number of events per hour.

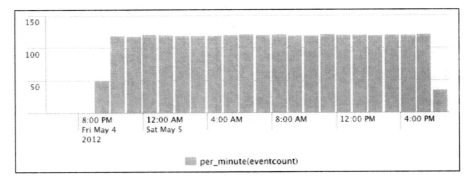

This scale looks in line with our one-hour query, as we are now looking at the event count per minute.

Like in the *Calculating average requests per minute* section, we could also ignore minutes that had no data. We could accomplish that as shown in the following code:

```
earliest=-24h sourcetype=impl_splunk_gen
   | bucket span=1m _time
   | stats count by _time
   | timechart span=1h avg(count)
```

This approach does not penalize incomplete hours, for instance, the current hour. The graph looks like this:

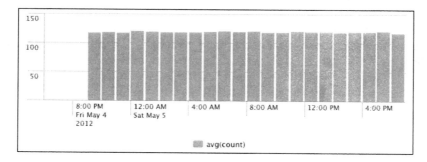

This gives us a better understanding of events for the *current* hour, but is arguably not entirely truthful about the *first* hour in the graph.

Rebuilding top

The `top` command is very simple to use, but is actually doing a fair amount of interesting work. I often start with `top`, then switch to `stats count`, but then wish for something that `top` provides automatically. This exercise will show you how to recreate all of the elements, so that you might pick and choose what you need.

Let's recreate the `top` command by using other commands.

Here is the query that we will replicate:

```
sourcetype="impl_splunk_gen" error
   | top useother=t limit=5 logger user
```

The output looks like this:

	logger ⇕	user ⇕	count ⇕	percent ⇕
1	BarClass	mary	773	18.812363
2	BarClass	jacky	422	10.270139
3	BarClass	bob	394	9.588708
4	BarClass	linda	391	9.515697
5	BarClass	Bobby	381	9.272329
6	OTHER	OTHER	1748	42.540764

To build `count`, we can use `stats` like this:

```
sourcetype="impl_splunk_gen" error
  | stats count by logger user
```

This gets us most of the way to our end goal:

	logger ⇕	user ⇕	count ⇕
1	AuthClass	Bobby	103
2	AuthClass	bob	68
3	AuthClass	extrauser	33
4	AuthClass	jacky	81
5	AuthClass	linda	79
6	AuthClass	mary	148
7	BarClass	Bobby	381
8	BarClass	bob	394
9	BarClass	extrauser	162
10	BarClass	jacky	422
11	BarClass	linda	391
12	BarClass	mary	773
13	FooClass	Bobby	104
14	FooClass	bob	87
15	FooClass	extrauser	43
16	FooClass	jacky	90
17	FooClass	linda	81
18	FooClass	mary	146
19	LogoutClass	Bobby	88
20	LogoutClass	bob	74
21	LogoutClass	extrauser	28
22	LogoutClass	jacky	82
23	LogoutClass	linda	80
24	LogoutClass	mary	171

To calculate the percentage that `top` includes, we will first need the total number of events. The `eventstats` command lets us add statistics to every row, without replacing the rows.

```
sourcetype="impl_splunk_gen" error
  | stats count by logger user
  | eventstats sum(count) as totalcount
```

This adds our `totalcount` column in the result:

	logger ⇕	user ⇕	count ⇕	totalcount ⇕
1	AuthClass	Bobby	103	4109
2	AuthClass	bob	68	4109
3	AuthClass	extrauser	33	4109
4	AuthClass	jacky	81	4109
5	AuthClass	linda	79	4109
6	AuthClass	mary	148	4109
7	BarClass	Bobby	381	4109
8	BarClass	bob	394	4109
9	BarClass	extrauser	162	4109
10	BarClass	jacky	422	4109
11	BarClass	linda	391	4109
12	BarClass	mary	773	4109
13	FooClass	Bobby	104	4109
14	FooClass	bob	87	4109
15	FooClass	extrauser	43	4109
16	FooClass	jacky	90	4109
17	FooClass	linda	81	4109
18	FooClass	mary	146	4109
19	LogoutClass	Bobby	88	4109
20	LogoutClass	bob	74	4109
21	LogoutClass	extrauser	28	4109
22	LogoutClass	jacky	82	4109
23	LogoutClass	linda	80	4109
24	LogoutClass	mary	171	4109

Now that we have our total, we can calculate the percentage for each row. While we're at it, let's sort the results in descending order by `count`:

```
sourcetype="impl_splunk_gen" error
  | stats count by logger user
  | eventstats sum(count) as totalcount
  | eval percent=count/totalcount*100
  | sort -count
```

This gives us:

	logger ⬍	user ⬍	count ⬍	percent ⬍	totalcount ⬍
1	BarClass	mary	773	18.812363	4109
2	BarClass	jacky	422	10.270139	4109
3	BarClass	bob	394	9.588708	4109
4	BarClass	linda	391	9.515697	4109
5	BarClass	Bobby	381	9.272329	4109
6	LogoutClass	mary	171	4.161596	4109
7	BarClass	extrauser	162	3.942565	4109
8	AuthClass	mary	148	3.601850	4109
9	FooClass	mary	146	3.553176	4109
10	FooClass	Bobby	104	2.531029	4109
11	AuthClass	Bobby	103	2.506693	4109
12	FooClass	jacky	90	2.190314	4109
13	LogoutClass	Bobby	88	2.141640	4109
14	FooClass	bob	87	2.117303	4109
15	LogoutClass	jacky	82	1.995619	4109
16	AuthClass	jacky	81	1.971283	4109
17	FooClass	linda	81	1.971283	4109
18	LogoutClass	linda	80	1.946946	4109
19	AuthClass	linda	79	1.922609	4109
20	LogoutClass	bob	74	1.800925	4109
21	AuthClass	bob	68	1.654904	4109
22	FooClass	extrauser	43	1.046483	4109
23	AuthClass	extrauser	33	0.803115	4109
24	LogoutClass	extrauser	28	0.681431	4109

If not for useother=t, we could simply end our query with head 5, which would return the first five rows. To accomplish the "other" row, we will have to label everything beyond row **5** with a common value, and collapse the rows using stats. This will take a few steps.

First, we need to create a counter field, which we will call rownum:

```
sourcetype="impl_splunk_gen" error
  | stats count by logger user
  | eventstats sum(count) as totalcount
  | eval percent=count/totalcount*100
  | sort -count
  | eval rownum=1
```

This gives us (only the first 10 rows are shown):

	logger ⇕	user ⇕	count ⇕	percent ⇕	rownum ⇕	totalcount ⇕
1	BarClass	mary	773	18.812363	1	4109
2	BarClass	jacky	422	10.270139	1	4109
3	BarClass	bob	394	9.588708	1	4109
4	BarClass	linda	391	9.515697	1	4109
5	BarClass	Bobby	381	9.272329	1	4109
6	LogoutClass	mary	171	4.161596	1	4109
7	BarClass	extrauser	162	3.942565	1	4109
8	AuthClass	mary	148	3.601850	1	4109
9	FooClass	mary	146	3.553176	1	4109
10	FooClass	Bobby	104	2.531029	1	4109

Next, using `accum`, we will increment the value of `rownum`:

```
sourcetype="impl_splunk_gen" error
    | stats count by logger user
    | eventstats sum(count) as totalcount
    | eval percent=count/totalcount*100
    | sort -count
    | eval rownum=1
    | accum rownum
```

This gives us (only the first 10 rows are shown):

	logger ⇕	user ⇕	count ⇕	percent ⇕	rownum ⇕	totalcount ⇕
1	BarClass	mary	773	18.812363	1	4109
2	BarClass	jacky	422	10.270139	2	4109
3	BarClass	bob	394	9.588708	3	4109
4	BarClass	linda	391	9.515697	4	4109
5	BarClass	Bobby	381	9.272329	5	4109
6	LogoutClass	mary	171	4.161596	6	4109
7	BarClass	extrauser	162	3.942565	7	4109
8	AuthClass	mary	148	3.601850	8	4109
9	FooClass	mary	146	3.553176	9	4109
10	FooClass	Bobby	104	2.531029	10	4109

Now using `eval`, we can label everything beyond row **5** as OTHER, and flatten
`rownum` **beyond 5:**

```
sourcetype="impl_splunk_gen" error
  | stats count by logger user
  | eventstats sum(count) as totalcount
  | eval percent=count/totalcount*100
  | sort -count
  | eval rownum=1
  | accum rownum
  | eval logger=if(rownum>5,"OTHER",logger)
  | eval user=if(rownum>5,"OTHER",user)
  | eval rownum=if(rownum>5,6,rownum)
```

This gives us (only the first 10 rows are shown):

	logger ⇕	user ⇕	count ⇕	percent ⇕	rownum ⇕	totalcount ⇕
1	BarClass	mary	773	18.812363	1	4109
2	BarClass	jacky	422	10.270139	2	4109
3	BarClass	bob	394	9.588708	3	4109
4	BarClass	linda	391	9.515697	4	4109
5	BarClass	Bobby	381	9.272329	5	4109
6	OTHER	OTHER	171	4.161596	6	4109
7	OTHER	OTHER	162	3.942565	6	4109
8	OTHER	OTHER	148	3.601850	6	4109
9	OTHER	OTHER	146	3.553176	6	4109
10	OTHER	OTHER	104	2.531029	6	4109

Next, we will recombine the values using `stats`. Events are sorted by the fields listed
after `by`, which will maintain our original order:

```
sourcetype="impl_splunk_gen" error
  | stats count by logger user
  | eventstats sum(count) as totalcount
  | eval percent=count/totalcount*100
  | sort -count
  | eval rownum=1
  | accum rownum
  | eval logger=if(rownum>5,"OTHER",logger)
  | eval user=if(rownum>5,"OTHER",user)
  | eval rownum=if(rownum>5,6,rownum)
  | stats
      sum(count) as count
      sum(percent) as percent
      by rownum logger user
```

This gives us:

rownum ‡	logger ‡	user ‡	count ‡	percent ‡
1	BarClass	mary	773	18.812363
2	BarClass	jacky	422	10.270139
3	BarClass	bob	394	9.588708
4	BarClass	linda	391	9.515697
5	BarClass	Bobby	381	9.272329
6	OTHER	OTHER	1748	42.540764

We're almost done! All that's left to do is hide the `rownum` column. We can use `fields` for this purpose:

```
sourcetype="impl_splunk_gen" error
    | stats count by logger user
    | eventstats sum(count) as totalcount
    | eval percent=count/totalcount*100
    | sort -count
    | eval rownum=1
    | accum rownum
    | eval logger=if(rownum>5,"OTHER",logger)
    | eval user=if(rownum>5,"OTHER",user)
    | eval rownum=if(rownum>5,6,rownum)
    | stats
        sum(count) as count
        sum(percent) as percent
        by rownum logger user
    | fields - rownum
```

This finally gives us what we are after:

logger ‡	user ‡	count ‡	percent ‡
BarClass	mary	773	18.812363
BarClass	jacky	422	10.270139
BarClass	bob	394	9.588708
BarClass	linda	391	9.515697
BarClass	Bobby	381	9.272329
OTHER	OTHER	1748	42.540764

And we're done. Just a reminder of what we were reproducing:

```
top useother=t limit=5 logger user
```

That is a pretty long query to replicate a one liner! While completely recreating `top` is not something practically needed, hopefully this example sheds some light on how to combine commands in interesting ways.

Summary

I hope this chapter was enlightening, and has sparked some ideas that you can apply to your own data. As stated in the introduction, Splunk Answers (`http://answers.splunk.com`) is a fantastic place to find examples and general help. You can ask your questions there, and contribute answers back to the community.

In the next chapter, we will use more advanced features of Splunk to help extend the search language, and enrich data at search time.

6
Extending Search

In this chapter, we will look at some of the features that Splunk provides
to go beyond its already powerful search language. We will cover the following
with the help of examples:

- Tags and event types that help you categorize events, both for search
  and reporting
- Lookups that allow you to add external fields to events as though they
  were part of the original data
- Macros that let you reuse snippets of search in powerful ways
- Workflow actions that let you build searches and links based on field
  values in an event
- External commands that allow you to use Python code to work with
  search results

In this chapter, we will investigate a few of the many commands included in Splunk.
We will write our own commands in *Chapter 12, Extending Splunk*.

Using tags to simplify search

Tags allow you to attach a "marker" to fields and event types in Splunk. You can then
search and report on these tags later. Let's attach a tag to a couple of users
who are administrators. Start with the following search:

```
sourcetype="impl_splunk_gen"
  | top user
```

This search gives us a list of our users such as **mary**, **linda**, **Bobby**, **jacky**, **bob**, and **extrauser**:

user ⬍	count ⬍	percent ⬍
mary	39044	31.695417
linda	19641	15.944311
Bobby	19593	15.905346
jacky	19503	15.832285
bob	19460	15.797378
extrauser	5944	4.825263

Let's say that in our group, `linda` and `jacky` are administrators. Using a standard search, we can simply search for these two users like this:

```
sourcetype="impl_splunk_gen" (user=linda OR user=jacky)
```

Searching for these two users while going forward will still work, but instead if we search for the tag value, we can avoid being forced to update multiple saved queries in the future.

To create a tag, first we need to locate the field.

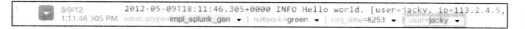

If the **user** field isn't already visible, click on it in the field picker, and then click on **Select and show in results**:

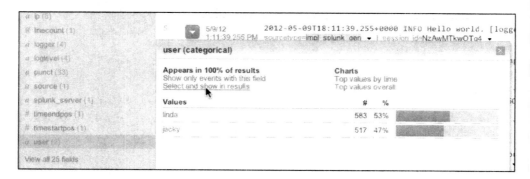

With the menu now visible, we can tag this value of the **user** field:

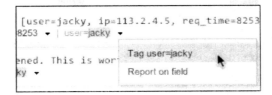

We are presented with the **Tag This Field** dialog as shown in the following screenshot. Let's tag `user=jacky` with `admin`:

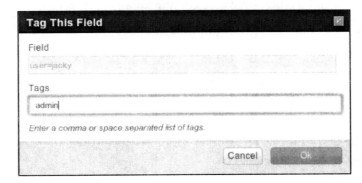

We now see our tag next to this field:

o world. [user=jacky, ip=113.2.4.
| req_time=8253 ▾ | user=jacky admin ▾

Once this is done, follow the steps used for `user=jacky` for `user=linda`.

With these two users tagged, we can search for the tag value instead of the actual usernames:

```
sourcetype="impl_splunk_gen" tag::user="admin"
```

Under the covers, this query is unrolled into exactly the same query we started with. The advantage is that if this tag is added to new values or removed from existing ones, no queries have to be updated.

Some other interesting features of tags are as follows:

- Tags can be searched globally simply by using `tag=tag_name`; in this case `tag=admin`. Using this capability, you can apply any tag to any field or event type, and simply search for the tag. This is commonly used in security applications to tag hosts, users, and event types that need special monitoring.

- Any field or event type can have any number of tags. Simply choose the tag editor and enter multiple tag values separated by spaces.

- To remove a tag, simply edit the tags again and remove the value(s) you want to remove.

- Tags can also be edited in **Manager** at **Manager | Tags**.

Using event types to categorize results

An event type is essentially a simple search definition, with no pipes or commands. To define an event type, first make a search. Let's search for:

```
sourcetype="impl_splunk_gen" logger="AuthClass"
```

Let's say these events are login events. To make an event type, choose **Event type...** from the **Create** menu, as shown here:

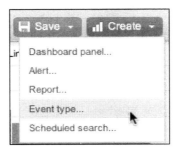

This presents us with a dialog, where we can assign a **Name** string and optionally any **Tags(s)** to this event type, as shown in the following screenshot:

Let's name our event type login.

We can now search for the same events using the event type:

```
eventtype=login
```

Event types can be used as part of another search, as follows:

```
eventtype=login loglevel=error
```

Event type definitions can also refer to other event types. For example, let's assume that all login events that have a loglevel value of ERROR are in fact failed logins.

We can now save this into another event type using the same steps as mentioned previously. Let's call it failed_login. We can now search for these events using the following:

```
eventtype="failed_login"
```

Now, let's combine this event type with the users that we tagged as admin in the previous section:

```
eventtype="failed_login" tag::user="admin"
```

This will find all failed logins for administrators. Let's now save this as yet another event type, failed_admin_login. We can now search for these events, as follows:

```
eventtype="failed_admin_login"
```

As a final step, let's tag this event type. First, make sure the field **eventtype** is visible. Your events should look like this:

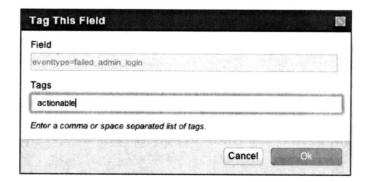

Notice the three values of **eventtype** in this case. We are searching only for eventtype=failed_admin_login, but this event also matches the definitions of eventtype=failed_login and eventtype=login. Also notice our tagged user. We are not searching for the admin tag, but jacky matches tag::user=admin, so the value is tagged accordingly.

Following the steps in the previous section, tag eventtype=failed_admin_login with the value actionable:

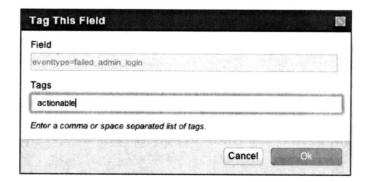

We can now search for these events with the following query:

```
tag::eventtype="actionable"
```

This technique is very useful for building up definitions of events that should appear in alerts and reports. For example, consider the following query:

```
tag::eventtype="actionable"
  | table _time eventtype user
```

This will now give us a very useful report, shown as follows:

_time ⇕	eventtype ⇕	user ⇕
1 5/14/12 12:43:02.202 PM	failed_admin_login failed_login login	jacky
2 5/14/12 12:42:16.394 PM	failed_admin_login failed_login login	jacky
3 5/14/12 12:40:17.947 PM	failed_admin_login failed_login login	jacky
4 5/14/12 12:39:30.712 PM	failed_admin_login failed_login login	linda
5 5/14/12 12:39:17.054 PM	failed_admin_login failed_login login	linda

Think about the ways that these event types are being used in this seemingly simple query:

- **Search**: An event type definition is defined as a search, so it seems only natural that you can search for events that match an event type definition.
- **Categorization**: As events are retrieved, if the events match the definition of *any* event type, those events will have that event type's name added to the eventtype field.
- **Tagging**: Since event types can also be tagged, tag values assigned to certain event types can be used for both search and categorization. This is extremely powerful for assigning common tags to varied sets of results; for instance, events that belong in a report or should cause an alert.

For clarity, let's unroll this query to see what Splunk is essentially doing under the covers. The query is expanded from the tag and event type definitions, as follows:

- `tag::eventtype="actionable"`
- `eventtype="failed_admin_login"`
- `eventtype="failed_login" tag::user="admin"`
- `(eventtype=login loglevel=error) tag::user="admin"`
- `((sourcetype="impl_splunk_gen" logger="AuthClass") loglevel=error) tag::user="admin"`
- `((sourcetype="impl_splunk_gen" logger="AuthClass") loglevel=error) (user=linda OR user=jacky)`

Let's explain what happens at each step:

1. The initial search.
2. All event types that are tagged `actionable` are substituted. In this case, we only have one, but if there were multiple, they would be combined with OR.
3. The definition of the event type `failed_admin_login` is expanded.
4. The definition of `failed_login` is expanded.
5. The definition of `login` is expanded.
6. All values of `user` with the tag `admin` are substituted, separated by OR.

Any changes to tagged values or event type definitions will be reflected the next time they are used in any search or report.

Using lookups to enrich data

Sometimes, information that would be useful for reporting and searching is not located in the logs themselves, but is available elsewhere. Lookups allow us to enrich data, and even search against the fields in the lookup as if they were part of the original events.

The source of data for a lookup can be either a **Comma Separated Values (CSV)** file or a script. We will cover the most common use of a CSV lookup in the next section. We will cover scripted lookups in *Chapter 12, Extending Splunk*.

There are three steps for fully defining a lookup: creating the file, defining the lookup definition, and optionally wiring the lookup to run automatically.

Defining a lookup table file

A lookup table file is simply a CSV file. The first line is treated as a list of field names for all other lines.

Lookup table files are managed at **Manager | Lookups | Lookup table files**. Simply upload a new file and give it a filename, preferably ending in .csv.

The lookup file `users.csv` is included in `ImplementingSplunkDataGenerator`:

```
user,city,department,state
mary,Dallas,HR,TX
jacky,Dallas,IT,TX
linda,Houston,HR,TX
Bobby,Houston,IT,TX
bob,Chicago,HR,IL
```

With this file uploaded, we can immediately use it with the `lookup` command. In the simplest case, the format of the `lookup` command is as follows:

```
lookup [lookup definition or file name] [matching field]
```

An example of its usage is as follows:

```
sourcetype="impl_splunk_gen"
  | lookup users.csv user
```

We can now see all of the fields from the lookup file as if they were in the events:

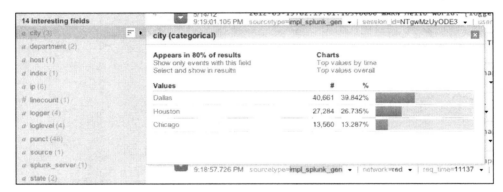

We can use these fields in reports:

```
sourcetype="impl_splunk_gen"
  | lookup users.csv user
  | stats count by user city state department
```

This will produce results as shown in the following screenshot:

	user ⇕	city ⇕	state ⇕	department ⇕	count ⇕
1	Bobby	Houston	TX	IT	13632
2	bob	Chicago	IL	HR	13560
3	jacky	Dallas	TX	IT	13411
4	linda	Houston	TX	HR	13652
5	mary	Dallas	TX	HR	27250

This is all that is required to use a CSV lookup to enrich data, but if we do a little more configuration work, we can make the lookup even more useful.

Defining a lookup definition

Though you can access a lookup immediately by the filename, defining the lookup allows you to set other options, reuse the same file, and later make the lookup run automatically. Creating a definition also eliminates a warning message that appears when simply using the filename.

Navigate to **Manager | Lookups | Lookup definitions** and click on the **New** button.

Stepping through these fields, we have:

- **Destination app**: This is where the lookup definition will be stored. This matters because you may want to limit the scope of a lookup to a particular application for performance reasons.

- **Name**: This is the name that you will use in search strings.

- **Type**: The options here are **File-based** or **External**. We will cover **External**, or scripted, in *Chapter 12, Extending Splunk*.

- **Lookup file**: We have chosen **users.csv** in this case.

- **Configure time-based lookup**: Using a time-based lookup, you can have a value that changes at certain points in time while going forward. For instance, if you built a lookup of what versions of software were deployed to what hosts at what time, you could generate a report on errors or response times by the software version.

- **Advanced options**: This simply exposes the remaining fields.

- **Minimum matches**: This defines the number of items in the lookup that must be matched. With a value of 1, the value of **Default matches** will be used if no match is found.

- **Maximum matches**: This defines the maximum number of matches before stopping. For instance, if there were multiple entries for each user in our lookup file, this value would limit the number of rows that would be applied to each event.

- **Default matches**: This value will be used to populate all fields from the lookup when no match is found, and **Minimum matches** is greater than 0.

After clicking on **Save**, we can use our new lookup in the following manner:

```
sourcetype="impl_splunk_gen"
    | lookup userslookup user
    | stats count by user city state department
```

This will produce results as shown in the following screenshot:

user ⇕	city ⇕	state ⇕	department ⇕	count ⇕
Bobby	Houston	TX	IT	13436
bob	Chicago	IL	HR	13315
extrauser	unknown	unknown	unknown	4171
jacky	Dallas	TX	IT	13184
linda	Houston	TX	HR	13443
mary	Dallas	TX	HR	26819

Notice that extrauser now appears in the table since it has values for city, state, and department.

Lookup tables have other features, including wildcard lookups, CIDR lookups, and temporal lookups. We will use those features in later chapters.

Defining an automatic lookup

Automatic lookups are, in this author's opinion, one of the coolest features in Splunk. Not only are the contents of the lookup added to events as if they were always there, but you can also search against the fields in the lookup file as if they were part of the original event.

To define the automatic lookup, navigate to **Manager | Lookups | Automatic lookups** and click on the **New** button:

Let's step through the fields in this definition:

- **Destination app**: This is the application where the definition will live. We'll discuss the implications of this choice in *Chapter 7, Working with Apps*.
- **Name**: This name is used in the configuration. It should not contain spaces or special characters. We will discuss its significance in *Chapter 10, Configuring Splunk*.
- **Lookup table**: This is the name of the lookup definition.
- **Apply to**: This lets us choose which events are acted upon. The usual case is **sourcetype**, which must match a sourcetype name exactly. Alternatively, you can specify **source** or **host**, with or without wildcards.

- **Lookup input fields**: This defines the fields that will be queried in the lookup file. One field must be specified, but multiple fields can be specified. Think of this as a join in a database. The left side is the name of the field in the lookup file. The right side is the name of the existing field in our events.

- **Lookup output fields**: This section lets you decide what columns to include from the lookup file and optionally overrides the names of those fields. The left side is the name of the field in the lookup file. The right side is the field to be created in the events. If left blank, the default behavior is to include all fields from the lookup, using the names defined in the lookup file.

- **Overwrite field values**: If this option is selected, any existing field values in an event will be overwritten by a value with the same name from the lookup file.

After clicking on **Save**, we see the listing of **Automatic lookups**. Initially, the **Sharing** option is **Private**, which will cause problems if you want to share searches with others. To share the lookup, first click on **Permissions**.

This presents us with the **Permissions** page. Change the value of **Object should appear in** to **All apps**. We will discuss these permissions in greater detail in *Chapter 10, Configuring Splunk*.

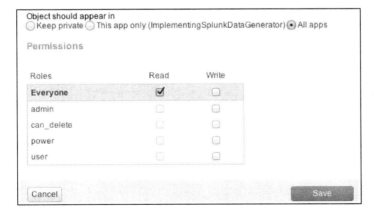

We now have a fully automatic lookup, enriching the source type `impl_splunk_gen` based on the value of `user` in each event. To show the power of this lookup, let's search for a field in the lookup file, as if it were part of the events:

```
source="impl_splunk_gen" department="HR" | top user
```

Even though `department` isn't in our events at all, Splunk will reverse the lookup, find the values of `user` that are in `department`, and run the search for those users. This returns the following result:

user ‡	count ‡	percent ‡
mary	6376	49.894358
bob	3206	25.088035
linda	3197	25.017607

Let's combine this search with an event type that we defined earlier. To find the most recent failed login for each member of HR, we can run:

```
source="impl_splunk_gen" department="HR" eventtype="failed_login"
  | dedup user
  | table _time user department city state
```

This returns:

_time ‡	user ‡	department ‡	city ‡	state ‡
5/14/12 11:07:48.570 PM	bob	HR	Chicago	IL
5/14/12 11:04:53.993 PM	linda	HR	Houston	TX
5/14/12 11:04:49.755 PM	mary	HR	Dallas	TX

The `dedup` command simply says to keep only one event for each value of `user`. As events are returned in the "most recent first" order, this query will return the most recent login for each `user`.

We will configure more advanced lookups in later chapters.

Troubleshooting lookups

If you are having problems with a lookup, very often the problem is with permissions. Check permissions at all three of these paths:

- **Manager | Lookups | Lookup table files**
- **Manager | Lookups | Lookup definitions**
- **Manager | Lookups | Automatic lookups**

Once permissions are squared away, be sure to keep the following points in mind:

- Check your spelling of the fields.
- By default, lookup values are case sensitive.
- If your installation is using multiple indexers, it may take some time for the lookup files and definitions to be distributed to your indexers, particularly if the lookup files are large or you have installed many apps that have assets to be distributed.
- A rule of thumb is that a lookup file should not have more than two million rows. If a lookup is too large, an external lookup script may be required.

Using macros to reuse logic

A **macro** serves the purpose of replacing bits of search language with expanded phrases. Using macros can help you reuse logic and greatly reduce the length of queries.

Let's use one of our examples from *Chapter 5, Advanced Search Examples*, as our example case:

```
sourcetype="impl_splunk_web" user=mary
   | transaction maxpause=5m user
   | stats avg(duration) avg(eventcount)
```

Creating a simple macro

Let's take the last two lines of our query and convert them to a macro. First, navigate to **Manager | Advanced search | Advanced search | Search macros** and click on **New**.

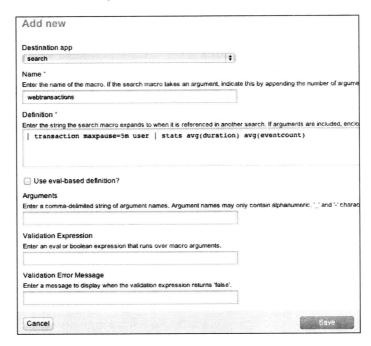

Walking through our fields, we have:

- **Destination app**: This is where the macro will live.
- **Name**: This is the name we will use in our searches.
- **Definition**: This is the text that will be placed in our search.
- **Use eval-based definition?**: If checked, the **Definition** string is treated as an `eval` statement instead of raw text. We'll use this option later.
- The remaining fields are used if arguments are specified. We will use these in our next example.

After clicking on **Save**, our macro is now available for use. We can use it like this:

```
sourcetype="impl_splunk_web" user=mary `webtransactions`
```

`webtransactions` is enclosed by backticks. This is similar to the usage of backticks on a Unix command line, where a program can be executed to generate an argument. In this case, `webtransactions` is simply replaced with the raw text defined in the macro, recreating the query we started with.

Creating a macro with arguments

Let's collapse the entire search into a macro that takes two arguments, the user and a value for maxpause.

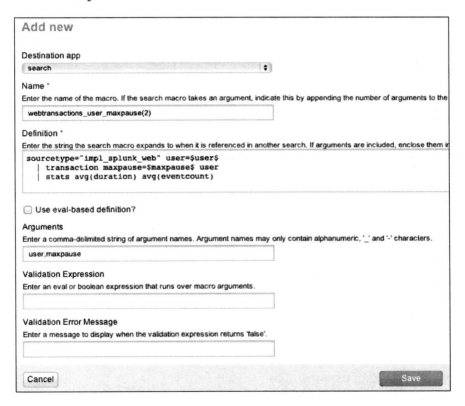

Be sure to remove newlines from your search definition. Macros do not appear to work with embedded newlines.

Walking through our fields, we have:

- **Name**: This is the name we will use in our searches. The parentheses and integer (2) specify how many arguments this macro expects.
- **Definition**: We have defined the entire query in this case. The variables are defined as $user$ and $maxpause$. We can use these names because we have defined the variables under **Arguments**.
- **Arguments**: This list assigns variable names to the values handed in to the macro.

After clicking on **Save**, our macro is now available for use. We can use it like this:

```
webtransactions_user_maxpause(mary,5m)
```

or

```
`webtransactions_user_maxpause("mary","5m")`
```

Using eval to build a macro

We will use this feature in conjunction with a workflow action later in this chapter. See the *Building a workflow action to show field context* section later in this chapter.

Creating workflow actions

Workflow actions allow us to create custom actions based on the values in search results. The two supported actions either run a search or link to a URL.

Running a new search using values from an event

To build a workflow action, navigate to **Manager** | **Fields** | **Workflow actions** and click on **New**. You are presented with this form:

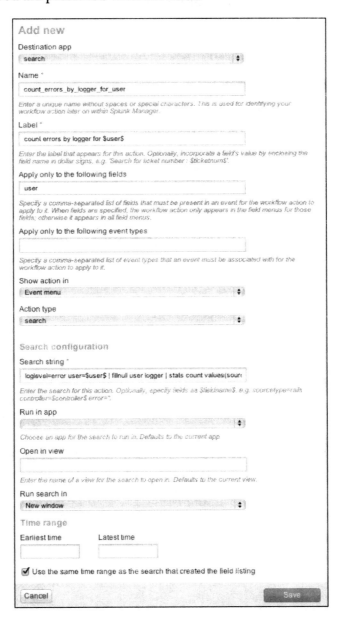

Let's walk through the following fields:

- **Destination app**: This is the app where the workflow action definition will live.

- **Name**: This is the name used in configuration files. This name cannot contain spaces, but underscores are fine.

- **Label**: This is what will appear in the menu. It can contain variables. In this case, we have included $user$, which will be populated with the value of the user field from the event.

- **Apply only to the following fields**: This workflow action will only appear on an event if all fields specified in this list have a value. **Show action in** will determine which menus can contain the workflow action.

- **Apply only to the following event types**: Only show this workflow action for events that match a particular event type. For instance, if you defined an event type called login, you might want a custom workflow action to search for all logins for this particular user over the last week.

- **Show action in**: The three options are **Event menu**, **Fields menus**, and **Both**.
    - The **Event menu** option is to the left of the event. If **Apply only to the following fields** is not empty, the workflow action will only be present if all of the fields specified are present in the event.
    - The **Fields menus** option falls to the right of each field under the events. If **Apply only to the following fields** is not empty, only the fields listed will contain the workflow action.
    - **Both** will show the workflow action in both places, following the same rules.

- **Action type**: The choices here are **search** or **link**. We have chosen **search**. We will try **link** in the next section.

- **Search string**: This is the search template to run. You will probably use field values here, but it is not required.

- **Run in app**: If left blank, the current app will be used, otherwise the search will be run in the app that is specified. You would usually want to leave this blank.

- **Open in view**: If left blank, the current view will be used. If you expect to use an events listing panel on dashboards, you probably want to set this to flashtimeline.

- **Run search in**: The choices here are **New window** or **Current window**.

- **Time range**: You *can* specify a specific time range here, either in epoch time or relative time. Leaving **Latest time** empty will search to the latest data available.

- **Use the same time range as the search that created the field listing**: In most cases, you will either check this checkbox or provide a value in at least **Earliest time**. If you do not, the query will run over all time, which is not usually what you want. It is also possible to specify the time frame in our query.

After we click on **Save**, we now see our action in the event workflow action menu like this:

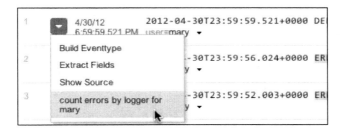

After we choose the option, a new window appears with our results, like this:

user ⬍	logger ⬍	count ⬍	values(sourcetype) ⬍
mary	0	131	impl_splunk_gen
mary	AuthClass	64	impl_splunk_gen
mary	BarClass	251	impl_splunk_gen
mary	FooClass	46	impl_splunk_gen
mary	LogoutClass	55	impl_splunk_gen

Linking to an external site

A workflow action can also link to an external site, using information from an event. Let's imagine that your organization has some other web-based tool. If that tool can accept arguments via GET or POST requests, then we can link directly to it from the Splunk results.

Create a new workflow action as we did in the previous example, but change **Action type** to **link**. The options change to those shown in the following screenshot:

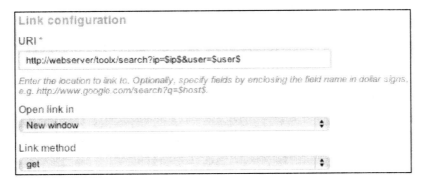

Splunk will encode any variables in the URL so that special characters survive. If you need a variable to not be encoded—for instance, if the value is actually part of the URL—add an exclamation point before the variable name, like this:

```
$!user$
```

If **Link method** is set to **post**, then more input fields appear, allowing you to specify post arguments like this:

Choosing this workflow action will open a new window with the URL we specified, either in the current window or in a new window according to the value of **Open link in**.

 The fields used by a workflow action can also come from automatic lookups. This is useful in cases where the external tool needs some piece of information that is not in your events, but can be derived from your events.

Building a workflow action to show field context

Show Source is available as a workflow action on all events. When chosen, it runs a query that finds events around the current event for the same `source` and `host`. While this is very useful, sometimes it would be nice to see events that have something else in common besides `source`, and to see those events in the regular search interface, complete with the timeline and field picker.

To accomplish this, we will make a workflow action and macro that work in tandem to build the appropriate query. This example is fairly advanced, so don't be alarmed if it doesn't make a lot of sense.

Building the context workflow action

First, let's build our workflow action. As before, make a workflow action with **Action type** set to **search**.

Let's step through our values, as follows:

- **Name**: This can be anything. Let's name it after our time frame.
- **Label**: This is what will appear in the menu. You may notice two special fields, @field_name and @field_value. These two fields only make sense when **Show action in** is set to **Fields menus**.

> There are a number of @variables available to workflow actions. Search http://docs.splunk.com/ for Create workflow actions in Splunk to find complete documentation.

- **Apply only to the following fields**: This can be blank or * to indicate all fields.
- **Show action in**: We have chosen **Fields menus** in this case.
- **Action type**: We are running a search. It's a fairly strange search, as we are using a macro, but it is still technically a search.
- **Search string**: The fact that this query is a macro doesn't matter to the workflow action, `context("$@field_name$", "$@field_value$", "$_time$", "-1m", "+5m")`. We will create the context macro next.
- **Run in app**: With nothing chosen, this macro will execute the search in the current app.
- **Open in view**: We want to make sure that our query executes in flashtimeline, so we explicitly set it.
- **Run search in**: We choose **New window**.
- **Time**: Contrary to the previous advice, we have left the time frame unspecified. We will be overriding the search times in the search itself. Anything specified here will be replaced.

After clicking on **Save**, the workflow action is available on all the field menus.

Choosing this menu item generates this search:

```
'context("ip", "1.22.3.3", "2012-05-16T20:23:59-0500", "-1m", "+5m")'
```

Let us consider our query definition:

```
'context("$@field_name$", "$@field_value$", "$_time$", "-1m", "+5m")'
```

We can see that the variables were simply replaced, and the rest of the query was left unchanged. _time is not in the format I would expect (I would have expected the epoch value), but we can work with it.

Building the context macro

When searching, you can specify the time ranges in the query itself. There are several fields that allow us to specify the time. They are as follows:

- earliest: This is the earliest time, inclusive. It can be specified as either a relative time or an epoch time in seconds.

- latest: This is the latest time, exclusive. Only events with a date *before* this time will be returned. This value can be specified as either a relative time or an epoch time in seconds.

- now: Using this field, you can redefine what relative values in earliest and latest are calculated against. It must be defined as epoch time in seconds.

Now, given our inputs, let's define our variable names:

- field_name = ip
- field_value = 1.22.3.3
- event_time = 2012-05-16T20:23:59-0500
- earliest_relative = -1m
- latest_relative = +5m

The query we want to run looks like this:

```
earliest=-1m latest=+5m now=[epoch event time] ip=1.22.3.3
```

The only value we don't have is now. To calculate this, there is a function available to eval called strptime. To test this function, let's use |stats to create an event, build an event_time field, and parse the value. Consider the following code:

```
|stats count
  | eval event_time="2012-05-16T20:23:59-0500"
  | eval now=strptime(event_time, "%Y-%m-%dT%H:%M:%S%z")
```

This gives us the following table:

count ⇕	event_time ⇕	now ⇕
1	0	2012-05-16T20.23.59-0500	1337217839.000000

> Good references for strptime formats can be found on modern
> Linux systems by running man strptime or man date, or by
> searching google.com. Splunk has several special extensions
> to strptime that can be found by searching for Enhanced
> strptime() support at http://docs.splunk.com/.

Now that we have our epoch value for now, we can build and test our query like this:

```
earliest=-1m latest=+5m now=1337217839 ip=1.22.3.3
```

This gives us a normal event listing, from one minute before our event to
five minutes after our selected event, only showing events that have the field
ip in common.

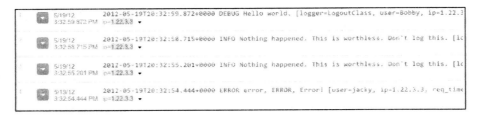

Now that we have our search, and our eval statement for converting the value
of now, we can actually build our macro in **Manager | Advanced search | Search
macros | Add new**.

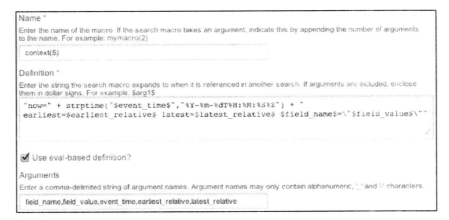

This macro is using a few interesting features, as follows:

- Macros can take arguments. The number of arguments is specified in the name of the macro by appending ([argument count]) to the name of the macro. In this case, we are expecting five arguments.

- The definition of a macro can actually be an eval statement. This means we can use eval functions to build our query based on some value handed to the macro. In this case, we are using strptime. Things to note about this feature are as follows:

  ○ The eval statement is expected to return a string. If your statement fails, for some reason, to return a string, the user will see an error.

  ○ The variable names specified are replaced before the eval statement is executed. This means that there may be issues with escaping the values in the variables, so some care is required to make sure whether your value contains quotes or not as is expected.

- **Use eval-based definition?** is checked to indicate that this macro is expected to be parsed as an eval statement.

- In the **Arguments** field, we specify names for the arguments handed in. These are the names we refer to in the **Definition** field.

After clicking on **Save**, we have a working macro. You might make adjustments to this workflow action to better suit your needs. Let's change the definition to sort events by ascending time, and prevent searching across indexes. Change the workflow action definition **Search string** to:

```
'context("$@field_name$", "$@field_value$", "$_time$", "-1m", "+5m")'
  index=$index$ | reverse
```

Let's expand this just for clarity, like this:

```
'context("$@field_name$", "$@field_value$", "$_time$", "-1m", "+5m")'
  index=$index$ | reverse
'context("ip", "1.22.3.3", "2012-05-16T20:23:59-0500", "-1m", "+5m")'
  index=implsplunk | reverse
earliest=-1m latest=+5m now=1337217839 ip=1.22.3.3
  index=implsplunk | reverse
```

You can create multiple workflow actions that specify different time frames, or include other fields, for instance host.

Using external commands

The Splunk search language is extremely powerful, but at times, it may be either difficult or impossible to accomplish some piece of logic by using nothing but the search language. To deal with this, Splunk allows external commands to be written in Python. A number of commands ship with the product, and a number of commands are available in apps at http://splunk-base.splunk.com/.

Let's try out a few of the included commands. The documentation for the commands is included with other search commands at http://docs.splunk.com/. You can find a list of all included commands, both internal and external, by searching for All search commands. We will write our own commands in *Chapter 12, Extending Splunk*.

Extracting values from XML

Fairly often, machine data is written in XML format. Splunk will index this data without any issue, but it has no native support for XML. Though XML is not an ideal logging format, it can usually be parsed simply enough. Two commands are included in the search app that can help us pull fields out of XML.

xmlkv

xmlkv uses regular expressions to create fields from tag names. For instance, given the following XML:

```
<doc><a>foo</a><b>bar</b></doc>
```

xmlkv will produce the fields a=foo and b=bar. To test, try this:

```
|stats count
  | eval _raw="<doc><a>foo</a><b>bar</b></doc>"
  | xmlkv
```

This produces a table, as shown in the following screenshot:

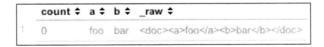

As this command is using regular expressions its advantage is that malformed or incomplete XML statements will still produce results.

Using an external command is significantly slower than using the native search language, particularly if you are dealing with large sets of data. If it is possible to build the required fields using `rex` or `eval`, it will execute faster and it will introduce a smaller load on your Splunk servers. For instance, in the previous example, the fields could be extracted using:

```
| rex "<a.*?>(?<a>.*?)<" | rex "<b.*?>(?<b>.*?)<"
```

XPath

XPath is a powerful language for selecting values from an XML document. Unlike `xmlkv`, which uses regular expressions, XPath uses an XML parser. This means that the event must actually contain a valid XML document.

For example, consider the following XML document:

```
<d>
  <a x="1">foo</a>
  <a x="2">foo2</a>
  <b>bar</b>
</d>
```

If we wanted the value for the a tag whose x attribute equals 2, the XPath code would look like this:

```
//d/a[@x='2']
```

To test this, let's use our `|stats` trick to generate a single event and execute the `xpath` statement:

```
|stats count
  | eval _raw="<d><a x='1'>foo</a><a x='2'>foo2</a><b>bar</b></d>"
  | xpath outfield=a "//d/a[@x='2']"
```

This generates an output, as shown in the following screenshot:

count ⬍	a ⬍	_raw ⬍
0	foo2	<d><a x='1'>foo</a><a x='2'>foo2</a>bar</d>

`xpath` will also retrieve multivalue fields. For instance, this `xpath` statement simply says to find any a field:

```
|stats count
  | eval _raw="<d><a x='1'>foo</a><a x='2'>foo2</a><b>bar</b></d>"
  | xpath outfield=a "//a"
```

The result of this query is as shown:

count ⬍	a ⬍	_raw ⬍
0	foo foo2	<d><a x='1'>foo</a><a x='2'>foo2</a>bar</d>

There are many XPath references available online. My favorite quick reference is at the Mulberry Technologies website: `http://www.mulberrytech.com/quickref/xpath2.pdf`.

Using Google to generate results

External commands can also act as data generators, similar to the `stats` command that we used to create test events. There are a number of these commands, but let's try a fun example, `google`. This command takes one argument, a search string, and returns the results as a set of events. Let's execute a search for `splunk`:

```
|google "splunk"
```

This produces a table, as shown in the following screenshot:

This example may not be terribly useful, but you can probably think of external sources that you would like to query as a starting point, or even to populate a subsearch for another Splunk query. We'll write an example data generator in *Chapter 12, Extending Splunk*.

Summary

In this chapter, we quickly covered tags, event types, lookups, macros, workflow actions, and external commands. I hope these examples and discussions will serve as starting points for your apps. More examples can be found in the official Splunk documentation at `http://docs.splunk.com/` and at `http://splunk-base.splunk.com/`.

In the next chapter, we will dive into creating and customizing our own apps.

7
Working with Apps

In this chapter, we will explore what makes up a Splunk app. We will:

- Inspect included apps
- Install apps from Splunkbase
- Build our own app
- Customize app navigation
- Customize app look and feel

Defining an app

In the strictest sense, an **app** is a directory of configurations and, sometimes, code. The directories and files inside have a particular naming convention and structure. All configurations are in plain text, and can be edited using your choice of text editor.

Apps generally serve one or more of the following purposes:

1. **A container for searches, dashboards, and related configurations**: This is what most users will do with apps. This is not only useful for logical grouping, but also for limiting what configurations are applied and at what time. This kind of app usually does not affect other apps.

2. **Providing extra functionality**: Many objects can be provided in an app for use by other apps. These include field extractions, lookups, external commands, saved searches, workflow actions, and even dashboards. These apps often have no user interface at all; instead they add functionality to other apps.

3. **Configuring a Splunk installation for a specific purpose**: In a distributed deployment, there are several different purposes that are served by the multiple installations of Splunk. The behavior of each installation is controlled by its configuration, and it is convenient to wrap those configurations into one or more apps. These apps completely change the behavior of a particular installation.

Included apps

Without apps, Splunk has no user interface, rendering it essentially useless. Luckily, Splunk comes with a few apps to get us started. Let's look at a few of these apps:

- **gettingstarted**: This app provides the help screens that you can access from the launcher. There are no searches, only a single dashboard that simply includes an HTML page.

- **search**: This is the app where users spend most of their time. It contains the main search dashboard that can be used from any app, external search commands that can be used from any app, admin dashboards, custom navigation, custom css, a custom app icon, a custom app logo, and many other useful elements.

- **splunk_datapreview**: This app provides the data preview functionality in the admin interface. It is built entirely using JavaScript and custom REST endpoints.

- **SplunkDeploymentMonitor**: This app provides searches and dashboards to help you keep track of your data usage and the health of your Splunk deployment. It also defines indexes, saved searches, and summary indexes. It is a good source for more advanced search examples.

- **SplunkForwarder** and **SplunkLightForwarder**: These apps, which are disabled by default, simply disable portions of a Splunk installation so that the installation is lighter in weight. We will discuss these in greater detail in *Chapter 11, Advanced Deployments*.

If you never create or install another app, and instead simply create saved searches and dashboards in the app search, you can still be quite successful with Splunk. Installing and creating more apps, however, allows you to take advantage of others' work, organize your own work, and ultimately share your work with others.

Installing apps

Apps can either be installed from Splunkbase or uploaded through the admin interface. To get started, let's navigate to **Manager | Apps**, or choose **Manage apps...** from the **App** menu as shown in the following screenshot:

Installing apps from Splunkbase

If your Splunk server has direct access to the Internet, you can install apps from Splunkbase with just a few clicks. Navigate to **Manager | Apps** and click on **Find more apps online**. The most popular apps will be listed as follows:

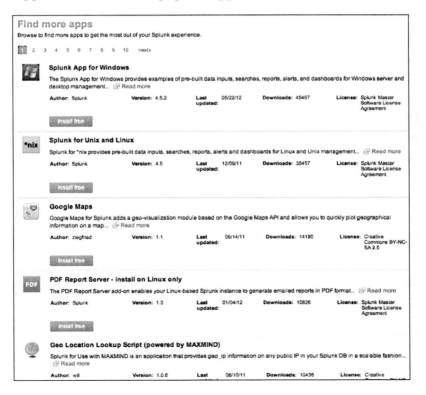

Let's install a pair of apps and have a little fun. First, install **Geo Location Lookup Script (powered by MAXMIND)** by clicking on the **Install free** button. You will be prompted for your splunk.com login. This is the same login that you created when you downloaded Splunk. If you don't have an account, you will need to create one.

Next, install the **Google Maps** app. This app was built by a Splunk customer and contributed back to the Splunk community. This app will prompt you to restart Splunk.

Once you have restarted and logged back in, check the **App** menu.

Google Maps is now visible, but where is Geo Location Lookup Script? Remember that not all apps have dashboards; nor do they necessarily have any visible components at all.

Using Geo Location Lookup Script

Geo Location Lookup Script provides a lookup script to provide geolocation information for IP addresses. Looking at the documentation, we see this example:

```
eventtype=firewall_event | lookup geoip clientip as src_ip
```

> You can find the documentation for any Splunkbase app by searching for it at splunkbase.com, or by clicking on **Read more** next to any installed app by navigating to **Manager | Apps | Browse more apps**.

Let's read through the arguments of the lookup command:

- geoip: This is the name of the lookup provided by **Geo Location Lookup Script**.

You can see the available lookups by going to **Manager** | **Lookups** | **Lookup definitions**.

- clientip: This is the name of the field in the lookup that we are matching against.

- as src_ip: This says to use the value of src_ip to populate the field before it; in this case, clientip. I personally find this wording confusing. In my mind, I read this as "using" instead of "as".

Included in the *ImplementingSplunkDataGenerator* app (available at http://packtpub.com/) is a sourcetype instance named impl_splunk_ips, which looks like this:

```
2012-05-26T18:23:44 ip=64.134.155.137
```

The IP addresses in this fictitious log are from one of my websites. Let's see some information about these addresses:

```
sourcetype="impl_splunk_ips"
  | lookup geoip clientip AS ip
  | top client_country
```

This gives us a table similar to the one shown in the following screenshot:

	client_country ⬍	count ⬍	percent ⬍
1	United States	447	71.634615
2	China	90	14.423077
3	Russian Federation	39	6.250000
4	Slovenia	15	2.403846
5	United Kingdom	14	2.243590
6	Ukraine	9	1.442308
7	South Africa	3	0.480769
8	Germany	2	0.320513
9	United Arab Emirates	1	0.160256
10	Turkey	1	0.160256

That's interesting. I wonder who is visiting my site from Slovenia!

Using Google Maps

Now let's do a similar search in the Google Maps app. Choose **Google Maps** from the **App** menu. The interface looks like the standard search interface, but with a map instead of an event listing. Let's try this remarkably similar (but not identical) query using a lookup provided in the **Google Maps** app:

```
sourcetype="impl_splunk_ips"
    | lookup geo ip
```

The map generated looks like this:

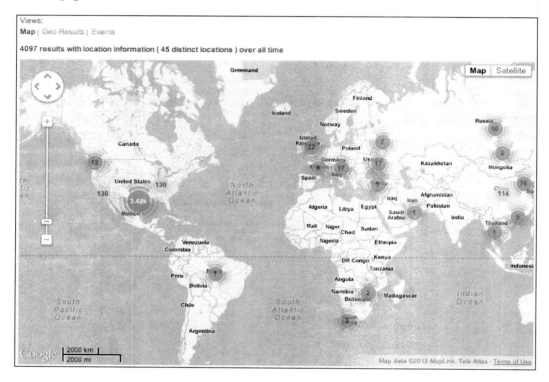

Unsurprisingly, most of the traffic to this little site came from my house in Austin, Texas. We'll use the Google Maps app for something more interesting in *Chapter 8, Building Advanced Dashboards*.

Installing apps from a file

It is not uncommon for Splunk servers to not have access to the Internet, particularly in a datacenter. In this case, follow these steps:

1. Download the app from `splunkbase.com`. The file will have a `.spl` or `.tgz` extension.
2. Navigate to **Manager | Apps**.
3. Click on **Install app from file**.
4. Upload the downloaded file using the form provided.
5. Restart if the app requires it.
6. Configure the app if required.

That's it. Some apps have a configuration form. If this is the case, you will see a **Set up** link next to the app when you go to **Manager | Apps**. If something goes wrong, contact the author of the app.

> If you have a distributed environment, in most cases the app only needs to be installed on your search head. The components that your indexers need will be distributed automatically by the search head. Check the documentation for the app.

Building your first app

For our first app, we will use one of the templates provided with Splunk. To get started, navigate to **Manager | Apps** and then click on **Create app**. The following page will open:

Set the fields as follows:

- Set **Name** to `Implementing Splunk App One`. This name will be visible on the home screen, in the **App** menu, and in the app banner in the upper left of the window.

- Set **Folder name** to `is_app_one`. This value will be the name of the app directory on the filesystem, so you should limit your name to letters, numbers, and underscores.

- Set **Visible** to **Yes**. If your app simply provides resources for other apps to use, there may be no reason for it to be visible.

- Set **Template** to **barebones**. The **barebones** template contains sample navigation and the minimal configuration required by an app. The **sample_app** template contains many example dashboards and configurations.

After clicking on **Save**, we can now visit our app by going to **Manager | Apps**, in the **App** menu, and in the **Home** app.

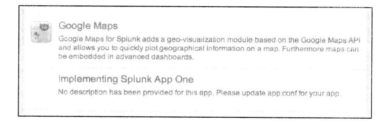

Now that we have our app, we can create searches and dashboards, and maintain them in our app. The simplest way to ensure that your objects end up in your app is to verify that the app banner is correct before creating objects or before entering the Splunk Manager. Our app banner looks like this:

splunk> Implementing Splunk App One

Create a dashboard called `Errors` using the following searches (refer back to *Chapter 4, Simple XML Dashboards*, for detailed instructions):

```
error sourcetype="impl_splunk_gen" | timechart count by user
error sourcetype="impl_splunk_gen" | top user
error sourcetype="impl_splunk_gen" | top logger
```

This produces the following result:

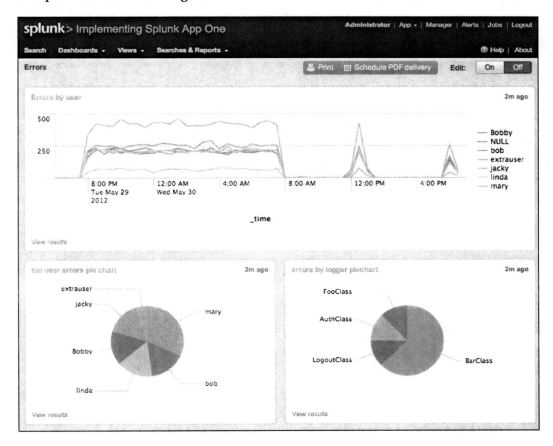

The searches appear under **Searches & Reports**, and our new dashboard appears in the navigation menu under **Views**:

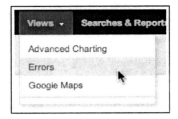

Editing navigation

Navigation is controlled by an XML file that can be accessed by going to **Manager |
User interface | Navigation menus**.

Nav name ⬍	Owner ⬍	App ⬍	Sharing ⬍	Status ⬍
default	No owner	is_app_one	App | Permissions	Enabled

There can only be one active navigation file per app, and it is always called default.
After clicking on the name, we see the XML provided by the **barebones** template:

```
<nav>
    <view name="flashtimeline" default='true' />
    <collection label="Dashboards">
        <view source="unclassified" match="dashboard"/>
        <divider />
    </collection>
    <collection label="Views">
        <view source="unclassified" />
        <divider />
    </collection>
    <collection label="Searches &amp; Reports">
        <collection label="Reports">
            <saved source="unclassified" match="report" />
        </collection>
        <divider />
        <saved source="unclassified" />
    </collection>
</nav>
```

The structure of the XML is essentially the following:

```
nav
  view
  saved
  collection
    view
    a href
    saved
    divider
    collection
      . . .
```

The logic of navigation is probably best absorbed by simply editing it and seeing what happens. You should keep a backup, as this XML is somewhat fragile and Splunk does not provide any kind of version control. Here are some general details about `nav`:

- Children of `nav` appear in the navigation bar.
- `collection`: Children of `collection` tags appear in a menu or submenu.

  If the child tags do not produce any results, the menu will not appear. The `divider` tag always produces a result, so it can be used to ensure that a menu appears.

- `view`: This tag represents a dashboard, with the following attributes:
    ○ `name` is the name of the dashboard filename, without `.xml`.
    ○ The first `view` element with the attribute `default='true'` will load automatically when the app is selected.
    ○ The label of each `view` is based on the contents of the `label` tag in the dashboard XML, not the name of the dashboard filename.
    ○ `match="dashboard"` selects all dashboards whose filename contains `dashboard`. If you want to group dashboards, you may want to follow a naming convention to make grouping more predictable.
    ○ `source="unclassified"` essentially means "all views that have not been previously associated to a menu". In other words, this will match dashboards that were not explicitly referenced by `name` or matched using the `match` attribute or a different `view` tag.

- `a href`: You can include standard HTML links of the form `<a href="http://a.b/c">`.

  The link is untouched and passed along as written.

- `saved`: This tag represents a saved search, with the following attributes:
    ○ `name` is equal to the name of a saved search.
    ○ `match="report"` selects all saved searches that have `report` in their names.
    ○ `source="unclassified"` essentially means "all searches that have not yet been previously associated to a menu". In other words, this will match searches that were not explicitly referenced by `name` or matched using the `match` attribute or a different `saved` tag.

Let's customize our navigation. We'll make a few changes like these:

- Create an entry specifically for our `errors` dashboard
- Add `default='true'` so that this dashboard loads by default
- Simplify the `Views` and `Searches` collections

These changes are reflected in the following code:

```
<nav>
    <view name="errors" default='true' />
    <view name="flashtimeline" />
    <collection label="Views">
        <view source="unclassified" />
    </collection>
    <collection label="Searches">
      <saved source="unclassified" />
    </collection>
</nav>
```

Our navigation now looks like this screenshot:

With this navigation in place, all new dashboards will appear under **Views**, and all new saved searches will appear under **Searches**.

Notice that **Advanced Charting** and **Google Maps** appear under **Views**. Neither of these dashboards are part of our app, but are visible because of the permissions in their respective apps. We will discuss permissions in more detail in the *Object permissions* section.

Customizing the appearance of your app

It is helpful to further customize the appearance of your application, if for no other reason than to make it more obvious which app is currently active.

Customizing the launcher icon

The launcher icon is seen both in the Home app and in Splunkbase, if you decide to share your app. The icon is a 36 x 36 PNG file named `appIcon.png`. I have created a simple icon for our sample app (please don't judge my art skills):

To use the icon follow these steps:

1. Navigate to **Manager | Apps.**
2. Click on **Edit properties** next to our app, **Implementing Splunk App One.**
3. Click on **Upload asset** and select the file.
4. Click on **Save.**

Our icon will now appear on the launcher screen, like in the following screenshot:

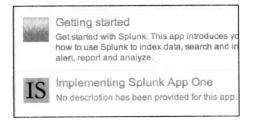

Using custom CSS

The look of the Splunk application is controlled via CSS. One common element to change is the application icon in the application bar. Follow these steps to do just that:

1. First, create a file named `application.css`. This file will be loaded on every dashboard of the application containing it. The CSS is listed later in this section.

 As of Splunk Version 4.3.2, the first time `application.css` is added to an app of Version 4.3.2, a restart is required before the file is served to the users. Subsequent updates do not require a restart.

2. Next, create a file named `appLogo.png`. This file can be called anything, as we will reference it explicitly in our CSS file. Borrowing CSS from the search app, we will make our file 155 x 43 pixels:

3. For each file, follow the same steps as for uploading the launcher icon:

    1. Navigate to **Manager | Apps.**
    2. Click on **Edit properties** next to our app, **Implementing Splunk App One.**
    3. Click on **Upload asset** and select the file.
    4. Click on **Save.**

Our CSS references a few classes in the application header bar:

```
.appHeaderWrapper h1 {
    display: none;
}

.appLogo {
    height: 43px;
    width: 155px;
    padding-right: 5px;
    float: left;
    background: url(appLogo.png) no-repeat 0 0;
}

.appHeaderWrapper {
    background: #612f00;
}
```

Let's step through these classes:

*   `.appHeaderWrapper h1`: By default, the name of the app appears as text in the upper-left corner. This definition hides that text.

- .appLogo: This sets the background of the upper-left block to our custom file. The height and width should match the dimensions of our logo.

- .appHeaderWrapper: This sets the background color of the top bar.

With everything in place, our top bar now looks like this:

Using custom HTML

In some apps, you will see static HTML blocks. This can be accomplished using both simple and complex dashboards.

Custom HTML in a simple dashboard

In a simple dashboard, you can simply insert an <html> element inside a <row> element, and include static HTML inline. For example, after uploading an image named graph.png, the following block can be added to any dashboard:

```
<row>
 <html>
  <table>
   <tr>
    <td><img src="/static/app/is_app_one/graph.png" /></td>
    <td>
     <p>Lorem ipsum ...</p>
     <p>Nulla ut congue ...</p>
     <p>Etiam pharetra ...</p>
    </td>
   </tr>
  </table>
 </html>
</row>
```

The XML would render this panel:

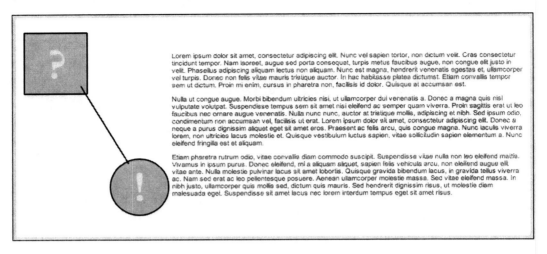

This approach has the advantage that no other files are needed. The disadvantage, however, is that you cannot build the HTML document in an external program and upload it untouched.

You could also reference custom CSS using this method by adding classes to application.css and then referencing those classes in your HTML block.

Using ServerSideInclude in a complex dashboard

You can also develop static pages as HTML documents, referencing other files in the same directory. Let's build a slightly more complicated page using graph.png, but also a style from application.css as follows:

1. Place graph.png and application.css into a directory.
2. Create a new HTML file. Let's name it intro.html.
3. Add any styles for your page to application.css.
4. Upload the new HTML file and modified CSS file.
5. Create the dashboard referencing the HTML file.

Starting with the HTML from our previous example, let's make it a complete document: move the image to a CSS style and add a class to our text, like this:

```
<html>
 <head>
  <link rel="stylesheet" type="text/css"
    href="application.css" />
```

```
   </head>
   <body>
    <table>
     <tr>
      <td class="graph_image"></td>
      <td>
       <p class="lorem">Lorem ipsum ...</p>
       <p class="lorem">Nulla ut congue ...</p>
       <p class="lorem">Etiam pharetra ...</p>
      </td>
     </tr>
    </table>
   </body>
  </html>
```

Maintaining the classes for the navigation bar, add our page classes to `application.css`, like this:

```
.appHeaderWrapper h1 {
    display: none;
}

.appLogo {
    height: 43px;
    width: 155px;
    padding-right: 5px;
    float: left;
    background: url(appLogo.png) no-repeat 0 0;
}

.appHeaderWrapper {
    background: #612f00;
}

.lorem {
    font-style:italic;
    background: #CCCCCC;
    padding: 5px;
}

.graph_image {
    height: 306px;
    width: 235px;
    background: url(graph.png) no-repeat 0 0;
}
```

We can now open this file in a browser. Clipped for brevity, the page looks like this:

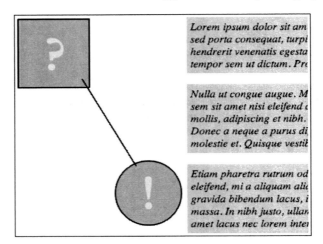

To include this external HTML document, we have to use advanced XML. We will cover advanced XML more thoroughly in *Chapter 8, Building Advanced Dashboards*.

First, build a minimal dashboard like this:

```
<view template="dashboard.html">
  <label>Included</label>
  <!-- chrome here -->
  <module
      name="ServerSideInclude"
      layoutPanel="panel_row1_col1">
    <param name="src">intro.html</param>
  </module>
</view>
```

 All "simple" XML dashboards are converted to "advanced" XML behind the scenes. We will take advantage of this later.

Now upload our files as we did before under the *Customizing the launcher icon* section. The page should render nearly identically as the file did in the browser, with the addition of the border around the panel:

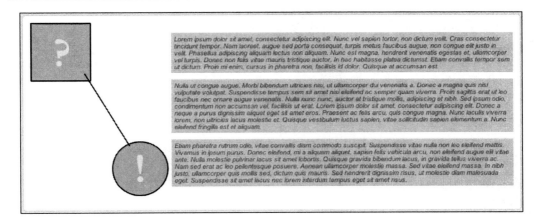

A few things to note from this overly simplified example are as follows:

1. Your CSS classes may end up merging with styles included by Splunk in unexpected ways. Using the developer tools in any modern browser will help greatly.

2. The navigation and dashboard title were excluded for brevity. They would normally go where we see `<!-- chrome here -->`. This is interesting because there are cases where you would want to exclude the navigation; something that cannot be done with simple XML.

3. The static files, such as `application.css`, can be edited directly on the filesystem, and the changes will be seen immediately. This is not true of the dashboard XML file. We will cover these locations later in the *App directory structure* section.

Object permissions

Almost all objects in Splunk have permissions associated with them. The permissions essentially have the following three options:

- **Private**: Only the user that created the search can see or use the object, and only in the app where it was created

- **App**: All users that have permission to read an object may use that object in the context of the app that contains that object

- **Global**: All users that have permission to read an object may use that object in any app

How permissions affect navigation

To see a visible instance of permissions in action, let's look at our navigation.
In our application, **Implementing Splunk App One**, our navigation looks like this:

If you recall the navigation XML we built before, this menu is controlled by the
following XML:

```
<collection label="Views">
  <view source="unclassified" />
</collection>
```

There is no mention of any of these dashboards. Here is where they are coming from:

- **Advanced Charting** is inherited from the **Search** app. Its permissions are set
  to **Global**.
- **Included** is from this app. Its permissions are set to **App**.
- **Google Maps** is inherited from the **Google Maps** app. Its permissions are set
  to **Global**.

 If the permissions of a dashboard or search are set to **Private**, a green
dot appears next to the name in the navigation.

Dashboards or searches shared from other apps can also be referenced by name.
For example, most apps, including ours, will include a link to `flashtimeline`,
which appears as **Search**, the label in that dashboard's XML:

```
<view name="flashtimeline" />
```

This allows us to use this dashboard in the context of our app so that all of the other
objects that are scoped solely to our app will be available.

How permissions affect other objects

Almost everything you create in Splunk has permissions. To see all objects, navigate
to **Manager | All configurations**.

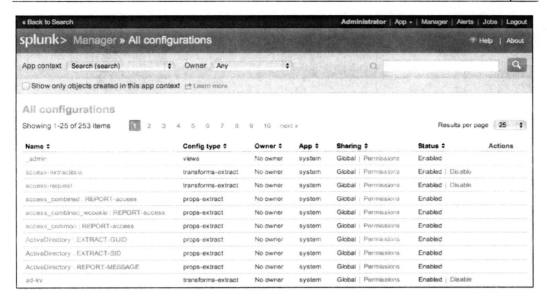

Everything with the value **system** in the **App** column ships with Splunk. These items live in $SPLUNK_HOME/etc/system. We will cover these different configuration types in *Chapter 10, Configuring Splunk*, but the important takeaway is that the **Sharing** settings affect nearly everything.

When you create new objects and configurations, it is important to share all related objects. For instance, in *Chapter 6, Extending Search*, we created lookups. It is important that all three parts of the lookup definition are shared appropriately, or users will be presented with error messages.

Correcting permission problems

If you see errors about permissions, it is more than likely that some object still has **Sharing** set to **Private**, or is shared at the **App** level but needs to be **Global**. Follow these steps to find the object:

1. Navigate to **Manager | All configurations**.
2. Change **App context** to **All**.
3. Sort by using the **Sharing** status. Click twice so that **Private** objects come to the top.
4. If there are too many items to look through, filter the list by adding terms to the search field in the upper-right corner, or changing the **App context** value.

5. Fix the permissions appropriately. In most cases, the permissions you want will look like this:

 You should choose **All apps** with care. For instance, when building a lookup, it is common to share the lookup table file and lookup definition across all apps. This allows the lookup to be used in searches by other apps. It is less common to share the Automatic lookup, as this can affect performance in other apps in unforeseen ways.

App directory structure

If you do much beyond building searches and dashboards, sooner or later you will need to edit files in the filesystem directly. All apps live in `$SPLUNK_HOME/etc/apps/`. On Unix systems, the default installation directory is `/opt/splunk`. On Windows, the default installation directory is `c:\Program Files\Splunk`. This is the value that `$SPLUNK_HOME` will inherit on startup.

Stepping through the most common directories, we have:

- `appserver`: This directory contains files that are served by the Splunk web app. The files that we uploaded in earlier sections of this chapter are stored in `appserver/static`.

- `bin`: This is where command scripts belong. These scripts are then referenced in `commands.conf`. This is also a common location for scripted inputs to live, though they can live anywhere.

- default and local: These two directories contain the vast majority of the configurations that make up an app. We will discuss these configurations and how they merge in *Chapter 10, Configuring Splunk*. Here is a brief look:

    ° Newly created, unshared objects live in $SPLUNK_HOME/etc/users/ USERNAME/APPNAME/local.

    ° Once an object is shared at the App or Global level, the object is moved to $SPLUNK_HOME/etc/APPNAME/local.

    ° Files in local take precedence over its equivalent value in default.

    ° Dashboards live in (default|local)/data/ui/views.

    ° Navigations lives in (default|local)/data/ui/nav.

    ° When editing files by hand, my general rule of thumb is to place configurations in local unless the app will be redistributed. We'll discuss this in more detail in the *Adding your app to Splunkbase* section.

- lookups: Lookup files belong in this directory. They are then referenced in (default|local)/transforms.conf.

- metadata: The files default.meta and local.meta in this directory tell Splunk how configurations in this app should be shared. It is generally much easier to edit these settings through the **Manager** interface.

Let's look at the contents of our is_app_one app, which we created earlier:

```
appserver/static/appIcon.png
appserver/static/application.css
appserver/static/appLogo.png
appserver/static/graph.png
appserver/static/intro.html
bin/README
default/app.conf
default/data/ui/nav/default.xml
default/data/ui/views/README
local/app.conf
local/data/ui/nav/default.xml
local/data/ui/views/errors.xml
local/data/ui/views/included.xml
local/savedsearches.conf
local/viewstates.conf
metadata/default.meta
metadata/local.meta
```

The file `metadata/default.meta`, and all files in `default/`, were provided in the template app. We created all of the other files. With the exception of the `png` files, all files are plain text.

Adding your app to Splunkbase

Splunkbase (`splunkbase.com`) is a wonderful community-supported site that Splunk put together for users and Splunk employees alike to share Splunk apps. The apps on Splunkbase are a mix of fully realized apps, add-ons of various sorts, and just example code. Splunk has good documentation for sharing apps at the following URL:

```
http://docs.splunk.com/Documentation/Splunk/latest/Developer/
ShareYourWork
```

Preparing your app

Before we upload our app, we need to make sure all of our objects are shared properly, move our files to `default`, and configure `app.conf`.

Confirming sharing settings

To see sharing settings for all our objects, navigate to **Manager | All configurations** and set the **App context** option:

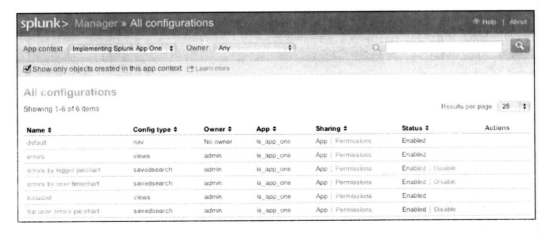

In the case of a self-contained app like ours, all objects should probably be set to **App** under **Sharing**. If you are building an app to share lookups or commands, the value should be **Global**.

Cleaning up our directories

When you upload an app, you should move everything out of local and into default. This is important because all changes a user makes will be stored in local. When your app is upgraded, all files in the app will be replaced, and the user's changes will be lost. The following Unix commands illustrate what needs to be done:

1. First, let's copy our app to another location, perhaps /tmp:

```
cp -r $SPLUNK_HOME/etc/apps/is_app_one /tmp/
```

2. Next, let's move everything from local to default. In the case of .xml files, we can simply move the files; but .conf files are a little more complicated, and we need to merge them manually. The following code does this:

```
cd /tmp/is_app_one
mv local/data/ui/nav/*.xml default/data/ui/nav/
mv local/data/ui/views/*.xml default/data/ui/views/
#move conf files, but don't replace conf files in default
mv -n local/*conf default/
```

3. Now we need to merge any .conf files that remain in local. The only configuration we have left is app.conf;

local/app.conf	default/app.conf
[ui]	[install] is_configured = 0
[launcher]	
	[ui]
[package] check_for_updates = 1	is_visible = 1 label = Implementing Splunk App One
	[launcher] author = description = version = 1.0

Configuration merging is additive, with any values from local added to the values in default. In this case, the merged configuration would be as follows:

```
[install]
is_configured = 0

[ui]
```

```
is_visible = 1
label = Implementing Splunk App One

[launcher]
author =
description =
version = 1.0

[package]
check_for_updates = 1
```

4. Place this merged configuration in default/app.conf and delete local/app.conf.

We will cover configuration merging extensively in *Chapter 10, Configuring Splunk*.

Packaging your app

To package an app, we need to be sure that there are a few values in default/app.conf, and only then build the archive.

First, edit default/app.conf like this:

```
[install]
is_configured = 0
build = 1

[ui]
is_visible = 1
label = Implementing Splunk App One

[launcher]
author = My name
description = My great app!
version = 1.0

[package]
check_for_updates = 1
id = is_app_one
```

build is used in all URLs, so it should be incremented to defeat browser caching. id should be a unique value in Splunkbase — you will be alerted if the value is not unique.

Next, we need to build a `tar` file compressed with `gzip`. With a modern version of `tar`, the command is simply the following:

```
cd /tmp
tar -czvf is_app_one.tgz is_app_one
#optionally rename as spl
mv is_app_one.tgz is_app_one.spl
```

The Splunk documentation (`http://docs.splunk.com/Documentation/Splunk/latest/AdvancedDev/PackageApp`) covers this extensively, including Mac and Windows procedures.

Uploading your app

Now that we have our archive, all we have to do is send it up to Splunkbase. First, click on the **upload an app** button.

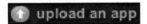

Then fill out the form shown in the following screenshot:

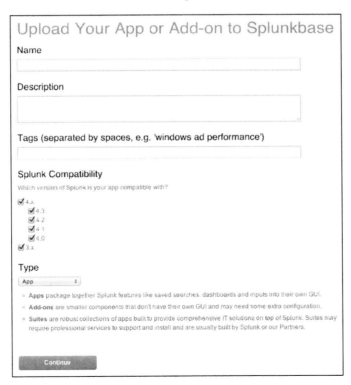

More than likely your app will not be compatible with Splunk 3.x, so uncheck the **3.x** checkbox.

Once Splunk personnel approve your app, it will appear in Splunkbase, ready for others to download.

Summary

In this chapter, we covered installing, building, customizing, and sharing apps. Apps are a loose concept in Splunk, with many different purposes served by a simple directory of files. Hopefully we have covered the basics well enough for you to get started on your own great apps. In later chapters, we will build even more complicated object types, as well as custom code to extend Splunk in unique ways.

In the next chapter, we will dig into advanced dashboards, both covering what can be done with Splunk alone, and what can be done with the help of a few popular apps.

8
Building Advanced Dashboards

In *Chapter 4, Simple XML Dashboards*, we covered building dashboards using simple XML. We first used the wizards provided in Splunk, and then edited the resultant XML. When you reach the limits of what can be accomplished with simple XML, one option is to dive into Splunk's advanced XML.

Reasons for working with advanced XML

Here are a few reasons to use advanced XML:

1. **More control over layout**: With advanced XML, you have better control over where form elements and chrome appear, and somewhat improved control over the placement of the output.

2. **Custom drilldowns**: It is only possible to create custom drilldowns from tables and charts using advanced XML.

3. **Access to more parameters**: The modules in simple XML actually use advanced XML modules, but many parameters are not exposed. Sometimes the desire is actually to disable features, and this is only possible by using advanced XML.

4. **Access to more modules**: There are many modules *not* available when using simple XML, for example the search bar itself. All extra modules provided by the apps at Splunkbase, for example *Google Maps*, are for use in advanced XML.

Reasons for not working with advanced XML

There are also a number of reasons to not work with advanced XML:

1. **Steep learning curve**: Depending on what technologies you are comfortable working with, and possibly on how well the rest of this chapter is written, the learning curve for advanced XML can be steep.

2. **No direct control over HTML**: If there is a particular HTML you want to produce from search results, this may not be as simple as you had hoped. Short of writing your own module, you must work within the bounds of the options provided to the existing modules, modify CSS with `application. css`, or modify the HTML using JavaScript.

3. **No direct control over logic**: If you need specific things to happen when you click on specific table cells, particularly based on other values in the same row, this can only be accomplished by modifying the document using JavaScript. This is possible, but it is not well documented. Examples can be found at `http://splunkbase.com` both in answers posts and sample applications. Check out `customBehaviors` in the third-party app *Sideview Utils* for an alternative.

 If you have specific layout or logic requirements, you may be better served using one of the Splunk APIs available at `http://dev. splunk.com` and writing applications in your favorite language.

Development process

When building dashboards, my approach is generally as follows:

1. Create the needed queries.
2. Add the queries to a simple XML dashboard. Use the GUI tools to tweak the dashboard as much as possible. Finish all graphical changes at this stage, if possible.
3. Convert the simple XML dashboard to a form if form elements are needed. Make all logic work with simple XML if possible.
4. Convert the simple XML dashboard to an advanced XML dashboard. There is no reverse conversion possible, so this should be done as late as possible, and only if needed.
5. Edit the advanced XML dashboard accordingly.

The idea is to take advantage of the Splunk GUI tools as much as possible, letting the simple XML conversion process add all of the advanced XML that you would have to otherwise find yourself. We covered steps 1-3 in the previous chapters. Step 4 is covered in the *Converting simple XML to advanced XML* section.

Advanced XML structure

Before we dig into the modules provided, let's look at the structure of the XML itself and cover a couple of concepts.

The tag structure of an advanced XML document is essentially:

```
view
  module
    param
    . . .
    module
    . . .
```

The main concept of Splunk's XML structure is that the effects of modules flow downstream to child modules. This is a vital concept to understand. The XML structure has almost nothing to do with layout, and everything to do with the flow of data.

Let's look at a simple example like this:

```
<view
    template="dashboard.html">

  <label>Chapter 8, Example 1</label>

  <module
      name="HiddenSearch"
      layoutPanel="panel_row1_col1"
      autoRun="True">
    <param name="earliest">-1d</param>
    <param name="search">error | top user</param>

    <module name="SimpleResultsTable"></module>

  </module>

</view>
```

This document produces a sparse dashboard with one panel like this:

user ‡	count ‡	percent ‡
mary	1668	31.376975
Bobby	871	16.384500
jacky	851	16.008277
bob	844	15.876599
linda	828	15.575621
extrauser	254	4.778029

Let's step through this example line by line.

- `<view`: Open the outer tag. This tag begins all advanced XML dashboards.
- `template="dashboard.html">`: Set the base HTML template. Dashboard layout templates are stored in `$SPLUNK_HOME/share/splunk/search_mrsparkle/templates/view/`. Among other things, the templates define the panels available for use in `layoutPanel`.
- `<label>Chapter 8, Example 1</label>`: Set the label used by navigation.
- `<module`: Begin our first module declaration.
- `name="HiddenSearch"`: The name of the module to use. `HiddenSearch` runs a search but displays nothing, relying instead on child modules to render the output.
- `layoutPanel="panel_row1_col1"`: This states where in the dashboard to display our panel. It seems strange to put this attribute on a module that displays nothing, but `layoutPanel` must be specified on every immediate child of `view`. See the *Understanding layoutPanel* section later for more details.
- `autoRun="True">`: Without this attribute, the search does not run when the dashboard loads, and instead waits for user interaction from form elements. Since we have no form elements, we need this attribute to see the results.
- `<param name="earliest">-1d</param>`: It is very important to specify a value for `earliest`, as the query will by default run over All time.

 `param` values affect only the `module` tag they are nested directly inside.

- `<param name="search">error | top user</param>`: The actual query to run.

- `<module name="SimpleResultsTable"></module>`: This module simply displays a table of the events produced by a parent module. Since there are no `param` tags specified, the defaults for this module will be used.

- `</module>`: Close the `HiddenSearch` module. This is required for valid XML, but it also implies that the scope of influence for this module is closed. To reiterate, only the downstream modules of the `HiddenSearch` module will receive the events it produces.

- `</view>`: Close the document.

This is a very simple dashboard. It lacks navigation, form elements, job status, and drilldowns. Adding all of these things is initially somewhat complicated to understand. Luckily, you can build a dashboard in simple XML, convert it to advanced XML, and then modify the provided XML as needed.

Converting simple XML to advanced XML

Let's go back to one of the dashboards we created in *Chapter 4, Simple XML Dashboards*, `errors_user_form`. We built this before our app, so it still lives in the Search app. In my instance, this URL is `http://mysplunkserver:8000/en-US/app/search/errors_user_form`.

Just to refresh, the simple XML behind this dashboard looks like:

```
<?xml version='1.0' encoding='utf-8'?>
<form>

  <fieldset>
    <input type="text" token="user">
      <label>User</label>
    </input>
    <input type="time" />
  </fieldset>

  <label>Errors User Form</label>

  <row>
    <chart>
      <searchString>
        sourcetype="impl_splunk_gen" loglevel=error user="$user$"
        | timechart count as "Error count" by network
```

```
      </searchString>
      <title>
        Dashboard - Errors - errors by network timechart
      </title>
      <option name="charting.chart">line</option>
    </chart>
  </row>

  <row>
    <chart>
      <searchString>
        sourcetype="impl_splunk_gen" loglevel=error user="$user$"
        | bucket bins=10 req_time | stats count by req_time
      </searchString>
      <title>
        Error count by req_times
      </title>
      <option name="charting.chart">pie</option>
    </chart>
    <chart>
      <searchString>
        sourcetype="impl_splunk_gen" loglevel=error user="$user$"
        | stats count by logger
      </searchString>
      <title>Errors by logger</title>
      <option name="charting.chart">pie</option>
    </chart>
  </row>

  <row>
    <event>
      <searchString>
        sourcetype="impl_splunk_gen" loglevel=error user="$user$"
      </searchString>
      <title>Error events</title>
      <option name="count">10</option>
      <option name="displayRowNumbers">true</option>
      <option name="maxLines">10</option>
      <option name="segmentation">outer</option>
      <option name="softWrap">true</option>
    </event>
  </row>

</form>
```

In the simple XML, the layout and logic flow are tied together.

Before this simple XML is rendered to the user, Splunk first dynamically converts it to advanced XML in memory. We can access that advanced XML by appending `?showsource=1` to any URL, like this:

```
http://mysplunkserver:8000/en-US/app/search/errors_user_
form?showsource=1
```

This produces a page with a tree view of the module structure like this:

View source: errors_user_form (Errors User Form)

Properties

- *template*: dashboard.html
- *autoCancelInterval*: 90
- *objectMode*: SimpleForm
- *label*: Errors User Form
- *stylesheet*: None
- *onunloadCancelJobs*: True
- *isVisible*: True

Module tree

Collapse all | Expand all | Toggle all

- AccountBar_0_0_0 *appHeader*
  - AccountBar config
- AppBar_0_0_1 *navigationHeader*
  - AppBar config
- Message_0_0_2 *messaging*
  - Message config
- Message_1_0_3 *messaging*
  - Message config
- TitleBar_0_0_4 *viewHeader*
  - TitleBar config
- ExtendedFieldSearch_0_0_5 *viewHeader*
  - ExtendedFieldSearch config
  - TimeRangePicker_0_1_0
    - TimeRangePicker config
    - SubmitButton_0_2_0
      - SubmitButton config
      - HiddenSearch_0_3_0 *panel_row1_col1*
        - HiddenSearch config
        - ViewstateAdapter_0_4_0
          - ViewstateAdapter config
          - HiddenFieldPicker_0_5_0
            - HiddenFieldPicker config
            - JobProgressIndicator_0_6_0
              - JobProgressIndicator config
              - EnablePreview_0_7_0
                - EnablePreview config
                - HiddenChartFormatter_0_8_0
                  - HiddenChartFormatter config

This is followed by a textbox containing the raw XML like this:

XML source

```
<view autoCancelInterval="90" isVisible="true" objectMode="SimpleForm" onunloadCancelJobs="true"
template="dashboard.html">
  <label>Errors User Form</label>
  <module name="AccountBar" layoutPanel="appHeader"/>
  <module name="AppBar" layoutPanel="navigationHeader"/>
  <module name="Message" layoutPanel="messaging">
   <param name="filter">*</param>
   <param name="clearOnjobDispatch">False</param>
   <param name="maxSize">1</param>
  </module>
  <module name="Message" layoutPanel="messaging">
   <param name="filter">splunk.search.job</param>
   <param name="clearOnjobDispatch">True</param>
   <param name="maxSize">1</param>
  </module>
  <module name="TitleBar" layoutPanel="viewHeader">
   <param name="actionsMenuFilter">dashboard</param>
  </module>
  <module name="ExtendedFieldSearch" layoutPanel="viewHeader">
   <param name="replacementMap">
    <param name="arg">
     <param name="user"/>
    </param>
   </param>
```

An abbreviated version of the advanced XML version of errors_user_form follows:

```
<view
...   template="dashboard.html">
  <label>Errors User Form</label>
  <module name="AccountBar" layoutPanel="appHeader"/>
  <module name="AppBar" layoutPanel="navigationHeader"/>
  <module name="Message" layoutPanel="messaging">
...<module name="Message" layoutPanel="messaging">
...<module name="TitleBar" layoutPanel="viewHeader">
...<module name="ExtendedFieldSearch" layoutPanel="viewHeader">
    <param name="replacementMap">
      <param name="arg">
        <param name="user"/>
      </param>
    </param>
    <param name="field">User</param>
    <param name="intention">
...   <module name="TimeRangePicker">
        <param name="searchWhenChanged">False</param>
        <module name="SubmitButton">
          <param name="allowSoftSubmit">True</param>
          <param name="label">Search</param>
          <module
              name="HiddenSearch"
```

```
              layoutPanel="panel_row1_col1"
              group="Dashboard - Errors - errors by network timechart"
              autoRun="False">
          <param name="search">
            sourcetype="impl_splunk_gen"
            loglevel=error user="$user$"
            | timechart count as "Error count" by network
          </param>
          <param name="groupLabel">
            Dashboard - Errors - errors by network timechart
          </param>
          <module name="ViewstateAdapter">
            <param name="suppressionList">
              <item>charting.chart</item>
            </param>
            <module name="HiddenFieldPicker">
              <param name="strictMode">True</param>
              <module name="JobProgressIndicator">
                <module name="EnablePreview">
                  <param name="enable">True</param>
                  <param name="display">False</param>
                  <module name="HiddenChartFormatter">
                    <param name="charting.chart">line</param>
                    <module name="JSChart">
                      <param name="width">100%</param>
                      <module name="Gimp"/>
                      <module name="ConvertToDrilldownSearch">
                        <module name="ViewRedirector">
...                   </module>
                      <module name="ViewRedirectorLink">
...       </module>
          <module
              name="HiddenSearch"
              layoutPanel="panel_row2_col1"
              group="Error count by req_times"
              autoRun="False">
            <param name="search">
              sourcetype="impl_splunk_gen" loglevel=error
              user="$user$"
              | bucket bins=10 req_time | stats count by req_time
            </param>
            <param name="groupLabel">Error count by req_times</param>
...       </module>
```

```
            <module
                name="HiddenSearch"
                layoutPanel="panel_row2_col2"
                group="Errors by logger"
                autoRun="False">
              <param name="search">
                sourcetype="impl_splunk_gen"
                loglevel=error user="$user$"
                | stats count by logger
              </param>
              <param name="groupLabel">Errors by logger</param>
...         </module>
            <module
                name="HiddenSearch"
                layoutPanel="panel_row3_col1"
                group="Error events"
                autoRun="False">
              <param name="search">
                sourcetype="impl_splunk_gen"
                loglevel=error
                user="$user$"
              </param>
              <param name="groupLabel">Error events</param>
              <module name="ViewstateAdapter">
...             <module name="HiddenFieldPicker">
...               <module name="JobProgressIndicator"/>
                  <module name="Paginator">
                    <param name="count">10</param>
                    <module name="EventsViewer">
...                   <module name="Gimp"/>
...                 </module>
...
...
</view>
```

This XML is more verbose than we actually need, but luckily it is easier to delete code than to create it.

Module logic flow

The main concept of nested modules is that parent (upstream) modules affect child (downstream) modules. Looking at the first panel, the full module flow is:

```
<module name="ExtendedFieldSearch">
  <module name="TimeRangePicker">
    <module name="SubmitButton">
      <module name="HiddenSearch">
```

```
<module name="ViewstateAdapter">
  <module name="HiddenFieldPicker">
    <module name="JobProgressIndicator">
      <module name="EnablePreview">
        <module name="HiddenChartFormatter">
          <module name="JSChart">
            <module name="ConvertToDrilldownSearch">
              <module name="ViewRedirector">
              <module name="ViewRedirectorLink">
```

 A reference for the modules installed in your instance of Splunk is available at /modules. In my case, the full URL is http://mysplunkserver:8000/modules.

Let's step through these modules in turn and discuss what they are each accomplishing:

- ExtendedFieldSearch: This provides a textbox for entry. The parameters for this module are complicated, and represent arguably the most complicated aspect of advanced XML—**intentions**. Intentions affect child modules, specifically HiddenSearch. We will cover intentions later.

- TimeRangePicker: This provides the standard time picker. It affects child HiddenSearch modules that do not have times specified either using param values or in the query itself. The precedence of times used in a query are:
    - Times specified in the query itself
    - Times specified via earliest and latest param values to the search module
    - A value provided by TimeRangePicker

- SubmitButton: This draws the **Search** button and fires off any child search modules when clicked.

- HiddenSearch: As we saw before, this runs a query and produces events for downstream modules. In this case, autoRun is set to false, so that the query waits for the user.

- ViewstateAdapter: A **viewstate** describes what settings a user has selected in the GUI, for instance, sort order, page size, or chart type. Any time you change a chart setting or pick a time range, you create a viewstate that is saved by Splunk. This module is used to access an existing viewstate, or to suppress specific viewstate settings. By suppressing specific settings, the default or specified values of child modules will be used instead. This module is rarely needed unless you are using a saved search with an associated viewstate.

- `HiddenFieldPicker`: This module limits what fields are accessible by downstream modules. This is useful when running a query that produces many fields, but only certain fields are needed. This would affect the fields shown below events in an events listing, or the columns displayed in a table view. This module is rarely needed.

- `JobProgressIndicator`: This module displays a progress bar until the job is completed. In this case, because of the placement of the module in the XML, it will appear above the results. This module does not affect downstream modules, so it can be listed on its own.

- `EnablePreview`: This module allows you to specify whether searches should refresh with incomplete results while the query is running. The default appears to be true for Splunk-provided modules, but this module allows you to control this behavior. This module does not affect downstream modules, so could be listed on its own.

[Disabling preview can improve the performance dramatically, but provides no information until the query is complete, which is less visually appealing, particularly during a long-running query.]

- `HiddenChartFormatter`: This module is where the chart settings are specified. These settings affect any child modules that draw charts.

- `JSChart`: This draws a chart using JavaScript. Prior to Splunk 4.3, all charts were drawn using Flash. The `FlashChart` module is still included, for backward compatibility.

- `ConvertToDrilldownSearch`: This module takes the values from a click on a parent module and produces a query based on the query that produced the results. This usually works, but not always, depending on the complexity of the query. We will build a custom drilldown search later.

- `ViewRedirector`: This module accepts the query from its upstream module and redirects the user to `viewTarget`, with the query specified in the URL. Usually, `flashtimeline` is specified as the `viewTarget` param, but it could be any dashboard. The query will affect a `HiddenSearch` or `SearchBar` module.

- `ViewRedirectorLink`: This module sends the user to a new search page with the search results for this module.

Thinking about what we have seen in this flow, we could say that modules can:

- Generate events
- Modify a query

- Modify the behavior of a downstream module
- Display an element on the dashboard
- Handle actions produced by clicks

It is also possible for a module to:

- Post process the events produced by a query
- Add custom JavaScript to the dashboard

Understanding layoutPanel

In an advanced XML dashboard, which panel a module is drawn to is determined by the value of the layoutPanel attribute. This separation of logic and layout can be useful — for instance, allowing you to reuse data generated by a query with multiple modules — but displays the results on different parts of the page.

A few rules about this attribute are as follows:

- The layoutPanel attribute *must* appear on all *immediate* children of <view>.
- The layoutPanel attribute *can* appear on descendant child module tags.
- If a module does not have a layoutPanel attribute, it will inherit the value from the closest upstream module that does.
- Modules that have visible output are added to their respective layoutPanel attribute in the order they appear in the XML.
- Modules "flow" in the panel they are placed. Most modules take the entire width of the panel, but some do not, and flow left to right before wrapping.

Looking through our XML, we find these elements with the layoutPanel attribute like this:

```
<module name="AccountBar" layoutPanel="appHeader"/>
<module name="AppBar" layoutPanel="navigationHeader"/>
<module name="Message" layoutPanel="messaging">

<module name="TitleBar" layoutPanel="viewHeader">
<module name="ExtendedFieldSearch" layoutPanel="viewHeader">
  <module name="TimeRangePicker">
    <module name="SubmitButton">

      <module name="HiddenSearch" layoutPanel="panel_row1_col1">
       . . .
```

```
<module name="HiddenSearch" layoutPanel="panel_row2_col1">
  . . .
<module name="HiddenSearch" layoutPanel="panel_row2_col2">
  . . .
<module name="HiddenSearch" layoutPanel="panel_row3_col1">
  . . .
```

The first set of the `layoutPanel` values are panels included in the "chrome" of the page. This displays the account information, the navigation, and any messages to the user. The second set of modules make up the title and form elements. Notice that `TimeRangePicker` and `SubmitButton` have no `layoutPanel` value, but will inherit from `ExtendedFieldSearch`.

The results panels all begin with a `HiddenSearch` module. All of the children of each of these modules inherit this `layoutPanel` value.

Panel placement

For your dashboard panels, you will almost always use a `layoutPanel` value of the form `panel_rowX_colY`.

A simple visualization of the layout produced by our modules would look like:

panel_row1_col1¤	¤
panel_row2_col1¤	panel_row2_col2¤	¤
panel_row3_col1¤	¤

In our simple XML version of this dashboard, the layout was tied directly to the order of the XML, like this:

```
<row>
  <chart></chart>
</row>

<row>
  <chart></chart>
  <chart></chart>
</row>

<row>
  <event></event>
</row>
```

Just to reiterate, the simple XML structure translates to:

```
<row>
  <chart></chart> == panel_row1_col1
</row>

<row>
  <chart></chart> == panel_row2_col1
  <chart></chart> == panel_row2_col2
</row>

<row>
  <event></event> == panel_row3_col1
</row>
```

There is another extension available, _grp1, which allows you to make columns inside a panel. We will try that out in the *Creating a custom drilldown* section later.

Reusing a query

One example of separating layout from data would be using a single query to populate both a table and a chart. The advanced XML for this could look like the following:

```
<view template="dashboard.html">
  <label>Chapter 8 - Reusing a query</label>

  <module
      name="StaticContentSample"
      layoutPanel="panel_row1_col1">
    <param name="text">Text above</param>
  </module>

  <module
      name="HiddenSearch"
      layoutPanel="panel_row1_col1"
      autoRun="True">
    <param name="search">
      sourcetype="impl_splunk_gen" loglevel=error | top user
    </param>
    <param name="earliest">-24h</param>

    <module name="HiddenChartFormatter">
      <param name="charting.chart">pie</param>
```

```
       <module name="JSChart"></module>

       <module
           name="StaticContentSample"
           layoutPanel="panel_row1_col1">
           <!-- this layoutPanel is unneeded, but harmless -->
         <param name="text">Text below</param>
       </module>
     </module>

     <module name="SimpleResultsTable"
         layoutPanel="panel_row1_col2"></module>

   </module>
 </view>
```

This XML will render a dashboard like the following screenshot:

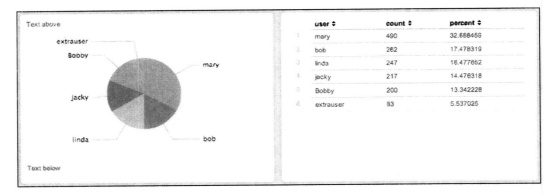

There are some things to notice in this XML:

- The data produced by `HiddenSearch` is used by both child modules.
- `JSChart` inherits `layoutPanel="panel_row1_col1"` from `HiddenSearch`.
- `SimpleResultsTable` has its own `layoutPanel` attribute set to `panel_row1_col2`, so the table draws to the right.
- Both `StaticContentSample` modules specify `layoutPanel="panel_row1_col1"`, and therefore appear in the same panel as the chart. Though they are at different depths in the XML, the order drawn follows the order seen in the XML.

Using intentions

Intentions allow you to affect downstream searches, using values provided by other modules, for instance, form fields or the results of a click. There are a number of available intention types, but we will cover the two most common, `stringreplace` and `addterm`. You can see examples of other types of intentions in the *UI Examples* app available at `http://splunkbase.com`.

stringreplace

This is the most common intention to use, and maps directly to the only available action in simple XML—variable replacement. Let's look at our search field from our advanced XML example:

```
<module name="ExtendedFieldSearch" layoutPanel="viewHeader">
  <param name="replacementMap">
    <param name="arg">
      <param name="user"/>
    </param>
  </param>
  <param name="field">User</param>
  <param name="intention">
    <param name="name">stringreplace</param>
    <param name="arg">
      <param name="user">
        <param name="fillOnEmpty">True</param>
      </param>
    </param>
  </param>
```

Stepping through the params we have:

- `field`: This is the label for the field displayed in the dashboard.

- `replacementMap`: This parameter names the variable that the `ExtendedFieldSearch` module is creating. I have been told that the nested nature means nothing, and we should simply copy and paste the entire block of XML, changing nothing but the value of the deepest `param`, in this case to `user`.

- `intention`: Intentions have specific structures that build blocks of query from a structured XML. In the case of `stringreplace` (which is the most common use case), we can essentially copy the entire XML and once again change nothing but the value of the third-level `param`, which is currently `user`. `fillOnEmpty` determines whether to make the substitution when the `user` variable is empty.

All of this code simply says to replace $user$ in any searches with the value of the input field. Our first HiddenSearch looks like the following:

```
<module name="HiddenSearch" ...
  <param name="search">
      sourcetype="impl_splunk_gen"
      loglevel=error user="$user$"
      | timechart count as "Error count" by network
  </param>
```

The value of $user$ will be replaced and the query will be run.

 If you want to see exactly what is happening, you can insert a SearchBar module as a child of the form elements, and it will render the resulting query. For an example, see the code of the dashboard drilldown_chart1 in the *UI Examples* app available at http://splunkbase.com.

addterm

This intention is useful for adding search terms to a query, with or without user interaction. For example, let's say you always want to ensure that a particular value of the field source is queried. You can then modify the query that will be run, appending a search term. Here is an example from the dashboard advanced_lister_with_searchbar in the *UI Examples* app available at http://splunkbase.com:

```
<module name="HiddenIntention">
  <param name="intention">
    <param name="name">addterm</param>
    <param name="arg">
      <param name="source">*metrics.log</param>
    </param>
    <!-- tells the addterm intention to put our
         term in the first search clause no matter what. -->
    <param name="flags"><list>indexed</list></param>
  </param>
```

Stepping through the params:

- name: This parameter sets the type of intention, in this case addterm.

- arg: This is used to set the field to add to the query.

  - The nested param tag sets the fieldname and value to use in the query. In this case, source="*metrics.log" will be added to the query.

○ Variables can be used in either the `name` attribute or body of this nested `param` tag. We will see an example of this under the *Creating a custom drilldown* section.

- `flags`: Every example of `addterm` that I can find includes this attribute, exactly as written. It essentially says that the term to be added to the search should be added before the first pipe symbol, not at the end of the full query. For example, consider the following query:

```
error | top logger
```

This param would amend our query like this:

```
error source="*metrics.log" | top logger
```

Creating a custom drilldown

A drilldown is a query built using values from a previous query. The module `ConvertToDrilldownSearch` will build a query automatically from the table or graph that it is nested inside. Unfortunately, this only works well when the query is fairly simple, and when you want to see raw events. To build a custom drilldown, we combine intentions and the nested nature of modules.

Building a drilldown to a custom query

Looking back at our chart in the *Reusing a query* section, let's build a custom drilldown that shows the top instances of another field when it is clicked on.

Here is an example dashboard that draws a chart and then runs a custom query when clicked on:

```
<view template="dashboard.html">
  <label>Chapter 8 - Drilldown to custom query</label>
  <!-- chrome -->
  <module
      name="HiddenSearch"
      layoutPanel="panel_row1_col1"
      autoRun="True"
      group="Errors by user">
    <param name="search">
      sourcetype="impl_splunk_gen" loglevel=error | top user
    </param>
    <param name="earliest">-24h</param>
```

```
    <!-- draw the chart -->
    <module name="HiddenChartFormatter">
      <param name="charting.chart">pie</param>
      <module name="JSChart">

        <!-- nested modules are invoked on click -->
        <!-- create a new query -->
        <module name="HiddenSearch">
          <param name="search">
            sourcetype="impl_splunk_gen" loglevel=error
            | top logger
          </param>

          <!-- create an intention using the value from the chart.
               Use addterm to add a user field to the query. -->
          <module name="ConvertToIntention">
            <param name="intention">
              <param name="name">addterm</param>
              <param name="arg">
                <param name="user">$click.value$</param>
              </param>
              <param name="flags">
                <item>indexed</item>
              </param>
            </param>

            <!-- Send the user to flashtimeline
                 with the new query. -->
            <module name="ViewRedirector">
              <param name="viewTarget">flashtimeline</param>
            </module>
          </module>
        </module>
      </module>
    </module>
  </module>
</view>
```

Everything should look very similar up until the JSChart module. Inside this module we find a HiddenSearch module. The idea is that the downstream modules of display modules are not invoked until the display module is clicked. HiddenSearch in this case is used to build a query, but instead of the query being handed to a display module, it is handed to the ViewRedirector module.

The "magical" field in all of this is `click.value`. This field contains the value that was clicked on in the chart.

Let's look at what this dashboard renders:

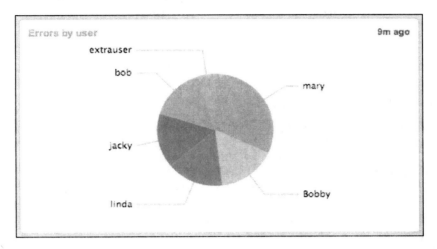

The resulting query when we click on the slice of the pie for the user **bob** looks like:

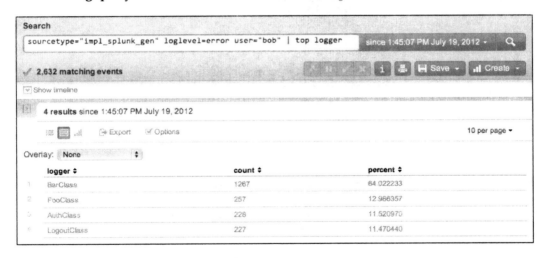

Look back to the *addterm* section for more details on how this intention works.

Building a drilldown to another panel

Another option for a drilldown is to draw a new panel on the same dashboard. This lets you create various drilldowns without redrawing the screen, which might be less jarring to the user. Here is the XML:

```
<?xml version="1.0"?>
<view template="dashboard.html">
  <label>Chapter 8 - Drilldown to new graph</label>
  <!-- chrome should go here -->
  <module
      name="HiddenSearch"
      layoutPanel="panel_row1_col1"
      autoRun="True"
      group="Errors by user">
    <param name="search">
      sourcetype="impl_splunk_gen" loglevel=error | top user
    </param>
    <param name="earliest">-24h</param>
    <module name="HiddenChartFormatter">
      <param name="charting.chart">pie</param>

      <!-- draw the first chart -->
      <module name="JSChart">

        <!-- the modules inside the chart will wait for
             interaction from the user -->
        <module name="HiddenSearch">
          <param name="earliest">-24h</param>
          <param name="search">
            sourcetype="impl_splunk_gen" loglevel=error
            user="$user$" | timechart count by logger
          </param>
          <module name="ConvertToIntention">
            <param name="intention">
              <param name="name">stringreplace</param>
              <param name="arg">
                <param name="user">
                  <param name="value">$click.value$</param>
                </param>
              </param>
            </param>

            <!-- print a header above the new chart -->
```

```
            <module name="SimpleResultsHeader">
              <param name="entityName">results</param>
              <param name="headerFormat">
                Errors by logger for $click.value$
              </param>
            </module>

            <!-- draw the chart. We have not specified another
                 layoutPanel, so it will appear below the first
                 chart -->
            <module name="HiddenChartFormatter">
              <param name="charting.chart">area</param>
              <param name="chart.stackMode">stacked</param>
              <module name="JSChart"/>
            </module>
          </module>
        </module>
      </module>
    </module>
  </module>
</view>
```

Here's what the dashboard looks like after clicking on **bob** in the pie chart:

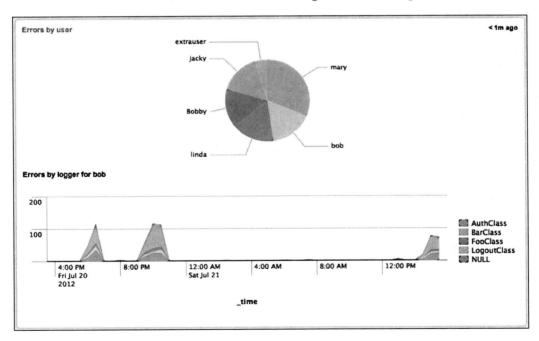

Building a drilldown to multiple panels using HiddenPostProcess

Taking the last dashboard further, let's build a number of panels from a single custom drilldown query. As we covered in *Chapter 4, Simple XML Dashboards*, search results can be post processed, allowing you to use the same query results multiple ways. In advanced XML, this is accomplished using the `HiddenPostProcess` module. We will also add the chrome for our first complete dashboard. Here is an abbreviated example. The complete dashboard is in the `Chapter8_drilldown_to_new_graph_with_postprocess.xml` file in the *Implementing Splunk App One* app:

```
<view template="dashboard.html">
  <label>Chapter 8 - Drilldown to new graph with postprocess</label>

<!-- The chrome at the top of the dashboard
     containing navigation and the app header -->
  <module name="AccountBar" layoutPanel="appHeader"/>
  <module name="AppBar" layoutPanel="navigationHeader"/>
  <module name="Message" layoutPanel="messaging">
    <param name="filter">*</param>
    <param name="clearOnJobDispatch">False</param>
    <param name="maxSize">1</param>
  </module>
  <module name="DashboardTitleBar" layoutPanel="viewHeader"/>
  <module name="Message" layoutPanel="navigationHeader">
    <param name="filter">splunk.search.job</param>
    <param name="clearOnJobDispatch">True</param>
    <param name="maxSize">1</param>
    <param name="level">warn</param>
  </module>

!-- Begin our initial search
    which will populate our pie chart -->
  <module
      name="HiddenSearch" layoutPanel="panel_row1_col1"
      autoRun="True" group="Errors by user">
    <param name="search">
      sourcetype="impl_splunk_gen" loglevel=error | top user
    </param>
    <param name="earliest">-24h</param>

    <module name="HiddenChartFormatter">
      <param name="charting.chart">pie</param>
      <module name="JSChart">

<!-- Initially, only the pie chart will be drawn
     After a click on a user wedge, this nested query will run -->
        <module name="HiddenSearch">
```

```
          <param name="earliest">-24h</param>
          <param name="search">
            sourcetype="impl_splunk_gen" loglevel=error
            user="$user$" | bucket span=30m _time
            | stats count by logger _time
          </param>
          <module name="ConvertToIntention">
            <param name="intention">
              <param name="name">stringreplace</param>
              <param name="arg">
                <param name="user">
                  <param name="value">$click.value$</param>
...

<!-- The remaining modules are downstream from the pie chart
     and are invoked when a pie wedge is clicked -->
          <module name="SimpleResultsHeader"
              layoutPanel="panel_row2_col1">
            <param name="entityName">results</param>
            <param name="headerFormat">
              Errors by logger for $click.value$
            </param>
          </module>

<!-- The SingleValue modules -->
          <module name="HiddenPostProcess">
            <param name="search">
              stats sum(count) as count by logger
              | sort -count | head 1
              | eval f=logger + " is most common (" + count + ")" |
table f </param>
              <module name="SingleValue"
                  layoutPanel="panel_row2_col1"></module>
          </module>
...
<!-- The chart -->
          <module name="HiddenPostProcess">
            <param name="search">
              timechart span=30m sum(count) by logger
            </param>
            <module name="HiddenChartFormatter">
              <param name="charting.chart">area</param>
              <param name="chart.stackMode">stacked</param>
              <module
                name="JSChart"
                layoutPanel="panel_row4_col1_grp1"/>
            </module>
          </module>

<!-- The table -->
```

```
            <module name="HiddenPostProcess">
              <param name="search">
                stats sum(count) as count by logger
              </param>
              <module name="SimpleResultsTable"
                  layoutPanel="panel_row4_col1_grp2"/>
            </module>
  ...
        </module>
    </view>
```

This dashboard contains the chrome, which is very useful as it displays the errors in your intentions and query statements. After clicking on **bob**, this is what we see:

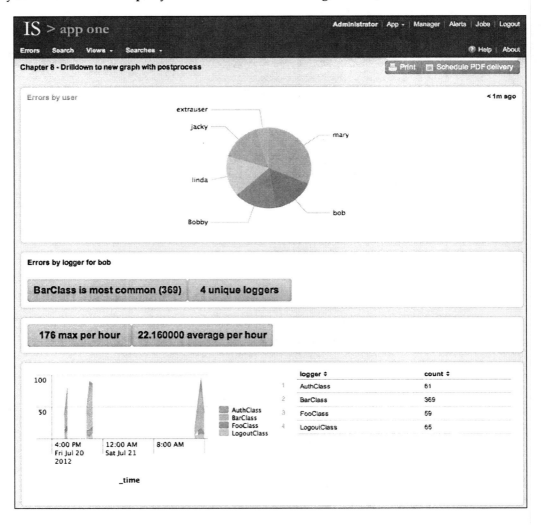

Let's step through the new queries. The initial query is the same:

```
sourcetype="impl_splunk_gen" loglevel=error | top user
```

The next query may seem strange, but there's a good reason for this:

```
sourcetype="impl_splunk_gen" loglevel=error user="$user$"
| bucket span=30m _time
| stats count by logger _time
```

If you look back to *Chapter 5, Advanced Search Examples*, we used `bucket` and `stats` to slice events by `_time` and other fields. This is a convenient way to break down events for post processing, where one or more of the post-process queries uses `timechart`. This query produces a row with the field `count` for every unique value of `logger` in each 30-minute period.

 Post processing has a limit of 10,000 events. To accommodate this limit, all aggregation possible should be done in the initial query. Ideally, only what is needed by all child queries should be produced by the initial query. It is also important to note that all fields needed by post-process queries must be returned by the initial query.

The first `HiddenPostProcess` builds a field for a module we haven't used yet, `SingleValue`, which takes the first value it sees and renders that value in a rounded rectangle.

```
stats sum(count) as count by logger
| sort -count
| head 1
| eval f=logger + " is most common (" + count + ")"
| table f
```

The query is additive, so the full query for this module is essentially:

```
sourcetype="impl_splunk_gen" loglevel=error user="bob"
| bucket span=30m _time
| stats count by logger _time
| stats sum(count) as count by logger
| sort -count
| head 1
| eval f=logger + " is most common (" + count + ")"
| table f
```

The remaining `SingleValue` modules do similar work to find the count of unique loggers, the max errors per hour, and the average errors per hour. To step through these queries, simply copy each piece and add it to a query in search.

Other things to notice in this dashboard are:

- `grp` builds columns inside a single panel, for instance, in `layoutPanel="panel_row4_col1_grp2"`

- `SingleValue` modules do not stack vertically, but rather flow horizontally, overflowing onto the next line when the window width is reached

- `span` used in the `bucket` statement is the minimum needed by any post-process statements, but as large as possible to minimize the number of events returned

Third-party add-ons

There are many excellent apps available at `http://splunkbase.com`, a number of which provide custom modules. We will cover two of the most popular, *Google Maps* and *Sideview Utils*.

Google Maps

As we saw in *Chapter 7, Working with Apps*, the *Google Maps* app provides a dashboard and lookup for drawing results on a map. The underlying module is also available to use in your own dashboards.

Here is a very simple dashboard that uses the `GoogleMaps` module:

```
<?xml version="1.0"?>
<view template="search.html">

  <!-- chrome -->
  <label>Chapter 8 - Google Maps Search</label>
  <module name="AccountBar" layoutPanel="appHeader"/>
  <module name="AppBar" layoutPanel="navigationHeader"/>
  <module name="Message" layoutPanel="messaging">
    <param name="filter">*</param>
    <param name="clearOnJobDispatch">False</param>
    <param name="maxSize">1</param>
  </module>

  <!-- search -->
  <module name="SearchBar" layoutPanel="splSearchControls-inline">
    <param name="useOwnSubmitButton">False</param>
    <module name="TimeRangePicker">
      <param name="selected">Last 60 minutes</param>
      <module name="SubmitButton">
```

```
    <!-- map -->
    <module
        name="GoogleMaps"
        layoutPanel="resultsAreaLeft"
        group="Map" />
    </module>
  </module>
 </module>
</view>
```

This code produces a search bar with a map under it, as seen here in the following screenshot:

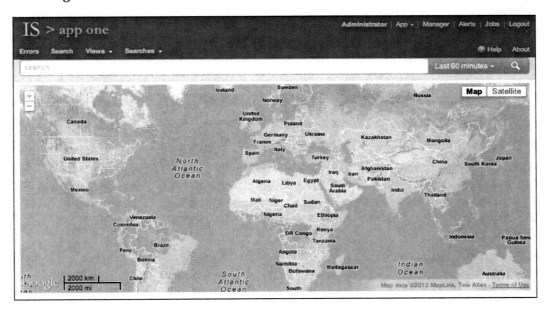

When using the `GoogleMaps` module, you would usually convert some set of values to geographic coordinates. This is usually accomplished using the `geoip` lookup (see *Chapter 7, Working with Apps*, for examples) to convert IP addresses to locations, or by using a custom lookup of some sort.

Just to show that the data can come from anywhere, let's make a graph by setting the `_geo` field on events from one of our example source types:

```
sourcetype="impl_splunk_gen" req_time
   | eventstats max(req_time) as max
   | eval lat=(req_time/max*360)-180
   | eval lng=abs(lat)/2-15
   | eval _geo=lng+","+lat
```

This query will produce a "V" from our random `req_time` field, as shown in the following screenshot. See the maps documentation at `splunkbase.com` for more information about the `_geo` field:

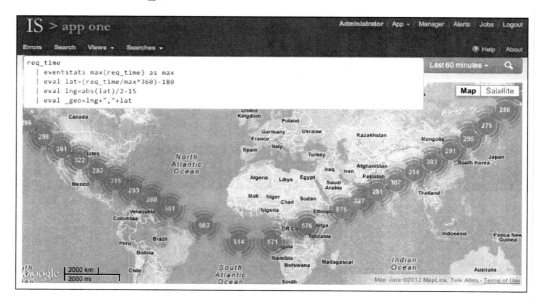

This is a very simplistic example, using the default settings for nearly everything. For a more complete example, see the **Google Maps** dashboard included with the **Google Maps** app. You can see the source code in the manager, or by using the `showsource` attribute. On my server, that URL would be `http://mysplunkserver:8000/en-US/app/maps/maps?showsource=1`.

Sideview Utils

Sideview Utils is a third-party app for Splunk that provides an alternative set of modules for most of what you need to build an interactive Splunk dashboard. These modules remove the complexity of intentions, make it much easier to build forms, make it possible to use variables in HTML, and make it much simpler to hand values between panels and dashboards.

We will use a few of the modules to build forms and link multiple dashboards together based on URL values.

An older but still functional version of `SideviewUtils` is available through Splunkbase. You can download the latest version from `http://sideviewapps.com/`, which adds a number of features, including a visual editor for assembling dashboards.

The Sideview Search module

Let's start with a simple search:

```xml
<?xml version="1.0"?>
<view template="dashboard.html">

  <!-- add sideview -->
  <module layoutPanel="appHeader" name="SideviewUtils"/>

  <!-- chrome -->
  <label>Chapter 8 - Sideview One</label>
  <module name="AccountBar" layoutPanel="appHeader"/>
  <module name="AppBar" layoutPanel="navigationHeader"/>
  <module name="Message" layoutPanel="messaging">
    <param name="filter">*</param>
    <param name="clearOnJobDispatch">False</param>
    <param name="maxSize">1</param>
  </module>

  <!-- search -->
  <module
      name="Search"
      autoRun="True"
      group="Chapter 8 - Sideview One"
      layoutPanel="panel_row1_col1">
    <param name="earliest">-1h</param>
    <param name="search">source="impl_splunk_gen" | top user</param>

    <!-- chart -->
    <module name="HiddenChartFormatter">
      <param name="charting.chart">pie</param>
      <module name="JSChart"/>
    </module>
  </module>
</view>
```

This dashboard renders identically to the first panel, previously described in
the *Building a drilldown to a custom query* section. There are two things to notice
in this example:

1. The `SideviewUtils` module is needed to include the code needed by
   all *Sideview Utils* apps.

2. We use the alternative `Search` module as a replacement for the
   `HiddenSearch` module to illustrate our first `SideviewUtils` module.
   In this simplistic example, `HiddenSearch` would still work.

Linking views with Sideview

Starting from our simple dashboard, let's use the `Redirector` module to build a link. This link could be to anything, but we will link to another Splunk dashboard, which we will build next. Here's the XML:

```
...
<module name="JSChart">
  <module name="Redirector">
    <param name="arg.user">$click.value$</param>
    <param name="url">chapter_8_sideview_2</param>
  </module>
</module>
...
```

After clicking on **mary**, a new URL is built using the user value. In my case, the URL is:

```
http://mysplunkserver:8000/en-US/app/is_app_one/chapter_8_
sideview_2?user=mary
```

The dashboard referenced does not exist yet, so this URL will return an error. Let's create the second dashboard now.

Sideview URLLoader

The `URLLoader` module provides the ability to set variables from the query string of a URL, a very useful feature. For our next dashboard, we will draw a table showing the error counts for the `user` value provided in the URL:

```
<view template="dashboard.html">

  <!-- add sideview -->
  <module name="SideviewUtils" layoutPanel="appHeader"/>

  <!-- chrome -->
  <label>Chapter 8 - Sideview Two</label>
  <module name="AccountBar" layoutPanel="appHeader"/>
  <module name="AppBar" layoutPanel="navigationHeader"/>
  <module name="Message" layoutPanel="messaging">
    <param name="filter">*</param>
    <param name="clearOnJobDispatch">False</param>
    <param name="maxSize">1</param>
```

```
    </module>

    <!-- search -->
    <module
        name="URLLoader"
        layoutPanel="panel_row1_col1"
        autoRun="True">
      <module name="HTML">
        <param name="html"><![CDATA[
          <h2>Errors by logger for $user$.</h2>
          ]]>
        </param>
      </module>
      <module name="Search" group="Chapter 8 - Sideview Two">
        <param name="earliest">-1h</param>
        <param name="search">
          source="impl_splunk_gen" user=$user$
          | top logger
        </param>

        <!-- table -->
        <module name="SimpleResultsTable">
          <param name="drilldown">row</param>
          <module name="Redirector">
            <param name="url">chapter_8_sideview_3</param>
            <param name="arg.logger">
              $click.fields.logger.rawValue$
            </param>
            <param name="arg.user">$user$</param>
            <param name="arg.earliest">
              $search.timeRange.earliest$
            </param>
          </module>
        </module>
      </module>
    </module>
  </module>
</view>
```

 It is very important that autoRun="true" be placed in one module, most likely URLLoader, and that it exists only in a single module.

With the value of *user* as *mary* in our URL, this dashboard creates the simple view:

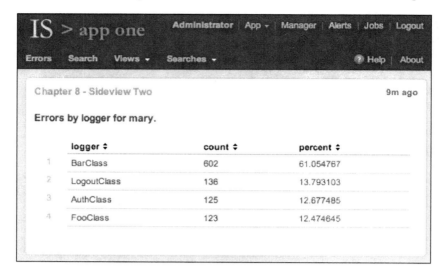

Looking at the modules in this example that are of interest, we see:

- `SideviewUtils`: This module is required to use any of the other `Sideview` modules. It is invisible to the user, but is still required.

- `URLLoader`: This module takes any values specified in the URL query string and turns them into variables to be used by the descendant modules. Our URL contains `user=mary`, so `$user$` will be replaced with the value `mary`.

- `HTML`: This module draws a snippet of HTML inline. Variables from `URLLoader` and from form elements are replaced.

- `Search`: This replacement for `HiddenSearch` understands variables from `URLLoader` and form elements. This completely obviates the need for intentions. In our case, `$user$` will be replaced.

- `Redirector`: In this example, we are going to hand along two values to the next dashboard—user from `URLLoader`, and `logger` from the table itself. A few things to notice:

  ○ `logger` will be populated with `$click.fields.logger.rawValue$`.

  ○ When a table is clicked on, the variable `click.fields` contains all fields from the row of the table clicked on.

  ○ `rawValue` makes sure the unescaped value is returned. As the Sideview docs say: *Rule of Thumb - for displaying in headers and sending via redirects, use $foo.rawValue$. For searches, use foo.*

This rule applies to values in `Redirector`, not in display.

- ○ `search.timeRange` contains information about the times used by this search, whether it comes from the URL, a `TimeRangePicker`, or params to the `Search` module. `arg.earliest` will add the value to the URL.

With a click on the table row for **LogoutClass**, we are taken to the following URL:

```
http://mysplunkserver:8000/en-US/app/is_app_one/chapter_8_sideview_3?
user=mar&ylogger=LogoutClass&earliest=1344188377
```

We will create the dashboard at this URL in the next section.

Sideview forms

For our final dashboard using `Sideview` modules, we will build a dashboard with a form that can be prefilled from a URL, and allows changing the time range. The advantage of this dashboard is that it can be used as a destination of a click without being linked to from elsewhere. If the user accesses this dashboard directly, the default values specified in the dashboard will be used instead. Let's look at the code:

```xml
<?xml version="1.0"?>
<view template="dashboard.html">

  <!-- add sideview -->
  <module name="SideviewUtils" layoutPanel="appHeader"/>

  <!-- chrome -->
  <label>Chapter 8 - Sideview Three</label>
  <module name="AccountBar" layoutPanel="appHeader"/>
  <module name="AppBar" layoutPanel="navigationHeader"/>
  <module name="Message" layoutPanel="messaging">
    <param name="filter">*</param>
    <param name="clearOnJobDispatch">False</param>
    <param name="maxSize">1</param>
  </module>

  <!-- URLLoader -->
  <module
      name="URLLoader"
      layoutPanel="panel_row1_col1"
```

```
            autoRun="True">

    <!-- form -->

    <!-- user dropdown -->
    <module name="Search" layoutPanel="panel_row1_col1">
      <param name="search">
        source="impl_splunk_gen" user user="*"
        | top user
      </param>
      <param name="earliest">-24h</param>
      <param name="latest">now</param>

      <module name="Pulldown">
        <param name="name">user</param>
        <!-- use valueField in SideView 2.0 -->
        <param name="searchFieldsToDisplay">
          <list>
            <param name="value">user</param>
            <param name="label">user</param>
          </list>
        </param>
        <param name="label">User</param>
        <param name="float">left</param>

        <!-- logger textfield -->
        <module name="TextField">
          <param name="name">logger</param>
          <param name="default">*</param>
          <param name="label">Logger:</param>
          <param name="float">left</param>
          <module name="TimeRangePicker">
            <param name="searchWhenChanged">True</param>
            <param name="default">Last 24 hours</param>

            <!-- submit button -->
            <module name="SubmitButton">
              <param name="allowSoftSubmit">True</param>

              <!-- html -->
              <module name="HTML">

                <param name="html"><![CDATA[
                  <h2>Info for user $user$, logger $logger$.</h2>
                ]]></param>
              </module>
```

```
        <!-- search 1 -->
        <module
            name="Search"
            group="Chapter 8 - Sideview Three">
          <param name="search">
            source="impl_splunk_gen" user="$user$"
            logger="$logger$"
            | fillnull value="unknown" network
            | timechart count by network
          </param>

          <!-- JobProgressIndicator -->
          <module name="JobProgressIndicator"/>

          <!-- chart -->
          <module name="HiddenChartFormatter">
            <param name="charting.chart">area</param>
            <param name="charting.chart.stackMode">
              stacked
            </param>
            <module name="JSChart"/>
          </module>
        </module>

        <!-- search 2 -->
        <module
            name="Search"
            group="Chapter 8 - Sideview Three">
          <param name="search">
            source="impl_splunk_gen" user="$user$"
            logger="$logger$"
            | fillnull value="unknown" network
            | top network
          </param>

          <!-- table -->
          <module name="SimpleResultsTable"/>
        </module>
      </module>
     </module>
    </module>
   </module>
  </module>
</view>
```

This draws a dashboard like this:

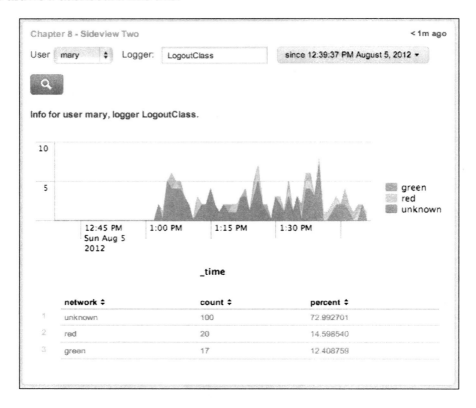

There are quite a few things to cover in this example, so let's step through portions of the XML.

Include `SideviewUtils` to enable the other `Sideview` modules. In this case, `URLLoader`, `HTML`, `Pulldown`, `Search`, and `TextField` are `Sideview` modules.

```
<module layoutPanel="appHeader" name="SideviewUtils"/>
```

Wrap everything in `URLLoader` so that we get values from the URL:

```
<module
    name="URLLoader"
    layoutPanel="panel_row1_col1"
    autoRun="True">
```

Start a search to populate the `user` dropdown. This query will find all users in the last 24 hours:

```
<module name="Search" layoutPanel="panel_row1_col1">
  <param name="search">
    source="impl_splunk_gen" user user="*"
    | top user
  </param>
  <param name="earliest">-24h</param>
  <param name="latest">now</param>
```

 Using a query to populate a dropdown can be very expensive, particularly as your data volumes increase. You may need to precalculate these values, either storing the values in a CSV using `outputcsv` and `inputcsv`, or using a summary index. See *Chapter 9, Summary Indexes and CSV Files*, for examples of summary indexing and using CSV files for transient data.

This module draws the user selector. The menu is filled by the `Search` module previously, but notice that the value selected is from our URL value:

```
<module name="Pulldown">
    <!-- use valueField in SideView 2.0 -->
  <param name="searchFieldsToDisplay">
    <list>
      <param name="value">user</param>
      <param name="label">user</param>
    </list>
  </param>
  <param name="name">user</param>
  <param name="label">User</param>
  <param name="float">left</param>
```

Next is a text field for our logger. This is a Sideview version of `ExtendedFieldSearch`. It will prepopulate using upstream variables:

```
<module name="TextField">
  <param name="name">logger</param>
  <param name="default">*</param>
  <param name="label">Logger:</param>
  <param name="float">left</param>
```

The `TimeRangePicker` module will honor the values earliest and latest in the URL. Note that `searchWhenChanged` must be `True` to work properly in this case. As a rule of thumb, `searchWhenChanged` should always be `True`.

```
<module name="TimeRangePicker">
    <param name="searchWhenChanged">True</param>
    <param name="default">Last 24 hours</param>
```

The `SubmitButton` module will kick off a search when values are changed. `allowSoftSubmit` allows outer modules to start the query, either by choosing a value or hitting return in a text field.

```
<module name="SubmitButton">
    <param name="allowSoftSubmit">True</param>
```

Next are two `Search` modules, each containing an output module:

```
<module
    name="Search"
    group="Chapter 8 - Sideview Three">
  <param name="search">
    source="impl_splunk_gen" user="$user$"
    logger="$logger$"
    | fillnull value="unknown" network
    | timechart count by network
  </param>

  <!-- JobProgressIndicator -->
  <module name="JobProgressIndicator"/>

  <!-- chart -->
  <module name="HiddenChartFormatter">
    <param name="charting.chart">area</param>
    <param name="charting.chart.stackMode">
      stacked
    </param>
    <module name="JSChart"/>
  </module>
</module>

<!-- search 2 -->
<module
```

```
        group="Chapter 8 - Sideview Three"
        name="Search">
<param name="search">
    source="impl_splunk_gen" user="$user$"
    logger="$logger$"
    | fillnull value="unknown" network
    | top network
</param>

<!-- table -->
<module name="SimpleResultsTable">
    <param name="drilldown">row</param>
</module>
```
  . . .

For greater efficiency, these two searches could be combined into one query and the PostProcess module used.

Summary

We have covered an enormous amount of ground in this chapter. The toughest concepts we touched on were module nesting, the meaning of layoutPanel, intentions, and an alternative to intentions with *SideView Utils*. As with many skills, the best way to become proficient is to dig in, and hopefully have some fun along the way! The examples in this chapter should give you a head start.

In the next chapter, we will cover summary indexing, a powerful part of Splunk that can improve the efficiency of your queries greatly.

Summary Indexes and CSV Files

9

As the number of events retrieved by a query increases, performance decreases linearly. Summary indexing allows you to calculate statistics in advance, then run reports against these "roll ups", dramatically increasing performance.

Understanding summary indexes

A **summary index** is a place to store events calculated by Splunk. Usually, these events are aggregates of raw events broken up over time, for instance, how many errors occurred per hour. By calculating this information on an hourly basis, it is cheap and fast to run a query over a longer period of time, for instance, days, weeks, or months.

A summary index is usually populated from a saved search with **Summary indexing** enabled as an action. This is not the only way, but is certainly the most common.

On disk, a summary index is identical to any other Splunk index. The difference is solely the source of data. We create the index through configuration or through the GUI like any other index, and we manage the index size in the same way.

 Think of an index like a table, or possibly a tablespace in a typical SQL database. Indexes are capped by size and/or time, much like a tablespace, but all the data is stored together, much like a table. We will discuss index management in *Chapter 10, Configuring Splunk*.

Creating a summary index

To create an index, navigate to **Manager | Indexes | Add new**.

Add new

Index settings

Index name *

summary_impl_splunk

Set index name (e.g., INDEX_NAME). Search using index=INDEX_NAME.

Home path

Hot/warm db path. Leave blank for default ($SPLUNK_DB/INDEX_NAME/db).

Cold path

Cold db path. Leave blank for default ($SPLUNK_DB/INDEX_NAME/colddb).

Thawed path

Thawed/resurrected db path. Leave blank for default ($SPLUNK_DB/INDEX_NAME/thaweddb).

Max size (MB) of entire index

500000

Maximum target size of entire index.

Max size (MB) of hot/warm/cold bucket

auto

Maximum target size of buckets. Enter 'auto_high_volume' for high-volume indexes.

Frozen archive path

Frozen bucket archive path. Set this if you want Splunk to automatically archive frozen buckets.

Cancel   Save

For now, let's simply give our new index a name and accept the default values. We will discuss these settings under the *indexes.conf* section in *Chapter 10, Configuring Splunk*. I like to put the word `summary` at the beginning of any summary index, but the name does not matter. I would suggest you follow some naming convention that makes sense to you.

Now that we have an index to store events in, let's do something with it.

When to use a summary index

When the question you want to answer requires looking at all or most events for a given source type, very quickly the number of events can become huge. This is what is generally referred to as a "dense search".

For example, if you want to know how many page views happened on your website, the query to answer this question must inspect every event. Since each query uses a processor, we are essentially timing how fast our disk can retrieve the raw data and how fast a single processor can decompress that data. Doing a little math:

1,000,000 hits per day /

10,000 events processed per second =

100 seconds

If we use multiple indexers, or possibly buy much faster disks, we can cut this time, but only linearly. For instance, if the data is evenly split across four indexers, without changing disks, this query will take roughly 25 seconds.

If we use summary indexing, we should be able to improve our times dramatically. Let's assume we have calculated hit counts per five minutes. Now doing the math:

*24 hours * 60 minutes per hour / 5 minute slices =*

288 summary events

If we then use those summary events in a query, the math looks like:

288 summary events /

10,000 events processed per second =

.0288 seconds

This is a significant increase in performance. In reality, we would probably store more than 288 events. For instance, let's say we want to count events by their HTTP response code. Assuming there are 10 different status codes we see on a regular basis, we have:

*24 hours * 60 minutes per hour / 5 minute slices * 10 codes =*

2880 events

The math then looks like:

2,880 summary events /

10,000 events processed per second =

.288 seconds

That's still a significant improvement over 100 seconds.

When to not use a summary index

There are several cases where summary indexes are either inappropriate or inefficient. Consider the following:

- **When you need to see the original events**: In most cases, summary indexes are used to store aggregate values. A summary index could be used to store a separate copy of events, but this is not usually the case. The more events you have in your summary index, the less advantage it has over the original index.

- **When the possible number of categories of data is huge**: For example, if you want to know the top IP addresses seen per day, it may be tempting to simply capture a count of every IP address seen. This can still be a huge amount of data, and may not save you a lot of search time, if any. Likewise, simply storing the top 10 addresses per slice of time may not give an accurate picture over a long period of time. We will discuss this scenario under the *Calculating top for a large time frame* section.

- **When it is impractical to slice the data across sufficient dimensions**: If your data has a large number of dimensions or attributes, and it is useful to slice the data across a large number of these dimensions, then the resulting summary index may not be sufficiently smaller than your original index to bother with.

- **When it is difficult to know the acceptable time slice**: As we set up a few summary indexes, we have to pick the slice of time to which we aggregate. If you think 1 hour is an acceptable time slice, and you find out later that you really need 10 minutes of resolution, it is not the easiest task to recalculate the old data into these 10-minute slices. It is, however, very simple to later change your 10-minute search to one hour, as the 10-minute slices should still work for your hourly reports.

Populating summary indexes with saved searches

A search to populate a summary index is much like any other saved search (see *Chapter 2, Understand Search,* for more detail on creating saved searches). The differences are that this search will run periodically and the results will be stored in the summary index. Let's build our first summary search by following these steps:

1. Start with a search that produces some statistic:

   ```
   source="impl_splunk_gen" | stats count by user
   ```

2. Save this search as summary - count by user.

3. Edit the search in **Manager** by navigating to **Manager | Searches and reports | summary – count by user**. The **Save search...** wizard provides a link to the manager on the last dialog in the wizard.

4. Set the appropriate times. This is a somewhat complicated discussion. See the *How latency affects summary queries* section discussed later.

Let's look at the following fields:

- **Search**: `source="impl_splunk_gen" | stats count by user`

  This is our query. Later we will use `sistats`, a special summary index version of `stats`.

- **Start time**: `-62m@m`

  It may seem strange that we didn't simply say `-60m@m`, but we need to take latency into account. See the *How latency affects summary queries* section discussed later for more details.

- **Finish time**: `-2m@m`

- **Schedule and Alert | Schedule this search**: This checkbox needs to be checked for the query to run on a schedule.

- **Schedule type**: **Cron**

- **Cron schedule**: `2 * * * *`

  This indicates that the query runs on minute 2 of every hour, every day. To accommodate for latency, **Cron schedule** is shifted after the beginning of the hour along with the start and finish times. See the *How latency affects summary queries* section discussed later for more details.

- **Summary indexing | Enable**: This checkbox enables writing the output to another index.

- **Select the summary index**: `summary_impl_splunk`

  This is the index to write our events to.

 Non-admin users are only allowed to write to the index summary. This ability is controlled by the `indexes_edit` capability, which only the admin role has enabled by default. See *Chapter 10, Configuring Splunk,* for a discussion on roles and capabilities.

- **Add fields**: Using these fields, you can store extra pieces of information in your summary index. This can be used to group results from multiple summary results, or to tag results.

Using summary index events in a query

After the query to populate the summary index has run for some time, we can use the results in other queries.

If you're in a hurry, or need to report against slices of time before the query was created, you will need to "backfill" your summary index. See the *How and when to backfill summary data* section for details about calculating summary values for past events.

First, let's look at what actually goes into the summary index:

```
08/15/2012 10:00:00, search_name="summary - count by user",
search_now=1345046520.000, info_min_time=1345042800.000, info_max_
time=1345046400.000, info_search_time=1345050512.340, count=17,
user=mary
```

Breaking this event down, we have:

- `08/15/2012 10:00:00`: This is the time at the beginning of this block of data. This is consistent with how `timechart` and `bucket` work.
- `search_name="summary - count by user"`: This is the name of the search. This is usually the easiest way to find the results you are interested in.
- `search_now ... info_search_time`: These are informational fields about the summary entry, and are generally not useful to users.
- `count=17, user=mary`: The rest of the entry will be whatever fields were produced by the populating query. There will be one summary event per row produced by the populating query.

Now let's build a query against this data. To start the query, we need to specify the name of the index and the name of the search:

```
index="summary_impl_splunk" search_name="summary - count by user"
```

On my machine, this query loads 48 events, compared to the 22,477 original events.

Using `stats`, we can quickly find the statistics by `user`:

```
index="summary_impl_splunk" | stats sum(count) count by user
```

This produces a very simple table, as shown in the following screenshot:

user ⬍	sum(count) ⬍	count ⬍
Bobby	12113	16
bob	11845	16
extrauser	3612	16
jacky	12158	16
linda	12057	16
mary	24092	16

We are calculating sum(count) and count in this query, which you might expect to produce the same number, but they are doing very different things:

- sum(count): If you look back at our raw event, count contains the number of times that user appeared in that slice of time. We are storing the raw value in this count field. See the *Using sistats, sitop, and sitimechart* section for a completely different approach.

- count: This actually represents the number of events in the summary index. The generator that is producing these events is not very random, so all users produce at least one event per hour.

Producing a timechart is no more complicated:

```
index="summary_impl_splunk" | timechart span=1h sum(count) by user
```

This produces our graph as shown in the following screenshot:

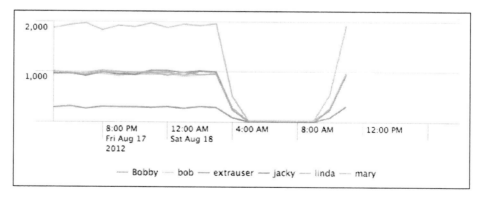

The main thing to remember here is that *we cannot make a graph more detailed than the schedule of our populating query*. In this case, the populating query uses a span of one hour. 1 hour is granular enough for most daily reports, and certainly fine for weekly or monthly reports, but it may not be granular enough for an operations dashboard.

The following are a few other interesting queries you could make with this simple set of data:

```
index="summary_impl_splunk" search_name="summary - count by user"
   | stats avg(count) as "Average events per hour"
```

The previous code snippet tells us the average number of events per slice of time, which we know is an hour. Adding `bucket` and another `stats` command, we can calculate for a custom period of time, as follows:

```
index="summary_impl_splunk" search_name="summary - count by user"
   | bucket span=4h _time
   | stats sum(count) as count by _time
   | stats avg(count) as "Average events per 4 hours"
```

This query would give us the user with the maximum number of events in a given hour, and the hour it happened in:

```
index="summary_impl_splunk" search_name="summary - count by user"
   | stats first(_time) as _time max(count) as max by user
   | sort -max
   | head 1
   | rename max as "Maximum events per hour"
```

Using sistats, sitop, and sitimechart

So far we have used the `stats` command to populate our summary index. While this works perfectly well, the `si*` variants have a couple of advantages:

- The remaining portion of the query does not have to be rewritten. For instance, `stats count` still works as if you were counting the raw events.

- `stats` functions that require more data than what happened in that slice of time will still work. For example, if your time slices each represent an hour, it is not possible to calculate the average value for a day using nothing but the average of each hour. `sistats` keeps enough information to make this work.

There are a few fairly serious disadvantages to be aware of:

- The query using the summary index *must* use a subset of the functions and split fields that were in the original populating query. If the subsequent query strays from what is in the original `sistats` data, the results may be unexpected and difficult to debug. For example:

  ○ The following code works fine:

  ```
  source="impl_splunk_gen"
      | sitimechart span=1h avg(req_time) by user
      | stats avg(req_time)
  ```

  ○ The following code returns unpredictable and wildly incorrect values:

  ```
  source="impl_splunk_gen"
      | sitimechart span=1h avg(req_time) by user
      | stats max(req_time)
  ```

  Notice that `avg` went into `sistats`, but we tried to calculate `max` from the results.

- Using `dc` (distinct count) with `sistats` can produce huge events. This happens because to accurately determine unique values over slices of time, all original values must be kept. One common use case is to find the top IP addresses that hit a public facing server. See the *Calculating top for a large time frame* section for alternate approaches to this problem.

- The contents of the summary index are quite difficult to read as they are not meant to be used by humans.

To see how all of this works, let's build a few queries. We start with a simple `stats` query as follows:

```
sourcetype=impl_splunk_gen
    | stats count max(req_time) avg(req_time) min(req_time) by user
```

This produces results like you would expect:

user ◆	count ◆	max(req_time) ◆	avg(req_time) ◆	min(req_time) ◆
Bobby	11459	12239	6136.885004	1
bob	11294	12237	6107.613410	2
extrauser	3464	12239	6128.628753	6
jacky	11473	12236	6142.702905	1
linda	11375	12237	6107.128160	2
mary	23098	12239	6131.918991	1

Now, we could save this and send it straight to the summary index, but the results are not terribly nice to use, and the average of the average would not be accurate. On the other hand, we can use the `sistats` variant as follows:

```
sourcetype=impl_splunk_gen
    | sistats count max(req_time) avg(req_time) min(req_time) by user
```

The results have a lot of extra information not meant for humans as shown in the following screenshot:

	psrsvd_ct_req_time ⇕	psrsvd_gc ⇕	psrsvd_nc_req_time ⇕	psrsvd_nn_req_time ⇕	psrsvd_nx_req_time ⇕	pars
1	8609	11459	8609	1	12239	
2	8531	11294	8531	2	12237	
3	3464	3464	3464	6	12239	
4	8674	11473	8674	1	12236	
5	8505	11375	8505	2	12237	
6	17282	23098	17282	1	12239	

Splunk knows how to deal with these results, and can use them in combination with the `stats` functions as if they were the original results. You can see how `sistats` and `stats` work together by chaining them together, as follows:

```
sourcetype=impl_splunk_gen
    | sistats
        count max(req_time) avg(req_time) min(req_time)
        by user
    | stats count max(req_time) avg(req_time) min(req_time) by user
```

Even though the `stats` function is not receiving the original events, it knows how to work with these `sistats` summary events. We are presented with exactly the same results as the original query, as shown in the following screenshot:

	user ⇕	count ⇕	max(req_time) ⇕	avg(req_time) ⇕	min(req_time) ⇕
1	Bobby	11459	12239	6136.885004	1
2	bob	11294	12237	6107.613410	2
3	extrauser	3464	12239	6126.628753	6
4	jacky	11473	12236	6142.702905	1
5	linda	11375	12237	6107.128160	2
6	mary	23098	12239	6131.918991	1

`sitop` and `sitimechart` work in the same fashion.

Let's step through the procedure to set up summary searches as follows:

1. Save the query using `sistats`.

    ```
    sourcetype=impl_splunk_gen
        | sistats count max(req_time) avg(req_time) min(req_time) by
    user
    ```

2. Set the times accordingly, as we saw previously in the *Populating summary indexes with saved searches* section. See the *How latency affects summary queries* section for more information.

3. Build a query that queries the summary index, as we saw previously in the *Using summary index events in a query* section. Assuming we saved this query as `testing sistats`, the query would be: `index="summary_impl_splunk"` `search_name="testing sistats"`.

4. Use the original `stats` function against the results, as follows:

    ```
    index="summary_impl_splunk" search_name="testing sistats"
        | stats count max(req_time) avg(req_time) min(req_time) by user
    ```

This should produce exactly the same results as the original query.

The `si*` variants still seem somewhat magical to me, but they work so well that it is in your own best interest to dive in and trust the magic. Be very sure that your functions and fields are a subset of the original!

How latency affects summary queries

Latency is the difference between the time assigned to an event (usually parsed from the text) and the time it was written to the index. Both times are captured, in `_time` and `_indextime`, respectively.

This query will show us what our latency is:

```
sourcetype=impl_splunk_gen
    | eval latency = _indextime - _time
    | stats min(latency) avg(latency) max(latency)
```

In my case, these statistics look as shown in the following screenshot:

min(latency) ⬍	avg(latency) ⬍	max(latency) ⬍
-0.465	31.603530	72.390

The latency in this case is exaggerated, because the script behind `impl_splunk_gen` is creating events in chunks. In most production Splunk instances, the latency is usually just a few seconds. If there is any slowdown, perhaps because of network issues, the latency may increase dramatically, and so it should be accounted for.

This query will produce a table showing the time for every event:

```
sourcetype=impl_splunk_gen
   | eval latency = _indextime - _time
   | eval time=strftime(_time,"%Y-%m-%d %H:%M:%S.%3N")
   | eval indextime=strftime(_indextime,"%Y-%m-%d %H:%M:%S.%3N")
   | table time indextime latency
```

The previous query produces the following table:

	time ⇕	indextime ⇕	latency ⇕
51	2012-08-22 21:38:11.107	2012-08-22 21:38:33.000	21.893
52	2012-08-22 21:38:11.011	2012-08-22 21:38:33.000	21.989
53	2012-08-22 21:38:10.546	2012-08-22 21:38:33.000	22.454
54	2012-08-22 21:38:10.433	2012-08-22 21:38:33.000	22.567
55	2012-08-22 21:38:10.419	2012-08-22 21:38:33.000	22.581
56	2012-08-22 21:38:09.588	2012-08-22 21:38:33.000	23.412
57	2012-08-22 21:38:08.955	2012-08-22 21:38:33.000	24.045
58	2012-08-22 21:38:08.502	2012-08-22 21:38:33.000	24.498
59	2012-08-22 21:38:07.867	2012-08-22 21:38:33.000	25.133

To deal with this latency, you should add enough delay in your query that populates the summary index. The following are a few examples:

Confidence	Time slice	Earliest	Latest	cron
2 minutes	1 hour	-62m@m	-2m@m	2 * * * *
15 minutes	1 hour	-1h@h	-0h@h	15 * * * *
5 minutes	5 minutes	-10m@m	-5m@m	*/5 * * * *
1 hour	15 minutes	-75m@m	-60m@m	*/15 * * * *
1 hour	24 hours	-1d@d	-0d@d	0 1 * * *

Sometimes you have no idea when your logs will be indexed, as when they are delivered in batches on unreliable networks. This is what I would call "unpredictable latency". For one possible solution, take a look at the app *indextime search* available at `http://splunkbase.com`.

How and when to backfill summary data

If you are building reports against summary data, you of course need enough time represented in your summary index. If your report represents only a day or two, then you can probably just wait for the summary to have enough information. If you need the report to work sooner rather than later, or the time frame is longer, then you can backfill your summary index.

Using fill_summary_index.py to backfill

The `fill_summary_index.py` script allows you to backfill the summary index for any time period you like. It does this by running the saved searches you have defined to populate your summary indexes, but for the time periods you specify.

To use the script, follow the given procedure:

1. Create your scheduled search, as detailed previously in the *Populating summary indexes with saved searches* section.

2. Log in to the shell on your Splunk instance. If you are running a distributed environment, log in to the search head.

3. Change directories to the Splunk `bin` directory. `cd $SPLUNK_HOME/bin`.

   `$SPLUNK_HOME` is the root of your Splunk installation. The default installation directory is `/opt/splunk` on Unix operating systems, and `c:\Program Files\Splunk` on Windows.

4. Run the `fill_summary_index` command. An example from inside the script is as follows:

   ```
   ./splunk cmd python fill_summary_index.py -app is_app_one -name
   "summary - count by user" -et -30d -lt now -j 8 -dedup true -auth
   admin:changeme
   ```

Let's break down these arguments in the following manner:

- `./splunk cmd`: This essentially sets environment variables so that whatever runs next has the appropriate settings to find Splunk's libraries and included Python modules.
- `python fill_summary_index.py`: This runs the script itself using the Python executable and modules included with the Splunk distribution.
- `-app is_app_one`: This is the name of the app that contains the summary populating queries in question.
- `-name "summary - count by user"`: The name of the query to run. `*` will run all summary queries contained in the app specified.
- `-et -30d`: This is the earliest time to consider. The appropriate times are determined and used to populate the summary index.
- `-lt now`: This is the latest time to consider.
- `-j 8`: This determines how many queries to run simultaneously.
- `-dedup true`: This is used to determine whether there are no results already for each slice of time. Without this flag, you could end up with duplicate entries in your summary index. For some statistics this wouldn't matter, but for most it would.

> If you are concerned that you have summary data that is incomplete, perhaps because summary events were produced while an indexer was unavailable, you should investigate the `delete` command to remove these events first. The `delete` command is not efficient, and should be used sparingly, if at all.

- `-auth admin:changeme`: The `auth` to run the query.

When you run this script, it will run the query with the appropriate times, as if the query had been run at those times in the past. This can be a very slow process, particularly if the number of slices is large. For instance, slices every 5 minutes for a month would be *30 * 24 * (60/5) = 8,640* queries.

Using collect to produce custom summary indexes

If the number of events destined for your summary index could be represented in a single report, we can use the `collect` function to create our own summary index entries directly. This has the advantage that we can build our index in one shot, which could be much faster than running the backfill script, which must run one search per slice of time. For instance, if you want to calculate 15-minute slices over a month, the script will fire off 2,880 queries.

If you dig into the code that actually produces summary indexes, you will find that it uses the `collect` command to store events into the specified index. The `collect` command is available to us, and with a little knowledge, we can use it directly.

First, we need to build a query that slices our data by buckets of time as follows:

```
source="impl_splunk_gen"
  | bucket span=1h _time
  | stats count by _time user
```

This gives us a simple table as shown in the following screenshot:

	_time ‡	user ‡	count ‡
1	8/22/12 8:00:00.000 PM	Bobby	549
2	8/22/12 8:00:00.000 PM	bob	565
3	8/22/12 8:00:00.000 PM	extrauser	168
4	8/22/12 8:00:00.000 PM	jacky	551
5	8/22/12 8:00:00.000 PM	linda	588
6	8/22/12 8:00:00.000 PM	mary	1115
7	8/22/12 9:00:00.000 PM	Bobby	960
8	8/22/12 9:00:00.000 PM	bob	979
9	8/22/12 9:00:00.000 PM	extrauser	294
10	8/22/12 9:00:00.000 PM	jacky	942

Notice that there is a row per slice of time, and each user that produced events during that slice of time.

Let's add a few more fields for interest:

```
source="impl_splunk_gen"
  | bucket span=1h _time
  | eval error=if(loglevel="ERROR",1,0)
  | stats count avg(req_time) dc(ip) sum(error) by _time user
```

This gives us a table as shown in the following screenshot:

_time ⬍	user ⬍	count ⬍	avg(req_time) ⬍	dc(ip) ⬍	sum(error) ⬍
1	8/22/12 8:00:00.000 PM	Bobby	549	5918.018913	6	144
2	8/22/12 8:00:00.000 PM	bob	565	6002.448357	6	117
3	8/22/12 8:00:00.000 PM	extrauser	168	6125.517857	6	40
4	8/22/12 8:00:00.000 PM	jacky	551	6005.267123	6	143
5	8/22/12 8:00:00.000 PM	linda	588	6215.339326	6	130
6	8/22/12 8:00:00.000 PM	mary	1115	6039.061078	6	292
7	8/22/12 9:00:00.000 PM	Bobby	960	6144.366255	6	227
8	8/22/12 9:00:00.000 PM	bob	979	6413.421622	6	229
9	8/22/12 9:00:00.000 PM	extrauser	294	6129.421769	6	88
10	8/22/12 9:00:00.000 PM	jacky	942	6115.462518	6	227

Now, to get ready for our summary index, we switch to `sistats`, and add a `search_name` field as the saved search would. Use `testmode` to make sure everything is working as expected, as follows:

```
source="impl_splunk_gen"
  | bucket span=1h _time
  | eval error=if(loglevel="ERROR",1,0)
  | sistats count avg(req_time) dc(ip) sum(error) by _time user
  | eval search_name="summary - user stats"
  | collect index=summary_impl_splunk testmode=true
```

The results of this query show us what will actually be written to the summary index, but as this is not designed for humans, let's simply test the round trip by adding the original `stats` statement to the end, as follows:

```
source="impl_splunk_gen"
  | bucket span=1h _time
  | eval error=if(loglevel="ERROR",1,0)
  | sistats count avg(req_time) dc(ip) sum(error) by _time user
  | eval search_name="summary - hourly user stats - collect test"
  | collect index=summary_impl_splunk testmode=true
  | stats count avg(req_time) dc(ip) sum(error) by _time user
```

If we have done everything correctly, the results should be identical to the original table:

	_time ⬍	user ⬍	count ⬍	avg(req_time) ⬍	dc(ip) ⬍	sum(error) ⬍
1	8/22/12 8:00:00.000 PM	Bobby	549	5918.018913	6	144
2	8/22/12 8:00:00.000 PM	bob	565	6002.448357	6	117
3	8/22/12 8:00:00.000 PM	extrauser	168	6125.517857	6	40
4	8/22/12 8:00:00.000 PM	jacky	551	6005.267123	6	143
5	8/22/12 8:00:00.000 PM	linda	588	6215.339326	6	130
6	8/22/12 8:00:00.000 PM	mary	1115	6039.061078	6	292
7	8/22/12 9:00:00.000 PM	Bobby	960	6144.366255	6	227
8	8/22/12 9:00:00.000 PM	bob	979	6413.421622	6	229
9	8/22/12 9:00:00.000 PM	extrauser	294	6129.421769	6	88
10	8/22/12 9:00:00.000 PM	jacky	942	6115.462518	6	227

To actually run this query, we simply remove `testmode` from `collect`, as follows:

```
source="impl_splunk_gen"
  | bucket span=1h _time
  | eval error=if(loglevel="ERROR",1,0)
  | sistats count avg(req_time) dc(ip) sum(error) by _time user
  | eval search_name="summary - user stats"
  | collect index=summary_impl_splunk
```

> Beware that you will end up with duplicate values if you use the `collect` command over a time frame that already has results in the summary index. Either use a custom time frame to ensure you do not produce duplicates, or investigate the `delete` command, which as mentioned earlier, is not efficient, and should be avoided if possible.

No results will be available until the query is complete and the file created behind the scenes is indexed. On my installation, querying one month of data, the query inspected 2.2 million events in 173 seconds, producing 2,619 summary events. Let's use the summary data now:

```
index=summary_impl_splunk
search_name="summary - hourly user stats - collect test"
  | timechart sum(error) by user
```

This will give us a neat graph as shown in the following screenshot:

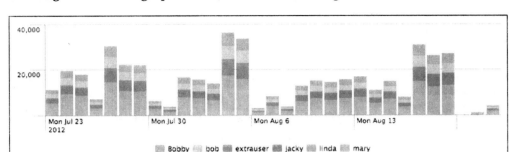

Because this is created from the summary, instead of three minutes, this query completes in 1.5 seconds.

In this specific case, using `collect` was four times faster than using the `fill_summary_index.py` script. That said, it is much easier to make a mistake, so be very careful. Rehearse with `collect testmode=true` and a trailing `stats` or `timechart` command.

Reducing summary index size

If the saved search populating a summary index produces too many results, the summary index is less effective at speeding up searches. This usually occurs because one or more of the fields used for grouping has more unique values than is expected.

One common example of a field that can have many unique values is the URL in a web access log. The number of URL values might increase in instances where:

- The URL contains a session ID
- The URL contains search terms
- Hackers are throwing URLs at your site trying to break in
- Your security team runs tools looking for vulnerabilities

On top of this, multiple URLs can represent exactly the same resource, as follows:

- `/home/index.html`
- `/home/`
- `/home/index.html?a=b`
- `/home/?a=b`

We will cover a few approaches to flatten these values. These are just examples and ideas, as your particular case may require a different approach.

Using eval and rex to define grouping fields

One way to tackle this problem is to make up a new field from the URL using `rex`. Perhaps you only really care about hits by directories. We can accomplish this with `rex`, or if needed, multiple `rex` statements.

Looking at the fictional source type `impl_splunk_web`, we see results that look like the following:

```
2012-08-25T20:18:01 user=bobby GET /products/x/?q=10471480 uid=Mzg2NDc0OA

2012-08-25T20:18:03 user=user3 GET /bar?q=923891 uid=MjY1NDI5MA

2012-08-25T20:18:05 user=user3 GET /products/index.html?q=9029891
uid=MjY1NDI5MA

2012-08-25T20:18:08 user=user2 GET /about/?q=9376559 uid=MzA4MTc5OA
```

URLs are tricky, as they might or might not contain certain parts of the URL. For instance, the URL may or may not have a query string, may or may not have a page, and may or may not have a trailing slash. To deal with this, instead of trying to make an all encompassing regular expression, we will take advantage of the behavior of `rex`, which is to make no changes to the event if the pattern does not match. Consider the following query:

```
sourcetype="impl_splunk_web"
    | rex "\s[A-Z]+\s(?P<url>.*?)\s"
    | rex field=url "(?P<url>.*)\?"
    | rex field=url "(?P<url>.*/)"
    | stats count by url
```

In our case, this will produce the following report:

url ⬍	count ⬍
/	5741
/about/	2822
/contact/	2847
/products/	5653
/products/x/	5637
/products/y/	2786

Stepping through these `rex` statements we have:

- `rex "\s[A-Z]+\s(?P<url>.*?)\s"`: This pattern matches a space followed by uppercase letters, followed by a space, and then captures all characters until a space into the field `url`. The `field` attribute is not defined, so the `rex` statement matches against the `_raw` field. The values extracted look like the following:

  ○ `/products/x/?q=10471480`

  ○ `/bar?q=923891`

  ○ `/products/index.html?q=9029891`

  ○ `/about/?q=9376559`

- `rex field=url "(?P<url>.*)\?"`: Searching the field `url`, this pattern matches all characters until a question mark. If the pattern matches, the result replaces the contents of the field `url`. If the pattern doesn't match, `url` stays the same. The values of `url` become:

  ○ `/products/x/`

  ○ `/bar`

  ○ `/products/index.html`

  ○ `/about/`

- `rex field=url "(?P<url>.*/)"`: Once again, while searching the field `url`, this pattern matches all characters until and including the last slash. The values of `url` are then:

  ○ `/products/x/`

  ○ `/`

  ○ `/products/`

  ○ `/about/`

This should effectively reduce the number of possible URLs, and hopefully make our summary index more useful and efficient. It may be that you only want to capture up to three levels of depth. You could accomplish that with this `rex` statement:

```
rex field=url "(?P<url>/(?:[^/]/){,3})"
```

The possibilities are endless. Be sure to test as much data as you can when building your summary indexes.

Using a lookup with wildcards

Splunk lookups also support wildcards, which we can use in this case. One advantage is that we can define arbitrary fields for grouping, independent of the values of url.

For a lookup wildcard to work, first we need to set up our url field and the lookup:

1. Extract the url field. The rex pattern we used before should work: \s[A-Z]+\s(?P<url>.*?)\s. See *Chapter 3, Tables, Charts, and Fields,* for detailed instructions on setting up a field extraction. Don't forget to set permissions on the extraction.

2. Create our lookup file. Let's call the lookup file flatten_summary_lookup.csv. Use the following contents for our example log:

   ```
   url,section
   /about/*,about
   /contact/*,contact
   /*/*,unknown_non_root
   /*,root
   *,nomatch
   ```

 If you create your lookup file in Excel on a Mac, be sure to save the file using the format Windows Comma Separated (.csv).

3. Upload the lookup table file, create our lookup definition, and automatic lookup. See the *Using lookups to enrich data* section in *Chapter 6, Extending Search,* for detailed instructions. The automatic lookup definition should look like the following screenshot (the value of **Name** doesn't matter):

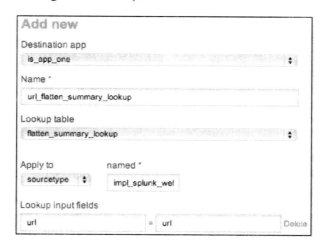

4. Set the permissions on all of the objects. I usually opt for **All Apps** for **Lookup table files** and **Lookup definitions**, and **This app only** for **Automatic lookups**. See *Chapter 6, Extending Search*, for details.

5. Edit `transforms.conf`. As of Splunk 4.3, not all features of lookups can be defined through the admin interface. To access these features, the configuration files that actually drive Splunk must be edited manually. We will cover configuration files in great detail in *Chapter 10, Configuring Splunk*, but for now, let's add two lines to one file and move on:

    1. Edit `$SPLUNK_HOME/etc/apps/is_app_one/local/transforms.conf`. The name of the directory `is_app_one` may be different depending on what app was active when you created your lookup definition. If you can't find this file, check your permissions and the **App** column in the admin interface.

    2. You should see these two lines, or something similar, depending on what you named your **Lookup table file** and **Lookup definition** instances:

```
[flatten_summary_lookup]
filename = flatten_summary_lookup.csv
```

   If you do not see these lines in this file, check your permissions.

    1. Add two more lines below `filename`:

```
match_type = WILDCARD(url)
max_matches = 1
```

   These two lines effectively say:

* `match_type = WILDCARD(url)`: When evaluating the field `url`, honor wildcard characters. Without this setting, matches are always exact.

* `max_matches = 1`: Stop searching after the first match. By default, up to 10 matches are allowed. We want to match only the first line that matches, effectively using the lookup like a `case` statement.

If everything is wired up properly, we should now be able to run the search:

```
sourcetype=impl_splunk_web | stats count by section
```

This should give us the following simple report:

section ⬍	count ⬍
1 about	2822
2 contact	2847
3 root	5741
4 unknown_non_root	14076

To see in greater detail what is really going on, let's try the following search:

```
sourcetype=impl_splunk_web
    | rex field=url "(?P<url>.*)\?"
    | stats count by section url
```

The `rex` statement is included to remove the query string from the value of `url` created by our extracted field. This gives us the following report:

section ⬍	url ⬍	count ⬍
1 about	/about/	2822
2 contact	/contact/	2847
3 root	/bar	2847
4 root	/foo	2894
5 unknown_non_root	/products/	5653
6 unknown_non_root	/products/x/	5637
7 unknown_non_root	/products/y/	2786

Looking back at our lookup file, our matches appear to be as follows:

url	pattern	section
/about/	/about/*	about
/contact/	/contact/*	contact
/bar	/*	root
/foo	/*	root
/products/	/*/*	unknown_non_root
/products/x/	/*/*	unknown_non_root
/products/y/	/*/*	unknown_non_root

If you read the lookup file from top to bottom, the first pattern that matches wins.

Using event types to group results

Another approach for grouping results to reduce summary index size would be to use event types in creative ways. For a refresher on event types, see *Chapter 6, Extending Search*.

This approach has the following advantages:

- All definitions are defined through the web interface
- It is possible to create arbitrarily complex definitions
- You can easily search for only those events that have defined section names
- You can place events in multiple groups if desired

The disadvantages to this approach are as follows:

- This is a non-obvious approach.
- It is not simple to not place events in multiple groups if more than one event type matches. For instance, if you want a page to match /product/x/* but not /product/*, this is not convenient to do.

The following is the procedure to create these event types:

1. For each section, create an event type, as follows:

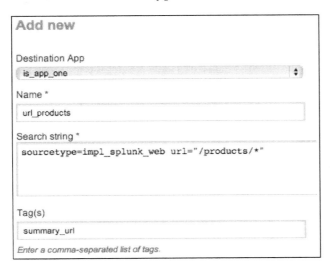

2. Set the permissions to either **This app only** or **Global**, depending on the scope.
3. Repeat this for each section you want to summarize. The **Clone** link in **Manager** makes this process much faster.

With our event types in place, we can now build queries. The **Tag** value that we included means we can search easily for only those events that match a section, like the following:

```
tag::eventtype="summary_url" | top eventtype
```

The previous code returns a table as shown in the following screenshot:

eventtype ⬍	count ⬍	percent ⬍
bogus	19745	100.000000
url_products	14076	71.288934
url_contact	2847	14.418840
url_about	2822	14.292226

Our results contain the new event types that we created, along with an unwanted event type, **bogus**. Remember that all event type definitions that match an event are attached. This is very powerful, but sometimes is not what you expect. The **bogus** event type definition is *, which means it matches everything. The **bogus** event type was added purely to illustrate the point and has no practical use.

Let's create a new field from our summary event type name, then aggregate based on the new field:

```
tag::eventtype="summary_url"
   | rex field=eventtype "url_(?P<section>.*)"
   | stats count by section
```

The previous code gives us the results we are looking for, as shown in the following screenshot:

section ⬍	count ⬍
about	2822
contact	2847
products	14076

This search finds only events that have defined event types, which may be what you want. To group all other results into an "other" group, we instead need to search for all events in the following manner:

```
sourcetype=impl_splunk_web
   | rex field=eventtype "url_(?P<section>.*)"
   | fillnull value="other" section
   | stats count by section
```

The previous code then produces the following report:

	section ‡	count ‡
1	about	2822
2	contact	2847
3	other	5741
4	products	14076

Hopefully these examples will be food for thought when it comes to collapsing your results into more efficient summary results.

Calculating top for a large time frame

One common problem is to find the top contributors out of some huge set of unique values. For instance, if you want to know what IP addresses are using the most bandwidth in a given day or week, you may have to keep track of the total of request sizes across millions of unique hosts to definitively answer this question. When using summary indexes, this means storing millions of events in the summary index, quickly defeating the point of summary indexes.

Just to illustrate, let's look at a simple set of data:

Time	1.1.1.1	2.2.2.2	3.3.3.3	4.4.4.4	5.5.5.5	6.6.6.6
12:00	99	100	100	100		
13:00	99		100	100	100	
14:00	99	100		101	100	
15:00	99		99	100	100	
16:00	99	100			100	100
total	495	300	299	401	400	100

If we only stored the top three IPs per hour, our data set would look like the following:

Time	1.1.1.1	2.2.2.2	3.3.3.3	4.4.4.4	5.5.5.5	6.6.6.6
12:00		100	100	100		
13:00			100	100	100	
14:00		100		101	100	
15:00			99	100	100	
16:00		100			100	100
total		300	299	401	400	100

According to this data set, our top three IP addresses are 4.4.4.4, 5.5.5.5, and 2.2.2.2. The actual largest value was for 1.1.1.1, but it was missed because it was never in the top three.

To tackle this problem, we need to keep track of more data points for each slice of time. But how many?

Using our generator data, let's count a random number and see what kind of results we see. In my data set, it is the following query:

```
source="impl_splunk_gen" | top req_time
```

When run over a week, this query gives me the following results:

	req_time ⇕	count ⇕	percent ⇕
1	10	402	0.072102
2	34	383	0.068694
3	15	377	0.067618
4	118	374	0.067080
5	26	373	0.066901
6	21	370	0.066362
7	18	366	0.065645
8	46	365	0.065466
9	140	365	0.065466
10	291	363	0.065107

How many unique values were there? The following query will tell us that:

```
source="impl_splunk_gen" | stats dc(req_time)
```

This tells us there are 12,239 unique values of req_time. How many different values are there per hour? The following query will calculate the average unique values per hour:

```
source="impl_splunk_gen"
    | bucket span=1h _time
    | stats dc(req_time) as dc by _time
    | stats avg(dc)
```

This tells us that each hour there are an average of 3,367 unique values of req_time. So, if we stored every count of every req_time for a week, we will store *3,367 * 24 * 7 = 565,656* values. How many values would we have to store per hour to get the same answer we received before?

The following is a query that attempts to answer that question:

```
source="impl_splunk_gen"
  | bucket span=1h _time
  | stats count by _time req_time
  | sort 0 _time -count
  | streamstats count as place by _time
  | where place<50
  | stats sum(count) as count by req_time
  | sort 0 -count
  | head 10
```

Breaking this query down we have:

- source="impl_splunk_gen": This finds the events.
- | bucket span=1h _time: This floors our _time field to the beginning of the hour. We will use this to simulate hourly summary queries.
- | stats count by _time req_time: This generates a count per req_time per hour.
- | sort 0 _time -count: This sorts and keeps all events (that's what 0 means), first ascending by _time then descending by count.
- | streamstats count as place by _time: This loops over the events, incrementing place, and starting the count over when _time changes. Remember that we flattened _time to the beginning of each hour.
- | where place<50: This keeps the first 50 events per hour. These will be the largest 50 values of count per hour, since we sorted descending by count.
- | stats sum(count) as count by req_time: This adds up what we have left across all hours.
- | sort 0 -count: This sorts the events in descending order by count.
- | head 10: This shows the first 10 results.

How did we do? Keeping the top 50 results per hour, my results look as shown in the following screenshot:

req_time ⇕	count ▾
10	139
257	125
101	109
103	109
140	107
46	107
15	98
21	98
24	97
211	96

That really isn't close. Let's try this again. We'll try `where place<1000`. This gives us the following results:

req_time ⇕	count ▾
10	401
34	367
15	361
26	356
101	354
118	351
18	350
21	349
46	345
291	344

That is much closer, but we're still not quite there. After experimenting a little more, `place<2000` was enough to get the expected top 10. This is better than storing 3,367 rows per hour. This may not seem like a big enough difference to bother, but increase the number of events by 10 or 100, and it can make a huge difference.

To use these results in a summary index, you would simply eliminate results going into your data set. One way to accomplish this might be:

```
source="impl_splunk_gen"
  | sitop req_time
  | streamstats count as place
  | where place<2001
```

The first row produced by `sitop` contains the total value.

Another approach, using a combination of `eventstats` and `sistats`, is as follows:

```
source="impl_splunk_gen"
  | eventstats count by req_time
  | sort 0 -req_time
  | streamstats count as place
  | where place<2001
  | sistats count by req_time
```

Luckily, this is not a terribly common problem, so most of this complexity can be avoided. For another option, see the *Storing a running calculation* section.

Storing raw events in a summary index

Sometimes it is desirable to copy events to another index. I have seen a couple of reasons for doing this, namely:

- **Differing retention**: If some special events need to be kept indefinitely, but the index where they are initially captured rolls off after some period of time, they can be captured into a summary index

- **Enrichment**: Sometimes the enrichment of data is too expensive to happen with every query, or it is important to capture events with the values from a lookup as the values existed at a particular point in time

The process is essentially the same as creating any summary index events. Follow these steps:

1. Create a populating query.
2. Add interesting fields using the `fields` command.
3. Add a `search_name` field to the search definition.
4. Include `_time`, but rename `_raw` to raw.

Let's capture all errors that `mary` sees, enriched with some extra data. First, create the query:

```
sourcetype=impl_splunk_gen mary error
| eval raw=_raw
| table _time raw department city
```

Save the query and edit the summary info:

summary - mary errors

Search *

```
sourcetype=impl_splunk_gen error mary | fields
department city
```

Description

Time range

Start time   Finish time

```
-2m@m
```
```
-1m@m
```

Time specifiers: y, mon, d, h, m, s
Learn more

Schedule and alert

☑ Schedule this search

Schedule type

```
Basic                                                    ▲▼
```

Run every

```
minute                                                   ▲▼
```

Summary indexing

☑ Enable

Select the summary index

```
summary_impl_splunk                                      ▲▼
```

Only indexes that you can write to are listed.

Add fields

search_name	=	summary - mary errors	Delete
	=		Delete

Add another field

You can then search against the summary index using the `search_name` value you provided:

```
index=summary_impl_splunk search_name="summary - mary errors"
```

The events in the summary index look almost identical to the original event, with the addition of the fields specified:

```
09/03/2012 203:11:59 -0600, search_name="summary - mary errors",
search_now=1346641919.000, info_min_time=1346641919.000, info_max_
time=1346641919.000, info_search_time=1346641919.588, city=Dallas,
department=HR, raw="2012-09-03T03:11:59.107+0000 DEBUG error, ERROR,
Error! [logger=LogoutClass, user=mary, ip=3.2.4.5, req_time=1414]"
```

With the addition of the `table` command, we can see the extra fields that were added using the `fields` command:

```
index=summary_impl_splunk search_name="summary - mary errors"
  | table _time department city search_name
```

The previous search renders the following table:

	_time ⬍	department ⬍	city ⬍	search_name ⬍
1	9/2/12 10:08:54.946 PM	HR	Dallas	summary - mary errors
2	9/2/12 10:08:50.093 PM	HR	Dallas	summary - mary errors
3	9/2/12 10:08:47.942 PM			summary - mary errors
4	9/2/12 10:08:46.304 PM	HR	Dallas	summary - mary errors
5	9/2/12 10:08:41.989 PM	HR	Dallas	summary - mary errors
6	9/2/12 10:08:35.099 PM	HR	Dallas	summary - mary errors
7	9/2/12 10:08:25.719 PM	HR	Dallas	summary - mary errors
8	9/2/12 10:08:24.545 PM			summary - mary errors
9	9/2/12 10:08:24.211 PM	HR	Dallas	summary - mary errors
10	9/2/12 10:08:22.395 PM	HR	Dallas	summary - mary errors

This process is fairly complicated, so luckily adding events to a summary index is not commonly needed.

Using CSV files to store transient data

Sometimes it is useful to store small amounts of data outside of a Splunk index. Using the `inputcsv` and `outputcsv` commands, we can store tabular data in CSV files on the filesystem.

Pre-populating a dropdown

If a dashboard contains a dynamic dropdown, you must use a search to populate the dropdown. As the amount of data increases, the query to populate the dropdown will run more and more slowly, even from a summary index. We can use a CSV file to store just the information needed, simply adding new values when they occur.

First, we build a query to generate the CSV file. This query should be run over as much data as possible:

```
source="impl_splunk_gen"
   | stats count by user
   | outputcsv user_list.csv
```

Next, we need a query to run periodically that will append any new entries to the file. Schedule this query to run periodically as a saved search:

```
source="impl_splunk_gen"
   | stats count by user
   | append [inputcsv user_list.csv]
   | stats sum(count) as count by user
   | outputcsv user_list.csv
```

To then use this in our dashboard, our populating query will simply be:

```
|inputcsv user_list.csv
```

Simple dashboard XML using this query would look like the following:

```
<input type="dropdown" token="sourcetype">
  <label>User</label>
  <populatingSearch fieldForValue="user" fieldForLabel="user">
     |inputcsv user_list.csv
  </populatingSearch>
</input>
```

Creating a running calculation for a day

If the number of events per day is in the millions or tens of millions, querying all events for that day can be extremely expensive. For that reason, it makes sense to do part of the work on smaller periods of time.

Using a summary index to store these interim values can sometimes be overkill if those values are not needed for long. In the *Calculating top for a large time frame* section, we ended up storing thousands of values every few minutes. If we simply wanted to know the top 10 per day, this might be seen as a waste. To cut down on the noise in our summary index, we can use a CSV as cheap interim storage.

The steps are essentially to:

1. Periodically query recent data and update the CSV.
2. Capture top values in summary at the end of the day.
3. Empty the CSV file.

Our periodic query looks like the following:

```
source="impl_splunk_gen"
    | stats count by req_time
    | append [inputcsv top_req_time.csv]
    | stats sum(count) as count by req_time
    | sort 10000 -count
    | outputcsv top_req_time.csv
```

Let's break the query down line by line:

- `source="impl_splunk_gen"`: This is the query to find the events for this slice of time.

- `| stats count by req_time`: This helps calculate the count by `req_time`.

- `| append [inputcsv top_req_time.csv]`: This loads the results generated so far from the CSV file, and adds the events to the end of our current results.

- `| stats sum(count) as count by req_time`: This uses `stats` to combine the results from our current time slice and the previous results.

- `| sort 10000 -count`: This sorts the results descending by `count`. The second word, `10000`, specifies that we want to keep the first 10,000 results.

- `| outputcsv top_req_time.csv`: This overwrites the CSV file.

Schedule the query to run periodically, perhaps every 15 minutes. Follow the same rules about latency as discussed in the *How latency affects summary queries* section.

When the rollup is expected, perhaps each night at midnight, schedule two more queries a few minutes apart, as follows:

- `| inputcsv top_req_time.csv | head 100`: Save this as a query adding to a summary index, as in the *Populating summary indexes with saved searches* section
- `| stats count |outputcsv top_req_time.csv`: This query will simply overwrite the CSV file with a single line

Summary

In this chapter, we have explored the use of summary indexes and the commands surrounding them. While summary indexes are not always the answer, they can be very useful for particular problems. We also explored alternative approaches using CSV files for interim storage.

Summary indexes have long been a hotbed of development at Splunk, and I know there has been major work done for Splunk 5, increasing the speed of some summary queries dramatically.

In our next chapter we will dive into the configuration files that drive Splunk.

10
Configuring Splunk

Everything that controls Splunk lives in configuration files sitting in the filesystem of each instance of Splunk. These files are unencrypted, easily readable, and easily editable. Almost all of the work that we have done so far has been accomplished through the web interface, but everything actually ends up in these configuration files.

While the web interface does a lot, there are many options that are not represented in the admin interface. There are also some things that are simply easier to accomplish by editing the files directly.

In this chapter, we will cover:

- Locating configuration files
- Merging configurations
- Debugging configurations
- Common configurations and their parameters

Locating Splunk configuration files

Splunk's configuration files live in `$SPLUNK_HOME/etc`. This is reminiscent of Unix's `/etc` directory but is instead contained within Splunk's directory structure. This has the advantage that the files don't have to be owned by `root`. In fact, the entire Splunk installation can run as an unprivileged user (assuming you don't need to open a port below 1024 or read files only readable by another user).

The directories that contain configurations are:

- `$SPLUNK_HOME/etc/system/default`: The default configuration files that ship with Splunk. Never edit these files as they will be overwritten each time you upgrade.

- `$SPLUNK_HOME/etc/system/local`: This is the location of global configuration overrides specific to this host. There are very few configurations that need to live here—most configurations that do live here are created by Splunk itself. In almost all cases, you should make your configuration files inside of an app.

- `$SPLUNK_HOME/etc/apps/$app_name/default`: This is the proper location for configurations in an app that will be shared either through Splunkbase or otherwise.

- `$SPLUNK_HOME/etc/apps/$app_name/local`: This is where most configurations should live and where all non-private configurations created through the web interface will be placed.

- `$SPLUNK_HOME/etc/users/$user_name/$app_name/local`: When a search configuration is created through the web interface, it will have a permission setting of **Private** and will be created in a user-/app-specific configuration file. Once permissions are changed, the configuration will move to the corresponding directory named `$app_name/local`.

There are a few more directories that contain files that are not `.conf` files. We'll talk about those later in this chapter, under the *User interface resources* section.

The structure of a Splunk configuration file

The `.conf` files used by Splunk look very similar to `.ini` files. A simple configuration looks like this:

```
#settings for foo
[foo]
bar=1
la = 2
```

Let's look at the following couple of definitions:

- **stanza**: A stanza is used to group attributes. Our stanza in this example is `[foo]`. A common synonym for this is **section**. Keep in mind the following key points:
    - A stanza name must be unique in a single file
    - Order does not matter

- **attribute**: An attribute is a name-value pair. Our attributes in this example are `bar` and `la`. A common synonym is **parameter**. Keep in mind the following key points:

    ○ The attribute name must not contain whitespace or the equals sign
    ○ Each attribute belongs to the stanza defined above; if the attribute appears above all stanzas, the attribute belongs to the stanza `[default]`
    ○ The attribute name must be unique in a single stanza but not in a configuration
    ○ Each attribute must have its own line and can only use one line
    ○ Spaces around the equal sign do not matter

These are a few rules that may not apply in other implementations:

- Stanza and property names are *case sensitive*
- The comment character is #
- Bare attributes at the top of a file are added to the `[default]` stanza
- Any attributes in the stanza `[default]` are added to all stanzas that do not have an attribute with that name already

Configuration merging logic

Configurations in different locations merge behind the scenes into one "super" configuration. Luckily, the merging happens in a predictable way and is fairly easy to learn, and there is a tool to help us preview this merging.

Merging order

Merging order is slightly different depending on whether the configuration is being used by the search engine or another part of Splunk. The difference is whether there is an active user and app.

Merging order outside of search

Configurations being used outside of search are merged in a fairly simple order. These configurations include what files to read, what indexed fields to create, what indexes exist, and deployment server and client configurations as well as other settings. These configurations merge in this order:

1. `$SPLUNK_HOME/etc/system/default`: This directory contains the base configurations that ship with Splunk.

Never make changes in `$SPLUNK_HOME/etc/system/default` as your changes will be lost when you upgrade Splunk.

2. `$SPLUNK_HOME/etc/apps/*/default`: Configurations are "overlaid" in reverse ASCII order by app directory name. a beats z.

3. `$SPLUNK_HOME/etc/apps/*/local`

4. `$SPLUNK_HOME/etc/system/local`

   ° The configurations in this directory are applied last.

   ° Outside of search, these configurations cannot be overridden by an app configuration. Apps are a very convenient way to compartmentalize control and distribute configurations. This is particularly relevant if you use the deployment server, which we will cover in *Chapter 11*, *Advanced Deployments*.

 Do *not* edit configurations in `$SPLUNK_HOME/etc/system/local` unless you have a very specific reason. An app is almost always the correct place for configuration.

A little pseudo code to describe this process might look like this:

```
$conf = new Configuration('$SPLUNK_HOME/etc/')

$conf.merge( 'system/default/$conf_name' )

for $this_app in reverse(sort(@all_apps)):
  $conf.merge( 'apps/$this_app/default/$conf_name' )

for $this_app in reverse(sort(@all_apps)):
  $conf.merge( 'apps/$this_app/local/$conf_name' )

$conf.merge( 'system/local/$conf_name' )
```

Merging order when searching

When searching, configuration merging is slightly more complicated. When running a search, there is always an active user and app, and they come into play. The logical order looks like this:

1. `$SPLUNK_HOME/etc/system/default`

2. `$SPLUNK_HOME/etc/system/local`

3. `$SPLUNK_HOME/etc/apps/not app`

   ° Each app, other than the current app, is looped through in ASCII order of the directory name (not the visible app name). Unlike merging outside of search, *z* beats *a*.

   ° All configuration attributes that are shared globally are applied, first from `default` and then from `local`.

4. `$SPLUNK_HOME/etc/apps/app`

   ° All configurations from `default` and then `local` are merged.

5. `$SPLUNK_HOME/etc/users/user/app/local`

Maybe a little pseudo code would be clearer:

```
$conf = new Configuration('$SPLUNK_HOME/etc/')

$conf.merge( 'system/default/$conf_name' )
$conf.merge( 'system/local/$conf_name' )

for $this_app in sort(@all_apps):
  if $this_app != $current_app:
    $conf.merge_shared( 'apps/$this_app/default/$conf_name' )
    $conf.merge_shared( 'apps/$this_app/local/$conf_name' )

$conf.merge( 'apps/$current_app/default/$conf_name' )
$conf.merge( 'apps/$current_app/local/$conf_name' )

$conf.merge( 'users/$current_user/$current_app/local/$conf_name' )
```

Configuration merging logic

Now that we know what configurations will merge in what order, let's cover the logic for how they actually merge. The logic is fairly simple.

- The configuration name, stanza name, and attribute name must match exactly
- The last configuration added wins

The best way to understand configuration merging is through examples.

Configuration merging example 1

Say we have the base configuration `default/sample1.conf`:

```
[foo]
bar=10
la=20
```

And say we merge a second configuration, `local/sample1.conf`:

```
[foo]
bar=15
```

The resulting configuration would be:

```
[foo]
bar=15
la=20
```

The things to notice are as follows:

- The second configuration does not simply replace the prior configuration
- The value of `bar` is taken from the second configuration
- The lack of a `la` property in the second configuration does not remove the value from the final configuration

Configuration merging example 2

Say we have the base configuration `default/sample2.conf`:

```
[foo]
bar = 10
la=20

[pets]
cat = red
Dog=rex
```

And say we merge a second configuration, `local/sample2.conf`:

```
[pets]
cat=blue
dog=fido
fish = bubbles
```

```
[foo]
bar= 15

[cars]
ferrari =0
```

The resulting configuration would be:

```
[foo]
bar=15
la=20

[pets]
cat=blue
dog=rex
Dog=fido
fish=bubbles

[cars]
ferrari=0
```

Things to notice in this example:

- The order of the stanzas does not matter
- The spaces around the equal signs do not matter
- Dog does not override dog as all stanza names and property names are case sensitive
- The cars stanza is added fully

Configuration merging example 3

Let's do a little exercise, merging four configurations from different locations. In this case, we are not in search, so we will use the rules from the *Merging order outside of search* section. Let's step through a few sample configurations:

- For $SPLUNK_HOME/etc/apps/d/default/props.conf we have:

```
[web_access]
MAX_TIMESTAMP_LOOKAHEAD = 25
TIME_PREFIX = ^\[

[source::*.log]
BREAK_ONLY_BEFORE_DATE = true
```

- For `$SPLUNK_HOME/etc/system/local/props.conf` we have:

```
BREAK_ONLY_BEFORE_DATE = false

[web_access]
TZ = CST
```

- For `$SPLUNK_HOME/etc/apps/d/local/props.conf` we have:

```
[web_access]
TZ = UTC

[security_log]
EXTRACT-<name> = \[(?P<user>.*?)\]
```

- For `$SPLUNK_HOME/etc/apps/b/default/props.conf` we have:

```
[web_access]
MAX_TIMESTAMP_LOOKAHEAD = 20
TIME_FORMAT = %Y-%m-%d $H:%M:%S

[source::*/access.log]
BREAK_ONLY_BEFORE_DATE = false
```

I've thrown a bit of a curveball here by placing the files out of merging order. These configurations would actually merge in this order:

```
$SPLUNK_HOME/etc/apps/d/default/props.conf
$SPLUNK_HOME/etc/apps/b/default/props.conf
$SPLUNK_HOME/etc/apps/d/local/props.conf
$SPLUNK_HOME/etc/system/local/props.conf
```

Stepping through each merge, the configuration would look like this:

1. We start with `$SPLUNK_HOME/etc/apps/d/default/props.conf`:

```
[web_access]
MAX_TIMESTAMP_LOOKAHEAD = 25
TIME_PREFIX = ^\[

[source::*.log]
BREAK_ONLY_BEFORE_DATE = true
```

2. We then merge `$SPLUNK_HOME/etc/apps/b/default/props.conf`:

```
[web_access]
MAX_TIMESTAMP_LOOKAHEAD = 30
TIME_PREFIX = ^\[
TIME_FORMAT = %Y-%m-%d $H:%M:%S
```

```
[source::*.log]
BREAK_ONLY_BEFORE_DATE = true
```

[source::*/access.log]
BREAK_ONLY_BEFORE_DATE = false

Even though [source::*.log] and [source::*/access.log] both match a file called access.log, they will not merge in the configuration because the stanza names do not match exactly. This logic is covered later under **An overview of Splunk .conf files | props.conf | Stanza types**.

3. We then merge $SPLUNK_HOME/etc/apps/d/local/props.conf:

```
[web_access]
MAX_TIMESTAMP_LOOKAHEAD = 30
TIME_PREFIX = ^\[
TIME_FORMAT = %Y-%m-%d $H:%M:%S
```
TZ = UTC

```
[source::*.log]
BREAK_ONLY_BEFORE_DATE = true
```

```
[source::*/access.log]
BREAK_ONLY_BEFORE_DATE = false
```

[security_log]
EXTRACT-<name> = \[(?P<user>.*?)\]

4. We finally merge the globally overriding $SPLUNK_HOME/etc/system/local/props.conf file:

[default]
BREAK_ONLY_BEFORE_DATE = false

```
[web_access]
MAX_TIMESTAMP_LOOKAHEAD = 25
TIME_PREFIX = ^\[
TIME_FORMAT = %Y-%m-%d $H:%M:%S
```
TZ = CST
BREAK_ONLY_BEFORE_DATE = false

```
[source::*.log]
BREAK_ONLY_BEFORE_DATE = true
```

```
[source::*/access.log]
```

```
BREAK_ONLY_BEFORE_DATE = false


[security_log]
EXTRACT-<name> = \[(?P<user>.*?)\]
BREAK_ONLY_BEFORE_DATE = false
```

The setting with the biggest impact here is the bare attribute BREAK_ONLY_BEFORE_
DATE = false. It is first added to the [default] stanza and then is added to *all*
stanzas that do not already have any value.

 As a general rule, avoid using the [default] stanza or bare word
attributes. The final impact may not be what you expect.

Configuration merging example 4 (search)

In this case, we *are* in search, so we will use the more complicated merging order.
Assuming that we are currently working in the app d, let's merge the same
configurations again. For simplicity, we are assuming that all attributes are shared
globally. We will merge the same configurations listed previously in example 3.

With d as our current app , we will now merge in this order:

```
$SPLUNK_HOME/etc/system/local/props.conf
$SPLUNK_HOME/etc/apps/b/default/props.conf
$SPLUNK_HOME/etc/apps/d/default/props.conf
$SPLUNK_HOME/etc/apps/d/local/props.conf
```

Stepping through each merge, the configuration will look like this:

1. We start with $SPLUNK_HOME/etc/system/local/props.conf:

   ```
   BREAK_ONLY_BEFORE_DATE = false


   [web_access]
   TZ = CST
   ```

2. Now, we merge the default for apps other than our current app (which, in
   this case, is only one configuration) $SPLUNK_HOME/etc/apps/b/default/
   props.conf:

   ```
   BREAK_ONLY_BEFORE_DATE = false


   [web_access]
   MAX_TIMESTAMP_LOOKAHEAD = 20
   TIME_FORMAT = %Y-%m-%d $H:%M:%S
   TZ = CST
   ```

```
[source::*/access.log]
BREAK_ONLY_BEFORE_DATE = false
```

3. Next, we merge our current app default $SPLUNK_HOME/etc/apps/d/
   default/props.conf:

```
BREAK_ONLY_BEFORE_DATE = false

[web_access]
MAX_TIMESTAMP_LOOKAHEAD = 25
TIME_PREFIX = ^\[
TIME_FORMAT = %Y-%m-%d $H:%M:%S
TZ = CST

[source::*/access.log]
BREAK_ONLY_BEFORE_DATE = false

[source::*.log]
BREAK_ONLY_BEFORE_DATE = true
```

4. Now we merge our current app local $SPLUNK_HOME/etc/apps/d/local/
   props.conf:

```
BREAK_ONLY_BEFORE_DATE = false

[web_access]
MAX_TIMESTAMP_LOOKAHEAD = 25
TIME_PREFIX = ^\[
TIME_FORMAT = %Y-%m-%d $H:%M:%S
TZ = UTC

[source::*/access.log]
BREAK_ONLY_BEFORE_DATE = false

[source::*.log]
BREAK_ONLY_BEFORE_DATE = true

[security_log]
EXTRACT-<name> = \[(?P<user>.*?)\]
```

5. And finally, we apply our default stanza to stanzas that don't already have
   the attribute:

```
BREAK_ONLY_BEFORE_DATE = false
```

```
[web_access]
MAX_TIMESTAMP_LOOKAHEAD = 25
TIME_PREFIX = ^\[
TIME_FORMAT = %Y-%m-%d $H:%M:%S
TZ = UTC
BREAK_ONLY_BEFORE_DATE = false

[source::*/access.log]
BREAK_ONLY_BEFORE_DATE = false

[source::*.log]
BREAK_ONLY_BEFORE_DATE = true

[security_log]
EXTRACT-<name> = \[(?P<user>.*?)\]
BREAK_ONLY_BEFORE_DATE = false
```

I know this is fairly confusing, but with practice, it will make sense. Luckily, `btool`, which we will cover next, makes it easier to see.

Using btool

To help preview merged configurations, we call on `btool`, a command-line tool that prints the merged version of configurations. The Splunk site has one of my favorite documentation notes of all time, as follows:

> *Note: btool is not tested by Splunk and is not officially supported or guaranteed. That said, it's what our Support team uses when trying to troubleshoot your issues.*

With that warning in mind, `btool` has never steered me wrong. The tool has a number of functions, but the only one I have ever used is `list`, like so:

```
$SPLUNK_HOME/bin/splunk cmd btool props list
```

This produces 5,277 lines of output, which I won't list here. Let's list the stanza `impl_splunk_gen` by adding it to the end of the command line, thus:

```
/opt/splunk/bin/splunk cmd btool props list impl_splunk_gen
```

This will produce an output such as this:

```
[impl_splunk_gen]
ANNOTATE_PUNCT = True
BREAK_ONLY_BEFORE =
BREAK_ONLY_BEFORE_DATE = True
```

```
... truncated ...
LINE_BREAKER_LOOKBEHIND = 100
LOOKUP-lookupusers = userslookup user AS user OUTPUTNEW
MAX_DAYS_AGO = 2000
... truncated ...
TRUNCATE = 10000
TZ = UTC
maxDist = 100
```

Our configuration file at $SPLUNK_HOME/etc/apps/
ImplementingSplunkDataGenerator/local/props.conf contains only the
following lines:

```
[impl_splunk_web]
LOOKUP-web_section = flatten_summary_lookup url AS url OUTPUTNEW
EXTRACT-url = \s[A-Z]+\s(?P<url_from_app_local>.*?)\s
EXTRACT-foo = \s[A-Z]+\s(?P<url_from_app>.*?)\s
```

So where did the rest of this configuration come from? With the use of the --debug
flag, we can get more details.

```
/opt/splunk/bin/splunk cmd btool props list impl_splunk_gen --debug
```

This produces the following query:

```
Implementi [impl_splunk_gen]
system     ANNOTATE_PUNCT = True
system     BREAK_ONLY_BEFORE =
system     BREAK_ONLY_BEFORE_DATE = True
... truncated ...
system     LINE_BREAKER_LOOKBEHIND = 100
Implementi LOOKUP-lookupusers = userslookup user AS user OUTPUTNEW
system     MAX_DAYS_AGO = 2000
... truncated ...
system     TRUNCATE = 10000
Implementi TZ = UTC
system     maxDist = 100
```

The first column, though truncated, tells us what we need to know. The vast majority
of these lines are defined in system, most likely in system/default/props.conf.
The remaining items from our file are labeled Implementi, which is the beginning
of our app directory, ImplementingSplunkDataGenerator.

If you ever have a question about where some setting is coming from, btool will
save you a lot of time. Also, check out the app *Splunk on Splunk* at Splunkbase for
access to btool from the Splunk web interface.

An overview of Splunk .conf files

If you have spent any time in the filesystem investigating Splunk, you have seen many different files ending in .conf. In this section, we will give a quick overview of the most common .conf files. The official documentation is the best place to look for a complete reference of files and attributes.

 The quickest way to find the official documentation is with your favorite search engine by searching for splunk filename.conf. For example, a search for splunk props.conf pulls up the Splunk documentation for props.conf first in every search engine I tested.

props.conf

The stanzas in props.conf define which events to match based on host, source, and sourcetype. These stanzas are merged into the master configuration based on the uniqueness of stanza and attribute names, as with any other configuration, but there are specific rules governing when each stanza is applied to an event and in what order. Stated as simply as possible, attributes are sorted by type, then by priority, and then by ASCII value.

We'll cover those rules under the *Stanza types* section. First, let's look at common attributes.

Common attributes

The full set of attributes allowed in props.conf is vast. Let's look at the most common attributes and try to break them down by the time when they are applied.

Search-time attributes

The most common attributes that users will make in props.conf are field extractions. When a user defines an extraction through the web interface, it ends up in props.conf, like so:

```
[my_source_type]
EXTRACT-foo = \s(?<bar>\d+)ms
EXTRACT-cat = \s(?<dog>\d+)s
```

This configuration defines the fields bar and dog for the source type my_source_type. Extracts are the most common search-time configurations. Any of the stanza types listed under the *Stanza types* section can be used, but source type is definitely the most common.

Other common search time attributes include:

- `REPORT-foo = bar`: This attribute is a way to reference stanzas in `transforms.conf` but apply them at search time instead of index time. This approach predates `EXTRACT` and is still useful for a few special cases. We will cover this case later under the *transforms.conf* section.

- `KV_MODE = auto`: This attribute allows you to specify whether Splunk should automatically extract fields in the form `key=value` from events. The default value is `auto`. The most common change is to disable automatic field extraction for performance reasons by setting the value to `none`. Other possibilities are `multi`, `json`, and `xml`.

- `LOOKUP-foo = mylookup barfield`: This attribute lets you wire up a lookup to automatically run for some set of events. The lookup itself is defined in `transforms.conf`.

Index-time attributes

As discussed in *Chapter 3, Indexed fields versus extracted fields*, it is possible to add fields to the metadata of events. This is accomplished by specifying a transform in `transforms.conf`, and an attribute in `props.conf`, to tie the transformation to specific events.

The attribute in `props.conf` looks like this: `TRANSFORMS-foo = bar1,bar2`. This attribute references stanzas in `transforms.conf` by name, in this case, `bar1` and `bar2`. These transform stanzas are then applied to the events matched by the stanza in `props.conf`.

Parse-time attributes

Most of the attributes in `props.conf` actually have to do with parsing events. To successfully parse events, a few questions need to be answered, such as these:

- When does a new event begin? Are events multiline? Splunk will make fairly intelligent guesses, but it is best to specify an exact setting. Attributes that help with this include:
  - `SHOULD_LINEMERGE = false`: If you know your events will never contain the newline character, setting this to `false` will eliminate a lot of processing.
  - `BREAK_ONLY_BEFORE = ^\d\d\d\d-\d\d-\d\d`: If you know that new events always start with a particular pattern, you can specify it using this attribute.

- ° TRUNCATE = 1024: If you are certain you only care about the first n characters of an event, you can instruct Splunk to truncate each line. What is considered a line can be changed with the next attribute.

- ° LINE_BREAKER = ([\r\n]+)(?=\d{4}-\d\d-\d\d): The most efficient approach to multiline events is to redefine what Splunk considers a line. This example says that a line is broken on any number of newlines followed by a date of the form 1111-11-11. The big disadvantage to this approach is that, if your log changes, you will end up with garbage in your index until you update your configuration. Try the *props helper* app available at Splunkbase for help making this kind of configuration.

- Where is the date? If there is no date, see DATETIME_CONFIG further down this bullet list. The relevant attributes are:

  - ° TIME_PREFIX = ^\[: By default, dates are assumed to fall at the beginning of the line. If this is not true, give Splunk some help and move the cursor past the characters preceding the date. This pattern is applied to each line, so if you have redefined LINE_BREAKER correctly, you can be sure only the beginnings of actual multiline events are being tested.

  - ° MAX_TIMESTAMP_LOOKAHEAD = 30: *Even if you change no other setting, you should change this one.* This setting says how far after TIME_PREFIX to test for dates. With no help, Splunk will take the first 150 characters of each line and then test regular expressions to find anything that looks like a date. The default regular expressions are pretty lax, so what it finds may look more like a date than the actual date. If you know your date is never more than *n* characters long, set this value to *n* or *n+2*. Remember that the characters retrieved come *after* TIME_PREFIX.

- What does the date look like? These attributes will be of assistance here:

  - ° TIME_FORMAT = %Y-%m-%d %H:%M:%S.%3N %:z: If this attribute is specified, Splunk will apply strptime to the characters immediately following TIME_PREFIX. If this matches, then you're done. This is by far the most efficient and least error-prone approach. Without this attribute, Splunk actually applies a series of regular expressions until it finds something that looks like a date.

- ○ `DATETIME_CONFIG = /etc/apps/a/custom_datetime.xml`: As mentioned, Splunk uses a set of regular expressions to determine the date. If `TIME_FORMAT` is not specified, or won't work for some strange reason, you can specify a different set of regular expressions or disable time extraction completely by setting this attribute to `CURRENT` (the indexer clock time) or `NONE` (file modification time, or if there is no file, clock time). I personally have never had to resort to a custom `datetime.xml` file, though I have heard of it being done.

- The **Data preview** function available when adding data through the manager interface builds a good, usable configuration. The generated configuration does not use `LINE_BREAKER`, which is definitely safer but less efficient. Here is a sample stanza using `LINE_BREAKER` for efficiency:

```
[mysourcetype]
TIME_FORMAT = %Y-%m-%d %H:%M:%S.%3N %:z
MAX_TIMESTAMP_LOOKAHEAD = 32
TIME_PREFIX = ^\[
SHOULD_LINEMERGE = False
LINE_BREAKER = ([\r\n]+)(?=\[\d{4}-\d{1,2}-\d{1,2}\s+\
d{1,2}:\d{1,2}:\d{1,2})
TRUNCATE = 1024000
```

This configuration would apply to log messages that looked like this:

```
[2011-10-13 13:55:36.132 -07:00] ERROR Interesting message.
More information.
And another line.
[2011-10-13 13:55:36.138 -07:00] INFO All better.
[2011-10-13 13:55:37.010 -07:00] INFO More data
  and another line.
```

Let's step through how these settings affect the first line of this sample configuration:

- `LINE_BREAKER` states that a new event starts when one or more newline characters is followed by a bracket and series of numbers and dashes, in the pattern `[1111-11-11 11:11:11]`.

- `SHOULD_LINEMERGE=False` tells Splunk to not bother trying to recombine multiple lines.

- `TIME_PREFIX` moves the cursor to the character after the `[` character.

- `TIME_FORMAT` is tested against the characters at the current cursor location. If it succeeds, we are done.

- If `TIME_FORMAT` fails, `MAX_TIMESTAMP_LOOKAHEAD` characters are read from the cursor position (after `TIME_PREFIX`) and the regular expressions from `DATE_CONFIG` are tested.

- If the regular expressions fail against the characters returned, the time last parsed from an event is used. If there is no last time parsed, the modification date from the file would be used, if known; otherwise, the current time would be used.

This is the most efficient and precise way to parse events in Splunk, but also the most brittle. If your date format changes, you will almost certainly have junk data in your index. Only use this approach if you are confident the format of your logs will not change without your knowledge.

Input time attributes

There are only a couple of attributes in `props.conf` that matter at the input stage, but they are generally not needed:

- `CHARSET = UTF-16LE`: When reading data, Splunk has to know the character set used in the log. Most applications write their logs using either `ISO-8859-1` or `UTF-8`, which the default settings handle just fine. Some Windows applications write logs in 2-byte Little Endian, which is indexed as garbage. Setting `CHARSET = UTF-16LE` takes care of the problem. Check the official documentation for a list of supported encodings.

- `NO_BINARY_CHECK = true`: If Splunk believes that a file is binary, it will not index the file at all. If you find that you have to change this setting to convince Splunk to read your files, it is likely that the file is in an unexpected character set. You might try other `CHARSET` settings before enabling this setting.

Stanza types

Now that we have looked at common attributes, let's talk about the different types of stanzas in `props.conf`. Stanza definitions can take the three following forms:

- `[foo]`
  - This is the exact name of a source type and is the most common type of stanza to be used; the source type of an event is usually defined in `inputs.conf`
  - Wildcards are not allowed

- `[source::/logs/.../*.log]`

    ◦ This matches the `source` attribute, which is usually the path to the log where the event came from

    ◦ `*` matches a file or directory name

    ◦ `...` matches any part of a path

- `[host::*nyc*]`

    ◦ This matches the `host` attribute, which is usually the value of `hostname` on a machine running Splunk Forwarder

    ◦ `*` is allowed

Precedence across types follows this order:

1. Source.

2. Host.

3. Source type.

For instance, say an event has the following fields:

```
sourcetype=foo_type
source=/logs/abc/def/gh.log
host=dns4.nyc.mycompany.com
```

Given this configuration snippet and our preceding event:

```
[foo_type]
TZ = UTC

[source::/logs/.../*.log]
TZ = MST

[host::*nyc*]
TZ = EDT
```

`TZ = MST` would be used during parsing, because the source stanza takes precedence.

To extend this example, say we have this snippet:

```
[foo_type]
TZ = UTC
TRANSFORMS-a = from_sourcetype

[source::/logs/.../*.log]
```

```
TZ = MST
BREAK_ONLY_BEFORE_DATE = True
TRANSFORMS-b = from_source

[host::*nyc*]
TZ = EDT
BREAK_ONLY_BEFORE_DATE = False
TRANSFORMS-c = from_host
```

The attributes applied to our event would therefore be:

```
TZ = MST
BREAK_ONLY_BEFORE_DATE = True
TRANSFORMS-a = from_sourcetype
TRANSFORMS-b = from_source
TRANSFORMS-c = from_host
```

Priorities inside a type

If there are multiple source or host stanzas that match a given event, the order in which settings are applied also comes into play. A stanza with a pattern has a priority of 0, while an exact stanza has a priority of 100. Higher priorities win. For instance, say we have the following stanza:

```
[source::/logs/abc/def/gh.log]
TZ = UTC

[source::/logs/.../*.log]
TZ = CDT
```

Our TZ value will be UTC since the exact match of source::/logs/abc/def/gh.log has a higher priority.

When priorities are identical, stanzas are applied by ASCII order. For instance, say we have this configuration snippet:

```
[source::/logs/abc/.../*.log]
TZ = MST

[source::/logs/.../*.log]
TZ = CDT
```

The attribute TZ=CDT would win because /logs/.../*.log is first in ASCII order. This may seem counterintuitive since /logs/abc/.../*.log is arguably a better match. The logic for determining what makes a better match, however, can quickly become fantastically complex, so ASCII order is a reasonable approach.

You can also set your own value of priority, but luckily, it is rarely needed.

Attributes with class

As you dig into configurations, you will see attribute names of the form FOO-bar. The word after the dash is generally referred to as the class. These attributes are special in a few ways:

- Attributes merge across files like any other attribute
- Only one instance of each class will be applied, according to the rules described previously
- The final set of attributes is applied in ASCII order by the value of class

Once again, say we are presented with an event with the following fields:

```
sourcetype=foo_type
source=/logs/abc/def/gh.log
host=dns4.nyc.mycompany.com
```

And say that this is the configuration snippet:

```
[foo_type]
TRANSFORMS-a = from_sourcetype1, from_sourcetype2

[source::/logs/.../*.log]
TRANSFORMS-c = from_source_b

[source::/logs/abc/.../*.log]
TRANSFORMS-b = from_source_c

[host::*nyc*]
TRANSFORMS-c = from_host
```

The surviving transforms would then be:

```
TRANSFORMS-c = from_source_b
TRANSFORMS-b = from_source_c
TRANSFORMS-a = from_sourcetype1, from_sourcetype2
```

To determine the order in which the transforms are applied to our event, we sort the stanzas according to the values of their classes, in this case, c, b, and a. This gives us:

```
TRANSFORMS-a = from_sourcetype1, from_sourcetype2
TRANSFORMS-b = from_source_c
TRANSFORMS-c = from_source_b
```

The transforms are then combined into a single list and executed in this order:

```
from_sourcetype1, from_sourcetype2, from_source_c, from_source_b
```

The order of transforms usually doesn't matter but is important to understand if you want to chain transforms and create one field from another. We'll try this later, in the *transforms.conf* section.

inputs.conf

This configuration, as you might guess, controls how data makes it into Splunk. By the time this data leaves the input stage, it still isn't an event but has some base metadata associated with it: *host*, *source*, *sourcetype*, and optionally *index*. This base metadata is then used by the parsing stage to break the data into events according to the rules defined in `props.conf`:

Input types can be broken down into files, network ports, and scripts. First, we will look at attributes that are common to all inputs.

Common input attributes

These common bits of metadata are used in the parsing stage to pick the appropriate stanzas in `props.conf`.

- `host`: By default, `host` will be set to the hostname of the machine producing the event. This is usually the correct value, but it can be overridden when appropriate.
- `source`: This field is usually set to the path to the file or network port that an event came from, but this value can be hardcoded.
- `sourcetype`: This field is almost always set in `inputs.conf` and is the primary field for determining which set of parsing rules in `props.conf` to apply to these events.

 It is very important to set `sourcetype`. In the absence of a value, Splunk will create automatic values based on `source`, which can easily result in an explosion of `sourcetype` values.

- `index`: This field says what index to write events to. If it is omitted, the default index will be used.

All of these values can be modified using transforms, the only caveat being that these transforms are applied *after* the parsing step. The practical consequence of this is that you cannot apply different parsing rules to different events in the same file, for instance, different time formats on different lines.

Files as inputs

The vast majority of events in Splunk come from files. Usually, these events are read from the machine where they are produced and as the logs are written. Very often, the entire input's stanza will look like this:

```
[monitor:///logs/interesting.log*]
sourcetype=interesting
```

This is often all that is needed. This stanza is saying:

- Read all logs that match the pattern /logs/interesting.log*, and going forward, watch them for new data
- Name the source type interesting
- Set the source to the name of the file in which the log entry was found
- Default the host to the machine where the logs originated
- Write the events to the default index

These are usually perfectly acceptable defaults. If sourcetype is omitted, Splunk will pick a default source type based on the filename, which you don't want—your source type list will get very messy very fast.

Using patterns to select rolled logs

You may notice that the previous stanza ended in *. This is important because it gives Splunk a chance to find events that were written to a log that has recently rolled. If we simply watch /logs/interesting.log, it is likely that events will be missed at the end of the log when it rolls, particularly on a busy server.

Will we end up with duplicate events after the log rolls to interesting.log.1 or interesting.log.2012-09-17? The answer is "almost certainly not". This is because Splunk does not use filenames to determine what files have been read but instead does so by using checksums on the contents of the files. This means that logs can be renamed or even moved to a different filesystem on the same server, and they will still be recognized as the same file.

There are specific cases where Splunk can get confused, but in the vast majority of cases, the default mechanisms do exactly what you would hope. See the *When to use crcSalt* section further on for a discussion about special cases.

Using blacklist and whitelist

It is also possible to use a blacklist and whitelist pattern for more complicated patterns. The most common use case is to blacklist files that should not be indexed, for instance, `gz` and `zip` files. It can be done as follows:

```
[monitor:///opt/B/logs/access.log*]
sourcetype=access
blacklist=.*.gz
```

This stanza would still match `access.log.2012-08-30`, but if we had a script that compressed older logs, Splunk would not try to read `access.log.2012-07-30.gz`.

Conversely, you can use a whitelist to apply very specific patterns, like so:

```
[monitor:///opt/applicationserver/logs]
sourcetype=application_logs
whitelist=(app|application|legacy|foo)\.log(\.\d{4})?
blacklist=.*.gz
```

This whitelist would match `app.log`, `application.log`, `legacy.log.2012-08-13`, and `foo.log`, among others. The blacklist will negate any `gz` files.

Since `logs` is a directory, the default behavior will be to recursively scan that directory.

Selecting files recursively

The layout of your logs or your application may dictate a recursive approach. For instance, say we have these stanzas:

```
[monitor:///opt/*/logs/access.log*]
sourcetype=access

[monitor:///opt/.../important.log*]
sourcetype=important
```

The character `*` will match a single file or directory, while `...` will match any depth. This will match the files you want, with the caveat that all of `/opt` will continually be scanned.

Splunk will continually scan all directories from the first wildcard in a monitor path!

If /opt contains many files and directories, which it almost certainly does, Splunk will use an unfortunate amount of resources scanning all directories for matching files, constantly using memory and CPU. I have seen a single Splunk process watching a large directory structure use 2 gigabytes of memory. A little creativity can take care of this, but it is something to be aware of.

The takeaway is that if you know the possible values for *, you are better off writing multiple stanzas. For instance, assuming our directories in /opt are A and B, the following stanzas will be far more efficient:

```
[monitor:///opt/A/logs/access.log*]
sourcetype=access

[monitor:///opt/B/logs/access.log*]
sourcetype=access
```

It is also perfectly acceptable to have stanzas matching files and directories that simply don't exist. This causes no errors, but be careful to not include patterns that are so broad that they match unintended files.

Following symbolic links

When scanning directories recursively, the default behavior is to follow symbolic links. Often this is very useful, but it can cause problems if a symbolic link points to a large or slow file system. To control this behavior, simply set:

```
followSymlink = false
```

It's probably a good idea to put this on all of your monitor stanzas until you know you need to follow a symbolic link.

Setting the value of host from source

The default behavior of using the hostname from the machine forwarding the logs is almost always what you want. If, however, you are reading logs for a number of hosts, you can extract the hostname from source using host_regex or host_segment. For instance, say we have the path:

```
/nfs/logs/webserver1/access.log
```

To set host to webserver1, you could use either:

```
[monitor:///nfs/logs/*/access.log*]
sourcetype=access
host_segment=3
```

Or:

```
[monitor:///nfs/logs/*/access.log*]
sourcetype=access
host_regex=/(.*?)/access\.log
```

host_regex could also be used to extract the value of host from the filename.

It is also possible to reset host using a transform, with the caveat that this will occur after parsing, which means any settings in props.conf that rely on matching host will already have been applied.

Ignoring old data at installation

It is often the case that when Splunk is installed, months or years of logs are sitting in a directory where logs are currently being written. Logs that are appended to infrequently may also have months or years of events that are no longer interesting and would be wasteful to index.

The best solution is to set up archive scripts to compress any logs older than a few days, but in a large environment, this may be difficult to do. Splunk has two settings that help ignore older data, but be forewarned: once these files have been ignored, there is no simple way to change your mind later. If, instead, you compress older logs and blacklist the compressed files as explained in the *Using blacklist and whitelist* section, you can simply decompress at a later stage, any files you would like to index. Let's look at a sample stanza:

```
[monitor:///opt/B/logs/access.log*]
sourcetype = access
ignoreOlderThan = 14d
```

In this case, ignoreOlderThan says to ignore, forever, all events in any files whose modification date is older than 14 days. If the file is updated in the future, any *new* events will be indexed.

The followTail attribute lets us ignore all events written so far, instead starting at the end of each file. Let's look at an example:

```
[monitor:///opt/B/logs/access.log*]
sourcetype = access
followTail = 1
```

Splunk will note the length of files matching the pattern, but `followTail` instructs Splunk to ignore everything currently in these files. Any new events written to the files will be indexed. Remember that there is no easy way to alter this if you change your mind later.

It is not currently possible to say "ignore all *events* older than X", but since most logs roll on a daily basis, this is not commonly a problem.

When to use crcSalt

To keep track of what files have been seen before, Splunk stores a checksum of the first 256 bytes of each file it sees. This is usually plenty, as most files start with a log message, which is *almost* guaranteed to be unique.

This breaks down when the first 256 bytes are not unique on the same server. I have seen two cases where this happens, as follows:

1. Logs that start with a common header containing product version information, for instance:

   ```
   ==================================================================
   == Great product version 1.2 brought to you by Great company  ==
   == Server kernel version 3.2.1                                 ==
   ```

2. A server writing many thousands of files with low time resolution, for instance:

   ```
   12:13:12 Session created
   12:13:12 Starting session
   ```

To deal with these cases, we can add the path to the log to the checksum, or "salt our crc". This is accomplished like so:

```
[monitor:///opt/B/logs/application.log*]
sourcetype = access
crcSalt = <SOURCE>
```

It says to include the full path to this log in the checksum.

This method will only work if your logs have a unique name. The easiest way to accomplish this is to include the current date in the name of the log when it is created. You may need to change the pattern for your log names so that the date is always included and the log is not renamed.

 Do not use `crcSalt` if your logs change names!

If you enable `crcSalt` in an input where it was not already enabled, you will re-index all the data! You need to ensure that the old logs are moved aside or compressed and blacklisted before enabling this setting in an existing configuration.

Destructively indexing files

If you receive logfiles in `batch`, you can use the `batch` input to consume logs and then *delete* them. This should only be used against a copy of the logs. See the following example:

```
[batch:///var/batch/logs/*/access.log*]
sourcetype=access
host_segment=4
move_policy = sinkhole
```

This stanza would index the files in the given directory and then delete the files. Be very sure this is what you want to do!

Network inputs

In addition to reading files, Splunk can listen to network ports. The stanzas take the following form:

```
[protocol://<remote host>:<local port>]
```

The remote host portion is rarely used, but the idea is that you can specify different input configurations for specific hosts. The usual stanzas look like this:

- `[tcp://1234]`: Specify that we will listen to port `1234` for TCP connections. Anything can connect to this port and send data in.

- `[tcp-ssl://importanthost:1234]`: Listen on TCP using SSL, and apply this stanza to the host `importanthost`. Splunk will generate self-signed certificates the first time it is launched.

- `[udp://514]`: This is generally used for receiving **syslog** events. While this does work, it is generally considered best practice to use a dedicated syslog receiver, such as rsyslog or syslogng. See *Chapter 11, Advanced Deployments*, for a discussion on this subject.

- `[splunktcp://9997]` or `[splunktcp-ssl://9997]`: In a distributed environment, your indexers will receive events on the specified port. It is a custom protocol used between Splunk instances. This stanza is created for you when you use the **Manager** page at **Manager | Forwarding and receiving | Receive data**.

For `tcp` and `udp` inputs, the following attributes apply:

- `source`: If not specified, `source` will default to `protocol:port`, for instance, `udp:514`.

- `sourcetype`: If not specified, `sourcetype` will also default to `protocol:port`, but this is generally not what you want. It is best to specify a source type and create a corresponding stanza in `props.conf`.

- `connection_host`: With network inputs, what value to capture for `host` is somewhat tricky. Your options essentially are:

  - `connection_host = dns`, which uses reverse DNS to determine the hostname from the incoming connection. When reverse DNS is configured properly, this is usually your best bet. This is the default.

  - `connection_host = ip`, which sets the host field to the IP address of the remote machine. This is your best choice when reverse DNS is unreliable.

  - `connection_host = none`, which uses the hostname of the Splunk instance receiving the data. This option can make sense when all traffic is going to an interim host.

  - `host = foo`, which sets the hostname statically.

  - It is also common to reset the value of `host` using a transform, for instance with syslog events. This happens after parsing, though, so is too late to change things such as time zone based on the host.

- `queueSize`: This value specifies how much memory Splunk is allowed to set aside for an input queue. A common use for a queue is to capture spikey data until the indexers can catch up.

- `persistentQueueSize`: This value specifies a persistent queue that can be used to capture data to disk if the in-memory queue fills up.

If you find yourself building a particularly complicated setup around network ports, I would encourage you to talk to Splunk support as there may be a better way to accomplish your goals.

Native Windows inputs

One nice thing about Windows is that system logs and many application logs go to the same place. Unfortunately, that place is not a file, so native hooks are required to access these events. Splunk makes those inputs available using stanzas of the form [WinEventLog:LogName]. For example, to index the Security log, the stanza simply looks like this:

```
[WinEventLog:Security]
```

There are a number of supported attributes, but the defaults are reasonable. The only attribute I have personally used is current_only, which is the equivalent of followTail for monitor stanzas. For instance, this stanza says to monitor the Application log, but to start reading from now:

```
[WinEventLog:Application]
current_only = 1
```

This is useful when there are many historical events on the server.

The other input available is **Windows Management Instrumentation (WMI)**. With WMI, you can:

- Monitor native performance metrics, like you would find in Windows Performance Monitor
- Monitor the Windows Event Log API
- Run custom queries against the database behind WMI
- Query remote machines

 Though it is theoretically possible to monitor many Windows servers using WMI and a few Splunk forwarders, this is not advised. The configuration is complicated, does not scale well, introduces complicated security implications, and is not thoroughly tested. Also, reading Windows Event Logs via WMI produces different output than the native input, and most apps that expect Windows events will not function as expected.

The simplest way to generate the inputs.conf and wmi.conf configurations needed for Windows Event Logs and WMI is to install Splunk for Windows on a Windows host and then configure the desired inputs through the web interface. See the official Splunk documentation for more examples.

Scripts as inputs

Splunk will periodically execute processes and capture the output. For example, here is input from the ImplementingSplunkDataGenerator app:

```
[script://./bin/implSplunkGen.py 2]
interval=60
sourcetype=impl_splunk_gen_sourcetype2
source=impl_splunk_gen_src2
host=host2
index=implSplunk
```

Things to notice in this example are as follows:

- The present working directory is the root of the app that contains inputs.conf.
- Files that end with .py will be executed using the Python interpreter included with Splunk. This means the Splunk Python modules are available. To use a different Python module, specify the path to Python in the stanza.
- Any arguments specified in the stanza will be handed to the script as if executed at the command line.
- interval specifies how often this script should be run, in seconds.
    - If the script is still running, it will not be launched again.
    - Long-running scripts are fine. Since only one copy of a script will run at a time, the interval will instead indicate how often to check whether the script is still running.
    - This value can also be specified in cron format.

Any programming language can be used, as long as it can be executed at the command line. Splunk simply captures the standard output from whatever is executed.

Included with Splunk for Windows are scripts for querying WMI. One sample stanza looks like this:

```
[script://$SPLUNK_HOME\bin\scripts\splunk-wmi.path]
```

Things to note are:

- Windows paths require backslashes instead of slashes.
- $SPLUNK_HOME will expand properly.

transforms.conf

`transforms.conf` is where we specify transformations and lookups that can then be applied to any event. These transforms and lookups are referenced by name in `props.conf`.

For our examples in the later subsections, we will use this event:

```
2012-09-24T00:21:35.925+0000 DEBUG [MBX] Password reset called.
[old=1234, new=secret, req_time=5346]
```

We will use it with these metadata values:

```
sourcetype=myapp
source=/logs/myapp.session_foo-jA5MDkyMjEwMTIK.log
host=vlbmba.local
```

Creating indexed fields

One common task accomplished with `transforms.conf` is the creation of new indexed fields. Indexed fields are different from extracted fields in that they must be created at index time and can be searched for whether the value is in the raw text of the event or not. It is usually preferable to create extracted fields instead of indexed fields. See *Chapter 3, Indexed fields versus extracted fields*, for a deeper discussion about when indexed fields are beneficial.

 Indexed fields are only applied to events that are indexed after the definition is created. There is no way to backfill a field without reindexing.

Creating a loglevel field

The format of a typical stanza in `transforms.conf` looks like this:

```
[myapp_loglevel]
REGEX = \s([A-Z]+)\s
FORMAT = loglevel::$1
WRITE_META = True
```

This will add to our events the field `loglevel=DEBUG`. This is a good idea if the values of `loglevel` are common words outside of this location, for instance `ERROR`.

Stepping through this stanza, we have:

- `[myapp_loglevel]`: The stanza can be any unique value, but it is in your best interest to make the name meaningful. This is the name referenced in `props.conf`.

- `REGEX = \s([A-Z]+)\s`: This is the pattern to test against each event that is handed to us. If this pattern does not match, this transform will not be applied.

- `FORMAT = loglevel::$1`: Create the field `loglevel`. Under the covers, all indexed fields are stored using a `::` delimiter, so we have to follow that form.

- `WRITE_META = True`: Without this attribute, the transform won't actually create an indexed field and store it with the event.

Creating a session field from source

Using our event, let's create another field, `session`, which appears to only be in the value of `source`.

```
[myapp_session]
SOURCE_KEY = MetaData:Source
REGEX = session_(.*?)\.log
FORMAT = session::$1
WRITE_META = True
```

Note the attribute `SOURCE_KEY`. The value of this field can be any existing metadata field or another indexed field that has already been created. See the *Attributes with class* subsection within the *props.conf* section for a discussion about transform execution order. We will discuss these fields in the *Modifying metadata fields* subsection.

Creating a "tag" field

It is also possible to create fields simply to tag events that would be difficult to search for otherwise. For example, if we wanted to find all events that were slow, we could search for:

```
sourcetype=myapp req_time>999
```

Without an indexed field, this query would require parsing every event that matches `sourcetype=myapp` over the time that we are interested in. The query would then discard all events whose `req_time` value was 999 or less.

If we know ahead of time that a value of `req_time>999` is bad, and we can come up with a regular expression to specify what bad is, we can tag these events for quicker retrieval. Say we have this `transforms.conf` stanza:

```
[myapp_slow]
REGEX = req_time=\d{4,}
FORMAT = slow_request::1
WRITE_META = True
```

This `REGEX` will match any event containing `req_time=` followed by four or more digits.

After adding `slow_request` to `fields.conf` (see the *fields.conf* section), we can search for `slow_request=1` and find all slow events very efficiently. This will not apply to events that were indexed before this transform existed. If the events that are slow are uncommon, this query will be *much* faster.

Creating host categorization fields

It is common, to have parts of a hostname mean something in particular. If this pattern is well known and predictable, it may be worthwhile to pull the value out into fields. Working from our fictitious `host` value, `vlbmba.local` (which happens to be my laptop), we might want to create fields for `owner` and `hosttype`. Out stanza might look like this:

```
[host_parts]
SOURCE_KEY = MetaData:Host
REGEX = (...)(...)\.
FORMAT = host_owner::$1 host_type::$2
WRITE_META = True
```

With our new fields, we can now easily categorize errors by whatever information is encoded into the hostname. Another approach would be to use a lookup, which has the advantage of being retroactive. This approach has the advantage of faster searches for the specific fields.

Modifying metadata fields

It is sometimes convenient to override the main metadata fields. We will look at one possible reason for overriding each base metadata value.

Remember that transforms are applied after parsing, so changing metadata fields via transforms cannot be used to affect which `props.conf` stanzas are applied for date parsing or line breaking. For instance, with syslog events that contain the hostname, you cannot change the time zone because the date has already been parsed before the transforms are applied.

The keys provided by Splunk include:

- `_raw` (this is the default value for `SOURCE_KEY`)
- `MetaData:Source`
- `MetaData:Sourcetype`
- `MetaData:Host`
- `_MetaData:Index`

Overriding host

If your hostnames are appearing differently from different sources, for instance, syslog versus Splunk Forwarders, you can use a transform to normalize these values. Given our hostname `vlbmba.local`, we may want to only keep the portion to the left of the first period. The stanza would look like this:

```
[normalize_host]
SOURCE_KEY = MetaData:Host
DEST_KEY = MetaData:Host
REGEX = (.*?)\.
FORMAT = host::$1
```

This will replace our hostname with `vlbmba`. Note these two things:

- `WRITE_META` is not included because we are not adding to the metadata of this event; we are instead overwriting the value of a core metadata field
- `host::` must be included at the beginning of the format

Overriding source

Some applications will write a log for each session, conversation, or transaction. One problem this introduces is an explosion of `source` values. The values of `source` will end up in `$SPLUNK_HOME/var/lib/splunk/*/db/Sources.data`—one line per unique value of `source`. This file will eventually grow to a huge size, and Splunk will waste a lot of time updating it, causing unexplained pauses. A new setting in `indexes.conf` called `disableGlobalMetadata`, can also eliminate this problem.

To flatten this value, we could use a stanza like this:

```
[myapp_flatten_source]
SOURCE_KEY = MetaData:Source
DEST_KEY = MetaData:Source
REGEX = (.*session_).*.log
FORMAT = source::$1x.log
```

This would set the value of `source` to `/logs/myapp.session_x.log`, which would eliminate our growing source problem.

If the value of `session` is useful, the transform in the *Creating a session field from source* section could be run before this transform to capture the value. Likewise, a transform could capture the entire value of `source` and place it into a different metadata field.

A huge number of logfiles on a filesystem introduces a few problems, including running out of inodes and the memory used by the Splunk process tracking all of the files. As a general rule, a cleanup process should be designed to archive older logs.

Overriding sourcetype

It is not uncommon to change the `sourcetype` field of an event based on the contents of the event, particularly from syslog. In our fictitious example, we want a different source type for events that contain `[MBX]` after the log level so that we can apply different extracts to these events. The following examples will do this work:

```
[mbx_sourcetype]
DEST_KEY = MetaData:Sourcetype
REGEX = \d+\s[A-Z]+\s\([MBX\])
FORMAT = sourcetype::mbx
```

Use this functionality carefully as it easy to go conceptually wrong, and this is difficult to fix later.

Routing events to a different index

At times, you may want to send events to a different index, either because they need to live longer than other events or because they contain sensitive information that should not be seen by all users. This can be applied to any type of event from any source, be it a file, network, or script.

All that we have to do is match the event and reset the index.

```
[contains_password_1]
DEST_KEY = _MetaData:Index
REGEX = Password reset called
FORMAT = sensitive
```

Things to note are:

- In this scenario, you will probably make multiple transforms, so be sure to make the name unique
- `DEST_KEY` starts with an underscore
- `FORMAT` does not start with `index::`
- The index `sensitive` must exist on the machine indexing the data, or the event will be lost

Lookup definitions

A simple lookup simply needs to specify a filename in transforms.conf, thus:

```
[testlookup]
filename = test.csv
```

Assuming `test.csv` contains the columns `user` and `group`, and our events contain the field `user`, we can reference this lookup by using the `lookup` command in search, as follows:

```
* | lookup testlookup user
```

Or, we can wire this lookup to run automatically in `props.conf`, thus:

```
[mysourcetype]
LOOKUP-testlookup = testlookup user
```

That's all you need to get started, and this probably covers most cases. See the *Using lookups to enrich data* section in *Chapter 6, Extending Search*, for instructions on creating lookups.

Wildcard lookups

In *Chapter 9, Summary Indexes and CSV Files*, we edited transforms.conf but did not explain what was happening. Let's take another look. Our transform stanza looks like this:

```
[flatten_summary_lookup]
filename = flatten_summary_lookup.csv
match_type = WILDCARD(url)
max_matches = 1
```

Stepping through what we added, we have:

- `match_type = WILDCARD(url)`: This says that the value of the field url in the lookup file may contain wildcards. In our example, the URL might look like `/contact/*` in our CSV file.

- `max_matches = 1`: By default, up to 10 entries that match in the lookup file will be added to an event, with the values in each field being added to a multivalue field. In this case, we only want the first match to be applied.

CIDR wildcard lookups

CIDR wildcards look very similar to text-based wildcards but use Classless Inter-Domain Routing rules to match lookup rows against an IP address. Let's try an example.

Say we have this lookup file:

```
ip_range,network,datacenter
10.1.0.0/16,qa,east
10.2.0.0/16,prod,east
10.128.0.0/16,qa,west
10.129.0.0/16,prod,west
```

It has this corresponding definition in `transforms.conf`:

```
[ip_address_lookup]
filename = ip_address_lookup.csv
match_type = CIDR(ip_range)
max_matches = 1
```

And, there are a few events such as these:

```
src_ip=10.2.1.3 user=mary
src_ip=10.128.88.33 user=bob
src_ip=10.1.35.248 user=bob
```

We could use our lookup to enrich these events like so:

```
src_ip="*"
  | lookup ip_address_lookup ip_range as src_ip
  | table src_ip user datacenter network
```

This would match the appropriate IP address and give us a table like this one:

	src_ip ⬍	user ⬍	datacenter ⬍	network ⬍
1	10.2.1.3	mary	east	prod
2	10.128.88.33	bob	west	qa
3	10.1.35.248	bob	east	qa

The query also shows that you could use the same lookup for different fields by using the as keyword in the `lookup` call.

Using time in lookups

A temporal lookup is used to enrich events based on when the event happened. To accomplish this, we specify the beginning of a time range in the lookup source and then specify a format for this time in our lookup configuration. Using this mechanism, lookup values can change over time, even retroactively.

Here is a very simple example to attach a `version` field based on time. Say we have the following CSV file:

```
sourcetype,version,time
impl_splunk_gen,1.0,2012-09-19 02:56:30 UTC
impl_splunk_gen,1.1,2012-09-22 12:01:45 UTC
impl_splunk_gen,1.2,2012-09-23 18:12:12 UTC
```

We then use the lookup configuration in `transforms.conf` to specify which field in our lookup will be tested against the time in each event and what the format of the time field will be:

```
[versions]
filename = versions.csv
time_field = time
time_format = %Y-%m-%d %H:%M:%S %Z
```

With this in place, we can now use our lookup in search, like so:

```
sourcetype=impl_splunk_gen error
  | lookup versions sourcetype
  | timechart count by version
```

This would give us a chart of errors (by version) over time, like so:

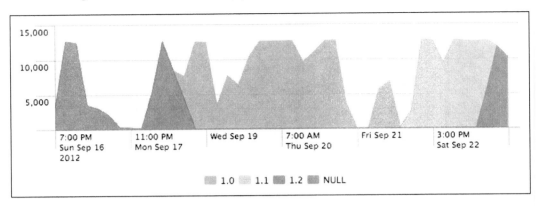

Other use cases include tracking deployments across environments and tracking activity from disabled accounts.

Using REPORT

Attributes of the format REPORT-foo in props.conf call stanzas in transforms.conf at search time, which means that they cannot affect metadata fields. EXTRACT definitions are more convenient to write as they live entirely in a single attribute in props.conf, but there are a couple of things that can only be done using a REPORT attribute paired with a transform defined in transforms.conf.

Creating multivalue fields

Assuming some value might happen multiple times in a given event, an EXTRACT definition can only match the first occurrence. For example, say we have the event:

```
2012-08-25T20:18:09 action=send a@b.com c@d.com e@f.com
```

We could pull the first e-mail address using the following extraction:

```
EXTRACT-email = (?i)(?P<email>[a-zA-Z0-9._]+@[a-zA-Z0-9._]+)
```

This would set the field email to a@b.com. Using a REPORT attribute and transform stanza, we can capture all of the e-mail addresses using the MV_ADD attribute.

The props stanza would look like this:

```
REPORT-mvemail = mvemail
```

The `transforms.conf` stanza would then look like this:

```
[mvemail]
REGEX = (?i)([a-zA-Z0-9._]+@[a-zA-Z0-9._]+)
FORMAT = email::$1
MV_ADD = true
```

The `MV_ADD` attribute also has the effect that, if some other configuration has already created the `email` field, all values that match will be added to the event.

Creating dynamic fields

Sometimes, it can be useful to dynamically create fields from an event. For instance, say we have an event such as:

```
2012-08-25T20:18:09 action=send from_335353("a@b.com") to_223523("c@d.
com") cc_39393("e@f.com") cc_39394("g@h.com")
```

It would be nice to pull `from`, `to`, and `cc` as fields, but we may not know all of the possible field names. This stanza in `transforms.conf` would create the fields we want, dynamically:

```
[dynamic_address_fields]
REGEX=\s(\S+)_\S+\("(.*?)"\)
FORMAT = $1::$2
MV_ADD=true
```

While we're at it, let's put the numeric value after the field name into a value:

```
[dynamic_address_ids]
REGEX=\s(\S+)_(\S+)\("
FORMAT = $1::$2
MV_ADD=true
```

This gives us multivalue fields like the ones in the following screenshot:

action ⇕	cc ⇕	from ⇕	to ⇕
send	e@f.com g@h.com 39393 39394	a@b.com 335353	c@d.com 223523

One thing that we cannot do is add extra text into the FORMAT attribute. For instance, in the second case, it would be nice to use a FORMAT attribute such as this one:

```
FORMAT = $1_id::$2
```

Unfortunately, this will not function as we hope and will instead create the field id.

Chaining transforms

As covered before in the *Attributes with class* section, transforms are executed in a particular order. In most cases, this order does not matter, but there are occasions when you might want to chain transforms together, with one transform relying on a field created by a previous transform.

A good example is the source flattening that we used previously, in the *Overriding source* section. If this transform happened before our transform in the *Creating a session field from source* section, our session field would always have the value x.

Let's reuse two transforms from previous sections and then create one more transform. We will chain them to pull the first part of session into yet another field. Say we have these transforms:

```
[myapp_session]
SOURCE_KEY = MetaData:Source
REGEX = session_(.*?)\.log
FORMAT = session::$1
WRITE_META = True

[myapp_flatten_source]
SOURCE_KEY = MetaData:Source
DEST_KEY = MetaData:Source
REGEX = (.*session_).*.log
FORMAT = source::$1x.log

[session_type]
SOURCE_KEY = session
REGEX = (.*?)-
FORMAT = session_type::$1
WRITE_META = True
```

To ensure that these transforms run in order, the simplest thing would be to place them in a single TRANSFORMS attribute in props.conf, like so:

```
[source:*session_*.log]
TRANSFORMS-s = myapp_session,myapp_flatten_source,session_type
```

We can use `source` from our sample event specified inside `tranforms.conf` like this:

```
source=/logs/myapp.session_foo-jA5MDkyMjEwMTIK.log
```

Stepping though the transforms, we have:

- `myapp_session`: Reading from the metadata field, `source`, creates the indexed field `session` with the value `foo-jA5MDkyMjEwMTIK`
- `myapp_flatten_source`: Resets the metadata field, `source`, to `/logs/myapp.session_x.log`
- `session_type`: Reading from our newly indexed field, `session`, creates the field `session_type` with the value `foo`

This same ordering logic can be applied at search time using the EXTRACT and REPORT stanzas. This particular case needs to be calculated as indexed fields, if we want to search for these values, since the values are part of a metadata field.

Dropping events

Some events are simply not worth indexing. The hard part is figuring out which ones these are and making very sure you're not wrong. Dropping too many events can make you blind to real problems at critical times and can introduce more problems than tuning Splunk to deal with the greater volume of data in the first place.

With that warning stated, if you know what events you do not need, the procedure for dropping events is pretty simple. Say we have an event such as this one:

```
2012-02-02 12:24:23 UTC TRACE Database call 1 of 1,000. [...]
```

I know absolutely that, in this case and for this particular source type, I do not want to index TRACE level events.

In `props.conf`, I create a stanza for my source type, thus:

```
[mysourcetype]
TRANSFORMS-droptrace=droptrace
```

Then, I create the following transform in `transforms.conf`:

```
[droptrace]
REGEX=^\d{4}-\d{2}-\d{2}\s+\d{1,2}:\d{2}:\d{1,2}\s+[A-Z]+\sTRACE
DEST_KEY=queue
FORMAT=nullQueue
```

This REGEX attribute is purposefully as strict as I can make it. It is vital that I do not accidentally drop other events, and it is better for this brittle pattern to start failing and to let through TRACE events rather than for it to do the opposite.

fields.conf

We need to add to fields.conf any indexed fields we create, or they will not be searched efficiently, or may even not function at all. For our examples in the *transforms.conf* section, fields.conf would look like this:

```
[session_type]
INDEXED = true

[session]
INDEXED = true

[host_owner]
INDEXED = true

[host_type]
INDEXED = true

[slow_request]
INDEXED = true

[loglevel]
INDEXED = true
```

These stanzas instruct Splunk to not look in the body of the events for the value being queried. Take, for instance, the following search:

```
host_owner=vlb
```

Without this entry, the actual query would essentially be:

```
vlb | search host_owner=vlb
```

With the expectation that the value vlb is in the body of the event, this query simply won't work. Adding the entry to fields.conf fixes this.

In the case of loglevel, since the value is in the body, the query will work, but it will not take advantage of the indexed field, instead only using it to filter events after finding all events that contain the bare word.

outputs.conf

This configuration controls how Splunk will forward events. In the vast majority of cases, this configuration exists on Splunk Forwarders, sending their events to Splunk indexers. An example would look like this:

```
[tcpout]
defaultGroup = nyc

[tcpout:nyc]
autoLB = true
server = 1.2.3.4:9997,1.2.3.6:9997
```

It is possible to use transforms to route events to different server groups, but it is not commonly used as it introduces a lot of complexity that is generally not needed.

indexes.conf

Put simply, indexes.conf determines where data is stored on disk, how much is kept, and for how long. An index is simply a named directory with a specific structure. Inside this directory structure, there are a few metadata files and subdirectories; the subdirectories are called **buckets** and actually contain the indexed data.

A simple stanza looks like this:

```
[implSplunk]
homePath    = $SPLUNK_DB/implSplunk/db
coldPath    = $SPLUNK_DB/implSplunk/colddb
thawedPath = $SPLUNK_DB/implSplunk/thaweddb
```

Let's step through these attributes:

- homePath : This is the location for recent data.
- coldPath: This is the location for older data.
- thawedPath: This is a directory where buckets can be restored. It is an unmanaged location. This attribute must be defined, but I for one, have never actually used it.

An aside about the terminology of buckets is probably in order. It is as follows:

- hot: This is a bucket that is currently open for writing. It lives in homePath.
- warm: This is a bucket that was created recently but is no longer open for writing. It also lives in homePath.

- `cold`: This is an older bucket that has been moved to `coldPath`. It is moved when `maxWarmDBCount` has been exceeded.

- `frozen`: For most installations, this simply means deleted. For customers who want to archive buckets, `coldToFrozenScript` or `coldToFrozenDir` can be specified to save buckets.

- `thawed`: A thawed bucket is a frozen bucket that has been brought back. It is special in that it is not managed, and it is not included in **All time** queries. When using `coldToFrozenDir`, only the raw data is typically kept, so `splunk rebuild` will need to be used to make the bucket searchable again.

How long data stays in an index is controlled by these attributes:

- `frozenTimePeriodInSecs`: This setting dictates the oldest data to keep in an index. A bucket will be removed when its newest event is older than this value. The default value is approximately 6 years.

- `maxTotalDataSizeMB`: This setting dictates how large an index can be. The total space used across all hot, warm, and cold buckets will not exceed this value. The oldest bucket is always frozen first. The default value is 500 gigabytes.

It is generally a good idea to set both of these attributes. `frozenTimePeriodInSecs` should match what users expect. `maxTotalDataSizeMB` should protect your system from running out of disk space.

Less commonly used attributes include:

- `coldToFrozenDir`: If specified, buckets will be moved to this directory instead of being deleted. This directory is not managed by Splunk, so it is up to the administrator to make sure that the disk does not fill up.

- `maxHotBuckets`: A bucket represents a slice of time and will ideally span as small a slice of time as is practical. I would never set this value to less than 3, but ideally, it should be set to `10`.

- `maxDataSize`: This is the maximum size for an individual bucket. The default value is set by processor type and is generally acceptable. The larger a bucket, the fewer buckets have to be opened to complete a search, but the more disk space will be needed before a bucket can be frozen. The default is `auto`, which will never top 750 MB. The setting `auto_high_volume`, which equals 1 GB on 32-bit systems and 10 GB on 64-bit systems, should be used for indexes that receive more than 10 GB a day.

We will discuss sizing multiple indexes in *Chapter 11, Advanced Deployments*.

authorize.conf

This configuration stores definitions of capabilities and roles. These settings affect search and the web interface. They are generally managed through the interface at **Manager | Access controls**, but a quick look at the configuration itself may be useful.

A role stanza looks like this:

```
[role_power]
importRoles = user
schedule_search = enabled
rtsearch       = enabled
srchIndexesAllowed = *
srchIndexesDefault = main
srchDiskQuota   = 500
srchJobsQuota   = 10
rtSrchJobsQuota = 20
```

Let's step through these settings:

- `importRoles`: This is a list of roles to import capabilities from. The set of capabilities will be the merging of capabilities from imported roles and added capabilities.
- `schedule_search` and `rtsearch`: These are two capabilities enabled for the role `power` that were not necessarily enabled for the imported roles.
- `srchIndexesAllowed`: What indexes this role is allowed to search. In this case, all are allowed.
- `srchIndexesDefault`: What indexes to search by default. This setting also affects the data shown on **Search | Summary**. If you have installed the `ImplementingSplunkDataGenerator` app, you will see `impl_splunk_*` source types on this page even though this data is actually stored in the `implsplunk` index.
- `srchDiskQuota`: Whenever a search is run, the results are stored on disk until they expire. The expiration can be set explicitly when creating a saved search, but the expiration is automatically set for interactive searches. Users can delete old results from the **Jobs** view.
- `srchJobsQuota`: Each user is limited to a certain number of concurrently running searches. The default is 3. Users with the `power` role are allowed 10, while those with the `admin` role are allowed 50.
- `rtSrchJobsQuota`: Similarly, this is the maximum number of concurrently running real-time searches. The default is 6.

savedsearches.conf

This configuration contains saved searches and is rarely modified by hand.

times.conf

This configuration holds definitions for time ranges that appear in the time picker.

commands.conf

This configuration specifies commands provided by an app. We will use this in *Chapter 12, Extending Splunk*.

web.conf

The main settings changed in this file are the port for the web server, the SSL certificates, and whether to start the web server at all.

User interface resources

Most Splunk apps consist mainly of resources for the web application. The app layout for these resources is completely different from all other configurations

Views and navigation

Like `.conf` files, view and navigation documents take precedence in the following order:

1. `$SPLUNK_HOME/etc/users/$username/$appname/local`: When a new dashboard is created, it lands here. It will remain here until the permissions are changed to **App** or **Global**.

2. `$SPLUNK_HOME/etc/apps/$appname/local`: Once a document is shared, it will be moved to this directory.

3. `$SPLUNK_HOME/etc/apps/$appname/default`: Documents can only be placed here manually. You should do this if you are going to share an app.

Unlike `.conf` files, these documents *do not* merge.

Within each of these directories, views and navigation end up under the directories `data/ui/views` and `data/ui/nav`, respectively. So, given a view `foo`, for the user `bob`, in the app `app1`, the initial location for the document will be:

`$SPLUNK_HOME/etc/users/bob/app1/local/data/ui/views/foo.xml`

Once the document is shared, it will be moved to:

`$SPLUNK_HOME/etc/apps/app1/local/data/ui/views/foo.xml`

Navigation follows the same structure, but the only navigation document that is ever used is called `default.xml`, for instance:

`$SPLUNK_HOME/etc/apps/app1/local/data/ui/nav/default.xml`

You can edit these files directly on the disk instead of through the web interface, but Splunk will probably not see the changes without a restart—unless you use a little trick. To reload changes to views or navigation made directly on disk, load the URL `http://mysplunkserver:8000/debug/refresh`, replacing `mysplunkserver` appropriately. If all else fails, restart Splunk.

Appserver resources

Outside of views and navigation, there are a number of resources that the web application will use. For instance, applications and dashboards can reference CSS and images, as we did in *Chapter 7, Working with Apps*. These resources are stored under `$SPLUNK_HOME/etc/apps/$appname/appserver/`. There are a few directories that appear under this directory, as follows:

- `static`: Any static files that you would like to use in your application are stored here. There are a few magic documents that Splunk itself will use, for instance, `appIcon.png`, `screenshot.png`, `application.css`, and `application.js`. Other files can be referenced using includes or templates. See the *Using ServerSideInclude in a complex dashboard* section in *Chapter 7, Working with* Apps for an example of referencing includes and static images.

- `event_renderers`: Event renderers allow you to run special display code for specific event types. We will write an event renderer in *Chapter 12, Extending Splunk*.

- `templates`: It is possible to create special templates using the `mako` template language. It is not commonly done.

- `modules`: This is where new modules that are provided by apps are stored. Examples of this include the `Google Maps` and `Sideview Utils` modules. See `http://dev.splunk.com` for more information about building your own modules or use existing modules as an example.

Metadata

Object permissions are stored in files located at `$SPLUNK_HOME/etc/apps/$appname/metadata/`. The two possible files are `default.meta` and `local.meta`.

These files:

- Are only relevant to the resources in the app where they are contained
- Do merge, with entries in `local.meta` taking precedence
- Are generally controlled by the admin interface
- Can contain rules that affect all configurations of a particular type, but this entry must be made manually

In the absence of these files, resources are limited to the current app.

Let's look at `default.meta` for is_app_one, as created by Splunk:

```
# Application-level permissions
[]
access = read : [ * ], write : [ admin, power ]

### EVENT TYPES
[eventtypes]
export = system

### PROPS
[props]
export = system

### TRANSFORMS
[transforms]
export = system


### LOOKUPS
[lookups]
```

```
export = system


### VIEWSTATES: even normal users should be able to create shared
viewstates
[viewstates]
access = read : [ * ], write : [ * ]
export = system
```

Stepping through this snippet, we have:

- The [] stanza states that all users should be able to read everything in this app but that only users with the admin or power roles should be able to write to this app.

- The [eventtypes], [props], [transforms], and [lookups] states say that all configurations of each type in this app should be shared by all users in all apps, by default. export=system is equivalent to **Global** in the user interface.

- The [viewstates] stanza gives all users the right to share their viewstates globally. A **viewstate** contains information about dashboard settings made through the web application, for instance, chart settings. Without this, chart settings applied to a dashboard or saved search would not be available.

Looking at local.meta, we see settings created by the web application for the configurations we created through the web application.

```
[indexes/summary_impl_splunk]
access = read : [ * ], write : [ admin, power ]

[views/errors]
access = read : [ * ], write : [ admin, power ]
export = system
owner = admin
version = 4.3
modtime = 1339296668.151105000

[savedsearches/top%20user%20errors%20pie%20chart]
export = none
owner = admin
version = 4.3
modtime = 1338420710.720786000

[viewstates/flashtimeline%3Ah2v14xkb]
owner = nobody
```

```
version = 4.3
modtime = 1338420715.753642000

[props/impl_splunk_web/LOOKUP-web_section]
access = read : [ * ]
export = none
owner = admin
version = 4.3
modtime = 1346013505.279379000
```

```
. . .
```

You get the idea. The web application will make very specific entries for each object created. When distributing an application, it is generally easier to make blanket permissions in metadata/default.meta, as appropriate for the resources in your application.

For an application that simply provides dashboards, no metadata at all will be needed, as the default for all resources (apps) will be acceptable.

If your application provides resources to be used by other applications, for instance, lookups or extracts, your default.meta file might look like this:

```
### PROPS
[props]
export = system

### TRANSFORMS
[transforms]
export = system

### LOOKUPS
[lookups]
export = system
```

This states that everything in your props.conf and transforms.conf files, and all lookup definitions, are merged into the logical configuration of every search.

Summary

This chapter provided an overview of how configurations work and a commentary on the most common aspects of Splunk configuration. This is by no means a complete reference for these configurations, which I will leave to the official documentation. I find the easiest way to get to the official documentation for a particular file is to query your favorite search engine for `splunk configname.conf`.

In *Chapter 11, Advanced Deployments*, we will dig into distributed deployments, and look at how they are efficiently configured. What you have learned in this chapter will be vital to understanding what is considered best practice.

11
Advanced Deployments

When you first started Splunk, you probably installed it on one machine, imported some logs, and got to work searching. It is wonderful that you can try the product out so easily, but once you move into testing and production, things can get much more complicated, and a bit of planning will save you from trouble later.

In this chapter, we will discuss getting data in, the different parts of a distributed deployment, distributed configuration management, sizing your installation, security concerns, and backup strategies.

Planning your installation

There are a few questions that you need to answer to determine how many Splunk instances will be involved in your deployment:

- How much data will be indexed per day? How much data will be kept?

  The rule of thumb is 100 gigabytes per day per Splunk indexer, assuming you have fast disks. See the *Sizing indexers* section for more information.

- How many searches will be running simultaneously?

  This number is probably smaller than you think. This is not the number of users who may be using Splunk, but how many simultaneous queries are running. This varies by the type of queries your group runs.

- What are the sources of data?

  Where your data comes from can definitely affect your deployment. Planning for all of the possible data that you might want to consume can save you from trouble later. See the *Common data sources* section for examples.

- How many data centers do you need to monitor?

  Dealing with servers in multiple locations introduces another level of complexity, to which there is no single answer. See *Deploying the Splunk binary* section for a few example deployments.

- How will you deploy the Splunk binary?
- How will you distribute configurations?

We will touch on these topics and more.

Splunk instance types

In a distributed deployment, different Splunk processes will serve different purposes. There are four stages of processing that are generally spread across two to four layers. The stages of processing include:

- **input**: This stage consumes raw data, from log files, ports, or scripts
- **parsing**: This stage splits raw data into events, parses time, sets base metadata, runs transforms, and so on
- **indexing**: This stage stores the data and optimizes indexes
- **searching**: This stage runs queries and presents the results to the user

These different stages can all be accomplished in one process, but splitting them across servers can improve performance as log volumes and search load increase.

Splunk forwarders

Each machine that contains the log files generally runs a Splunk forwarder process. The job of this process is to read logs on that machine or to run scripted inputs. This installation is either:

- A full installation of Splunk, configured to forward data instead of indexing it
- **Splunk Universal Forwarder**, which is essentially Splunk with everything needed for indexing or searching removed

With a full installation of Splunk, the process can be configured as one of two kinds of forwarder:

- A **light forwarder** is configured to not parse events but instead to forward the raw stream of data to indexers. This installation has the advantages that it uses very few resources on the machine running the forwarder (unless the number of files being scanned is very large) and that the configuration is simple. It has the disadvantage that the indexers will do more work. If this is what you need, it is recommended that you use the Splunk Universal Forwarder.

- A **heavy forwarder** is configured to parse events, forwarding these parsed or "cooked" events to the indexers. This has the advantage that the indexer does less work but the disadvantage that more configurations need to be pushed to the forwarders. This configuration also uses approximately double the CPU and memory required for a light forwarder configuration.

For most customers, the Splunk Universal Forwarder is the right answer.

The most important configurations to a forwarder installation are:

- `inputs.conf`: This defines what files to read, network ports to listen to, or scripts to run.

- `outputs.conf`: This defines which indexer(s) should receive the data.

- `props.conf`: As discussed in *Chapter 10, Configuring Splunk*, very little of this configuration is relevant to the input stage, but much of it is relevant to the parse stage. The simplest way to deal with this complexity is to send `props.conf` everywhere so that whatever part of the configuration is needed is available. We will discuss this further in the *Using apps to organize configuration* section in this chapter.

- `default-mode.conf`: This configuration is used to disable processing modules. Most modules are disabled in the case of a light forwarder.

- `limits.conf`: The main setting here is `maxKBps`, which controls how much bandwidth each forwarder will use. The default setting for a light forwarder is very low to prevent flooding the network or overtaxing the forwarding machine. This value can usually be increased safely. It is often increased to the limits of the networking hardware.

We will discuss deploying the forwarder under the *Deploying the Splunk binary* section in this chapter.

Splunk indexer

In most deployments, indexers handle both parsing and indexing of events. If there is only one Splunk indexer, the search is typically handled on this server as well.

An **indexer**, as the name implies, indexes the data. It needs direct access to fast disks, whether they are local disks, SANs, or network volumes.

 In my experience, **NFS** does not work reliably for storing Splunk indexes or files. Splunk expects its disks to act like a local disk, which, at times, NFS does not. It is fine to read logs from NFS. **iSCSI** works very well for indexers, as does **SAN**.

The configurations that typically matter to a Splunk indexer are:

- `inputs.conf`: This configuration typically has exactly one input, `[splunktcp://9997]`. This stanza instructs the indexer to listen for connections from Splunk forwarders on port 9997.
- `indexes.conf`: This configuration specifies where to place indexes and how long to keep data. By default:
    - all data will be written to `$SPLUNK_HOME/var/lib/splunk`
    - the index will grow to a maximum size of 500 gigabytes before dropping the oldest events
    - the index will retain events for a maximum of six years before dropping the oldest events

    Events will be dropped when either limit is reached. We will discuss changing these values under the *Sizing indexers* section.

- `props.conf` and `transforms.conf`: If the indexer handles parsing, these configurations control how the data stream is broken into events, how the date is parsed, and what indexed fields are created, if any.
- `server.conf`: This contains the license server address.

 See the *Sizing indexers* section for a discussion about how many indexers you might need.

Splunk search

When there is only one Splunk server, search happens along with indexing. Until log volumes increase beyond what one server can handle easily, this is fine. In fact, splitting off the search instance might actually hurt performance as there is more overhead involved in running a distributed search.

Most configurations pertaining to search are managed through the web interface. The configuration specifically concerning distributed search is maintained at **Manager | Distributed search**.

Common data sources

Your data may come from a number of sources; these can be files, network ports, or scripts. Let's walk through a few common scenarios.

Monitoring logs on servers

In this scenario, servers write their logs to a local drive, and a forwarder process monitors these logs. This is the typical Splunk installation.

The advantages of this approach include:

- This process is highly optimized. If the indexers are not overworked, events are usually searchable within a few seconds.

- Slowdowns caused by network problems or indexer overload are handled gracefully. The forwarder process will pick up where it left off when the slowdown is resolved.

- The agent is light, typically using less than 100 megabytes of RAM and a few percent of one CPU. These values go up with the amount of new data written and the number of files being tracked. See inputs.conf in *Chapter 10, Configuring Splunk*, for details.

- Logs without a time zone specified will inherit the time zone of the machine running the forwarder. This is almost always what you want.

- The hostname will be picked up automatically from the host. This is almost always what you want.

The disadvantages of this approach include:

- The forwarder must be installed on each server. If you have a system for distributing software already, this is not a problem. We will discuss strategies under the *Deploying the Splunk binary* section.
- The forwarder process must have read rights to all logs to be indexed. This is usually not a problem but does require some planning.

This typical deployment looks like the following figure:

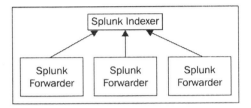

If your log volume exceeds 100 gigabytes of logs produced each day, you need to think about multiple indexers. We will talk about this further in the *Sizing indexers* section.

Monitoring logs on a shared drive

Some customers configure all servers to write their logs to a network share, NFS or otherwise. This setup can be made to work, but it is not ideal.

The advantages of this approach include:

- A forwarder does not need to be installed on each server that is writing its logs to the share.
- Only the Splunk instance reading these logs needs rights to the logs.

The disadvantages of this approach include:

- The network share can become overloaded and can become a bottleneck.
- If a single file has more than a few megabytes of unindexed data, the Splunk process will only read this one log until all data is indexed. If there are multiple indexers in play, only one indexer will be receiving data from this forwarder. In a busy environment, the forwarder may fall behind.
- Multiple Splunk forwarder processes do not share information about what files have been read. This makes it very difficult to manage a failover for each forwarder process without a SAN.

- Splunk relies on the modification time to determine whether the new events have been written to a file. File metadata may not be updated as quickly on a share.

- A large directory structure will cause the Splunk process reading logs to use a lot of RAM and a large percentage of the CPU. A process to move old logs away would be advisable so as to minimize the number of files Splunk must track.

This setup often looks like the following figure:

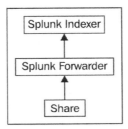

This configuration may look simple, but unfortunately, it does not scale easily.

Consuming logs in batch

Another less common approach is to gather logs periodically from servers after the logs have rolled. This is very similar to monitoring logs on a shared drive, except that the problems of scale are possibly even worse.

The advantages of this approach include:

- A forwarder does not need to be installed on each server that is writing its logs to the share.

The disadvantages of this approach include:

- When new logs are dropped, if the files are large, the Splunk process will only read events from one file at a time. When this directory is on an indexer, this is fine, but when a forwarder is trying to distribute events across multiple indexers, only one indexer will receive events at a time.

- The oldest events in the rolled log will not be loaded until the log is rolled and copied.

- An active log cannot be copied, as events may be truncated during the copy or Splunk may be confused and believe the update file is a new log, indexing the entire file again.

Sometimes this is the only approach possible, and in those cases, you should follow a few rules:

- Only copy complete logs to the watched directory.
- If possible, use `batch` stanzas in `inputs.conf`, instead of `monitor` stanzas, so that Splunk can delete files after indexing them.
- If possible, copy sets of logs to different Splunk servers, either to multiple forwarders that then spread the logs across multiple indexers, or possibly directly to watched directories on the indexers. Be sure to not copy the same log to multiple machines as Splunk has no mechanism for sharing file position information across instances.

Receiving syslog events

Another common source of data is **syslog**, usually from devices that have no filesystem or no support for installing software. These sources are usually devices or appliances, and usually send those events using UDP packets. Syslog management deserves a book of its own, so we will only discuss how to integrate syslog with Splunk at a high level.

Receiving events directly on the Splunk indexer

For very small installations, it may be acceptable to have your Splunk server listen directly for syslog events. This installation looks essentially like the following figure:

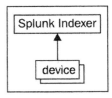

On the Splunk indexer, you would create an input for `syslog`, listening on `udp` or `tcp`. The `inputs.conf` configuration would look like:

```
[udp://514]
sourcetype = syslog
```

The advantage of this approach is its simplicity. The major caveat is that, if the Splunk process is down or busy for some reason, you will lose messages. Reasons for dropped events could include a heavy system load, large queries, a slow disk, network problems, or a system upgrade.

If your syslog events are important to you, it is worth the trouble to at least use a native syslog receiver on the same hardware, but you should ideally use separate hardware.

Using a native syslog receiver

The best practice is to use a standalone syslog receiver to write events to disk. Examples of syslog receivers include **syslog-ng** or **rsyslog**. Splunk is then configured to monitor the directories written by the syslog receiver.

> Ideally, the syslog receiver should be configured to write one file or directory per host. `inputs.conf` can then be configured to use `host_segment` or `host_regex` to set the value of `host`. This configuration has the advantage that `props.conf` stanzas can be applied by `host`, for instance, setting `TZ` by hostname pattern. This is not possible if `host` is parsed out of the log messages, as is commonly the case with syslog.

The advantages of a standalone process include:

- A standalone process has no other tasks to accomplish and is more likely to have the processor time to retrieve events from the kernel buffers before data is pushed out of the buffer
- The interim files act as a buffer so that, in the case of a Splunk slowdown or outage, events are not lost
- The syslog data is on disk, so it can be archived independently or queried with other scripts, as appropriate
- If a file is written for each host, the hostname can be extracted from the path to the file, and different parsing rules (for instance time zone) can be applied at that time

A small installation would look like the following figure:

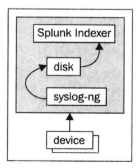

Since the configuration of the native syslog process is simple and unlikely to change, simply using another process on your single Splunk instance will add some level of protection from losing messages. A slow disk, high CPU load, or memory pressure can still cause problems, but you at least won't have to worry about restarting the Splunk process.

The next level of protection would be to use separate hardware to receive the syslog events and to use a Splunk forwarder to send the events to one or more Splunk indexers. That setup looks like the following figure:

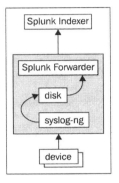

This single machine is still a single point of failure, but it has the advantage that the Splunk server holding the indexes can be restarted at will and will not affect the instance receiving the syslog events.

The next level of protection is to use a load balancer or a dynamic DNS scheme to spread the syslog data across multiple machines receiving the syslog events, which then forward the events to one or more Splunk indexers. That setup looks somewhat like the following figure:

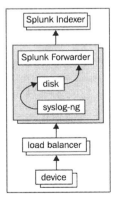

This setup is complicated but very resilient as only a large network failure will cause loss of events.

Receiving syslog with a Splunk forwarder

It is also possible to use Splunk instances to receive the syslog events directly, which then forward the forwarders to Splunk indexers. This setup might look somewhat like the following figure:

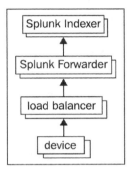

These interim Splunk forwarder processes can be configured with a large input buffer using the `queueSize` and `persistentQueueSize` settings in `inputs.conf`. Note that these interim forwarders cannot be light forwarders. There are a few advantages to this approach that I can think of:

- If these Splunk forwarder processes are in the data center with the device producing the events, the forwarder process will set the time zone of the events. If you have devices in data centers in multiple time zones, this can be very helpful.
- The work of parsing the events will be handled at this stage, offloading some work from the indexers.

One disadvantage is that any parsing rules that are relevant to events parsed by these interim forwarders must be installed at this layer, which may require a restart when there are changes.

Consuming logs from a database

Some applications are built to store their logs in a database. This has the advantage that the logs are centralized, but the disadvantage that it is difficult to scale beyond the limits of the database server. If the logs are pulled into Splunk, it is possible to take advantage of the Splunk interface and correlate these events with other logs.

The process to consume database logs is essentially:

1. Build the query to retrieve the appropriate events; something as follows:

    ```
    select date,id,log from log_table
    ```

2. Identify the field that you will use as your "pointer". This is usually either an ID field or a date field.

3. Modify the query to use this pointer field; use something such as the following code:

    ```
    select date,id,log from log_table where id>4567
    ```

4. Use scripted input to run this query, capture the pointer field, and print the results.

There are a number of applications in a number of languages available at `http://splunkbase.com` to get you started, but you can use any language and any tool you like.

The app I know the best is `jdbc scripted input`, which uses Java and a user-provided jdbc driver. Just to quickly illustrate how it is used, perform the following steps:

1. Ensure Java 1.5 or greater is installed.
2. Download the app.
3. Copy your jdbc driver JAR to `bin/lib`.
4. Duplicate `bin/example` to `bin/myapp`.
5. Modify `bin/myapp/query.properties` to look something like the following code:

    ```
    driverClass=com.mysql.jdbc.Driver
    connectionString=jdbc:mysql://mydb:3306/myapp?user=u&password=p
    iteratorField=id
    query=select date,id,log from entries where id>${id} order by id
    ```

6. Add a matching stanza to `inputs.conf`.

    ```
    [script://./bin/run.sh myapp]
    interval = 60
    sourcetype = myapp
    source = jdbc
    ```

That should be it. `iteratorField` is not needed if your query handles not retrieving duplicate data some other way.

Using scripts to gather data

A scripted input in Splunk is simply a process that outputs text. Splunk will run the script periodically, as configured in `inputs.conf`. Let's make a simple example.

The configuration `inputs.conf` inside your app would contain an entry as follows:

```
[script://./bin/user_count.sh]
interval = 60
sourcetype = user_count
```

The script in `bin/user_count.sh` could contain something as follows:

```
#!/bin/sh
DATE=$(date "+%Y-%m-%d %H:%M:%S")
COUNT=$(wc -l /etc/passwd | awk '{print "users="$1}')
echo $DATE $COUNT
```

This would produce output such as this:

```
2012-10-15 19:57:02 users=84
```

Good examples of this type of script are available in the Unix app available at `splunkbase.com`.

Please note that:

- New to Splunk 4.3: `interval` can be a cron schedule.
- If the name of the script ends in `.py`, Splunk will use its own copy of Python. Remember that there is no Python included with Universal Forwarder.
- Use `props.conf` to control event breaking as if this output was being read from a file.
- Set `DATETIME_CONFIG` to `CURRENT` if there is no date in the output.
- Set an appropriate `BREAK_ONLY_BEFORE` pattern if the events are multiline.
- Set `SHOULD_LINEMERGE` to `False` if the events are not multiline.
- Only one copy of each input stanza will run at a time. If a script should run continually, set `interval` to `-1`.

Sizing indexers

There are a number of factors that affect how many Splunk indexers you will need, but starting with a "model" system with typical usage levels, the short answer is 100 gigabytes of raw logs per day per indexer. In the vast majority of cases, the disk is the performance bottleneck, except in the case of very slow processors.

The measurements mentioned next assume that you will spread events across your indexers evenly, using the autoLB feature of the Splunk forwarder. We will talk more about this under *Indexer load balancing*.

The model system looks like this:

- 8 gigabytes of RAM

  If more memory is available, the operating system will use whatever Splunk does not use for the disk cache.

- Eight fast physical processors

  On a busy indexer, two cores will probably be busy most of the time, handling indexing tasks. It is worth noting the following:

  - More processors won't hurt but will probably not make much of a difference to an indexer as the disks holding indexes will probably not keep up with the increased search load. More indexers, each with its own disks, will have more impact.
  - Virtualized slices of cores or oversubscribed virtual hosts do not work well, as the processor is actually used heavily during search, mostly decompressing raw data.
  - Slow cores designed for highly threaded applications do not work well. For instance, you should avoid older Sun SPARC processors or slices of cores on AIX boxes.

- Disks performing 800 random IOPS (input/output operations per second)

  This is the value considered *fast* by Splunk engineering. Query your favorite search engine for splunk bonnie++ for discussions about how to measure this value. The most important thing to remember when testing your disks is that you must test enough data to defeat disk cache. Remember, if you are using shared disks, that the indexers will share the available IOPS.

- No more than four concurrent searches

  Please note that:

  - Most queries are finished very quickly
  - This count includes interactive queries and saved searches
  - Summary indexes and saved searches can be used to reduce the workload of common queries
  - Summary queries are simply saved searches

To test your concurrency on an existing installation, try this query:

```
index=_audit search_id action=search
    | transaction maxpause=1h search_id
    | concurrency duration=duration
    | timechart span="1h" avg(concurrency)
max(concurrency)
```

A formula for a rough estimate (assuming eight fast processors and 8 gigabytes of RAM per indexer) might look like this:

```
indexers needed =
[your IOPs] / 800 *
[gigs of raw logs produced per day] / 100 *
[average concurrent queries] / 4
```

The behavior of your systems, network, and users make it impossible to reliably predict performance without testing. These numbers are a rough estimate at best.

Let's say you work for a mid-sized company producing about 80 gigabytes of logs per day. You have some very active users, so you might expect four concurrent queries on average. You have good disks, which bonnie++ has shown to pull a sustained 950 IOPS. You are also running some fairly heavy summary indexing queries against your web logs, and you expect at least one to be running pretty much all the time. This gives us the following output:

```
950/800 IOPS *
80/100 gigs *
(1 concurrent summary query + 4 concurrent user queries) / 4
= 1.1875 indexers
```

You cannot really deploy 1.1875 indexers, so your choices are either to start with one indexer and see how it performs or to go ahead and start with two indexers. My advice would be to start with two indexers if at all possible. This gives you some fault tolerance, and installations tend to grow quickly as more data sources are discovered throughout the company. Ideally, when crossing the 100-gigabyte mark, it may make sense to start with three indexers and spread the disks across them. The extra capacity gives you the ability to take one indexer down and still have enough capacity to cover the normal load. See the discussion in the *Planning redundancy* section.

If we increase the number of average concurrent queries, increase the amount of data indexed per day, or decrease our IOPS, the number of indexers needed should scale more or less linearly.

If we scale up a bit more, say 120 gigabytes a day, 5 concurrent queries, and 2 summary queries running on average, we grow as follows:

```
950/800 IOPS *
120/100 gigs *
(2 concurrent summary query + 5 concurrent user queries) / 4
= 2.5 indexers
```

Three indexers would cover this load, but if one indexer is down, we will struggle to keep up with data from forwarders. Ideally, in this case, we should have four or more indexers.

Planning redundancy

The term redundancy can mean different things, depending on your concern. Splunk has features to help with some of these concerns but not others. In a nutshell, up to and including Version 4.3, Splunk is excellent at making sure data is captured but provides essentially no mechanism for reliably replicating data across multiple indexers. Splunk 5, not covered in this book, adds data replication features that can eliminate most of these concerns.

Indexer load balancing

Splunk forwarders are responsible for load balancing across indexers. This is accomplished most simply by providing a list of indexers in outputs.conf, as shown in the following code:

```
[tcpout:nyc]
server=nyc-splunk-index01:9997,nyc-splunk-index02:9997
```

If an indexer is unreachable, the forwarder will simply choose another indexer in the list. This scheme works very well and powers most Splunk deployments.

If the DNS entry returns multiple addresses, Splunk will balance between the addresses on the port specified.

By default, the forwarder will use auto load balancing, specified by autoLB=true. Essentially, the forwarder will switch between indexers on a timer. This is the only option available for the Universal Forwarder and light forwarder.

On a heavy forwarder, the setting autoLB=false will load balance by event. This is less efficient and can cause results to be returned in a non-deterministic manner, since the original event order is not maintained across multiple indexers.

Understanding typical outages

With a single Splunk instance, an outage—perhaps for an operating system upgrade—will cause events to queue on the Splunk forwarder instances. If there are multiple indexers, forwarders will continue to send events to the remaining indexers.

Let's walk through a simplified scenario. Given these four machines, with the forwarders configured to load balance their output across two indexers as shown in the following figure:

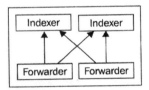

While everything is running, half of the events from each forwarder data will be sent to each indexer. If one indexer is down, we are left with only one indexer as shown in the figure:

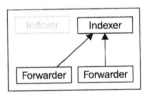

A few things happen in this case:

- All events will be sent to the remaining indexer.
- All events stored on our unavailable indexer will not be included in search results. Splunk 5 can help with this problem, at the cost of extra disks.
- Queries for recent events will work because these events will be stored on the remaining indexer, assuming the one indexer can handle the entire workload.

If our data throughput is more than a single indexer can handle, it will fall behind, which makes us essentially blind to new events until the other indexer comes back and we catch up.

As the size of our deployment increases, we can see that the impact of one indexer outage affects our results less, as shown in the following figure:

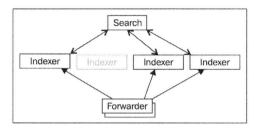

In this case, we have only lost 25 percent of our indexing capacity and have only lost access to 25 percent of our historical data. As long as three indexers can handle our indexing workload, our indexers will not fall behind and we will continue to have timely access to new events. As the number of indexers increases, the impact of one down indexer affects us less.

Working with multiple indexes

An **index** in Splunk is a storage pool for events, capped by size, time, or both. By default, all events will go to the index specified by `defaultDatabase`, which is called `main` but lives in a directory called `defaultdb`.

Directory structure of an index

Each index occupies a set of directories on disk. By default, these directories live in `$SPLUNK_DB`, which, by default, is located in `$SPLUNK_HOME/var/lib/splunk`. Looking at the following stanza for the `main` index:

```
[main]
homePath    = $SPLUNK_DB/defaultdb/db
coldPath    = $SPLUNK_DB/defaultdb/colddb
thawedPath = $SPLUNK_DB/defaultdb/thaweddb
maxHotIdleSecs = 86400
maxHotBuckets = 10
maxDataSize = auto_high_volume
```

If our Splunk installation lives at /opt/splunk, the index main is rooted at the path /opt/splunk/var/lib/splunk/defaultdb.

To change your storage location, either modify the value of SPLUNK_DB in $SPLUNK_HOME/etc/splunk-launch.conf or set absolute paths in indexes.conf.

splunk-launch.conf cannot be controlled from an app, which means it is easy to forget when adding indexers. For this reason, and for legibility, I would recommend using absolute paths in indexes.conf.

The homePath directories contain index-level metadata, hot buckets, and warm buckets. coldPath contains cold buckets, which are simply warm buckets that have aged out. See the upcoming sections *The lifecycle of a bucket* and *Sizing an index* for details.

When to create more indexes

There are several reasons for creating additional indexes. If your needs do not meet one of these requirements, there is no need to create more indexes. In fact, multiple indexes may actually hurt performance if a single query needs to open multiple indexes.

Testing data

If you do not have a test environment, you can use test indexes for staging new data. This then allows you to easily recover from mistakes by dropping the test index. Since Splunk will run on a desktop, it is probably best to test new configurations locally, if possible.

Differing longevity

It may be the case that you need more history for some source types than others. The classic example here is security logs, as compared to web access logs. You may need to keep security logs for a year or more but only need web access logs for a couple of weeks.

If these two source types are left in the same index, security events will be stored in the same buckets as web access logs and will age out together. To split these events up, you need to perform the following steps:

1. Create a new index called security, for instance.
2. Define different settings for the security index.
3. Update inputs.conf to use the new index for security source types.

For one year, you might make an `indexes.conf` setting such as this:

```
[security]
homePath    = $SPLUNK_DB/security/db
coldPath    = $SPLUNK_DB/security/colddb
thawedPath = $SPLUNK_DB/security/thaweddb
#one year in seconds
frozenTimePeriodInSecs = 31536000
```

For extra protection, you should also set `maxTotalDataSizeMB`, and possibly `coldToFrozenDir`.

> If you have multiple indexes that should age together, or if you will split `homePath` and `coldPath` across devices, you should use **volumes**. See the upcoming section, *Using volumes to manage multiple indexes*, for more information.

Then, in `inputs.conf`, you simply need to add `index` to the appropriate stanza as follows:

```
[monitor:///path/to/security/logs/logins.log]
sourcetype=logins
index=security
```

Differing permissions

If some data should only be seen by a specific set of users, the most effective way to limit access is to place this data in a different index and then limit access to that index by using a role. The steps to accomplish this are essentially as follows:

1. Define the new index.
2. Configure `inputs.conf` or `transforms.conf` to send these events to the new index.
3. Ensure the `user` role does *not* have access to the new index.
4. Create a new role that has access to the new index.
5. Add specific users to this new role. If you are using LDAP authentication, you will need to map the role to an LDAP group and add users to that LDAP group.

To route very specific events to this new index, assuming you created an index called `sensitive`, you can create a transform as follows:

```
[contains_password]
REGEX = (?i)password[=:]
DEST_KEY = _MetaData:Index
FORMAT = sensitive
```

You would then wire this transform to a particular `sourcetype` or `source` index in `props.conf`. See *Chapter 10, Configuring Splunk,* for examples.

Using more indexes to increase performance

Placing different source types in different indexes can help increase performance, if those source types are not queried together. The disks will spend less time seeking when accessing the source type in question.

If you have access to multiple storage devices, placing indexes on different devices can help increase performance even more by taking advantage of different hardware for different queries. Likewise, placing `homePath` and `coldPath` on different devices can help performance.

However, if you regularly run queries that use multiple source types, splitting those source types across indexes may actually hurt performance. For example, let's imagine you have two source types called `web_access` and `web_error`. We have the following line in `web_access`:

```
2012-10-19 12:53:20 code=500 session=abcdefg url=/path/to/app
```

And we have the following line in `web_error`:

```
2012-10-19 12:53:20 session=abcdefg class=LoginClass
```

If we want to combine these results, we could run a query like the following:

```
(sourcetype=web_access code=500) OR sourcetype=web_error
  | transaction maxspan=2s session
  | top url class
```

If `web_access` and `web_error` are stored in different indexes, this query will need to access twice as many buckets and will essentially take twice as long.

The lifecycle of a bucket

An index is made up of **buckets**, which go through a specific life cycle. Each bucket contains events from a particular period of time.

As touched on in *Chapter 10, Configuring Splunk*, the stages of this lifecycle are **hot, warm, cold, frozen**, and **thawed**. The only practical difference between hot and other buckets is that a hot bucket is being written to and has not necessarily been optimized. These stages live in different places on disk and are controlled by different settings in `indexes.conf`:

- `homePath` contains as many hot buckets as the integer value of `maxHotBuckets` and as many warm buckets as the integer value of `maxWarmDBCount`. When a hot bucket rolls, it becomes a warm bucket. When there are too many warm buckets, the oldest warm bucket becomes a cold bucket.

 Do not set `maxHotBuckets` too low. If your data is not parsing perfectly, dates that parse incorrectly will produce buckets with very large time spans. As more buckets are created, these buckets will overlap, which means all buckets will have to be queried every time, and performance will suffer dramatically. A value of five or more is safe.

- `coldPath` contains cold buckets, which are warm buckets that have rolled out of `homePath` once there are more warm buckets than the value of `maxWarmDBCount`. If `coldPath` is on the same device, only a move is required; otherwise, a copy is required.

- Once the values of `frozenTimePeriodInSecs`, `maxTotalDataSizeMB`, or `maxVolumeDataSizeMB` are reached, the oldest bucket will be frozen. By default, frozen means *deleted*. You can change this behavior by specifying either:

  - `coldToFrozenDir`: This lets you specify a location to move buckets once they have aged out. The index files will be deleted, and only the compressed raw data will be kept. This essentially cuts disk usage in half. This location is unmanaged, so it is up to you to watch your disk usage.

  - `coldToFrozenScript`: This lets you specify a script to perform some action when the bucket is frozen. The script is handed the path to the bucket about to be frozen.

- `thawedPath` can contain buckets that have been restored. These buckets are not managed by Splunk and are not included in **All time** searches. To search these buckets, their time range must be included explicitly in your search. I have never actually used this directory. Search `http://splunk.com` for `restore archived`, for procedures.

Sizing an index

To determine how much disk space is needed for an index, use the following formula:

```
(gigabytes per day) * .5 * (days of retention desired)
```

Likewise, to determine how many days you can store an index, the formula is essentially:

```
(device size in gigabytes) / ( (gigabytes per day) * .5 )
```

The `.5` represents a conservative compression ratio. The log data itself is usually compressed to 10 percent of its original size. The index files necessary to speed up search brings the size of a bucket closer to 50 percent of the original size, though it is usually smaller than this.

If you plan to split your buckets across devices, the math gets more complicated unless you use volumes. Without using volumes, the math is essentially as follows:

- `homePath = (maxWarmDBCount + maxHotBuckets) * maxDataSize`
- `coldPath = maxTotalDataSizeMB - homePath`

For example, say we are given these settings:

```
[myindex]
homePath = /splunkdata_home/myindex/db
coldPath = /splunkdata_cold/myindex/colddb
thawedPath = /splunkdata_cold/myindex/thaweddb
maxWarmDBCount = 50
maxHotBuckets = 6
maxDataSize = auto_high_volume #10GB on 64-bit systems
maxTotalDataSizeMB = 2000000
```

Filling in the preceding formula, we get these values:

```
homePath = (50 warm + 6 hot) * 10240 MB = 573440 MB
coldPath = 2000000 MB - homePath = 1426560 MB
```

If we use volumes, this gets simpler and we can simply set the volume sizes to our available space and let Splunk do the math.

Using volumes to manage multiple indexes

Volumes combine pools of storage across different indexes so that they age out together. Let's make up a scenario where we have five indexes and three storage devices.

The indexes are as follows:

Name	Data per day	Retention required	Storage needed
web	50 GB	no requirement	?
security	1 GB	2 years	730 GB * 50 percent
app	10 GB	no requirement	?
chat	2 GB	2 years	1,460 GB * 50 percent
web_summary	1 GB	1 years	365 GB * 50 percent

Now let's say we have three storage devices to work with, mentioned in the following table:

Name	Size
small_fast	500 GB
big_fast	1,000 GB
big_slow	5,000 GB

We can create volumes based on the retention time needed. security and chat share the same retention requirements, so we can place them in the same volumes. We want our hot buckets on our fast devices, so let's start there with the following configuration:

```
[volume:two_year_home]
#security and chat home storage
path = /small_fast/two_year_home
maxVolumeDataSizeMB = 300000

[volume:one_year_home]
#web_summary home storage
path = /small_fast/one_year_home
maxVolumeDataSizeMB = 150000
```

For the rest of the space needed by these indexes, we will create companion volume definitions on `big_slow`, thus:

```
[volume:two_year_cold]
#security and chat cold storage
path = /big_slow/two_year_cold
maxVolumeDataSizeMB = 850000  #([security]+[chat])*1024 - 300000

[volume:one_year_cold]
#web_summary cold storage
path = /big_slow/one_year_cold
maxVolumeDataSizeMB = 230000  #[web_summary]*1024 - 150000
```

Now for our remaining indexes, whose timeframe is not important, we will use `big_fast` and the remainder of `big_slow`, thus:

```
[volume:large_home]
#web and app home storage
path = /big_fast/large_home
maxVolumeDataSizeMB = 900000 #leaving 10% for pad

[volume:large_cold]
#web and app cold storage
path = /big_slow/large_cold
maxVolumeDataSizeMB = 3700000
#(big_slow - two_year_cold - one_year_cold)*.9
```

Given the sum of `large_home` and `large_cold` is 4,600,000 MB, and a combined daily volume of approximately `web` and `app` is 60,000 MB, we should retain approximately 153 days of web and app logs with 50 percent compression. In reality, the number of days retained will probably be larger.

With our volumes defined, we now have to reference them in our index definitions:

```
[web]
homePath = volume:large_home/web
coldPath = volume:large_cold/web
thawedPath = /big_slow/thawed/web

[security]
homePath = volume:two_year_home/security
coldPath = volume:two_year_cold/security
thawedPath = /big_slow/thawed/security
```

```
coldToFrozenDir = /big_slow/frozen/security

[app]
homePath = volume:large_home/app
coldPath = volume:large_cold/app
thawedPath = /big_slow/thawed/app

[chat]
homePath = volume:two_year_home/chat
coldPath = volume:two_year_cold/chat
thawedPath = /big_slow/thawed/chat
coldToFrozenDir = /big_slow/frozen/chat

[web_summary]
homePath = volume:one_year_home/web_summary
coldPath = volume:one_year_cold/web_summary
thawedPath = /big_slow/thawed/web_summary
```

 `thawedPath` cannot be defined using a volume and must be specified for Splunk to start.

For extra protection, we specified `coldToFrozenDir` for the indexes `security` and `chat`. The buckets for these indexes will be copied to this directory before deletion, but it is up to us to make sure the disk does not fill up. If we allow the disk to fill up, Splunk will stop indexing until space is made available.

This is just one approach to using volumes. You could overlap in any way that makes sense to you as long as you understand that the oldest bucket in a volume will be frozen first, no matter what index put the bucket in that volume.

Deploying the Splunk binary

Splunk provides binary distributions for Windows and a variety of Unix operating systems. For all Unix operating systems, a compressed tar file is provided. For some platforms, packages are also provided.

If your organization uses packages, such as `deb` or `rpm`, you should be able to use the provided packages in your normal deployment process. Otherwise, installation starts by unpacking the provided tar to the location of your choice.

The process is the same whether you are installing the full version of Splunk or the Splunk Universal Forwarder.

The typical installation process involves the following process:

1. Installing the binary.
2. Adding a base configuration.
3. Configuring Splunk to launch at boot.
4. Restarting Splunk.

 Having worked with many different companies over the years, I can honestly say that none of them used the same product or even methodology for deploying software. Splunk takes a hands-off approach to fit in as easily as possible into customer workflows.

Deploying from a tar file

To deploy from a tar file, the command depends on your version of tar. With a modern version of tar, you can run the following command:

```
tar xvzf splunk-4.3.x-xxx-Linux-xxx.tgz
```

Older versions may not handle gzip files directly, so you may have to run the following command:

```
gunzip -c splunk-4.3.x-xxx-Linux-xxx.tgz | tar xvf -
```

This will expand into the current directory. To expand into a specific directory, you can usually add -C, depending on the version of tar, as follows:

```
tar -C /opt/ -xvzf splunk-4.3.x-xxx-Linux-xxx.tgz
```

Deploying using msiexec

On Windows, it is possible to deploy Splunk using msiexec. This makes it much easier to automate deployment on a large number of machines.

To install silently, you can use the combination of AGREETOLICENSE and /quiet, as follows:

```
msiexec.exe /i splunk-xxx.msi AGREETOLICENSE=Yes /quiet
```

If you plan to use a deployment server, you can specify the following value:

```
msiexec.exe /i splunk-xxx.msi AGREETOLICENSE=Yes
DEPLOYMENT_SERVER="deployment_server_name:8089" /quiet
```

Or, if you plan to overlay an app that contains `deploymentclient.conf`, you can forego starting Splunk until that app has been copied into place, as follows:

```
msiexec.exe /i splunk-xxx.msi AGREETOLICENSE=Yes LAUNCHSPLUNK=0 /quiet
```

There are options available to start reading data immediately, but I would advise deploying input configurations to your servers instead of enabling inputs via installation arguments.

Adding a base configuration

If you are using Splunk's deployment server, this is the time to set up `deploymentclient.conf`. This can be accomplished in several ways as follows:

- On the command line by running the following code:

  ```
  $SPLUNK_HOME/bin/splunk set deploy-poll
  deployment_server_name:8089
  ```

- By placing a `deploymentclient.conf` in `$SPLUNK_HOME/etc/system/local/`

- By placing an app containing `deploymentclient.conf` in `$SPLUNK_HOME/etc/apps/`

The third option is what I would recommend because it allows overriding this configuration via a deployment server at a later time. We will work through an example later in the *Using Splunk deployment server* section.

If you are deploying configurations in some other way, for instance with puppet, be sure to restart the Splunk forwarder processes after deploying the new configuration.

Configuring Splunk to launch at boot

On Windows machines, Splunk is installed as a service that will start after installation and on reboot.

On Unix hosts, the `splunk` command line provides a way to create startup scripts appropriate for the operating system you are using. The command looks like this:

```
$SPLUNK_HOME/bin/splunk enable boot-start
```

To run Splunk as another user, provide the flag `-user`, as follows:

```
$SPLUNK_HOME/bin/splunk enable boot-start -user splunkuser
```

The startup command must still be run as root, but the startup script will be modified to run as the user provided.

 If you do not run Splunk as root, and you shouldn't if you can avoid it, be sure that the Splunk installation and data directories are owned by the user specified in the `enable boot-start` command. You can ensure this by using `chmod`, such as in `chmod -R splunkuser $SPLUNK_HOME`

On Linux, you could then start the command using `service splunk start`.

Using apps to organize configuration

When working with a distributed configuration, there are a number of ways to organize these configurations. The most obvious approach might be to organize configurations by machine type. For instance, put all configurations needed by web servers into one app and all configurations needed by database servers in another app. The problem with this approach is that any changes that affect both types of machines must be made in both apps, and mistakes will most likely be made.

The less fragile but more complicated approach is to normalize your configurations, ensuring that there is only one copy of each configuration spread into multiple apps.

Separate configurations by purpose

Stepping through a typical installation, you would have configuration apps named like the following:

- **inputs-sometype**

  For some logical set of inputs, you would create an app. You could use machine purpose, source type, location, operating system, or whatever makes sense in your situation. Normally, I would expect machine purpose or source type.

- **props-sometype**

  This grouping should correspond to the grouping of the inputs, more or less. You may end up with props apps for more than one type, for instance machine type and location.

- **outputs-datacenter**

  When deploying across data centers, it is common to place Splunk indexers in each data center. In this case, you would need an app per data center.

- **indexerbase**

  Assuming your indexers are configured similarly, it is handy to put all indexer configuration into an app and deploy it like any other app.

   All of these configurations are completely separate from search concerns, which should be stored in separate apps built and maintained through the Splunk web interface.

Let's imagine we have a distributed deployment across two data centers, east and west. Each data center has web servers, app servers, and database servers. In each data center we have two Splunk indexers. The apps for this setup could be as follows:

- inputs-web, inputs-app, and inputs-db
  - inputs.conf specifies the appropriate logs to monitor.
  - Each app should be distributed to each machine that is serving that purpose. If there are some machines that serve more than one purpose, they should receive all appropriate apps.

- props-web, props-app, and props-db
  - props.conf specifies how to parse the logs.
  - transforms.conf is included if there are relevant transforms.
  - Different portions of props.conf are needed at different stages of processing. Since it is difficult to know what stage is happening where, it is generally easiest to distribute these source type props apps everywhere.

- props-west, and props-east
  - Sometimes it is necessary to make configuration changes by location, for instance, configuring time zone on machines that are not set up properly. This can be accomplished by using the TZ setting in props.conf and sending this app to the appropriate data centers.

- outputs-west, and outputs-east
  - These would contain nothing but the outputs.conf configuration for the appropriate data center.

- indexerbase

  ○ Assuming all indexers are configured the same way, this app would contain a standard `indexes.conf` configuration, an `inputs.conf` configuration specifying the `splunktcp` port to listen to connections from Splunk forwarders, and `server.conf` specifying the address of the Splunk license server.

Let's look through an abbreviated listing of all of these files mentioned:

- For forwarders, we will need these apps:

```
inputs-web
  local/inputs.conf
    [monitor:///path/to/web/logs/access*.log]
    sourcetype = web_access
    index = web

    [monitor:///path/to/web/logs/error*.log]
    sourcetype = web_error
    index = web

inputs-app
  local/inputs.conf
    [monitor:///path/to/app1/logs/app*.log]
    sourcetype = app1
    index = app

    [monitor:///path/to/app2/logs/app*.log]
    sourcetype = app2
    index = app

inputs-db
  local/inputs.conf
    [monitor:///path/to/db/logs/error*.log]
    sourcetype = db_error

outputs-west
  local/outputs.conf
    [tcpout:west]
    server=spl-idx-west01.foo.com:9997,spl-idx-west02.foo.com:9997
    #autoLB=true is the default setting

outputs-east
  local/outputs.conf
    [tcpout:east]
    server=spl-idx-east01.foo.com:9997,spl-idx-east02.foo.com:9997
```

- All instances should receive these apps:

```
props-web
  local/props.conf
    [web_access]
    TIME_FORMAT = %Y-%m-%d %H:%M:%S.%3N %:z
    MAX_TIMESTAMP_LOOKAHEAD = 32
    SHOULD_LINEMERGE = False
    TRANSFORMS-squashpassword = squashpassword

    [web_error]
    TIME_FORMAT = %Y-%m-%d %H:%M:%S.%3N %:z
    MAX_TIMESTAMP_LOOKAHEAD = 32
    TRANSFORMS-squashpassword = squashpassword

  local/transforms.conf
    [squashpassword]
    REGEX = (?mi)^(.*)password[=:][^,&]+$
    FORMAT = $1password=########$2
    DEST_KEY = _raw

props-app
  local/props.conf
    [app1]
    TIME_FORMAT = %Y-%m-%d %H:%M:%S.%3N
    MAX_TIMESTAMP_LOOKAHEAD = 25
    BREAK_ONLY_BEFORE = ^\d{4}-\d{1,2}-\d{1,2}\s+\d{1,2}:\d{1,2}

    [app2]
    TIME_FORMAT = %Y-%m-%d %H:%M:%S.%3N
    MAX_TIMESTAMP_LOOKAHEAD = 25
    BREAK_ONLY_BEFORE = ^\d{4}-\d{1,2}-\d{1,2}\s+\d{1,2}:\d{1,2}

props-db
  local/props.conf
    [db_error]
    MAX_TIMESTAMP_LOOKAHEAD = 25

props-west
  local/props.conf
    [db_error]
    TZ = PST

    [web_error]
```

```
        TZ = PST

props-east
  local/props.conf
    [db_error]
    TZ = EST

    [web_error]
    TZ = EST
```

- **Finally, an app specifically for our indexers:**

```
indexerbase
  local/indexes.conf
    [volume:two_year_home]
    path = /small_fast/two_year_home
    maxVolumeDataSizeMB = 300000

    [volume:one_year_home]
    path = /small_fast/one_year_home
    maxVolumeDataSizeMB = 150000

    [volume:two_year_cold]
    path = /big_slow/two_year_cold
    maxVolumeDataSizeMB = 1200000

    [volume:one_year_cold]
    path = /big_slow/one_year_cold
    maxVolumeDataSizeMB = 600000

    [volume:large_home]
    path = /big_fast/large_home
    maxVolumeDataSizeMB = 900000

    [volume:large_cold]
    path = /big_slow/large_cold
    maxVolumeDataSizeMB = 3000000

    [web]
    homePath = volume:large_home/web
    coldPath = volume:large_cold/web
    thawedPath = /big_slow/thawed/web

    [app]
```

```
homePath = volume:large_home/app
coldPath = volume:large_cold/app
thawedPath = /big_slow/thawed/app

[main]
homePath = volume:large_home/main
coldPath = volume:large_cold/main
thawedPath = /big_slow/thawed/main
```

```
local/inputs.conf
  [splunktcp://9997]
```

```
local/server.conf
  [license]
  master_uri = https://spl-license.foo.com:8089
```

This is a minimal set of apps, but it should provide a decent overview of what is involved in configuring a distributed configuration. Next, we will illustrate where these apps should go.

Configuration distribution

As we have covered, in some depth, configurations in Splunk are simply directories of plain text files. Distribution essentially consists of copying these configurations to the appropriate machines and restarting the instances. You can either use your own system for distribution, such as puppet or simply a set of scripts, or use the deployment server included with Splunk.

Using your own deployment system

The advantage of using your own system is that you already know how to use it. Assuming that you have normalized your apps as described in the section *Using apps to organize configuration*, deploying apps to a forwarder or indexer consists of the following steps:

1. Set aside existing apps at `$SPLUNK_HOME/etc/apps/`.
2. Copy apps into `$SPLUNK_HOME/etc/apps/`.
3. Restart Splunk forwarder. Note that this needs to be done as the user that is running Splunk, either by calling the service script or calling `su`. On Windows, restart the `splunkd` service.

Assuming you already have a system for managing configurations, that's it.

If you are deploying configurations to indexers, be sure to only deploy configurations when downtime is acceptable, as you will need to restart the indexers to load the new configurations, ideally in a rolling manner. Do not deploy configurations until you are ready to restart as some (but not all) configurations will take effect immediately.

Using Splunk deployment server

If you do not have a system for managing configurations, you can use the deployment server included with Splunk.

Some advantages of the included deployment server are as follows:

- Everything you need is included in your Splunk installation
- It will restart forwarder instances properly when new app versions are deployed
- It is intelligent enough to not restart when unnecessary
- It will remove apps that should no longer be installed on a machine
- It will ignore apps that are not managed
- The logs for the deployment client and server are accessible in Splunk itself

Some disadvantages of the included deployment server are:

- As of Splunk 4.3, there are issues with scale beyond a few hundred deployment clients, at which point tuning is required
- The configuration is complicated and prone to typos

With these caveats out of the way, let's set up a deployment server for the apps we laid out before.

Step 1 – Deciding where your deployment server will run

For a small installation with less than a few dozen forwarders, your main Splunk instance can run the deployment server without issue. For more than a few dozen forwarders, a separate instance of Splunk makes sense.

Ideally, this instance would run on its own machine. The requirements for this machine are not large, perhaps 4 gigabytes of RAM and two processors, or possibly less. A VM would be fine.

Define a DNS entry for your deployment server, if at all possible. This will make moving your deployment server later much simpler.

If you do not have access to another machine, you could run another copy of Splunk on the same machine running some other part of your Splunk deployment. To accomplish this, follow these steps:

1. Install Splunk in another directory, perhaps /opt/splunk-deploy/splunk/.

2. Start this instance of Splunk by using /opt/splunk-deploy/splunk/bin/ splunk start. When prompted, choose different port numbers apart from the default and note what they are. I would suggest one number higher: 8090 and 8001.

3. Unfortunately, if you run splunk enable boot-start in this new instance, the existing startup script will be overwritten. To accommodate both instances, you will need to either edit the existing startup script, or rename the existing script so that it is not overwritten.

Step 2 – Defining your deploymentclient.conf configuration

Using the address of our new deployment server, ideally a DNS entry, we will build an app named deploymentclient-yourcompanyname. This app will have to be installed manually on forwarders but can then be managed by the deployment server.

This app should look somewhat like this:

```
deploymentclient-yourcompanyname
  local/deploymentclient.conf
    [deployment-client]

    [target-broker:deploymentServer]
    targetUri=deploymentserver.foo.com:8089
```

Step 3 – Defining our machine types and locations

Starting with what we defined under the *Separate configurations by purpose* section, we have, in the locations west and east, the following machine types:

* Splunk indexers
* db servers
* web servers
* app servers

Step 4 – Normalizing our configurations into apps appropriately

Let's use the apps we defined under the section *Separate configurations by purpose* plus the deployment client app we created in the section *Step 2 – Defining your deploymentclient.conf configuration*. These apps will live in `$SPLUNK_HOME/etc/deployment-apps/` on your deployment server.

Step 5 – Mapping these apps to deployment clients in serverclass.conf

To get started, I always start with `Example 2` from `$SPLUNK_HOME/etc/system/README/serverclass.conf.example`:

```
[global]

[serverClass:AppsForOps]
whitelist.0=*.ops.yourcompany.com
[serverClass:AppsForOps:app:unix]
[serverClass:AppsForOps:app:SplunkLightForwarder]
```

Let's assume we have the machines mentioned next. It is very rare for an organization of any size to have consistently named hosts, so I threw in a couple of rogue hosts at the bottom, as follows:

```
spl-idx-west01
spl-idx-west02
spl-idx-east01
spl-idx-east02
app-east01
app-east02
app-west01
app-west02
web-east01
web-east02
web-west01
web-west02
db-east01
db-east02
db-west01
db-west02
qa01
homer-simpson
```

The structure of `serverclass.conf` is essentially as follows:

```
[serverClass:<className>]
#options that should be applied to all apps in this class

[serverClass:<className>:app:<appName>]
#options that should be applied only to this app in this serverclass
```

Please note that:

- `<className>` is an arbitrary name of your choosing.
- `<appName>` is the name of a directory in `$SPLUNK_HOME/etc/deployment-apps/`.
- The order of stanzas does not matter. Be sure to update `<className>` if you copy an `:app:` stanza. This is by far the easiest mistake to make.

 It is important that configuration changes do not trigger a restart of indexers.

Let's apply this to our hosts, as follows:

```
[global]
restartSplunkd = True
#by default trigger a splunk restart on configuration change


####INDEXERS
##handle indexers specially, making sure they do not restart
[serverClass:indexers]
whitelist.0=spl-idx-*
restartSplunkd = False
[serverClass:indexers:app:indexerbase]
[serverClass:indexers:app:deploymentclient-yourcompanyname]
[serverClass:indexers:app:props-web]
[serverClass:indexers:app:props-app]
[serverClass:indexers:app:props-db]

#send props-west only to west indexers
[serverClass:indexers-west]
whitelist.0=spl-idx-west*
restartSplunkd = False
[serverClass:indexers-west:app:props-west]

#send props-east only to east indexers
```

```
[serverClass:indexers-east]
whitelist.0=spl-idx-east*
restartSplunkd = False
[serverClass:indexers-east:app:props-east]



####FORWARDERS
#send event parsing props apps everywhere
#blacklist indexers to prevent unintended restart
[serverClass:props]
whitelist.0=*
blacklist.0=spl-idx-*
[serverClass:props:app:props-web]
[serverClass:props:app:props-app]
[serverClass:props:app:props-db]

#send props-west only to west datacenter servers
#blacklist indexers to prevent unintended restart
[serverClass:west]
whitelist.0=*-west*
whitelist.1=qa01
blacklist.0=spl-idx-*
[serverClass:west:app:props-west]
[serverClass:west:app:deploymentclient-yourcompanyname]

#send props-east only to east datacenter servers
#blacklist indexers to prevent unintended restart
[serverClass:east]
whitelist.0=*-east*
whitelist.1=homer-simpson
blacklist.0=spl-idx-*
[serverClass:east:app:props-east]
[serverClass:east:app:deploymentclient-yourcompanyname]

#define our appserver inputs
[serverClass:appservers]
whitelist.0=app-*
whitelist.1=qa01
whitelist.2=homer-simpson
[serverClass:appservers:app:inputs-app]

#define our webserver inputs
[serverClass:webservers]
```

```
whitelist.0=web-*
whitelist.1=qa01
whitelist.2=homer-simpson
[serverClass:webservers:app:inputs-web]

#define our dbserver inputs
[serverClass:dbservers]
whitelist.0=db-*
whitelist.1=qa01
[serverClass:dbservers:app:inputs-db]

#define our west coast forwarders
[serverClass:fwd-west]
whitelist.0=app-west*
whitelist.1=web-west*
whitelist.2=db-west*
whitelist.3=qa01
[serverClass:fwd-west:app:outputs-west]

#define our east coast forwarders
[serverClass:fwd-east]
whitelist.0=app-east*
whitelist.1=web-east*
whitelist.2=db-east*
whitelist.3=homer-simpson
[serverClass:fwd-east:app:outputs-east]
```

You should organize the patterns and classes in a way that makes sense to your organization and data centers, but I would encourage you to keep it as simple as possible. I would strongly suggest opting for more lines than more complicated logic.

A few more things to note about the format of `serverclass.conf`:

- The number following whitelist and blacklist *must be sequential*, starting with zero. For instance, in the following example, `whitelist.3` will not be processed, since `whitelist.2` is commented:

```
[serverClass:foo]
whitelist.0=a*
whitelist.1=b*
# whitelist.2=c*
whitelist.3=d*
```

- whitelist.x and blacklist.x are tested against these values in the following order:
    - ° clientName as defined in deploymentclient.conf: This is not commonly used but is useful when running multiple Splunk instances on the same machine or when DNS is completely unreliable.
    - ° IP address: There is no CIDR matching, but you can use string patterns.
    - ° Reverse DNS: This is the value returned by DNS for an IP address. If your reverse DNS is not up to date, this can cause you problems, as this value is tested before the value of hostname, as provided by the host itself. If you suspect this, try ping <ip of machine> or something similar to see what the DNS is reporting.
    - ° Hostname as provided by forwarder: This is always tested after reverse DNS, so be sure your reverse DNS is up to date.

- When copying :app: lines, be very careful to update the <className> appropriately! This really is the most common mistake made in serverclass.conf.

Step 6 – Restarting the deployment server

If serverclass.conf did not exist, a restart of the Splunk instance running deployment server is required to activate the deployment server. After the deployment server is loaded, you can use the following command:

```
$SPLUNK_HOME/bin/splunk reload deploy-server
```

This command should be enough to pick up any changes to serverclass.conf and any changes in etc/deployment-apps.

Step 7 – Installing deploymentclient.conf

Now that we have a running deployment server, we need to set up the clients to call home. On each machine that will be running the deployment client, the procedure is essentially as follows:

1. Copy the deploymentclient-yourcompanyname app to $SPLUNK_HOME/etc/apps/.
2. Restart Splunk.

If everything is configured correctly you should see the appropriate apps appear in `$SPLUNK_HOME/etc/apps/`, within a few minutes. To see what is happening, look at the log `$SPLUNK_HOME/var/log/splunk/splunkd.log`.

If you have problems, enable debugging on either the client or the server by editing `$SPLUNK_HOME/etc/log.cfg`, followed by a restart. Look for the following lines:

```
category.DeploymentServer=WARN
category.DeploymentClient=WARN
```

Once found, change them to the following lines and restart Splunk:

```
category.DeploymentServer=DEBUG
category.DeploymentClient=DEBUG
```

After restarting Splunk, you will see the complete conversation in `$SPLUNK_HOME/var/log/splunk/splunkd.log`. Be sure to change the setting back once you no longer need the verbose logging!

Using LDAP for authentication

By default, Splunk authenticates using its own authentication system, which simply stores users and roles in flat files. The other two options available are LDAP and scripted authentication.

To enable LDAP authentication, perform the following steps:

1. Navigate to **Manager** | **Access controls** | **Authentication method**.
2. Check the **LDAP** checkbox.
3. Click on **Configure Splunk to use LDAP and map groups**.
4. Click on **New**.

You will then need the appropriate values to set up access to your LDAP server. Every organization sets up LDAP slightly differently, so I have never managed to configure this properly the first time. Your best bet is to copy the values from another application already configured in your organization.

Once LDAP is configured properly, you can map Splunk roles to LDAP groups through the admin interface. Whether to use an existing group or create Splunk-specific groups is of course up to your organization, but most companies I have worked with opted to create a specific group for each Splunk role. The common groups are often along the lines of: `splunkuser`, `splunkpoweruser`, `splunksecurity`, and `splunkadmin`. Rights are additive, so a user can be a member of as many groups as is appropriate.

New in Splunk 4.3 are the ability to use multiple LDAP servers at once, support for dynamic groups, support for nested groups, and more. The official documentation can be found at the following URL:

```
http://docs.splunk.com/Documentation/Splunk/latest/Security/
SetUpUserAuthenticationWithLDAP
```

Using Single Sign On

Single Sign On (SSO) lets you use some other web server to handle authentication for Splunk. For this to work, several assumptions are made, as follows:

- Your SSO system can act as an HTTP forwarding proxy, sending HTTP requests through to Splunk.
- Your SSO system can place the authenticated user's ID into an HTTP header.
- The IP of your server(s) forwarding requests is static.
- When given a particular username, Splunk will be able to determine what roles this user is a part of. This is usually accomplished using LDAP but could be accomplished by defining users directly through the Splunk UI or via a custom scripted authentication plugin.

Assuming all of these are true, the usual approach is to follow these steps:

1. Configure LDAP authentication in Splunk.
2. Configure your web server to send proxy requests through to Splunk: When this is configured properly, you should be able to use Splunk as if you were accessing the Splunk web application directly.
3. Configure your web server to authenticate: With this configured, your web server should ask for authentication, and you should still be asked for authentication by Splunk.
4. Look for the HTTP header containing the remote user: Proxying through your web server, change the URL to `http://yourproxyserver/debug/sso`. You should see your username under **Remote user HTTP header** or **Other HTTP headers**.
5. Configure SSO in `$SPLUNK_HOME/etc/system/local/web.conf`: You need to add three attributes to the `[settings]` stanza, as shown in the following code:

```
[settings]
SSOMode = strict
remoteUser = REMOTE-USER
trustedIP = 192.168.1.1,192.168.1.2
```

That should be it. The hardest part is usually convincing the web server to both authenticate and proxy. Use the /debug/sso page to help diagnose what is happening.

There can also be issues with punctuation in the header fieldname. If it's possible, removing any punctuation in the header name may eliminate unexpected problems.

Load balancers and Splunk

Some organizations that have invested heavily in load balancers like to use them whenever possible to centralize network management. There are three services Splunk typically exposes, mentioned in the following sections:

web

Usually on port 8000, the Splunk web server can be load balanced when configured with **search head pooling**. The load balancer should be configured to be "sticky", as the web server will still rely on user sessions tied to the web server the user started on.

See the *Multiple search heads* section for more information.

splunktcp

Usually on port 9997, splunktcp is itself stateless. Splunk auto load balancing is very well tested and very efficient but does not support complicated logic. For instance, you could use a load balancer to prefer connections to indexers in the same data center, only using indexers in another data center as a last resort.

The problem is that when only one address is provided to a Splunk forwarder, the forwarder will open one connection and keep it open indefinitely. This means that when an indexer is restarted, it will never receive a connection until forwarders are restarted.

The easy solution is to expose two addresses on your load balancer and list both of these addresses in outputs.conf. The two addresses must be either two different ports or two different IP addresses. Two different CNAMEs on the same port will not work, as Splunk resolves the addresses and collapses the list of IP addresses.

deployment server

Usually on port 8089, the deployment server listens using SSL, by default, with a self-signed certificate. There are a couple of problems with using a load balancer with the deployment server; they are as follows:

- The protocol is essentially REST over HTTP, but not quite. Use a TCP load balancer, not a load balancer that understands HTTP.

- While it is theoretically possible to load balance deployment servers, the issue is that, if the different deployment servers are out of sync, deployment clients may "flap", loading one set of apps and then the other. A better approach is probably running multiple deployment servers and using DNS or load balancers to ensure that certain sets of hosts always talk to a particular server.

Multiple search heads

Using the **search head pooling** feature, it is possible to run multiple **search head** instances. The feature requires a share of some sort behind the servers acting as search heads, which effectively means they must be in the same data center. The setup looks essentially like the following figure:

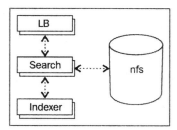

In short, the steps to configure the search are as follows:

1. Mount the NFS volume on each search head.
2. Enable the pooling feature on each instance.
3. Copy the existing configurations to the NFS volume.
4. Test the search heads.
5. Enable the load balancer.

The official documentation is available at `http://docs.splunk.com/Documentation/Splunk/latest/Deploy/Configuresearchheadpooling`.

Summary

We have touched upon a wide variety of subjects in this chapter, each of which possibly deserves a chapter of its own. Maybe that will be the next book.

We talked about the different purposes of Splunk instances, how to collect data from a variety of sources, how to install the Splunk binary, how to size your indexers, and how to manage the configuration of many instances, and finally, we touched upon a few advanced deployment topics.

In our final chapter, we will write some code to extend Splunk in a variety of ways.

12
Extending Splunk

While the core of Splunk is closed, there are a number of places where you can use scripts or external code to extend the default behaviors. In this chapter, we will write a number of examples, covering most of the places where external code can be added. Most code samples are written in Python, so if you are not familiar with Python, a reference may be useful.

We will cover:

- Writing scripts to create events
- Using Splunk from the command line
- Calling Splunk via REST
- Writing custom search commands
- Writing event type renderers
- Writing custom search action scripts

The examples used in this chapter are included in the app `ImplementingSplunkExtendingExamples`, which can be downloaded from the support page of the Packt Publishing website (`www.packtpub.com/support`).

Writing a scripted input to gather data

Scripted inputs allow you to run some piece of code on a scheduled basis, and capture the output as if it were simply being written to a file. It does not matter what language the script is written in, or where it lives, as long it is executable. We touched on this topic in the *Using scripts to gather data* section in *Chapter 11, Advanced Deployments*. Let's write a few more examples.

Capturing script output with no date

One common problem with script output is the lack of a predictable date or date format. In this situation, the easiest thing to do is to tell Splunk to not try to parse a date at all, and instead use the current date instead. Let's make a script that lists open network connections:

```python
from subprocess import Popen
from subprocess import PIPE
from collections import defaultdict
import re


def add_to_key(fieldname, fields):
    return " " + fieldname + "+" + fields[fieldname]

output = Popen("netstat -n -p tcp", stdout=PIPE,
               shell=True).stdout.read()

counts = defaultdict(int)
for l in output.splitlines():
    if "ESTABLISHED" in l:
        pattern = r"(?P<protocol>\S+)\s+\d+\s+\d+\s+"
        pattern += r"(?P<local_addr>.*?)[^\d](?P<local_port>\d+)\s+"
        pattern += r"(?P<remote_addr>.*)[^\d](?P<remote_port>\d+)"
        m = re.match(pattern, l)
        fields = m.groupdict()

        if "local_port" in fields and "remote_port" in fields:
            if fields["local_addr"] == fields["remote_addr"]:
                continue
            try:
                if int(fields["local_port"]) < 1024:
                    key = "type=incoming"
                    key += add_to_key("local_addr", fields)
                    key += add_to_key("local_port", fields)
                    key += add_to_key("remote_addr", fields)
                else:
                    key = "type=outgoing"
                    key += add_to_key("remote_addr", fields)
                    key += add_to_key("remote_port", fields)
                    key += add_to_key("local_addr", fields)
            except:
                print "Unexpected error:", sys.exc_info()[0]

            counts[key] += 1

for k, v in sorted(counts.items()):
    print k + " count=" + str(v)
```

Before we wire this up, we can test the command using the Python interpreter included with Splunk as follows:

```
$SPLUNK_HOME/bin/splunk cmd python connections.py
```

> If you are using any Splunk Python modules, you must use Python included with Splunk, as other Python installations will not find these modules.

On my machine, this produces:

```
type=outgoing remote_addr=17.149.36.120 remote_port=5223
  local_addr=192.168.0.20 count=1
type=outgoing remote_addr=17.158.10.104 remote_port=443
  local_addr=192.168.0.20 count=2
type=outgoing remote_addr=17.158.10.42 remote_port=443
  local_addr=192.168.0.20 count=5
type=outgoing remote_addr=17.158.8.23 remote_port=993
  local_addr=192.168.0.20 count=4
type=outgoing remote_addr=173.194.64.109 remote_port=993
  local_addr=192.168.0.20 count=8
type=outgoing remote_addr=199.47.216.173 remote_port=443
  local_addr=192.168.0.20 count=1
type=outgoing remote_addr=199.47.217.178 remote_port=443
  local_addr=192.168.0.20 count=1
type=outgoing remote_addr=50.18.31.239 remote_port=443
  local_addr=192.168.0.20 count=1
```

Now that we have a working script, we need two pieces of configuration, namely `inputs.conf` and `props.conf`. As we covered in *Chapter 11, Advanced Deployments*, you will want to place these configurations in different apps if you are going to distribute this input across a distributed environment.

`inputs.conf` should contain something like the following code:

```
[script://./bin/connections.py]
interval=60
sourcetype=connections
```

> If the script ends in `.py`, Splunk will automatically use the included Python interpreter. Otherwise, the script needs to be executable via the command line.
>
> If you want to use a different Python executable, you will need to specify the full path to Python as the script, and the script itself as an argument.

`props.conf` should then contain something as follows:

```
[connections]
SHOULD_LINEMERGE = false
DATETIME_CONFIG = CURRENT
```

This configuration requires each line to be treated as an event and to not even try to find something that looks like a date in this event.

Let's build a query using the output of this scripted input. A useful query might be ports open by domain name. This query uses `dnslookup` and then flattens `remote_host` to either a domain name or subnet:

```
index=implsplunk sourcetype=connections
   | fillnull value="-" remote_addr remote_port local_addr local_port
   | dedup remote_addr remote_port local_addr local_port
   | lookup dnslookup clientip as remote_addr
   | rex field=clienthost ".*\.(?<domain>[^\.]+\.[^\.]+)"
   | eval remote_host=coalesce(domain,remote_addr)
   | eval remote_host=replace(remote_host,"(.*)\.\d+$","\1.0")
   | stats sum(count) as count values(remote_port) as remote_ports
     by remote_host local_addr local_port
   | eval remote_ports=mvjoin(remote_ports, ", ")
```

On my laptop, I get the following results:

remote_host ‡	local_addr ‡	local_port ‡	count ‡	remote_ports ‡
138.108.7.0	172.16.14.25	-	2	80
172.16.14.0	172.16.14.25	-	8	55686, 55692, 55696, 61384, 61787, 61788, 61809, 62078
198.171.79.0	172.16.14.25	-	1	80
1e100.net	172.16.14.25	-	34	443, 80
206.33.35.0	172.16.14.25	-	1	1935
208.85.243.0	172.16.14.25	-	2	443, 80
209.170.117.0	172.16.14.25	-	3	80
akamaitechnologies.com	172.16.14.25	-	5	80
amazonaws.com	172.16.14.25	-	6	443
apple.com	172.16.14.25	-	1	5223

Capturing script output as a single event

When you want to capture the entire output of a script as a single event, the trick is to specify an impossible value for `LINE_BREAKER`. Let's write a shell script to output the different parts of `uname` with nice field names.

You can find the following script at
`ImplementingSplunkExtendingExamples/bin/uname.sh`:

```sh
#!/bin/sh

date "+%Y-%m-%d %H:%M:%S"
echo hardware=\"$(uname -m)\"
echo node=\"$(uname -n)\"
echo proc=\"$(uname -p)\"
echo os_release=\"$(uname -r)\"
echo os_name=\"$(uname -s)\"
echo os_version=\"$(uname -v)\"
```

This script produces output like the following code:

```
2012-10-30 19:28:05
hardware="x86_64"
node="mymachine.local"
proc="i386"
os_release="12.2.0"
os_name="Darwin"
os_version="Darwin Kernel Version 12.2.0: Sat Aug 25 00:48:52 PDT
2012; root:xnu-2050.18.24~1/RELEASE_X86_64"
```

You may notice that the last line definitely contains a date. Unless we specifically tell Splunk that the entire output is an event in one way or another, it will turn that last line into an event.

`inputs.conf` should contain something as follows:

```
[script://./bin/uname.sh]
interval = 0 0 * * *
sourcetype=uname
```

Notice the cron syntax for `interval`. This will run the script each day at midnight. An alternative would be to set the value to `86400`, which would run the script each time Splunk starts, and then every 24 hours thereafter.

`props.conf` should then contain something like the following:

```
[uname]
TIME_FORMAT = %Y-%m-%d %H:%M:%S
#treat each "line" as an event:
SHOULD_LINEMERGE = false
#redefine the beginning of a line to an impossible match,
#thus treating all data as one "line":
LINE_BREAKER = ((?!))
#chop the "line" at one megabyte, just in case:
TRUNCATE=1048576
```

Once installed, you can search for these events using `sourcetype=uname`, which produces output similar to the following screenshot:

```
1   11/10/12        2012-11-10 11:24:02
    11:24:02.000 AM hardware="x86_64"
                    node="vibmba.local"
                    proc="i386"
                    os_release="12.2.0"
                    os_name="Darwin"
                    os_version="Darwin Kernel Version 12.2.0: Sat Aug 25 00:48:52 PDT 2012; root:xnu-2050.18.24~1/RELEASE_X86_64"
```

Because we used the `fieldname="fieldvalue"` syntax and we quoted values with spaces and strange characters, these field values will be automatically extracted. We can then use these fields immediately for reporting. A useful query might be:

```
earliest=-24h sourcetype=uname
    | eventstats count by os_release os_name
    | search count<10
```

This query would find the rare `os_release os_name` combinations.

Making a long-running scripted input

Sometimes a process needs to be long running, for instance, if it is polling some external source, like a database. A simple example might be:

```
import time
import random
import sys

for i in range(1, 1000):
    print "%s Hello." % time.strftime('%Y-%m-%dT%H:%M:%S')
    #make sure python actually sends the output
    sys.stdout.flush()
    time.sleep(random.randint(1, 5))
```

This script will run for somewhere between 1,000 and 5,000 seconds and then exit. Since this is a long-running script, our choices are either to treat each line as an event as we did in the *Capturing script output with no date* section, or, if we know there is a date to use, configure the input like a regular log file. In this case, we can see that there is always a date, so we will rely on that. The output is, unsurprisingly, as follows:

```
2012-10-30T20:13:29 Hello.
2012-10-30T20:13:33 Hello.
2012-10-30T20:13:36 Hello.
```

`inputs.conf` should contain something similar to the following:

```
[script://./bin/long_running.py]
interval = 1
sourcetype=long_running
```

With `interval = 1`, Splunk will try to launch the script every second, but will only run one copy of the script at a time.

`props.conf` should then contain something like:

```
[long_running]
TIME_FORMAT = %Y-%m-%dT%H:%M:%S
MAX_TIMESTAMP_LOOKAHEAD = 21
BREAK_ONLY_BEFORE = ^\d{4}-\d{1,2}-\d{1,2}T\d{1,2}:
```

This will create a long-running process that can do whatever is appropriate.

> Though it is convenient to have Splunk execute scripts for you and capture the output, if the information you are capturing is vital, it may be safer to simply schedule the script with cron, direct its output to a file, and point Splunk at that file. This allows you to use the file in other ways; you can capture both standard output and errors, and the data will still be captured if Splunk is down. It, however, has the disadvantage that you have to clean up those logs yourself.

Using Splunk from the command line

Almost everything that can be done via the web interface can also be accomplished via the command line. For an overview, see the output of `/opt/splunk/bin/splunk help`. For help on a specific command, use `/opt/splunk/bin/splunk help [commandname]`.

The most common action to perform on the command line is search. For example, have a look at the following code:

```
$ /opt/splunk/bin/splunk search 'foo'
2012-08-25T20:17:54 user=user2 GET /foo?q=7148356 uid=MzA4MTc5OA
2012-08-25T20:17:54 user=user2 GET /foo?q=7148356 uid=MzA4MTc5OA
2012-08-25T20:17:54 user=user2 GET /foo?q=7148356 uid=MzA4MTc5OA
...
```

Things to note:

- By default, searches are performed over All time. Protect yourself by including `earliest=-1d` or an appropriate time range in your query.
- By default, Splunk will only output 100 lines of results. If you need more, use the `-maxout` flag.
- Search requires authentication, so the user will be asked to authenticate unless `-auth` is included as an argument.

Most use cases for the command line involve counting events for outputting to other systems. Let's try a simple `stats` call to count instances of the word `error` over the last hour by host:

```
$ /opt/splunk/bin/splunk search 'earliest=-1h error | stats count by
host'
```

This produces:

```
     host       count
------------    -----
host2            3114
vlb.local        3063
```

Things to notice in this case are:

- `earliest=-1h` is included to limit the query to the last hour.
- By default, the output is in a `table` format. This is nicer to read, but much harder to parse in another scripting language. Use `-output` to control the output format.
- By default, Splunk will render a preview of the results as results are retrieved. This slows down the overall execution. Disable preview with `-preview false`. Previews are not calculated when the script is not being called from an interactive terminal, for instance, when run from cron.

To retrieve the output as CSV, try the following code:

```
$ /opt/splunk/bin/splunk search 'earliest=-1h error | stats count by
host' -output csv -preview false
```

This gives us the following output:

```
count,host
3120,host2
3078,"vlb.local"
```

Note that if there are no results, the output will be empty.

Querying Splunk via REST

Splunk provides an extensive HTTP REST interface, which allows searching, adding data, adding inputs, managing users, and more. Documentation and SDKs are provided by Splunk at `http://dev.splunk.com/`.

To get an idea of how this REST interaction happens, let's step through a sample conversation to run a query and retrieve the results. The steps are essentially as follows:

1. Start the query (POST).
2. Poll for status (GET).
3. Retrieve results (GET).

We will use the command line program **cURL** to illustrate these steps. The SDKs make this interaction much simpler.

To start a query, the command is as follows:

```
curl -u user:pass -k https://yourserver:8089/services/search/jobs
  -d"search=search query"
```

This essentially says to POST `search=search query`. If you are familiar with HTTP, you might notice that this is a standard POST from an HTML form.

To run the query `earliest=-1h index="_internal" warn | stats count by host`, we need to URL encode the query. The command then is as follows:

```
$ curl -u admin:changeme -k https://localhost:8089/services/search/
jobs -d"search=search%20earliest%3D-1h%20index%3D%22_internal%22%20
warn%20%7C%20stats%20count%20by%20host"
```

If the query is accepted, we will receive XML that contains our search ID:

```
<?xml version='1.0' encoding='UTF-8'?>
<response><sid>1352061658.136</sid></response>
```

The contents of `<sid>` are then used to reference this job. To check the status of our job, we run the following code:

```
curl -u admin:changeme -k https://localhost:8089/services/search/
jobs/1352061658.136
```

This returns a large document with copious amounts of information about our job as follows:

```
<entry ...>
  <title>search earliest=-1h index="_internal" warn | stats count by
host</title>
```

```
   <id>https://localhost:8089/services/search/jobs/1352061658.136</id>
. . .
   <link href="/services/search/jobs/1352061658.136/events"
rel="events"/>
   <link href="/services/search/jobs/1352061658.136/results"
rel="results"/>
. . .
   <content type="text/xml">
     <s:dict>
. . .
       <s:key name="doneProgress">1.00000</s:key>
. . .
       <s:key name="eventCount">67</s:key>
. . .
       <s:key name="isDone">1</s:key>
. . .
       <s:key name="resultCount">1</s:key>
```

Interesting fields include `doneProgress`, `eventCount`, `resultCount`, and the field we are most interested in at this point, `isDone`. If `isDone` is not 1, we should wait and poll again later. Once `isDone=1`, we can retrieve our results from the URL specified in `<link rel="results">`.

To retrieve our results, we call the following:

```
curl -u admin:changeme -k https://localhost:8089/services/search/
jobs/1352061658.136/results
```

This returns the following XML output:

```
<?xml version='1.0' encoding='UTF-8'?>
<results preview='0'>
  <meta>
    <fieldOrder>
      <field>host</field>
      <field>count</field>
    </fieldOrder>
  </meta>
  <result offset='0'>
    <field k='host'>
      <value><text>vlb.local</text></value>
    </field>
    <field k='count'>
      <value><text>67</text></value>
    </field>
  </result>
</results>
```

The list of fields is contained in `meta/fieldOrder`. Each result will then follow this field order.

Though not necessary (since jobs expire on their own) we can save disk space on our Splunk servers by cleaning up after ourselves. Simply calling the DELETE method on the job URL will delete the results and reclaim the used disk space.

```
curl -u admin:changeme -k -X DELETE https://localhost:8089/services/
search/jobs/1352061658.136
```

Just to show the Python API action, here's a simple script:

```
import splunk.search as search
import splunk.auth as auth
import sys
import time

username = sys.argv[1]
password = sys.argv[2]
q = sys.argv[3]

sk = auth.getSessionKey(username, password)

job = search.dispatch("search " + q, sessionKey=sk)

while not job.isDone:
    print "Job is still running."
    time.sleep(.5)

for r in job.results:
    for f in r.keys():
        print "%s=%s" % (f, r[f])
    print "----------"

job.cancel()
```

This script uses the Python modules included with Splunk, so we must run it using Splunk's included Python as follows:

```
$ /opt/splunk/bin/splunk cmd python simplesearch.py admin changeme
'earliest=-7d index="_internal" warn | timechart count by source'
```

This produces output as follows:

```
_time=2012-10-31T00:00:00-0500
/opt/splunk/var/log/splunk/btool.log=0
/opt/splunk/var/log/splunk/searches.log=0
```

```
/opt/splunk/var/log/splunk/splunkd.log=31
/opt/splunk/var/log/splunk/web_service.log=0
_span=86400
_spandays=1
----------
_time=2012-11-01T00:00:00-0500
/opt/splunk/var/log/splunk/btool.log=56
/opt/splunk/var/log/splunk/searches.log=0
/opt/splunk/var/log/splunk/splunkd.log=87
/opt/splunk/var/log/splunk/web_service.log=2
_span=86400
_spandays=1
----------
. . .
```

For more examples and extensive documentation, check out
http://dev.splunk.com.

Writing commands

To augment the built-in commands, Splunk provides the ability to write commands in Python and Perl. You can write the commands to modify events, replace events, or even dynamically produce events.

When not to write a command

While external commands can be very useful, if the number of events to be processed is large, or if performance is a concern, it should be considered a last resort. You should make every effort to accomplish the task at hand using the search language built into Splunk, or other built-in features. For instance, if you need:

- Regular expressions — learn to use rex, regex, and extracted fields
- To calculate a new field, or modify an existing field — look into eval (search for splunk eval functions with your favorite search engine)
- To augment your results with external data — learn to use **lookups**, which can also be a script, if need be
- To read external data that changes periodically — consider using inputcsv

The performance issues introduced by external commands come from the following two places:

- The work involved with launching a Python process, exporting events as CSV to the Python process, and then importing the results back into the Splunk process.
- The actual code of the command. A command that queries some external data source, for instance a database, will be affected by the speed of that external source.

In my testing, I could not make a command run faster than the speed that is 50 percent slower than native commands. To test this, let's try a couple of searches as follows:

```
* | head 100000 | eval t=_time+1 | stats dc(t)
```

On my laptop, this query takes roughly four seconds to execute, when run on the command line with preview disabled, as shown in the following code:

```
# time /opt/splunk/bin/splunk search '* | head 100000 | eval t=_time+1
| stats dc(t)' -preview false
```

Now let's throw in a command included in our sample app:

```
* | head 100000 | echo | eval t=_time+1 | stats dc(t)
```

This increases the search time to slightly over six seconds, an increase of 50 percent. Included in the sample app are three variations on the echo app of varying complexity:

- `echo`: This command simply echoes the standard input to standard output.
- `echo_csv`: This command uses `csvreader` and `csvwriter`.
- `echo_splunk`: This command uses the Python modules provided with Splunk to gather the incoming events and then output the results. We will use these Python modules for our example commands.

Using each of these commands, the times are nearly identical, which tells me most of the time is spent shuttling the events in and out of Splunk.

 Adding `required_fields=_time` in `commands.conf` lowered times from 2.5x to 1.5x in this case. If you know the fields your command needs, this setting can dramatically increase performance.

When to write a command

Given the warning about performance, there are still times it will make sense to write a command. I can think of a few reasons:

- You need to perform a specific action that cannot be accomplished using internal commands
- You need to talk to an external system (though a lookup may be more efficient)
- You need to produce "events" out of thin air, perhaps from an external service or for testing

I'm sure you can think of your own reasons. Let's explore the nuts and bolts of different types of commands.

Configuring commands

Before we start writing commands, there is some setup that must be done for all commands. First, every command will need an entry in the commands.conf the of your app. Let's take a look at the following sample stanza:

```
[commandname]
filename = scriptname.py
streaming = false
enableheader = true
run_in_preview = true
local = false
retainsevents = false
```

Stepping through the following attributes:

- [commandname]: The command available to search will be the title of the stanza, in this case commandname.

- filename = scriptname.py: The script to run. It must live in the directory bin inside your app.

- streaming = false: By default, only one instance of each command will be run on the complete set of results. The assumption is that all events are needed for the script to do its work. If your script works on each event individually, set this value to true. This will eliminate the event limit, which by default is 50,000, as specified by maxresultrows in limits.conf.

- `enableheader = true`: By default, your script will receive a header that the Splunk Python modules know how to use. If this is set to `false`, your command will receive plain CSV.

- `run_in_preview = true`: By default, your command will be executed repeatedly while events are being retrieved, so as to update the preview in the GUI. This will have no effect on saved searches, but setting this to `false` can make a big difference in performance for interactive searches. This is particularly important if your command uses an external resource, as it will be called repeatedly.

- `local = false`: If you have a distributed environment, by default, your command will be copied to all indexers and executed there. If your command needs to be run on one machine, setting `local=true` will ensure the command only runs on the search head.

- `retainsevents = false`: By default, Splunk assumes that your command returns the transformed events, much like `stats` or `timechart`. Setting this to `true` will change the behavior to treat the results as regular events.

To make our commands available to other apps, for instance **Search**, we need to change the metadata in our app. Place the following two lines in the file `metadata/default.meta`:

```
[commands]
export = system
```

Finally, to use a newly configured command, we either need to restart Splunk or load the URL `http://yourserver/debug/refresh` in a browser. This may also be necessary after changing settings in `commands.conf`, but is not necessary after making changes to the script itself.

Adding fields

Let's start out with a simple command that does nothing more than add a field to each event. This example is stored in `ImplementingSplunkExtendingExamples/bin/addfield.py`:

```
#import the python module provided with Splunk
import splunk.Intersplunk as si

#read the results into a variable
results, dummyresults, settings = si.getOrganizedResults()
```

```
#loop over each result. results is a list of dict.
for r in results:
    #r is a dict. Access fields using the fieldname.
    r['foo'] = 'bar'

#return the results back to Splunk
si.outputResults(results)
```

Our corresponding stanza in commands.conf is as follows:

```
[addfield]
filename = addfield.py
streaming = true
retainsevents = true
```

We can use this command as follows:

```
* | head 10 | addfield | top foo
```

This gives us the result shown in the following screenshot:

foo ‡	count ‡	percent ‡
bar	10	100.000000

This could be accomplished much more efficiently by simply using eval foo="bar", but this illustrates the basic structure of a command.

Manipulating data

It is useful at times to modify the value of a field, particularly _raw. Just for fun, let's reverse the text of each event. We will also support a parameter that specifies whether to reverse the words or the entire value. You can find this example in ImplementingSplunkExtendingExamples/bin/reverseraw.py:

```
import splunk.Intersplunk as si
import re


#since we're not writing a proper class, functions need to be
#defined first
def reverse(s):
    return s[::-1]

#start the actual script
```

```
results, dummyresults, settings = si.getOrganizedResults()

#retrieve any options included with the command
keywords, options = si.getKeywordsAndOptions()

#get the value of words, defaulting to false
words = options.get('words', False)

#validate the value of words
if words and words.lower().strip() in ['t', 'true', '1', 'yes']:
    words = True
else:
    words = False

#loop over the results
for r in results:
    #if the words option is true, then reverse each word
    if words:
        newRaw = []
        parts = re.split('([^a-zA-Z\']+)', r['_raw'])
        for n in range(0, len(parts) - 2, 2):
            newRaw.append(reverse(parts[n]))
            newRaw.append(parts[n + 1])
        newRaw.append(reverse(parts[-1]))
        r['_raw'] = ''.join(newRaw)
    #otherwise simply reverse the entire value of _raw
    else:
        r['_raw'] = reverse(r['_raw'])

si.outputResults(results)
```

The `commands.conf` **stanza would look as follows:**

```
[reverseraw]
filename = reverseraw.py
retainsevents = true
streaming = true
```

Let us assume the following event:

```
2012-10-27T22:10:21.616+0000 DEBUG Don't worry, be happy. [user=linda,
ip=1.2.3., req_time=843, user=extrauser]
```

Using our new command:

```
* | head 10 | reverseraw
```

Running the previous command on the preceding event, we see the entire event reversed, as shown in the following code:

```
]resuartxe=resu ,348=emit_qer ,.3.2.1=pi ,adnil=resu[ .yppah eb ,yrrow
t'noD GUBED 0000+616.12:01:22T72-01-2102
```

We can then add the `words` argument:

```
* | head 10 | reverseraw words=true
```

We maintain the order of the words, as shown in the following code:

```
2012-10-27T22:10:21.616+0000 GUBED t'noD yrrow, eb yppah. [resu=adnil,
pi=1.2.3., qer_emit=843, resu=resuartxe]
```

For fun, let's reverse the event again:

```
* | head 10 | reverseraw words=true | reverseraw
```

This gives us the following output:

```
]extrauser=user ,348=time_req ,.3.2.1=ip ,linda=user[ .happy be ,worry
Don't DEBUG 0000+616.12:01:22T72-01-2102
```

happy be, worry Don't—Yoda could not have said it better.

Transforming data

So far, our commands have returned the original events with modifications to their fields. Commands can also transform data, much like the built-in functions `top` and `stats`. Let's write a function to count the words in our events. You can find this example in `ImplementingSplunkExtendingExamples/bin/countwords.py`:

```
import splunk.Intersplunk as si
import re
import operator
from collections import defaultdict


#create a class that does the actual work
class WordCounter:
    word_counts = defaultdict(int)
    unique_word_counts = defaultdict(int)
    rowcount = 0
    casesensitive = False
    mincount = 50
    minwordlength = 3

    def process_event(self, input):
```

```
            self.rowcount += 1
            words_in_event = re.findall('\W*([a-zA-Z]+)\W*', input)

            unique_words_in_event = set()
            for word in words_in_event:
                if len(word) < self.minwordlength:
                    continue    # skip this word, it's too short
                if not self.casesensitive:
                    word = word.lower()
                self.word_counts[word] += 1
                unique_words_in_event.add(word)

            for word in unique_words_in_event:
                self.unique_word_counts[word] += 1

    def build_sorted_counts(self):
        #create an array of tuples,
        #ordered by the count for each word
        sorted_counts = sorted(self.word_counts.iteritems(),
                               key=operator.itemgetter(1))
        #reverse it
        sorted_counts.reverse()

        return sorted_counts

    def build_rows(self):
        #build our results, which must be a list of dict
        count_rows = []
        for word, count in self.build_sorted_counts():
            if self.mincount < 1 or count >= self.mincount:
                unique = self.unique_word_counts.get(word, 0)
                percent = round(100.0 * unique / self.rowcount, 2)
                newrow = {'word': word,
                          'count': str(count),
                          'Events with word': str(unique),
                          'Event count': str(self.rowcount),
                          'Percent of events with word':
                          str(percent)}
                count_rows.append(newrow)
        return count_rows


#a helper method that doesn't really belong in the class
#return an integer from an option, or raise useful Exception
```

```
def getInt(options, field, default):
    try:
        return int(options.get(field, default))
    except Exception, e:
        #raise a user friendly exception
        raise Exception("%s must be an integer" % field)


#our main method, which reads the options, creates a WordCounter
#instance, and loops over the results
if __name__ == '__main__':
    try:
        #get our results
        results, dummyresults, settings = si.getOrganizedResults()
        keywords, options = si.getKeywordsAndOptions()

        word_counter = WordCounter()

        word_counter.mincount = getInt(options, 'mincount', 50)
        word_counter.minwordlength = getInt(options,
                                    'minwordlength', 3)

        #determine whether we should be case sensitive
        casesensitive = options.get('casesensitive', False)
        if casesensitive:
            casesensitive = (casesensitive.lower().strip() in
                            ['t', 'true', '1', 'y', 'yes'])
        word_counter.casesensitive = casesensitive

        #loop through the original results
        for r in results:
            word_counter.process_event(r['_raw'])

        output = word_counter.build_rows()
        si.outputResults(output)

    #catch the exception and show the error to the user
    except Exception, e:
        import traceback
        stack = traceback.format_exc()
        si.generateErrorResults("Error '%s'. %s" % (e, stack))
```

This is a larger script, but hopefully it is clear what is happening. Notice in this example a few new things:

- Most of the logic is in the class definition. This provides a better separation of Splunk-specific logic and business logic.
- Testing for __main__, as is the Python way.
- Exception handling.
- A nicer exception for failed parsing of integer arguments.
- Field names with spaces in them.

Our entry in `commands.conf` does not allow streaming, and does not retain events:

```
[countwords]
filename = countwords.py
retainsevents = false
streaming = false
```

We can then use our command as follows:

```
* | countwords
```

This will give us back a table, as shown in the following screenshot:

	count ⬍	Events with word ⬍	word ⬍	Event count ⬍	Percent of events with word ⬍
1	49680	21822	error	50000	43.64
2	47860	41870	user	50000	83.74
3	40075	40070	time	50000	80.14
4	40065	40065	req	50000	80.13
5	39971	39971	logger	50000	79.94
6	25310	12655	this	50000	25.31
7	25243	25243	barclass	50000	50.49
8	25211	25211	don	50000	50.42
9	16131	16131	network	50000	32.26
10	16056	16056	session	50000	32.11
11	13442	13442	mary	50000	26.88
12	12655	12655	worthless	50000	25.31
13	12655	12655	nothing	50000	25.31
14	12655	12655	happened	50000	25.31
15	12655	12655	log	50000	25.31
16	12584	12584	debug	50000	25.17
17	12556	12556	worry	50000	25.11
18	12556	12556	happy	50000	25.11
19	12523	12523	warn	50000	25.05
20	12426	12426	info	50000	24.85
21	12378	12378	hello	50000	24.76
22	12378	12378	world	50000	24.76
23	8106	8106	red	50000	16.21

With my test data, this produced 132 rows, representing 132 unique words at least 3 characters long in my not-so-random data set. **count** represents how many times each word occurred overall, while **Events with word** represents how many events contained the word at all.

 Notice the value **50000** in the **Event count** column. Even though my query found more than 300,000 events, only 50,000 make their way to the command. You can increase this limit by increasing `maxresultrows` in `limits.conf`, but be careful! This limit is for your protection.

Trying out our options as follows:

```
*  | head 1000
   | countwords casesensitive=true mincount=250 minwordlength=0
```

This query produces the following output:

	count ⇔	Events with word ⇔	word ⇔	Event count ⇔	Percent of events with word ⇔
1	1000	1000	T	1000	100.0
2	968	837	user	1000	83.7
3	801	801	logger	1000	80.1
4	799	799	ip	1000	79.9
5	798	796	time	1000	79.8
6	798	798	req	1000	79.8
7	531	459	ERROR	1000	45.9
8	490	490	BarClass	1000	49.0
9	473	473	Don	1000	47.3
10	473	473	t	1000	47.3
11	330	330	network	1000	33.0
12	304	304	session	1000	30.4
13	282	282	mary	1000	28.2
14	271	271	INFO	1000	27.1
15	268	268	error	1000	26.8
16	268	268	Error	1000	26.8
17	259	259	Hello	1000	25.9
18	259	259	world	1000	25.9
19	251	251	WARN	1000	25.1

Notice that we now see one-and two-letter words, have entries for both T and t, and our results stop when **count** drops below our value for `mincount`.

Just for completeness, to accomplish this command using built-in commands, you could do something like the following code:

```
* | rex max_match=1000 "\W*(?<word>[a-zA-Z]+)\W*"
  | eval id=1 | accum id | fields word id
  | eventstats count
  | mvexpand word
  | eval word=lower(word)
  | stats max(count) as event_count
          dc(id) as events_with_word
          count as word_count
          by word
  | sort -events_with_word
  | eval percent_events_containing =
          round(events_with_word/event_count*100.0,2)
  | rename word_count as count
      events_with_word as "Events with word"
      event_count as "Event count"
      percent_events_containing as "Percent of events with word"
  | table count "Events with word" word
      "Event count" "Percent of events with word"
```

There is probably a more efficient way to do this work using built-in commands, but this is what comes to mind initially.

Generating data

There are times when you want to create events out of thin air. These events could come from a database query, a web service, or simply some code that generates data useful in a query. Just to illustrate the plumbing, we will make a random number generator. You can find this example in ImplementingSplunkExtendingExamples/ bin/random_generator.py:

```
import splunk.Intersplunk as si
from random import randint

keywords, options = si.getKeywordsAndOptions()


def getInt(options, field, default):
    try:
        return int(options.get(field, default))
    except Exception, e:
        #raise a user friendly exception
        raise Exception("%s must be an integer" % field)

try:
    min = getInt(options, 'min', 0)
```

```
    max = getInt(options, 'max', 1000000)
    eventcount = getInt(options, 'eventcount', 100)

    results = []
    for r in range(0, eventcount):
        results.append({'r': randint(min, max)})

    si.outputResults(results)

except Exception, e:
    import traceback
    stack = traceback.format_exc()
    si.generateErrorResults("Error '%s'. %s" % (e, stack))
```

The entry in `commands.conf` then is as follows:

```
[randomgenerator]
filename = random_generator.py
generating = true
```

We can then use the command as follows:

```
|randomgenerator
```

Notice the leading pipe | symbol. This is the indication to run a command instead of running a search. Let's test the randomness of our Python:

```
|randomgenerator eventcount=100000 min=100 max=899
  | bucket r
  | chart count by r
```

This produces a graph, as shown in the following screenshot:

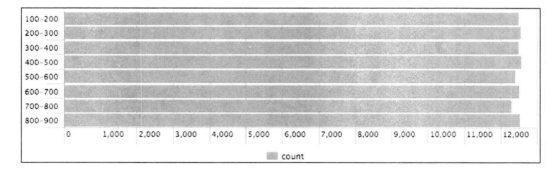

I guess that is not a bad distribution for 100,000 samples. Using Splunk's built-in commands, you could accomplish essentially the same thing using the following code:

```
index=_internal
    | head 100000
    | eval r=random()/2147483647*100000
    | bucket r
    | chart count by r
```

That is a very quick overview of commands, using fun demonstration commands to illustrate the plumbing required to execute your code. A number of samples ship with Splunk in `$SPLUNK_HOME/etc/apps/search/bin`.

Writing a scripted lookup to enrich data

We covered CSV lookups fairly extensively in *Chapter 6, Extending Search*, then touched on them again in *Chapter 9, Summary Indexes and CSV Files* and *Chapter 10, Configuring Splunk*. The capabilities built into Splunk are usually sufficient, but sometimes it is necessary to use an external data source or dynamic logic to calculate values. Scripted lookups have the following advantages over commands or CSV lookups:

- Scripted lookups are only run once per unique lookup value, as opposed to a command, which would run the command for every event
- The memory requirement of a CSV lookup increases with the size of the CSV file
- Rapidly changing values can be left in an external system and queried using the scripted lookup instead of being exported frequently

In the *Using a lookup with wildcards* section in *Chapter 9, Summary Indexes and CSV Files*, we essentially created a case statement through configuration. Let's implement that use case as a script, just to show how it would be done in Python. First, in `transforms.conf`, we need the following configuration:

```
[urllookup]
external_cmd = url_lookup.py
fields_list = url section call_count
```

The following are notes about this configuration:

- `fields_list` is the list of fields that will be sent to the script and the list of fields expected in the result
- `fields_list` must contain at least two fields or the script will fail silently

The script then looks as follows:

```python
import sys
import re
from csv import DictReader
from csv import DictWriter

patterns = []


def add_pattern(pattern, section):
    patterns.append((re.compile(pattern), section))

add_pattern('^/about/.*', 'about')
add_pattern('^/contact/.*', 'contact')
add_pattern('^/.*/.*', 'unknown_non_root')
add_pattern('^/.*', 'root')
add_pattern('.*', 'nomatch')


# return a section for this url
def lookup(url):
    try:
        for (pattern, section) in patterns:
            if pattern.match(url):
                return section
        return ''
    except:
        return ''


#set up our reader
reader = DictReader(sys.stdin)
fields = reader.fieldnames

#set up our writer
writer = DictWriter(sys.stdout, fields)
writer.writeheader()
```

```
#start our output
call_count = 0
for row in reader:
    call_count = call_count + 1

    if len(row['url']):
        row['section'] = lookup(row['url'])
        row['call_count'] = call_count
        writer.writerow(row)
```

In a nutshell, this script takes the value of url, tries each regular expression in sequence, and then sets the value of section accordingly. A few points about the preceding script follow:

- The script receives the raw CSV with the fields listed in transforms.conf, but only the fields that are needed for lookup will have a value. In our case, that is url.
- The field url must be present in the data, or mapped in the lookup command using the as option.
- call_count is included to show that this scripted lookup is more efficient than an external command, as the lookup will only receive one line of input per unique value of url.

Let's try it out:

```
index=impl splunk sourcetype="impl_splunk_web"
  | rex "\s[A-Z]+\s(?<url>.*?)\?"
  | lookup urllookup url
  | stats count values(call_count) by url section
```

This gives us the following results:

	url ⬍	section ⬍	count ⬍	values(call_count) ⬍
1	/about/	about	1443	1
2	/bar	root	1383	2
3	/contact/	contact	1389	3
4	/foo	root	1446	4
5	/products/	unknown_non_root	1364	5
6	/products/index.html	unknown_non_root	1389	6
7	/products/x/	unknown_non_root	2899	7
8	/products/y/	unknown_non_root	1430	8

The column **values(call_count)** tells us that our lookup script only received eight rows of input, one for each unique value of url. This is far better than 12,743 rows that an equivalent command would have received.

For more examples of scripted lookups, see $SPLUNK_HOME/etc/system/bin/ external_lookup.py and the MAXMIND app available in Splunkbase.

Writing an event renderer

Event renderers give you the ability to make a specific template for a specific event type. To read more about creating event types, see *Chapter 6, Extending Search*.

Event renderers use **mako** templates (http://www.makotemplates.org/). An event renderer is comprised of the following:

- A template stored at $SPLUNK_HOME/etc/apps/[yourapp]/appserver/ event_renderers/[template].html
- A configuration entry in event_renderers.conf
- An optional event type definition in eventtypes.conf
- Optional CSS classes in application.css

Let's create a few small examples. All the files referenced are included in $SPLUNK_ HOME/etc/apps/ImplementingSplunkExtendingExamples. These examples are not shared outside this app, so to see them in action, you will need to search from inside this app. Do this by pointing your browser at http://[yourserver]/app/ ImplementingSplunkExtendingExamples/flashtimeline.

Using specific fields

If you know the names of the fields you want to display in your output, your template can be fairly simple. Let's look at the following event type template_ example. The template is stored in appserver/event_renderers/template_ example.html:

```
<%page args="job, event, request, options">
<ul class="template_example">
  <li>
    <b>time:</b>
    ${i18n.format_datetime_microseconds(event.get('_time', event.
time))}
  </li>
  <li>
    <b>ip:</b>
    ${event.get('ip', '')}
```

```
      </li>
      <li>
        <b>logger:</b>
        ${event.get('logger', '')}
      </li>
      <li>
        <b>message:</b>
        ${event.get('message', '')}
      </li>
      <li>
        <b>req_time:</b>
        ${event.get('req_time', '')}
      </li>
      <li>
        <b>session_id:</b>
        ${event.get('session_id', '')}
      </li>
      <li>
        <b>user:</b>
        ${event.get('user', '')}
      </li>
      <li>
        <b>_raw:</b>
        ${event.get('_raw', '')}
      </li>
  </ul>
</%page>
```

This template outputs a `<ul>` block for each event, with the specific fields we want displayed. To connect this template to a specific event type, we need the following entry in `default/event_renderers.conf`:

```
[template_example]
eventtype = template_example
template = template_example.html
```

Finally, if we want to format our output, we can use the following CSS in `appserver/static/application.css`:

```
ul.template_example {
  list-style-type: none;
}

ul.template_example > li {
background-color: #dddddd;
  padding: 4px;
  margin: 1px;
}
```

To test our event type renderer, we need the configuration to be loaded. You can accomplish this by restarting Splunk or by pointing your browser to `http://[yourserver]/debug/refresh`.

At this point, we can run a query and apply the event type manually:

```
index="implsplunk" sourcetype="template_example"
  | eval eventtype="template_example"
```

This renders each event, as shown in the following screenshot:

To make this automatic, we can create an event type definition in `eventtypes.conf` as follows:

```
[template_example]
search = sourcetype=template_example
```

Now any query that finds events of `sourcetype=template_example` will be rendered using our template.

Table of fields based on field value

Since the template has access to everything in the event, you can use the fields in any way you like. The following example creates a horizontal table of fields, but lets the user specify a specific set of fields to display in a special field.

Our template, stored in `appserver/event_renderers/tabular.html`, looks as follows:

```
<%inherit file="//results/EventsViewer_default_renderer.html" />\
<%def name="event_raw(job, event, request, options, xslt)">\
<%
import sys
_fields = str(event.fields.get('tabular', 'host,source,sourcetype,line
count')).split(',')
```

```
head = ''
row = ''
for f in _fields:
    head += "<th>" + f + "</th>"
    row += "<td>" + str(event.fields.get(f, '-')) + "</td>"
%>
<table class="tabular_eventtype">
  <tr>
    ${head}
  </tr>
  <tr>
    ${row}
  </tr>
</table>
</%def>
```

Notice that we have extended the default event type renderer template, which means we will only change the rendering of the field _raw.

The entry in `event_renderers.conf` is as follows:

```
[tabular]
eventtype = tabular
template = tabular.html
```

Finally, our entries in `application.css` are as follows:

```
th.tabular_eventtype {
  background-color: #dddddd;
  border: 1px solid white;
  padding: 4px;
}

td.tabular_eventtype {
  background-color: #eeeeee;
  border: 1px solid white;
  padding: 4px;
}
```

We are not going to bother giving this event type a definition, but we can use it by setting the value of `eventtype` in the query. Let's try it out by running the following query:

```
index="implsplunk" | eval eventtype="tabular"
```

We see the following output, based on the default fields specified in the template:

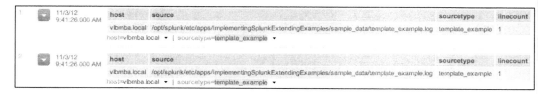

Notice that we still see the event number, the workflow actions menu, local time as rendered by Splunk, and the selected fields underneath our template output. We have really only overridden the rendering of `_raw`.

If we specify the fields we want in our table in the field `tabular`, the template will honor what we specify in our table:

```
index="implsplunk" sourcetype="template_example"
   | eval tabular="level,logger,message,foo,network"
   | eval eventtype="tabular"
```

This gives us the output shown in the following screenshot:

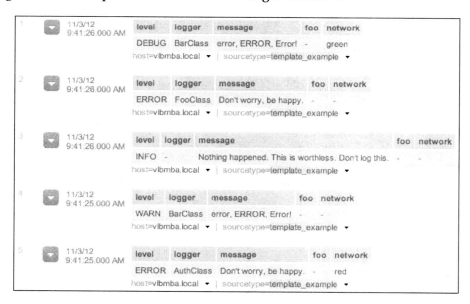

Any field that does not have a value is rendered as -, as per the following template code:

```
str(event.fields.get(f, '-'))
```

It would be much simpler to use the `table` command instead of writing an event renderer. This approach is only appropriate when you need a very specific rendering or still need access to `workflow` actions. For another approach, check out the `Table` and `Multiplexer` modules available in the app `Sideview Utils`.

Pretty print XML

In this example, we will use Python's `minidom` module to parse and "pretty print" XML, if possible. The template will look for a field called `xml`, or fallback to `_raw`. Let's look through the files included in `ImplementingSplunkExtendingExamples`.

The template file, located at `appserver/event_renderers/xml.html`, contains the following lines of code:

```
<%inherit file="//results/EventsViewer_default_renderer.html" />\
<%def name="event_raw(job, event, request, options, xslt)">\
<%
from xml.dom import minidom
import sys

def escape(i):
    return i.replace("<", "&lt;").replace(">", "&gt;")

_xml = str( event.fields.get('xml', event.fields['_raw']) )
try:
    pretty = minidom.parseString(_xml).toprettyxml(indent=' '*4)
    pretty = escape( pretty )
except Exception as inst:
    pretty = escape(_xml)
    pretty += "\n(couldn't format: " + str( inst ) + ")"
%>
<pre class="xml_eventtype">${pretty}</pre>
</%def>
```

Our entry in `event_renderers.conf` is as follows:

```
[xml]
eventtype = xml
template = xml.html
```

Our entry in `eventtypes.conf` is as follows:

```
[xml]
search = sourcetype="xml_example"
```

We can then simply search for our example source type as follows:

```
index="implsplunk" sourcetype="xml_example"
```

This renders the following output:

```
1   11/2/12
    8:03:15.000 AM   <bad><time>13:03:15</time><cat>dog</cat><e>egg</e><f /></d>
                     (couldn't format: mismatched tag: line 1, column 57)

                     host=vlbmba.local  ▼  | sourcetype=xml_example  ▼

2   11/1/12
    8:03:15.000 AM   <?xml version="1.0" ?>
                     <d>
                          <time>
                               13:03:15
                          </time>
                          <cat>
                               dog
                          </cat>
                          <e>
                               egg
                          </e>
                          <f/>
                     </d>

                     host=vlbmba.local  ▼  | sourcetype=xml_example  ▼

3   11/1/12
    8:03:15.000 AM   <?xml version="1.0" ?>
                     <reg>
                          <time>
                               13:03:15
                          </time>
                          <b>
                               5
                          </b>
                          <c>
                               dog
                          </c>
                          <e>
                               egg
                          </e>
                          <f>
                               fly
                          </f>
                     </reg>

                     host=vlbmba.local  ▼  | sourcetype=xml_example  ▼
```

The XML in the first event is invalid, so an error message is appended to the original value.

Writing a scripted alert action to process results

Another option for interfacing with an external system is to run a custom **Alert action** using the results of a saved search. Splunk provides a simple example in `$SPLUNK_HOME/bin/scripts/echo.sh`. Let's try it out and see what we get, using the following steps:

1. Create a saved search. For this test, do something cheap, such as the following:

   ```
   index=_internal | head 100 | stats count by sourcetype
   ```

2. Schedule the search to run at some point in the future. I set it to run every five minutes, just for this test.

3. Enable **Run a script** and type in `echo.sh`.

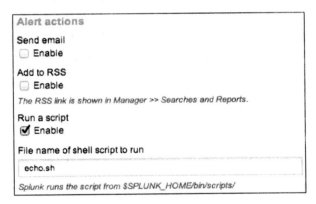

The script places the output into `$SPLUNK_HOME/bin/scripts/echo_output.txt`. In my case, the output is as follows:

```
'/opt/splunk/bin/scripts/echo.sh' '4' 'index=_internal | head 100
| stats count by sourcetype' 'index=_internal | head 100 | stats
count by sourcetype' 'testingAction' 'Saved Search [testingAction]
always(4)' 'http://vlbmba.local:8000/app/search/@go?sid=scheduler__
admin__search__testingAction_at_1352667600_2efa1666cc496da4' '' '/
opt/splunk/var/run/splunk/dispatch/scheduler__admin__search__
testingAction_at_1352667600_2efa1666cc496da4/results.csv.gz' 'sessionK
ey=7701c0e6449bf5a5f271c0abdbae6f7c'
```

Let's look through each argument in the bullets that follow:

- `$0` - script path:

  `'/opt/splunk/bin/scripts/echo.sh'`

- `$1` - number of events returned:

  `'4'`

- `$2` - search terms:

  `'index=_internal | head 100 | stats count by sourcetype'`

- `$3` - full search string:

  `'index=_internal | head 100 | stats count by sourcetype'`

- `$4` - saved search name:

  `'testingAction'`

- `$5` - the reason for the action:

  `'Saved Search [testingAction] always(4)'`

- `$6` - a link to the search results. The host is controlled in `web.conf`:

  `'http://vlbmba.local:8000/app/search/@go?sid=scheduler__admin__search__testingAction_at_1352667600_2efa1666cc496da4'`

- `$7` – deprecated:

  `''`

- `$8` - the path to the raw results, which are always gzipped:

  `'/opt/splunk/var/run/splunk/dispatch/scheduler__admin__search__testingAction_at_1352667600_2efa1666cc496da4/results.csv.gz'`

- `STDIN` - the session key when the search ran:

  `'sessionKey=7701c0e6449bf5a5f271c0abdbae6f7c'`

The typical use for scripted alerts is to send an event to a monitoring system. You could also imagine archiving these results for some compliance reason or to import into another system.

Let's make a fun example that copies the results to a file, and then issues a cURL statement. That script might look like:

```
#!/bin/sh
DIRPATH='dirname "$8"'
```

```
DIRNAME=`basename "$DIRPATH"`
DESTFILE="$DIRNAME.csv.gz"


cp "$8" /mnt/archive/alert_action_example_output/$DESTFILE


URL="http://mymonitoringsystem.mygreatcompany/open_ticket.cgi"
URL="$URL?name=$4&count=$1&filename=$DESTFILE"


echo Calling $URL
curl $URL
```

You would then place your script in $SPLUNK_HOME/bin/scripts on the server that will execute the script and refer to the script by name in **Alert actions**. If you have a distributed Splunk environment, the server that executes the scripts will be your search head.

If you need to perform an action for each row of results, then your script will need to open the results. The following is a Python script that loops over the contents of the gzip file and posts the results to a ticketing system, including a JSON representation of the event:

```python
#!/usr/bin/env python

import sys
from csv import DictReader
import gzip
import urllib
import urllib2
import json

#our ticket system url
open_ticket_url = "http://ticketsystem.mygreatcompany/ticket"

#open the gzip as a file
f = gzip.open(sys.argv[8], 'rb')

#create our csv reader
reader = DictReader(f)
for event in reader:
    fields = {'json': json.dumps(event),
              'name': sys.argv[4],
              'count': sys.argv[1]}
```

```
    #build the POST data
    data = urllib.urlencode(fields)

    #the request will be a post
    resp = urllib2.urlopen(open_ticket_url, data)
    print resp.read()

f.close()
```

Hopefully, these examples give you a starting point for your use case.

Summary

As we have seen in this chapter, there are a number of ways in which Splunk can be extended to input, manipulate, and output events. The search engine at the heart of Splunk is truly just the beginning. With a little creativity, Splunk can be used to extend existing systems, both as a data source and as a way to trigger actions.

Index

Symbols

A

 **Thank you for buying**
Implementing Splunk: Big Data Reporting and Development for Operational Intelligence

About Packt Publishing

Packt, pronounced 'packed', published its first book "*Mastering phpMyAdmin for Effective MySQL Management*" in April 2004 and subsequently continued to specialize in publishing highly focused books on specific technologies and solutions.

Our books and publications share the experiences of your fellow IT professionals in adapting and customizing today's systems, applications, and frameworks. Our solution based books give you the knowledge and power to customize the software and technologies you're using to get the job done. Packt books are more specific and less general than the IT books you have seen in the past. Our unique business model allows us to bring you more focused information, giving you more of what you need to know, and less of what you don't.

Packt is a modern, yet unique publishing company, which focuses on producing quality, cutting-edge books for communities of developers, administrators, and newbies alike. For more information, please visit our website: www.packtpub.com.

Writing for Packt

We welcome all inquiries from people who are interested in authoring. Book proposals should be sent to author@packtpub.com. If your book idea is still at an early stage and you would like to discuss it first before writing a formal book proposal, contact us; one of our commissioning editors will get in touch with you.

We're not just looking for published authors; if you have strong technical skills but no writing experience, our experienced editors can help you develop a writing career, or simply get some additional reward for your expertise.

Pentaho Data Integration 4 Cookbook

ISBN: 978-1-84951-524-5   Paperback: 352 pages

Over 70 recipes to solve ETL problems using Pentaho Kettle

1. Manipulate your data by exploring, transforming, validating, integrating, and more

2. Work with all kinds of data sources such as databases, plain files, and XML structures among others

3. Use Kettle in integration with other components of the Pentaho Business Intelligence Suite

Learning Highcharts

ISBN: 978-1-84951-908-3   Paperback: 300 pages

Create rich, intuitive, and interactive JavaScript data visualization for your web and enterprise development needs using this powerful charting library — Highcharts

1. Step-by-step instructions with real-live data to create bar charts, column charts and pie charts, to easily create artistic and professional quality charts

2. Learn tips and tricks to create a variety of charts such as horizontal gauge charts, projection charts, and circular ratio charts

3. Use and integrate Highcharts with jQuery Mobile and ExtJS 4, and understand how to run Highcharts on the server-side

Please check **www.PacktPub.com** for information on our titles

Oracle BI Publisher 11g: A Practical Guide to Enterprise Reporting

Create and deliver improved snapshots in time of your Enterprise data using Oracle BI Publisher 11g

Daniela Bozdoc

Oracle BI Publisher 11g: A Practical Guide to Enterprise Reporting

ISBN: 978-1-84968-318-0   Paperback: 254 pages

Create and deliver improved snapshots in time of your Enterprise data using Oracle BI Publisher 11g

1. A practical tutorial for improving your Enterprise reporting skills with Oracle BI Publisher 11g

2. Master report migration, template design, and E-Business Suite integration

3. A practical guide brimming with tips about all the new features of the 11g release

Oracle Hyperion Interactive Reporting 11 Expert Guide

Master advanced Dashboards, JavaScript and Computation features of Oracle Hyperion Interactive Reporting 11 and much more

Edward J. Cody   Emily M. Vose

Oracle Hyperion Interactive Reporting 11 Expert Guide

ISBN: 978-1-84968-314-2   Paperback: 276 pages

Master advanced Dashboards, JavaScript and Computation features of Oracle Hyperion Interactive Reporting 11 and much more

1. Walk through a comprehensive example of a simple, intermediate, and advanced dashboard with a focus on Interactive Reporting best practices.

2. Explore the data analysis functionally with an in-depth explanation of built-in and JavaScript functions.

3. Build custom interfaces to create batch programs and exports for automated reporting.

Please check **www.PacktPub.com** for information on our titles

CPSIA information can be obtained at www.ICGtesting.com
Printed in the USA
LVOW112009080513

332901LV00009B/99/P

Visit my website at www.meghanmarch.com

ABOUT CREOLE KINGPIN

New York Times bestselling author Meghan March goes back to New Orleans and the world of Lachlan Mount with a dangerous and bold new anti-hero.

The thing about ghosts is they're supposed to stay dead.
That's exactly what I am, but I can't stay away from Magnolia Marie Maison for one more day, let alone another year.
We've already got fifteen of those between us.
As it stands, she'll want to kill me as soon as she lays eyes on me.
And knowing her, she's completely up to the task.
But I'm a man on a mission, and I've got everything riding on this.
So, here I come, Magnolia. This ghost is ready for whatever you got.
After all, there's only one way I want this to end—'til death do us part.

Creole Kingpin is the first book in the Magnolia Duet. The story concludes in *Madam Temptress.*

CREOLE KINGPIN

Book One of the Magnolia Duet

Meghan March

Sinful Empire

SAVAGE TRILOGY:

Savage Prince

Iron Princess

Rogue Royalty

BENEATH SERIES:

Beneath This Mask

Beneath This Ink

Beneath These Chains

Beneath These Scars

Beneath These Lies

Beneath These Shadows

Beneath The Truth

DIRTY BILLIONAIRE TRILOGY:

Dirty Billionaire

Dirty Pleasures

Dirty Together

DIRTY GIRL DUET:

Dirty Girl

Dirty Love

REAL DUET:

Real Good Man

Real Good Love

REAL DIRTY DUET:

Real Dirty

Real Sexy

1
MAGNOLIA

"**O**ne card. You know the drill. I'm feeling strong energy coming off you today, Magnolia."

I pause midstride between the Saint Louis Cathedral and Jackson Square as Madame Celeste waves me over to her rickety card table. She has a shop a few streets over, but she sets up out here more than I think an elderly woman should. But then again, what the hell do I know? It's not like I could stop her anyway. Stubborn woman. I guess like recognizes like.

"You're only saying that because I didn't stop to say hi. I'm in a hurry," I tell her, my eyebrow popping up. Celeste and I go way back. She's been a fixture in the Quarter for as long as I can remember.

"Come see. There's always time for what the cards have to say."

My heels click on the stone pavers as I close the distance to her table. "I have an appointment, Celeste. I can't fuck around today." When something gleams in her otherworldly pale blue eyes in response, I huff out a breath. "Fine. Two minutes. One card. But I can't be late."

She holds out the deck, and I knock the top and shuffle quickly.

"Your life is about to change, *chère*."

My brow creases. "You haven't even flipped over the card," I say, giving her my best side-eye. Despite my words and the warm, sunny day, chills skitter up my spine, unleashing a raft of goose bumps along my exposed skin.

Celeste smiles, revealing the gap between her two front teeth. "I don't need the cards to feel the winds of change. You've been out of sorts for too long, Magnolia. The universe feels your energy and the questions you've been asking. Your answers are coming. All will be revealed."

I tip my head to the side and release another long breath of annoyance, but inside, I'm tense as hell. Celeste shouldn't know this shit. And, really, I shouldn't be buying into it. I'm a woman of the world, and no deck of cards is going to tell me what will happen in my life. I'm in control. That's the way this works.

Yet, here I sit.

"You don't need to give me the tourist song and dance, Celeste. Just flip the damn card."

"You feel it too," she says, and her eyes seem to glow. There's only one other person I've ever seen up close who had eyes that did the same trick, but they were a different color.

And we don't think about him. Not fucking ever.

"Right now, all I feel is how much I don't want to be late to this meeting I need to get to."

She winks at me and flips the card.

The Devil.

"Jesus fucking Christ, Celeste." I cut my gaze away from the card to her face. "You stop me and then flip over the Devil card?"

There's no hiding my discomfort in this moment. I scrub my hands up and down my arms to chase away the damn chill I shouldn't be feeling in this sunlight.

"You shuffled the deck, Magnolia. You brought the card up.

You can deny it all you want, but you feel it too, don't you? The unease that's been dogging your every step? You're letting everything that's happened to you eat you alive, and it's gotta stop." The woman sits up straighter and pulls back her thin shoulders. "It's time for change. You can't keep going on the way you are. You gotta make a choice."

The twisting knot in place of where my stomach used to be tightens to the point of discomfort. I've been carrying the weight of shit my whole life. That's nothing new to me. But Celeste is right. The last couple of years, shit's been getting real heavy.

Grief. Betrayal. Rage. Heartbreak.

Celeste hit the nail on the head—just like always. All those feelings swirling inside me have been slowly eating me alive. A girl like me can shake off a lot, but even I can only handle so much. Shooting and killing a man the way I did . . . it'll fuck you up.

I stare into Celeste's eerie eyes and force a smile to my crimson-painted lips. Bravado has always been one of my most valuable assets, a talent I can't live without.

"That's enough, Celeste. I'm fine. Shit always works out in the end."

She shakes her turban-covered head slowly from side to side. "Change is coming whether you want it or not. I know you like to dance with the devil, but watch yourself, girl. He always demands his due."

The hair rises on the back of my neck as I stand up. "Take care of yourself, Celeste. I'll see you later. I gotta go."

Her hand snakes out to grab my fingers, and I tense at her bony grip.

"All I want is for you to find peace. Peace *and love, chère*. Now go, but watch yourself. Those winds of change are blowing strong. I feel it in my bones."

With those foreboding last words, Celeste releases my hand, and I flex my fingers to shake off her predictions. I back away from the table, turning in the direction I was headed, making my way through the crowd of tourists who've gathered in front of musicians playing a tuba, a trumpet, and a trombone. Static rushes in my ears, drowning out the sound of the brass playing "When the Saints Go Marching In."

With my arms wrapped tightly around my middle, I pick my way across the gray stones beneath my feet, careful not to catch a heel in the cracks.

What the hell was that about? Change is coming whether I want it or not? As if that's news. It's the one thing I can always count on —*shit changes.*

Someone slams into me from the side, and my purse strap yanks against my shoulder.

"Not today, motherfucker," I bite out as my grip tightens, and I lock eyes on a kid who should definitely be in school. Then again, around that age, I wasn't either.

His eyes go wide before practically bulging out of his head when he gets a good look at me. I'm attractive. I have a body built for sin and a face to match.

My silky dark hair flutters in the breeze as I tilt my head at him. "You hear me? Not today."

The kid's head bobbles like one of those toys on a dashboard, and as if by magic, his hand releases my purse strap. "S-sorry, ma'am. I wasn't watching where I was going."

I spear him with a don't-fuck-with-me glare. "Right. And I was born yesterday."

He licks his lips and drops his gaze to my tits before backing away slowly. "You're fucking hot." At least this, he says to my face.

"Get your ass off the streets before you get picked up for all the shit you've done."

He nods, but it's unlikely my words will change a damn thing. The sorry excuse for a petty thief breaks eye contact after another beat before trotting away through the crowd. Probably off to find an unsuspecting victim.

At least it wasn't me.

You can't save them all, Mags. You can't save them all.

With that truth echoing in my brain, I start marching again, my focus on getting to this meeting before I'm actually late. Tardiness isn't something Mount tolerates, even from his wife's best friend. Him marrying Keira has definitely made my life easier, but it's clear where my bread is buttered, and I show proper respect. No one wants to wake the beast that man can be, especially not me. I'm all about self-preservation.

As I move to cross the street, dodging pedestrians, something catches my attention through the plate glass window of a building on the other side. An eerie greenish-gold gaze collides with mine.

Not. Possible.

Blinking, I spin around in the middle of the street, then rush toward the window to get a better look.

It can't be him. Not now. Not after all this time. That'd be like conjuring a damned ghost.

A small crowd of tourists blocks me as they gather around three boys drumming on five-gallon buckets, but I sidestep them to stare through the glass. Those haunting eyes I thought I saw? They're gone. And the seat where I thought I saw them? *Empty. Again.*

It's not the first time I've thought I saw the man those eyes belong to, but I'm always wrong.

He isn't coming back for you, and he never was. You've had fifteen years to get that through your damn head.

You'd think I'd learn. But old habits die hard, especially my habit of looking for *him* in every face I see.

"*Change is coming.*" Madame Celeste's words filter through my head as I stand on the sidewalk, staring at people eating brunch in the restaurant.

The scent of rich spices waft around me, and I swear I hear his voice.

"Some things don't happen twice in a lifetime, Magnolia. You're one of them."

Those words are from the past.

Fifteen years ago, I let myself forget who and what I was, and I made the ultimate mistake.

I fell in love.

Then he left and never came back. My heart has been black ever since.

Maybe Celeste is right. Maybe the devil is coming for me. Too bad it won't be the one I still think about in my weakest moments.

2
MAGNOLIA

"I'm here for an appointment," I tell the bartender as I check my watch. I'm still five minutes early, thank the good Lord.

The woman looks into the mirror hanging behind the bar and meets my gaze. With a tilt of her head, she motions for me to move toward the back of the room. A man approximately the size of a hundred-year-old sycamore stands between the scarred bar and a small doorway that leads into the office.

My pumps click on the concrete floor as I walk toward him.

"Appointment," is all I say in greeting to the man.

He gestures with his massive head and turns around. With his bulky frame, he has to turn sideways slightly to fit through the doorway. He pushes open the first door on the right, which leads into what looks like the manager's office, but I know better.

This ain't my first go-round.

Honestly, it kind of grates on me that I have to go through this whole song and dance to meet with the king of this city when I've been to his goddamned house so many times to see Keira. But this is Mount's way of reminding me that my friendship with her doesn't always give me special privileges. I'd call him an asshole, but I wouldn't be surprised if he could read my mind from here.

Mount is fucking scary. And yes, I knew that *before* they got together. But like I told Celeste, everything works out in the end. *Right?* A web of guilt winds its way around me for the choices I made that changed Keira's life. I may never shake that off completely.

Once inside the office, I pause while Señor Sycamore pats me down. "Gun and knife are in my purse," I tell him, holding the bag out in front of me.

He nods as he takes it and sets it on the desk. "It'll be here when he's done with you."

"You can keep the gun and knife, but I'd like my bag back."

Señor Sycamore shakes his head. "You don't need it."

I roll my eyes before I can think better of it. That's when the bookcase slides to the side, revealing a set of dimly lit stairs.

When I don't move immediately, he points a thick, branch-like index finger at it. "Don't keep him waiting."

"I'm going. I'm going." I shoot him a final glance before walking through the previously hidden doorway. I used to think this shit was cool, but now it's tedious.

When I'm halfway up the stairs, the bookcase slides shut, leaving me alone in pools of light coming from the sconces on the wood-paneled walls.

No escort? That's new.

Then again, what concern would Mount have about me doing a damn thing to cause trouble? He knows where my loyalty lies.

I reach the top of the stairs and study the row of doors along the side.

"Now where's he at?" I mumble as I keep walking.

Mount changes it up, and I don't know if he's behind door number one, two, or three.

Before I have to guess and start trying knobs, the one at the very end of the hall opens and the tall, dark, and dangerous man I've come here to meet stands there in a suit.

"I appreciate you coming."

I smile in response, rather than saying what I'm thinking. *Like I had any choice after I got the summons.*

When Mount waves his arm into the room, I stride forward and enter his infamous library. As soon as he shuts the door behind us, the room practically vibrates with the waves of power rolling off the man.

From past experience, I recall the big fireplace in the middle of the floor-to-ceiling bookshelves spins around, leading to a maze of hallways that eventually connects to Mount and Keira's private apartments, but I have a feeling that's not where we're going.

Confirming my suspicion, Mount motions toward one of the leather chairs. "Sit. We need to talk."

"Yes, sir." My show of respect doesn't come from a place of fear, but it's real all the same. I owe this man a lot for what he's done for me.

While I'm settling into the seat, he crosses to the sideboard and pours amber liquor into two glasses without asking me what I want. It's fine, because I know he's got whatever top-shelf Seven Sinners whiskey Keira has sampled lately.

Mount returns to the chairs and sits in the one beside mine before offering me the drink. I take it, hoping it's a good sign that he didn't drag me through the corridors to his other office—the Spartan one where the most serious business goes down.

"Thank you."

I'm dying to ask why he summoned me here, but Mount swirls his whiskey in his glass before taking a sip.

"You're welcome," he says as he crosses an ankle over his knee. A faint smile tugs at the corner of his mouth, and I'll bet he's thinking of Keira as he swallows.

I've never seen a woman have such an effect on a man. That's why I risked so much on them being perfect for each other. And I was right. Then again, I'm rarely wrong when it comes to things like that.

At least, with respect to other people. I have absolutely no sense when it comes to men for myself. Never have. Probably never will.

I'm thinking my favorite thought—that I should swear them off completely—when Mount finally speaks again.

"You've got trouble."

My mind tears away from my ruminations, and I turn to stare at him. "What kind of trouble?"

"The Feds are surveilling the house."

I set my whiskey on the table between us and shift in my seat to face him. We both know I don't technically own the house he's talking about anymore, but I still consider the women living in it to be my responsibility. "Well, fuck. Why?"

"Alberto Brandon."

I flip through my mental black book until a face and a bio come to mind. "Fifties. Prefers young blondes over his wife. Likes being called Daddy. Always flashed a lot of cash. Why are the Feds looking into him?"

Mount tastes his whiskey again before replying. "He's been moving a lot of money around in ways that particularly interest them, except they can't seem to find him. He's been MIA, and now his money is too. Hence, their interest in the house."

"Fuck," I whisper this time. "Do you think they'll bust it?"

He replies with a lift of his shoulders, as if he's not willing to say *I don't know* out loud.

I release a rush of breath and jam my fingers into my hair. "I'll tell Desiree. She'll have to be careful until the heat's gone."

When I mention the name of the girl who is buying the place from me through a bond for deed, Mount shakes his head.

"Not just careful. She needs to relocate for a while if you don't want her exposed."

"Shit. That bad?"

Mount's expression never changes. "Would I be telling you this if it wasn't?"

Slightly mortified, I pinch the bridge of my nose. "Of course not. You wouldn't waste your time. Thanks for the heads-up. I'll help Desiree deal with it."

"Good."

When Mount doesn't say more, I study him for a beat. "Is that all, sir?"

He meets my gaze for a long moment. "For now."

Even though I want to hug my arms around my middle so damn bad, I rise with my shoulders straight and my chin held high. "Thank you. I'll show myself out if we're done."

Something unsettling flashes in his dark eyes. "Done? Not by a long shot. But you can go. Keira wants to see you." He moves his hand and the fireplace turns, revealing his silent right-hand man who is built like a bull. "V will take you to her."

I rise, wishing Señor Sycamore from downstairs had let me bring my purse. But as soon as I have that thought, V lifts a hand, and I see the red leather strap dangling from his fingertips.

Fucking creepy how they read my goddamned mind.

There's a knock on the door through which I entered the room only minutes ago.

Mount meets my gaze. "That's my next appointment. Have a good one, Magnolia."

The unease that's followed me all day ramps up again as I walk toward the hidden passage. As soon as I step through it, the fireplace slowly spins. I turn toward V, but one sentence stops me cold.

No. Not the words. *The voice.*

Deep and rich with a hint of Creole flavor.

"You're a right hard man to find, Mount."

I whip around to stare through the crack that's narrowing with every passing second and catch a glimpse of those eyes that have haunted me for fifteen years.

"It's been a long time, Moses. Welcome back to New Orleans. To what do I owe the pleasure?"

3
MAGNOLIA

Oh. My. God.

What in the actual fuck is happening right now?

Moses Gaspard did *not* just walk into Mount's office behind me. *Did he?*

My breath catches, and my heart rate kicks up like I've just sprinted a hundred flights of stairs. I turn to stare at V with my mouth hanging open from the shock. "Did I just . . . Was he . . ."

V watches me like he's not certain what I'm about to do. That's fine, because I sure as hell don't know.

Even though the man rarely speaks, I point at the fireplace and ask, "Did you just see him? Did you? Tell me I'm not crazy right now."

V's gaze flicks to the fireplace and then back to my face, and I wait for him to give me a sign that I'm not hallucinating. He gives me a short nod as he hands me my purse.

"Jesus fucking Christ. What in God's name is going on here?"

V doesn't answer that question, but the little nod he gave me before was plenty.

Moses is back.

The memory of the eyes I thought I saw in the Quarter on my

way here resurfaces. *Did I enter another dimension when I woke up this morning? How is this happening* now?

Because Moses Gaspard left New Orleans a decade and a half ago and never looked back. Never called. Never wrote. Never kept the promises he made to me.

So, why the hell is he here now? And meeting with Mount?

V moves through the room, signaling with an arm that I should follow him, but my brain is scattered like broken Mardi Gras beads left in the gutters on Bourbon Street after a night of partying.

What is happening right now?

He grunts at me, clearly impatient with my lack of response to his gesture, but too damn bad. The man doesn't understand that my past just crashed into my present with the subtlety of a Mack truck slamming into a brick wall at full speed.

"Give me a minute, okay? Jesus."

He emits a low growl as I gather myself, glaring at the fucking fireplace. Goddamn Mount and all his hidey-holes and secret passages. I'm tempted to beat at that thing until I figure out how to open it back up and get the answers I'm owed.

But do I really want to see Moses? After all this time?

The pounding in my chest tells me I'm all too affected. I take a long, slow breath, hold it for a few beats, and release it. I repeat that again and again until V taps me on the arm.

I whip around to look at him. "Can't you see I'm dealing with some shit?"

He points in the opposite direction I'm facing and finally speaks. "Keira."

Fuck. That's right. He's taking me to see Keira.

Keira, who doesn't know about Moses. Because I never told her. Because I never told *anyone* what happened between us.

At first, I kept it to myself because I wanted to have something special that was just mine. And when he never came back or got in touch, I realized it wasn't worth the breath to tell anyone. Because it apparently didn't mean shit to him, so I started believing it didn't mean shit to me either. I decided he was basically a figment of my imagination, because nothing could be that good in real life.

As I give the fireplace one last hard look, I know something with certainty.

Mount did this on purpose. That motherfucker.

How could he know? I snort. That's right. I'm forgetting that Mount knows *everything.*

I haul in another breath and nod at V. "Lead the way. I'm ready. We'll forget this little episode ever happened. Deal?"

He lifts his chin, which I decide to take as a yes, especially since he walks away from me. I follow him, but can't help looking over my shoulder one more time at the fireplace standing between me and the man I'm pretty sure I could strangle with my bare hands right now.

How dare he just show up in my town after all this time like he's welcome?

Another thought nearly stops me in my tracks.

Why would Moses request an audience with the king first? What does that mean? Is he staying? Asking for permission to set up shop here?

I don't know what Moses has done for the last fifteen years, but after the first month of him being gone, I refused to let myself look for him. I did everything I could to erase him from my memory and scrub the phantom feeling of him from my skin.

When he didn't come back for me, his message was loud and clear. So I threw myself into building my empire so I could have what I wanted most—freedom and power.

To this day, I remember telling Moses how I was going to make enough money that no man could ever tell me what to do again. Short of answering Mount's summonses, I made that happen.

No man owns me.

No man controls me.

But why would Moses come back now?

V grunts from the hallway, letting me know to keep up. I clutch my handbag to my side as I follow him through a maze, not even caring about the hidden entrances that normally fascinate me.

When we finally reach corridors done in black, white, and gold, I know I'm getting close to Keira.

What am I going to tell her? Am I going to tell her?

Part of me wants to, but the other part . . .

How do I share my secret shame? That he didn't love me enough to come back for me. That I wasn't worth even a phone call or a check-in from time to time. That even a gangster realized you can't make a ho a housewife.

Moses nearly broke me once. I won't let him do it again. Whatever his reason for setting foot in my city, one thing is for sure—I'm not playing his game this time.

My heart clenches, trying to make a liar out of me.

Well, fuck that. My heart got me into trouble once, and I'm not going to let her throw my world into chaos again.

When V opens the door leading into an airy courtyard lined with brick walls, filled with greenery and a fountain, Keira looks up from a table, where she sits next to a little dark-haired dictator who takes after both her mother and father.

Aurora Mount is the princess of this castle. When she sees me, she lets out an earsplitting screech, her chubby arms waving in the air. Her hair, a deep auburn, sticks out in every direction, curling at the ends.

Keira scoops her up and rises to greet me. "Clearly, we're happy to see you." A bright smile lights up her green eyes as she laughs.

"And I'm always so damn happy to see you both." My words come out sounding normal, thank God.

I close the distance between us, reaching out to squeeze them in a hug. Then I steal the little miss, who clings to my neck with sticky fingers, making the transition from her mom to me like a monkey.

I welcome the distraction from my thoughts as I bounce her on my hip, blocking out thoughts of the man I just saw. "What have you been doing, Rory? Keeping your mama and daddy busy?"

Aurora offers a long-winded reply, but I only understand about ten percent of her baby talk.

Keira translates. "She's having snacks and they're the best ever, and if you want some, you're more than welcome to share them with her."

With Aurora's solid body in my arms, I glance at a small plate of kiddie treats on the table and back to the baby's chubby cheeks. "Thank you for the offer, princess. But they're all yours."

She smiles at me, and some of the bad juju following me through the halls of Mount's kingdom falls away. But not quickly enough, because Keira's green gaze sharpens on me with a laser focus.

"Something wrong? What did Lachlan want?"

It's still weird to hear her call the man I just met with *Lachlan*. It makes him sound almost human, and I'm not convinced he is.

"Nothing's wrong. He was just passing along some information." I give her a wink.

She should know better than to ask me to divulge anything Mount has said. If he wants her to know, he'll tell her.

I continue, changing the subject. "Damn, it's good to see you, though. *Shit*. Wait. Goddamn it, Keira, how do you not curse in front of this adorable freaking baby?"

Her lips press together as she studies me, which tells me I did a crap job of covering up what I was feeling by the time I walked into the courtyard. "It's a work in progress. You sure you're okay?"

Her questioning tone confirms my thought. Keira may be my

best friend, but we've always lived in two very different worlds. Hiding the truth from her is second nature to me. Short of that, I sugarcoat the shit out of most everything I tell her.

"How could I be anything but perfect with this angel in my arms?"

Keira's face changes completely as she smiles at her daughter with pure adoration. "She is pretty freaking magical. Until she starts screaming, and then only her daddy can make her stop."

I've only seen Mount with Aurora once, but that's all I needed to know without a doubt that the ruthless king of New Orleans is utterly and completely wrapped around his baby girl's finger. It almost made my black heart skip a beat, and that's saying something.

"I still don't know why you don't hate me, Ke-ke." I don't mean to say it, but it's something I think about a lot. Plus, my emotions are raw as hell with all that's happened in the last hour. Being dealt the Devil card. Meeting with the ruthless king. Catching sight of a ghost from my past.

Keira's smile changes, but it doesn't fade. "How could I? Without you, I wouldn't have everything I love most in my life."

Something burns behind my eyes, but there's no way it's tears. I don't cry. So I swallow the stupid returning lump and shrug a shoulder. "I'm happy for you, Ke-ke. I really am."

I peel Aurora off my neck and Keira takes her from me, raining kisses on her face before snuggling the baby against her body.

"Now if only we could see *you* this happy, Mags."

Fucking hell. I keep trying to turn this conversation in the direction of safe ground, but shit like this just makes me think of *him.*

My heart thumps hard as the vision of those greenish-gold eyes set in that golden-tanned face flashes through my brain once more.

Why the fuck is he here? After all this time?

The man best not think he's getting anywhere near me, because I don't want a damn thing to do with him.

"Mags?"

I press my lips together before forcing them into a smile. "Some of us just aren't built for that kind of happy. I'll settle for being gorgeous, rich, and in total control of my whole life."

This time, Keira's smile falters. "Do you miss Rafe?"

My head jerks back of its own volition. "Rafe? Hell no. That motherfucker is gone forever. If he comes back, we'll have *way* bigger problems to be worrying about." I slap three painted fingertips over my lips to cover the cursing. "Shit. *Crap.* I'm just gonna stop talking before Rory starts dropping f-bombs and her daddy looks to *me* for an explanation."

My mess-up does the trick, because Keira laughs again.

"He's just as guilty of it as you. I promise he'll never know." She nudges the heel of my pump with her toe. "It's been too long since I've seen you, though. What have you been doing?"

"My remodel has been a nightmare, but it's almost done. Less than a week to go, and I can finally move in. I can't wait for you to see it all finished."

"Finally! I can give you the housewarming gift I got you. I've been holding on to it since the week after you closed on the place."

That means she bought whatever it is almost ten months ago, when I purchased my very own house in the French Quarter. It's a small two-bedroom place whose charm had long since worn off or been covered up, but the moment I saw it, I knew it was mine.

I shake my head, because really, Keira's too fucking good for me. "Of course you went out and bought something, even when it was just a pit."

She brings her shoulders up to her ears. "Like you expect anything different from me."

"No, I guess I don't. I imagine you'll bring whiskey too, so I won't need to stock up for us."

This comment launches an exaggerated eye roll. "You never need to buy another bottle of Seven Sinners. You know that."

The taste of the whiskey is still on my tongue from Mount's office. "Much appreciated." When Aurora reaches out to grab some puffed cereal and shoves it in her mouth, I say, "Well, I should let you get back to what you're doing. I've gotta make a pass at Bernadette's before I head back to meet with the contractor about the punch list for the finish work."

"Already? But you just got here." Keira catches Aurora's hand before she flips her container of cereal onto the ground.

"You know me. I never stay still for long."

A gentle and warm expression crosses her face. "Whatever it is that's really going on with you . . . I can handle it, Mags. When you're ready to tell me, I'll be ready to listen."

The memory of Moses's glowing eyes flashes through my brain, and it takes everything I have to offer her a thin smile. "I'll let you know."

"Take care. We love you."

"And I love you right back." I lean in and press a kiss to Aurora's wild hair. "I'll see you two later."

As I turn to where V stands at the doorway, Aurora yells, "Yeeee!"

A pang of longing stabs me in my chest, where my heart should be. I'll never have that. I'll never know what it feels like to bring life into this world.

Then again, it's a fucked-up place, and God knows I'm not fit to be a mother anyway.

V shows me out of the inner sanctum a different way than we came in. Shockingly, he doesn't blindfold me so I can't see where we're going. I must have passed some kind of trust test since the last time I was here. He proves that further by handing my pink revolver and knife back to me before he opens the huge metal door.

The exit he takes me out leads to a different street than the one the bar is on. Sunshine beats down on my face, and I take a deep breath.

Moses is in that building, and I don't care. I won't let myself care.

As I walk past a shiny black Rolls Royce parked at the curb, I remind myself I'm an emotional fucking fortress. I only feel what I want to feel, and not a damn thing more.

Put that man out of your mind, Mags. He's got no business taking up your time or your thoughts.

Even though I know it's true, I struggle to not look back.

4
MAGNOLIA

"I don't know why you keep coming here." Bitchy Bernadette spits words at me from her recliner across the room, where she sits with a blanket over her lap as she watches her stories on TV.

"Glutton for punishment, I suppose. But then again, I really enjoy seeing how many new wrinkles you've gotten since the last time I stopped by. Run out of night cream, Aunt Bernie?"

She hisses, as in *actually* hisses like a snake. Considering she's as mean as one, it doesn't surprise me. "You were an ungrateful child, and now you're a perfectly awful woman. Get your whore ass out of my house."

That knocks loose the first real laugh I've had all day. "Bitch, I own this house, so my whore ass can come and go as I please."

She bares her teeth at me as Norma, the former maid who Bernadette treated *horribly* when she worked for her, comes to bring the bag of bones a tray for lunch. Or maybe dinner. Who the hell knows what schedule old people eat on anyway?

Bernadette's face pinches as she looks at the food and then back up at Norma. "Did you poison it? Is that why she's here? To finally watch me die? Because I'm ready. Been ready for years."

"Not today, Bernie," Norma says with a genuine smile. "Maybe tomorrow." The tables have turned, and Norma and I both find it fucking hilarious.

Bernadette had a fancy house and high standards. So high that she kicked me out when I was sixteen and got expelled from school after getting caught giving the history teacher a blowie in the supply closet. Not that anyone ever asked me *why* I did it or thought maybe *he* was the one in the wrong. I was out on my ass as soon as Bernadette got the call from the school.

She told me all along I was going to end up a whore like my mother, and I proved her right. What else was a homeless teenage girl going to do to support herself on the streets?

Fast forward nearly twenty years, and Bernadette got sucked into a series of phone scams that preyed on the elderly. She lost everything.

It must have been the worst day of her life when she had to call and ask me for money.

Bernadette glares at Norma's retreating back. "You love to torture me. Both of you."

I glance around the room of the house where she lives. "Yes, so much that I make sure you have everything you need and you never go hungry. You're lucky I don't restrict your food like you did mine when you thought I was getting fat at fourteen."

She grabs a carrot stick and crunches down hard on the end. "You should thank me for that. Look at you now."

I run my hands down my sides, letting them curve over my hips. "You're right. No thanks to you, I look fucking great."

"Get out of here with your filthy language. I shouldn't have to listen to this. It has to be elder abuse. I'm gonna get a lawyer and tell them everything. Just you wait."

I pluck a cherry tomato from her plate and pop it into my mouth. "Yeah, and what're you gonna pay him with? Your Social Security check barely keeps the lights on or buys groceries."

She shakes her head and hovers over her food so I can't steal more.

"It's good to see you're still kicking, Bernie. Just like the stubborn mule you are. I'll be back next week to check on you. Let Norma know if you need anything."

She ignores me as I strut out of the living room and into the small kitchen where Norma is washing silverware.

I cut the shit and get right to it. "How's she doing?"

Norma's frail shoulders rise and fall. "She's lonely, whether she'll admit it or not. She makes up reasons to complain so she'll have something to say to me. So . . . pretty much the same as always." She turns the water off and places the last spoon in the dish rack. "She's always full of energy after you come to visit, though. She doesn't mean what she says, you know?"

My eyebrows lift to my hairline. "Oh yes, she does. She was born mean, and she'll stay mean until the day she dies."

"You two best not be talking about me!" Bernadette calls from the other room. Being wheelchair bound after the last fall that broke her hip, she can't come find out.

I poke my head through the doorway. "Of course we're talking about you. Norma's telling me that there's hope of you being a decent human yet. I don't buy it."

"Go to hell." My great-aunt's slender middle finger flips me the bird.

"Already been there, Bernie. Try not to choke. No need to add ambulance bills to your upkeep."

I move back into the kitchen and give Norma a kiss on her papery cheek. "Thank you for taking such good care of her. You're a saint."

"You've done right by her, Ms. Magnolia, whether she'll admit it or not." Bernadette's caregiver squeezes my arm. "Have a blessed day."

"You too. Both of you."

5
MOSES

I *see you, mama. And I know you saw me earlier.*

I tap my thumb against the leather seat of the Rolls Royce Phantom, a car I picked up in New York for the drive down to NOLA, as the woman I haven't been able to get out of my mind in fifteen years picks her way down the cracked sidewalk of her French Quarter street. She stops in front of the gate of a bright yellow house with blue shutters to fish a set of keys out of her purse.

Sunshine for the home of a former woman of the night. Others might think it's an odd choice, but they don't understand her. Magnolia Marie Maison is a complex woman that no average man would ever be able to unravel.

Lucky for me, I'm far from average. I also plan to spend the rest of my life learning every last one of her secrets.

Magnolia inserts a key into the black metal gate that connects her property to the brick wall of the one beside it. It swings wide and she slips through the opening, glancing behind her as she pulls it shut. I savor the last glimpse of her as she disappears from view—a dress hugging those hot-as-hell curves and her shiny hair blowing in the breeze.

Anticipation rises within me, filling me with purpose, the likes of which I haven't felt in *years*. And, fuck, does that feel right. Like I'm finally alive for the first time since I walked away and left her behind.

I never planned to leave her alone for this long.

My fingers flex around the piece of alabaster in my hand.

A less certain man might wonder if she'd know who was sending it when she gets it, but I don't need to. Magnolia is a scarily intelligent woman. There will be no doubt in her mind where it came from, no matter who delivers it.

My blood pumps faster at the thought of what's coming next. War, most likely. But not over the streets like I've waged before. This time, it's going to be a battle for a barricaded heart.

Never before has anything been so fucking important.

I won't rest until she's mine.

Brace yourself, Magnolia. Another hurricane is coming.

6
MAGNOLIA

Every time I set foot in my new house, I feel like I can breathe easier. It's not big, but it's all mine, and there's not a single hint of promiscuity attached to it.

No client will ever come knocking.

No man will ever see the inside of my finished bedroom.

Leaving my condo behind is a fresh start in more ways than anyone could ever understand. Not that anyone has spent much time trying to understand me, beyond how they could get me to rescind my *I don't take clients anymore* edict.

My contractor is strangely absent, despite the fact that we're supposed to meet in five minutes to discuss the list of things he needs to complete before I hand him the final check. But that's okay. It gives me time to walk through the space and allow myself to daydream for a few minutes about what it's going to be like to live here.

An address in the French Quarter. Not too bad for a girl who's had to fight like a warrior to survive.

I spin on my heels, taking in the white subway tile of the kitchen backsplash above the massive copper farm sink. I can picture myself standing here, washing up after cooking a fantastic dinner *for one*.

It exudes peace, and that's something I haven't had nearly enough of so far in my life, but I'm banking on having it now. At least, I was until I saw him.

Thoughts of Moses spin through my brain, and I grit my teeth.

"What the hell is he doing back after all this time? And why the hell is he meeting with Mount?" I shake my head and look around the room, but the white walls don't have any answers for me. At least they'll keep all my secrets.

I'm upstairs, stepping over drop cloths to check out the progress in my small but luxe bathroom, when I finally hear the bell at the gate.

"It's about time, Rocco. You're *late*."

Tardiness isn't something I tolerate well, but I've learned my contractor doesn't work on my schedule. He works on his. Still, his price was right, and he hasn't tried to fuck me.

Points for him.

My heels click on the refinished hardwood as I make my way down the stairs and outside to the gate. I reach for the handle, not bothering to check the peephole. No one but Keira and Mount know I bought this place, which means I don't have to be constantly on guard. *Thank God for that.*

"What the fuck?" I mumble as I open the gate to find a street kid standing outside, bouncing from foot to foot.

"This is for you." He shoves something at me, and acting solely on instinct, I reach out to take the small but heavy object from him. As soon as he makes the transfer, he spins to leave.

"Hey!" I yell, but he sprints away. I look down at what he dropped into my hand. It's pure white, cool, and smooth to the touch.

Wait. Is that a *pawn? From a chess set?*

I shoot out the gate, letting it slam shut behind me as I take off after the kid, running with as much care as I can so I don't bite it in my designer pumps. He takes a right at the first corner, a couple of buildings down.

Why the fuck is he running? Who sent him?

I get three steps before I collide with a man turning the corner the kid just disappeared around.

He's startled too. "Whoa. Sorry. Didn't mean to slam into you."

"Don't worry about it," I say, trying to dodge around him, but he steps the same way, like we're freaking dancing. "Excuse me."

I move the other way, and he does too.

"Oh, jeez. Sorry. Really, I—"

By the time I get around him, the kid is gone.

"Fuck." I breathe the word out with a sigh.

The guy searches behind himself where I'm looking. "Shit. What'd I do? Are you okay?"

I finally look at his face, and just my luck, he's all golden blond and attractive as hell. Such a waste.

"Nothing. Don't worry about it." I wipe the hair out of my face and try to catch my breath. I'm no runner, that's for sure.

He looks down at me, concern in his predictably blue eyes. "Were you trying to catch that kid who bolted around the corner? Did he steal your purse or something? I can go after him."

I shake my head. "No. My purse is . . . *inside my fucking house.*" I release another long groan. "Shit."

The poster boy for the All-American man winces. "Crap. You locked yourself out?" he asks and scratches the back of his neck. "Damn. I would offer to help you get inside, but . . . I don't know how to use a lock pick or where you'd even get one. Clearly, my education is incomplete, because helping beautiful women should always be a top priority."

His comment is also way too predictable. The obvious flirting is nearly too much. "Don't worry about me, big shot. I'll be fine. Have a good one."

I turn to walk back to my gate, trying to figure out how the hell I'm going to break into my own damn house, when he grabs my arm.

That's a no-no. I jerk back immediately. "What the—"

As I glare at him, his hands go up in the air in surrender. "Sorry. I shouldn't have . . . I'm screwing this all up. I'm new here, and I'm lost. I'm looking for a café, but I left my phone at home, thinking I'd be more present and in the moment. Guess I forgot how much I need GPS to tell me where the hell to go."

My patience thinning, I roll my eyes. "Which café?"

"Café Envie."

I nod. "You're not far. Go to the next intersection and take a left. It's on the next corner, also on the left."

"It was really nice to meet you . . ." He trails off, clearly waiting for my name.

"A helpful stranger," I say, squeezing the chess piece in my hand and wanting this guy to get a move on.

His affable expression doesn't change much at my evasion. If anything, his smile widens. "All right, *stranger*. Thank you."

With a wink, he strides off down the street, and I wait until he turns the corner before I walk back to my gate, clutching the pawn. I don't need handsome men who think they're charming knowing where I live. My door is *closed* to them.

Thankfully, as I stop in front of my place, my contractor, Rocco, pulls up in his white pickup.

"Sorry I'm late. Got hung up in traffic. This fucking city."

At least one thing is going my way. "Good timing. I locked myself out."

"Ah, shit. That's no good. Come on, I'll let you in. Did you look around? What do you think?" He launches into a stream of chatter about what he's going to work on today, and everything he's finished since we last spoke.

I only listen to half of it. My mind is on the chess piece I tip over in my hand and the three initials on the bottom. *M. B. G.*

A flash from the past bursts into my brain, and I have to clutch the counter to stay upright as the vivid memory unfolds in my mind.

The most beautiful man I've ever seen in my life sits cross-legged on the floor of the house I was willing to die to save, across a chessboard from me, wearing a smile on his face guaranteed to melt even the blackest of hearts.

"A beautiful woman who plays chess like a master. I never guessed that'd be so damn sexy or my greatest weakness."

Moses.

Moses sent me a pawn.

What the fuck does it mean?

I'm his pawn? He's my pawn?

No . . .

He's making the first move.

7
MAGNOLIA

"**G**et it all done, and we won't have a problem." I give the order to Rocco with a firm voice, all business right now.

He smiles in return, with that appreciative look in his eye that plenty of men have had before him. But he ain't getting none of me. Not a single one of them are.

Not even the man who sent me a pawn.

You sure about that, Mags? The voice in my head, who I call Ho-It-All instead of Know-It-All, taunts me. Thankfully, I don't have time to think about the answer because Rocco replies.

"You know I will, Ms. Maison. You can count on me. You'll be moving in on time. I give you my word."

I offer him my hand, and when he shakes it, holding on a little longer than I'd like, I tug mine free from his grip. "Give my best to your wife, Rocco. I'll see you in a few days."

The reminder that he's a married man produces a ruddy hue just above the collar of his white T-shirt. "Of course. Have a good evening, Ms. Maison."

With that, I scoop up my handbag, toss the stupid pawn

inside, and stride out of my new digs like I don't have a care in the world.

But I do.

And I don't make it a half block before my cell vibrates in my bag.

I swear to Christ, if it's Moses, I'm going to give him a piece of my mind. Thinking he can come back here and walk into my life like it hasn't been fifteen fucking years of radio silence.

But I should know better. He never calls.

When I look down at the screen, it's a number I recognize.

Why the hell am I thinking about him constantly? He's in the past. Despite the fact he resurfaced today, he's dead and gone to me, just like the feelings I thought I once had.

But why now?

I don't answer that question either, choosing instead to answer the phone. "You got me."

"Oh, Mags. Thank you so much for picking up," Taylor, one of my top girls who still works for me, says in a rush as soon as I answer. "I . . . I've got a problem, and I don't know what to do."

I look both ways and then cross the street. "Lay it on me, girl."

"My last client seemed to think his appointment should have come with *other services* that are no longer included in my repertoire."

I release a long breath but keep marching. *I swear to Christ, this is why we shouldn't take male clients. Only women.*

"Who was it?"

"Baxter Frye. He paid for an eighty-minute massage. I gave him an eighty-minute massage." She's out of breath and sounds shaken.

I don't want to, but I know I have to ask. "And then what happened?"

"When I told him his treatment was over and that I'd wait in the other room until he dressed, he jumped off the massage table and started yelling that he didn't get his happy ending, and he

wasn't going to let me leave until he did." Her voice cracks as she tells the story.

I stop short, and a woman staring at her phone instead of where she's walking nearly runs into me.

"Where are you? You still there?" I'm poised, practically trembling with the energy rolling off me, ready to start sprinting for Baxter Frye's home to tear it down brick by brick with my bare hands if he's keeping my girl there against her will.

"No. I'm home. Safe."

My shoulders relax, but only slightly. This day has been one shit show after another. "Jesus *fuck*, girl. You could start with that next time."

"Sorry, Mags. I held him off with my stun gun and ran. I'm not working on him again. Ever."

I step around the corner and lean against the brick wall, staring up at the blue October sky. "You won't have to. Baxter Frye is off the client list *permanently*, and maybe every other fucking man in this town too." To myself, I add, *Especially ex-clients who think my girls still provide the services they used to. But I'm out of that fucking business.*

"Really?" Taylor sounds so young and hopeful, making me absolutely sure I'm making the right choice.

"Yeah, honey. Don't you worry. Mags has your back. I'll make sure Baxter knows what the fuck he's done, and I'll sort out what we're gonna do next." Nothing short of three or four vengeful ideas come to mind in short order.

"Thank you, Mags. I'm so sorry. I don't know what it is about me, but it seems like men just—"

"Stop right there, girl." I shift and clutch my purse to my side. "There ain't nothing about you that's wrong. It's just a man trying to take what isn't being freely given, and that's a fucking crime. This ain't about you, doll. This is about him. And I *will* take care of it."

"What would we do without you, Mags?"

I'm proud my girls have always been and always will be able to rely on me. "You don't have to wonder," I say, my elbow scraping against the rough wall as I lean. "I'm not going anywhere."

As I consider the words, a rush of disappointment floods me that I shouldn't be feeling. *What the hell? I love it here. NOLA is my home. Not somewhere I'm sad to be staying.*

"Thanks, Mags."

"I'm glad you're okay. We'll talk later, darlin'."

I hang up the phone and shake my head. I'm all out of sorts today. I should have known this would happen after Celeste pulled the fucking Devil card on me.

Scanning the intersection, I search for any sign of the Creole ghost who blew back into my life today, but there's nothing.

What the fuck do you want, Moses? Why now?

With a shake of my head, I push him out of my mind the best I can. Next stop, my condo. Then I'll give ol' Baxter Frye a call and let him know exactly how badly he fucked up.

No one crosses me or my girls. Not without paying a hefty price.

When I walk into my soon-to-be former home, the sight of the stacks of boxes puts a smile on my face.

"Only another week, and I'm out of here," I tell the room. It doesn't answer, and thank God for that.

If these walls could talk . . . well, I don't even want to think about what they'd say. I've made a lot of mistakes in my life, but they got me where I am, so I find it hard to regret most of them.

Some of them, though . . . some of them I regret a lot.

I set my purse on the sideboard and flip it open. The white pawn mocks me from where it's tucked inside. I reach for the whiskey and splash some into a glass before pulling the chess piece out to study it.

The liquor slides down my throat, just as smooth as the piece, but the whiskey is a hell of a lot more welcome. With the pawn in one hand and my glass in the other, I kick off my heels and pad across the tile floor to my sofa.

I haven't had a minute to myself since that street kid shoved the stupid thing at me, but now that I do . . . I don't know what to think.

Why now, Moses?

It makes no goddamned sense, and it certainly has nothing to do with me.

A man doesn't walk away from a woman for that long and come back thinking he's still got a shot with her. Then again, Moses wasn't *just any* man. Hell, I'm still not sure he's mortal, because he was nothing like anyone I've ever met—before or since.

And I need to stop thinking about him. No good can come of it. I'm not interested in anything he has to say.

Liar, liar. Pants on fire. Ho-It-All chimes in, and the mocking thought makes me think of the card Madame Celeste flipped over on the table before my meeting with Mount.

Okay then, fine. Maybe I want to know what he has to say, if only so I can shove those damn words right back down his sexy-ass throat.

My head jerks up, and I shake it as though the motion will clear out the thoughts of Moses. It doesn't work.

Remembering Baxter Frye does, though.

I set the pawn on my end table and cross the room to retrieve my phone before heading into my office. On the front wall, directly facing my desk, is a framed abstract painting of a woman rising out of the sea. I stop in front of it and give the frame a tug. It swings on a hinge connected to the left-hand side, revealing a safe behind it.

Spinning the knob, I put in the combination I know by heart

—08, 29, 05—but refuse to acknowledge that my choosing the date Katrina made landfall in my city has anything to do with Moses. When the safe unlocks, I find what I need inside.

A fat black book. It would be cliché if it weren't so amusing.

I collect it and return to my mirrored silver desk.

Before I open to the F section of the book, I pull open my desk drawer and flip the lid on a black lacquered box. From inside, I liberate a lighter and a joint. Once it's burning, I take a long hit, letting the smoke fill my lungs. A few more puffs, and a nice mellow buzz takes hold of me.

I reach for the whiskey and sip as I flip to Baxter's number. It's written in red ink, which I should have taken as a sign, but I thought the owner of a chain of well-known appliance stores would realize he had too much to lose to cause trouble.

Clearly, I misjudged him.

It doesn't happen all that often, but even I'm fallible when it comes to men, despite knowing them better than I know myself most days.

From another drawer, I pull out a disposable cell phone and punch in the number. As soon as it rings, I lean back in my white high-backed chair and prop my bare feet on my desk.

"Hello?" he says, answering on the third ring with a note of confusion.

"Oh, Baxter," I sing across the line.

"Who is this?"

"Do you have any idea in that tiny little brain of yours how many ways I could ruin your sorry life without so much as chipping my fingernail polish?"

The man on the other end of the line goes quiet.

"Oh, don't be shy now, Baxter. Where's your sense of adventure? Tell me about how much you like happy endings." It may be wrong, but I enjoy taunting him. It's easy to put weak men on their knees.

Then again, a good strong man wouldn't be in the position

he's in now. They wouldn't need to force a woman to do anything.

"W-what do you want?"

A tendril of his fear curls through the phone, and I grin.

"I just want to tell you a fairy tale. I can't recall all of it, but that's okay. I think you'll still get the gist. It goes something like this. Blah, blah, blah . . . and blah, blah, blah . . . and *poof*, Baxter ends up locked in a cage for *days*, and he's wondering if someone's going to let him out before he starves to death."

I take another hit while he breathes heavily over the line, at a loss for words.

"Now, the real question here, Baxter, is whether or not that fairy tale has a *happy ending*. Because I hear that you think you're entitled to one, and I just don't know if that's how this story ends. You wanna roll the dice with me and we can find out? Because I'm more than willing to put it to the test so we can know for sure."

There's a scraping noise from his end of the call, and several beats of silence before he speaks. "I . . . I made a mistake. I . . . It won't happen again."

"You're right. It won't happen again because you've been blackballed, Baxter."

"But—"

"Shut your *goddamned mouth* and listen." When he doesn't reply, I smile. "That's a good Baxter. Damn, it sounds like I'm talking to a dog. Which makes perfect sense, considering that's all you are. A fucking *mutt* who will be *put down* if you ever threaten another woman for the rest of your godforsaken life. You understand me, *Baxter*?"

He chokes and then answers, "Yes. I understand."

"Good boy, Baxter," I say, crooning to him like he is the mutt I just called him. Then I change my tone to steel. "Now, you have a lovely fucking evening, and just remember, I'm watching you. If you take one wrong step, we'll find out exactly how that story ends. And I'm pretty fucking sure you aren't going to like it."

I hang up the phone. *Entitled piece of shit.* I could fucking kill him. I take another drag, letting the weed soothe the anger bubbling inside me.

You handled it. Don't let emotion take over.

But the thought of Taylor's fear, even if it only lasted a few minutes, can't be so easily cowed. My fingers curl around the phone, and rage burns through my system.

I'm done with this life. Done with men who think they can take whatever they want. Done with putting girls in situations where they end up calling me, terrified out of their minds. I'm fucking done.

I let loose, flinging the phone as hard as I can against the opposite wall, but the shattering plastic does nothing to calm my temper.

"I have to get out of here." I shove out of my chair, joint in hand, as I stalk toward my bedroom to change.

Fuck men. Fuck Moses. Fuck everything.

I'm going to the club to see Desiree and handle shit myself. Just like I always do.

8
MAGNOLIA

When the car drops me off in front of the sprawling plantation house, I barely notice the massive trees with moss dangling from their limbs over the banks of the bayou. I'm not here to be filled with wonder and amazement like the new members who have been added to the roster since I bowed out of managing the club.

Then again, no one was surprised when I stepped aside a few years ago when my well-ordered life went through a proverbial wood chipper. Nothing is the same as it used to be, especially not me.

The sense of disquiet that's been haunting me all day chases me up the grand steps of the antebellum mansion. The doorman smiles beneath his mask when he sees me.

"Ms. Maison. It's a pleasure to see you this evening."

"Thank you, Gerard."

"Do you need a mask?" he asks, his gaze lingering on my face.

One of my eyebrows shoots up. "Do you think it's going to help me fly under the radar or something?" The question is more rhetorical than anything, because it doesn't seem to matter what I do. Everyone knows who I am wherever I go.

"Club rules," he says evenly, a reminder that I'm not part of the management anymore.

"Mine's inside." I have a locked cupboard in the ladies' dressing room, which contains all sorts of interesting things.

"Enjoy your evening, ma'am," Gerard says with a nod of approval.

The door sweeps open, and he gestures for me to enter. I step inside, barely noticing the shimmering crystal of the new chandelier or the throbbing bass beat of the music coming from upstairs. I don't turn and stare at the gold gilt covering the sconces on the walls or the art hanging between them.

That's not what I'm here for.

I head straight to the manager's office, turning three corners and clipping down a hallway. The door is closed, so I knock twice and wait.

The knob turns, and the door swings open a foot.

"Can I help— Oh, Magnolia. It's so good to see you. I didn't know you were coming tonight," Paige, the club's manager, says to me.

"Unscheduled visit. Business, not pleasure, darling," I tell her with a smile. "Is Desiree around?"

Paige nods. "Yes. I saw her on the monitors in the bar. Everything okay?"

"Everything's always okay in my world," I say, lying to her with a smile that hides everything I'm thinking and feeling.

"Good to hear. Also, good to see you. Enjoy your night."

I turn up the wattage of my smile. "You too, Paige. You too."

Thankful that I don't have to scour the entire club to track down Desiree, I pop into the ladies' dressing room, put on my mask, and take the back stairs up to the second floor. The large and stately room that houses the bar is the hub of all activity in the club. This is where most members' nights start and end.

It doesn't take me long to find Desiree. A small crowd of men surround her, no doubt dying to get the madam into bed. Like me after I took the reins of the house, Desiree doesn't take clients unless she feels so inclined. And it hasn't hurt business in the least. Exclusivity means big dollars in this world.

Rather than burst into her circle and have to talk to any of the men drooling over her, I belly up to the bar and lay my small clutch on the long expanse of wood.

"What can I get for you, Ms. Maison?"

"Three fingers of Seven Sinners. Neat." I shake my head at Paul and chuckle, vindicated. "I told Gerard it didn't matter if I wore a mask, and you just proved me right."

Paul's smile beams behind his half mask as he reaches for the bottle of whiskey. "He should know you're unforgettable."

The compliment is sweet, but the last thing I want to do is encourage Paul in any way. He's nearly thirty, but still way too innocent for a woman like me.

Oh, and what kind of man is right for you? Ho-It-All is back and hitting me with a question I'd do better not to contemplate.

As Paul pours the whiskey, I think about the answer.

A man who has some miles on him. Jaded. Scarred with battle wounds. Someone who is ready to ride off into the sunset and live a different life. Clean and brand new.

I stop short on that thought.

Ride off into the sunset? Really, Mags? Now you sound like a girl who believes in fairy tales and happily-ever-afters, and we know that's a waste of time.

"Here you go, Ms. Maison," Paul says as he slides the whiskey toward me.

As my hand curls around the glass, I open my mouth to thank him, but Desiree slips onto the bar stool next to me.

"Hey, boo."

I glance to my side. "Desi. You look good."

"Thanks. You too." She leans back on the stool, pushing her tits damn near out of her bustier as she arches her back.

Paul nearly swallows his tongue, even though he sees plenty

of skin in this place. Desiree is just that gorgeous with her blond mane and tip-tilted cat eyes. Poor kid doesn't stand a chance.

She orders a vodka rocks, and he nearly drops the bottle *and* the glass while making it. She shoots him a wink and then shifts her gaze to me. "What's happening, lady?"

She's making small talk, but what I have to say isn't small or fit to be discussed in this room.

"We need privacy."

Some of the languid grace of her posture dies. "What's wrong?"

"Privacy," I repeat. "You have a room for tonight?"

Worry lines her normally porcelain-smooth brow. "Of course."

"We'll talk there. Lead the way." I slide off the bar stool, and when Paul stares after Desiree as she struts away from the bar, I turn back to him for a beat. "Close your mouth, Paul. You'll drool in the drinks, bud."

His lips snap shut, and he busies himself with a towel, wiping down the surface of the bar.

With a quiet chuckle, I follow Desiree across the room. A current madam and a former madam heading to a private room at a sex club draw the eyes of everyone in the bar. No doubt the men are picturing us naked and grinding on each other already. I can't help but roll my eyes.

Less than three minutes later, I shut the door of the elegantly appointed room behind me. Inside is a four-poster bed with red silk cords tied to each corner post. A dark brown leather chair flanks the wall, next to an armoire that I know from experience is filled with a treasure trove of sex toys and implements.

Once we're alone, Desiree takes off her mask, and I do the same.

"What's going on, Mags?"

Thankfully, this place is regularly swept for bugs and listening devices, so I'm able to answer honestly. "Feds."

Desiree's dark brown eyes go wide. "Where?"

"Watching the house. You gotta lay low for a while. Put the girls on hotel mode. No clients in or out."

"Fuck." She huffs out the word before lowering herself into the armchair. When she looks up at me, I read fear on her face. "Why? What's going on?"

"Alberto Brandon apparently caught their notice, and they've been watching him. He led them right to you."

"Fuck," she repeats with a shake of her head. "That dirty old bastard barely tips, and now he brings the Feds down on us? As if it wasn't bad enough that he fell head over heels for Naya and wouldn't let her take any other clients." Her jaw works from side to side. "Come to think of it, the timing's real weird too. She told me she needed time off because she had to go out of town for a little bit. I haven't seen her in a damn week."

I tap a nail on the wood of the footboard. "They could have skipped town together if Brandon was worried he was in trouble. The Feds clearly don't know shit if they're watching the house."

"So, what should I do?"

"Cover your own ass and your girls'. Keep the clients away. The Feds will get bored when they don't see Brandon. Hopefully they'll move along."

She sips her vodka and lowers the glass. "What about your girls? You having them do anything different?"

I think about Taylor and the other girls who I've put through school so they could learn a trade and get out of the business. "They should be fine. All their appointments are off-site. There's nothing the Feds could pick them up for. Living in the house while they save money to get their own apartments isn't a crime."

"What about you? The house is still technically in your name while I'm paying on it. You think the Feds will come knocking on your door?"

"I guess we'll find out."

Desiree shakes her head. "I'm so sorry, Mags. Fuck. I didn't mean for this to happen."

"No apologies necessary, honey. Shit happens." I lean against the foot of the bed. "You didn't bring them down on us. Brandon did. So now we run damage control."

Desiree jams her hands into her hair. "Ugh. Men are fucking assholes. I could kick him in the balls right now."

"Amen, honey," I reply, thankful that my part in this mess is done. "You'll be fine. Now, get in touch with your girls, give them orders, and then get on with your night. I'll tell mine what's what and let you know when the heat dies down."

"You say it like it's so easy." Her tone is laced with frustration, and when she looks up at me, her expression resembles a lost little girl. "Then again, I'm sure for you it would be."

She needs a hug, but coddling her won't help. "Your house. Your call. You can handle it. Grow a pair and woman up. Besides, they don't want you. They want Brandon."

Desiree releases a long sigh. "True. Well, I guess I'd better get moving."

"Good girl," I tell her, and then slip my mask back on as I turn to leave the room.

"Mags?" Desiree's questioning tone stops me with my hand on the knob.

"What?"

"How did you know it was time to get out of the game?"

What is it with the hard questions tonight?

I meet Desiree's gaze and give it to her point-blank. "Baby, that's a question only you can answer. And the fact that you're asking it means you need to start thinking about a plan B."

❖

When I leave the private room, dozens of pairs of eyes follow me, but I don't pay them any mind. I came here to do what I needed to do, and now I'm getting the fuck out.

"If you wanna play, kitten," a man's voice says from over my shoulder, "I'll make you purr."

I turn around to look at him. "Kitten? Boy, I'm a goddamned lioness. Back the fuck off." A dark chuckle leaves my lips at the sight of his shocked face, and I exit the club with a smile.

9
MAGNOLIA

"Thank you for the ride, Lionel. I'll see you next time."

"Have a nice night, Ms. Maison. Take care."

I hand him a twenty as a tip and cross the sidewalk to the front entrance of my condo building.

One more week, and I'll be going home to the French Quarter, I think as I punch the button for the elevator that will take me up to the sixth floor.

I remember how excited I was to move here, because I was moving up in the world. It meant that I had *arrived*. Now I'm thrilled to get the hell out, because this place doesn't fit who I am anymore. And when I'm done with a person or a place, I'm *done*.

The elevator doors open, and I've only taken one step out when someone slams into me, ramming me back inside the car. Hot pain screams along my side.

"Hey!" I shriek out the protest and slam both palms into the guy who rushed me, pushing him off me and into the mirrored wall.

Fuck. He's wearing a mask. Bad sign.

I commit him to memory—around six feet tall, black balaclava, brown eyes—as his head smashes into the glass behind him.

"You fucking whore!"

That's when I see the knife. Glinting silver in the fluorescent lights of the elevator, dripping with my blood, it slashes out, no doubt aiming for my jugular as I jerk back into the corner, out of his reach. But that won't help me for long if I'm unarmed and trapped in here with him. That can only mean death.

Not today, motherfucker. Not today.

I twist to the side, reaching for the stiletto blade hidden at the small of my back. Before he realizes what I'm doing, I palm the knife and aim for his groin. I miss my intended target, but my blade sinks into the flesh of his upper thigh, and I twist the knife before yanking it free. He roars and stumbles back into the opposite corner of the elevator. Blood stains his jeans red, and I move as fast as I can, backing out of the car as I punch the down button.

He drops to his knees, his black gloves reaching for me, but the doors close before he can stop them.

Fuck. Fuck. Fuck.

My heart slams into my chest, but my brain shifts into survival mode.

I don't know who he was, why he was here, or what he wanted, but I know one thing for sure—I don't want anything to do with that knife-happy motherfucker, and I need to get the hell out of here.

The slice on my left side sears me with pain as it oozes blood. I cover it with my hand as I stop in front of my condo door and drop my clutch and the knife I didn't even realize I was still holding on the floor, letting my keys spill out. Once I have them in my sticky red fingers, I open the door as quickly as possible. Kicking my purse and the knife inside, I lock the dead bolt behind me.

But I'm not staying.

I hit my closet first and grab a duffel bag. It's already filled with everything I might need to make a run for it. Next stop is my office and the safe. I scoop up my book, cash, and weed and toss them inside the duffel. Finally, I rush into the bathroom and grab my first aid kit for *special* emergencies and a towel. I wrap the knife up and toss it into the bag too.

My side burns like a motherfucker, but I force the pain out of my mind as I wash my hands, slip on a black caftan over my clothes that swirls around my ankles, and snag a floppy hat.

I'm out of my condo in less than three minutes. On the way to the stairwell, I yank the fire alarm.

Chaos is good.

Moments later, I'm hustling down the stairs to the parking garage amid a crowd of frantic residents rushing outside.

My heels click against the pavement as I breathe in exhaust and gasoline fumes, but I don't go for my Lexus.

It's a gut feeling. Something I can't explain. But until I know if that dude in the elevator was coming for me or just anyone who happened to be riding up, I'm not taking any chances. My Lexus is too flashy and noticeable, and I'm feeling paranoid as shit right now. Instead, I trek to a corner spot and slide a key into the door of a black Honda Accord I keep for emergencies, complete with a car seat in the back to blend in.

I toss my duffel in the front seat and get the fuck out of Dodge before I can even hear the sirens that'll be coming next.

10
MOSES

People pour out every door of Magnolia's condo building as an alarm blares, and my unease hits new heights.

"Something isn't right," I tell Jules, who sits in the driver's seat.

"It's just a fire alarm. You want me to go in and check her place? She's probably outside already."

I shake my head. We hadn't seen Magnolia leave—sneaky woman—so it surprised us both when she got out of a car in front of the condo building a few minutes ago.

"No . . . timing is off. Something's wrong. We're both going in."

I'm out of the car before Jules can even get his door open. I don't ignore gut instincts, ever. That's how people get dead.

We catch the open front door as people stream out, and the first thing I notice in the lobby is a blood smear on the elevator door and a trail leading toward a door marked SERVICE, right beside it.

"What the fuck?" I point at it. "You follow the blood. I'm going to get her out if she isn't already."

Jules doesn't hesitate and goes into tracking mode. "Got it. On it."

We separate as I dash up five flights of stairs, dodging the people still coming down.

When I reach Magnolia's end of the hall, the first thing I notice is blood on her knob and door, and another smear on the floor.

"Fuck." Now my instincts are going wild. Doors are slamming around me as people run to get out of the building, but I know there's no fire. Whatever happened tonight, Magnolia's involved, and I gotta find her.

I pound on the door, but there's no answer. "Magnolia! Open the fucking door."

Still no answer.

I whip out a credit card, and a few seconds later, I'm inside. I should have known that she wasn't here, because the chain and dead bolt weren't set. And for her not to lock the dead bolt as she left? That tells me she hauled ass out of here as fast as she could.

The condo is loaded with boxes. It hasn't been tossed. No furniture is broken or lamps shattered. So, no sign of a struggle. *What the fuck happened then?*

I clear the rooms and then get the fuck out as fast as I came in, wiping the knob, door, and floor clean of blood and my prints.

My phone buzzes in my pocket, and I grab it. The display tells me it's Jules.

"Boss, we got a fucking problem."

"You find her?"

"No, but I got a dead body in the service hallway. Fucker got stabbed in the leg. Bled out."

"Femoral artery. Fuck. Get his prints and a picture of his face, then get the fuck out. We're going to find Magnolia."

11
MAGNOLIA

I t takes me over half an hour to get to my house in the Quarter, because I can't take the chance that anyone followed me. More than ever, I'm so fucking glad I never told anyone other than Mount and Keira that I bought this place.

But Moses knows.

I push the thought of him out of my mind. *Ain't got time for that. I've got bigger things to worry about.*

I park a block down and walk to my gate with my caftan swirling around my feet, my floppy hat fixed on my head, and my duffel bag over my shoulder. Once inside, I finally take a deep breath.

"Fuck, that hurts." My side is on fire where he cut me. But this ain't my first rodeo getting knifed, unfortunately. Hopefully, it's my last time, though. I'm thoroughly sick of this shit.

Carefully, I pick my way over drop cloths and head upstairs to my all-white bathroom. The bathroom that was never supposed to be stained with blood.

Too bad wishes don't all come true.

Once I'm inside, I drop the duffel on the floor and bend to unzip it, unleashing a sharp, burning sensation.

I grit my teeth as I dig in the bag. The first aid kit, whiskey, weed, and shotgun come out first. I lay the gun on the white marble countertop within reach, just in case that motherfucker manages to find me. Then I tug off the caftan, carefully peel up the hem of my crop top, and glance down at the wound. He sliced me right through the fucking band of my high-waisted black skirt.

Fucking asshole. I liked this skirt.

As I suspected from the pain, my inspection tells me the wound needs stitches. But that comes *after* the hefty swig of whiskey I take before slipping off my skirt.

Jesus, shit, that burns.

But it doesn't hurt as much as it's going to. I splash some of Keira's best whiskey on the cut and grit my teeth against the fiery pain.

"I'm getting too old for this bullshit," I murmur to the empty room with a shake of my head and a long sigh.

After digging into the first aid kit, I grab gauze and press it against the cut. The blood is clotting, so there's no chance I'll bleed out. Which means I have time to get my priorities in order and roll a nice fat blunt. Because I'm gonna need it.

Once I'm done, I light it and take a long hit, puffing hard to get it burning right. Smoke fills my lungs, and I wait a beat before blowing it out. I glance down at the suture kit, but reach for the whiskey again instead.

"This is gonna fucking suck," I murmur, then freeze.

Before he even speaks, I feel his presence. I jerk my head up to see Moses Buford Gaspard standing in the doorway of my goddamned bathroom.

"Your stitches are gonna be crooked as fuck if you drink that whole bottle before you start," he says with a lazy grin.

12
MOSES

Magnolia grabs the shotgun on the bathroom counter, racks it, and has the barrel pointed at me in less time than it would take most people to scream. But not Mags. She's one of a fucking kind.

I came here expecting the worst, but what I found was straight out of a twisted fantasy. With the shotgun cradled in her arms, a blunt hanging from her lips, and a bottle of whiskey by her side, Magnolia Maison is the goddamned woman of my dreams. Gorgeous. Capable. And so fucking sexy, even with the bleeding wound on her side.

"What the fuck are you doing here, Mob—Moses?" she spits out, almost calling me by that silly, long-lost nickname she gave me.

I forgot how her voice could sound with my name on her lips. *God, I missed that.* And then I damn near forget to breathe, but force myself to focus—on Mags and her injury.

"You need a real doctor for that?"

Her tiger eyes narrow, and I'm pretty fucking sure she'll pull the trigger if I say the wrong thing. "If I did, I would've gone to one. Now, get the fuck out of my house before I put in a hole in you that I can't sew up."

"Mags—"

"No," she says unequivocally. As usual, she doesn't take any shit from me. "I've already threatened one man's life and maimed another tonight. I'm not fucking afraid to hollow you out right here. So choose your words wisely, *Moses*, as you back the fuck out of this room."

I decide to test her. Probably because I'm a twisted son of a bitch. "Killed. Not maimed. You *killed* a man tonight."

A shadow ghosts across her face, and her lips press together around the blunt for a beat. Then, with that incredible self-control I've always found sexy as fuck, she relaxes and blows a cloud of smoke directly at my face.

"Get the fuck out."

"Who was he, Mags? You in trouble?"

Her tawny throat works as she swallows, and it's the sole sign that what happened tonight unsettled her. She's the strongest woman I've ever met, so it's no surprise she's not dissolving into tears.

She releases the shotgun with her right hand and flings her arm out. "Do I look like a damsel in distress to you? No one has ever mistaken me for Snow fucking White."

In her tight black crop top that shows off her tits and her skirt rolled down to her hips, she looks like temptation incarnate. But, still, I've gotta know she's safe. I didn't come back to claim her just to let someone else fuck up my plans.

"Was it random?"

Her glare carries enough heat that I feel the burn. "He called me a whore, so who the fuck knows."

My gaze drops to the cut again. "You need a hand? I've got two steady ones. At your service."

"I don't know what the fuck your game is," she says, shaking her head and gripping the shotgun tightly again. "But try to touch me, and I will fucking shoot you. I haven't needed your help in fifteen years, and I don't plan to ever need it again. So, despite whatever brought you here, you might as well drift right on back out of town."

Her finger caresses the trigger, and part of me is willing to bet that she hasn't shot me only because she doesn't want to mess up her new house. Not because she doesn't have the balls.

She sure as hell does. Of that I have no doubt.

I hold my hands up in surrender as I back out of the doorway. "All right, all right. I'm going. I just had to see for myself if you were okay. I wasn't about to let you bleed out somewhere all alone. Not on my watch."

Her glare strengthens to the power of a nuclear weapon. "I'm not *under your watch*. So, why the hell are you following me? Why the fuck are you even here?"

I curl my fingers around either side of the doorway and squeeze. I've got nothing to lose by giving her the truth, and after all these years, she deserves it. So that's what I do.

"I'm here for you, Mags. That's the only reason I'm back."

Her lower lip drops a half inch and the blunt nearly falls. Magnolia catches it and uses it to point at me. "Then leave. Because there's nothing for you here. Not now. So, fuck off."

I stay where I am. "Have dinner with me. Let me tell you—"

She pops the fat joint back in her mouth. "Motherfucker, no. I have nothing to say to you."

What. A. Woman.

"Tomorrow night. Eight o'clock. Arnaud's."

"Not a fucking chance. Go to hell."

I can't help the smile that's practically killing me to hide. "I'll wait for you until they kick me out."

She grabs the blunt, throws her head back, and that curtain of silky black hair goes flying as she bursts out laughing. "Try waiting fifteen fucking years, asshole." Her mirth dies as quickly as it started, and she snaps her mouth shut. But she can't take back what she said.

"You been waiting for me, mama? Because not a fucking day has gone by that I haven't thought about you."

After another deep drag, she puckers her lips again as she exhales, sending the cloud of smoke in my direction again. "I. Don't. Care. And don't fucking call me that. I'm nothing to you. Now, get the fuck out of my house before I shoot you."

She lifts the shotgun as her amber gaze, a perfect match for the whiskey in the glass, spears into me like the blade that got her. She's not fucking around, freshly painted walls or not.

"I'll be waiting."

She flips me off as she lowers the shotgun and reaches for the suture kit. I back away from the bathroom and show myself out of the house the same way I came in.

I'll wait an eternity for you, Magnolia . . . but I hope you don't make me.

With a backward glance at the light coming from the top right window of the house, I blow her a kiss that she'll never see.

13
MAGNOLIA

As soon as I hear the door click shut, I drop my head back to the wall I'm leaning against. My heart hammers like I've just run ten miles from the cops.

Jesus fucking Christ. What is he doing here? He shouldn't be here. Saying those things . . .

"I'm here for you, Mags. That's the only reason I'm back."

His words wash over me before I can stop them.

I pluck the blunt from my mouth and clench my teeth. "I'm not drunk or high enough to have imagined that shit, am I?" I ask the empty room, and the lack of an answer tells me I'm right.

I lied to Moses. I have plenty to say to him. I'm just not ready to hear what he wants to tell me. *Not at all.*

Nothing he can say to me can make up for fifteen years of wondering why the fuck he never came back for me like he said he would. Fifteen years of knowing that it was *easy* for him to leave me behind. Fifteen years of knowing I wasn't good enough for him. That I wasn't *worth it.* That'll fuck with a person.

"And how fucking dare he come back like this is something he can make right so damned easy?" I keep talking to the empty walls of my bathroom, but I wish there was someone to hear me. Even a fricking cat.

Maybe I should get a cat. A black one. Who hates men and has really sharp claws.

I set the shotgun down and reach for the bottle of whiskey. After a long pull, I nod to myself in the mirror.

Damn right. I'm getting a fucking cat. But first, I gotta sew myself up.

My hand is steady when I reach for the sutures and get set up. I sterilize the wound the best I can, and I go for it. As the needle punctures my flesh, I force my mind to go somewhere else. A trick I picked up at sixteen, when life on the streets should have killed me.

But instead of going to my happy place, it goes straight to the past . . . and Moses.

Fifteen years ago

"You sure you know what you're doing?" he asked as I pulled out the suture kit. The flashlight sat on the counter, reflecting in the mirror so I could see as much as possible.

I tilted my head at him. "You think I just keep this shit around for fun? Of course I know what I'm doing."

"All right, mama. Then stitch me up."

A thrill charged through me when he called me *mama*. I didn't know why. I should have thought it was weird, but coming from this man, it was sexy as hell. *He* was sexy as hell.

Don't think about fucking him while you're sewing him up. Neat stitches. Less scarring.

"This is gonna sting," I told him as my fingers hovered over the wound with the alcohol-soaked paper towels.

"Ain't my first poke."

I glanced down at the smooth golden skin of his chest, marked with scars that provided all the evidence I needed to know Moses hadn't had an easy life either. It made me feel like he could understand me in a way most people never would. In a way nobody ever wanted to.

I pressed the paper towels against the wound, and he hissed between his teeth but said nothing and didn't move. That strength and self-control was hot as fuck.

"All right. I'll make this as quick as I can."

His green-gold eyes flashed up at me. "Take all the time you need. I won't flinch."

Could this motherfucker be any sexier?

I believed the answer to that question was *fuck no*. My admiration probably had a hell of a lot to do with how he handled everything earlier tonight, but at that moment, I didn't care about all that. Honestly, I didn't even want to think about what would have happened if Moses hadn't been here.

"Okay. I'll make 'em neat and even."

"Good woman."

With his compliment warming me, I started working in the dim light, sewing closed a gash on his shoulder that he wouldn't have had if not for me.

Present day

As I tie off the last stitch, the vision of Moses a decade and a half ago, in my newly inherited whorehouse right after Hurricane Katrina, fades away.

I ain't got time to be dwelling on the past. Not anymore. Mama's got herself a brand-new house, and she's working on a future to match. No man will ever stand in the way of me getting the life I want.

Not even Moses Gaspard.

14
MAGNOLIA

I wake up to the sound of a door shutting. Groaning, I sit up from where I've been curled up on the bathroom floor, using my duffel bag as a pillow. My back, neck, and side ache like a son of a bitch.

"I'm too old for this shit," I mutter as I roll my head from side to side, trying to release the kink I got from sleeping in this position. *Damn.* Everything hurts.

"Someone up there? Ms. Maison?" Rocco calls from downstairs.

I clear my scratchy throat and answer. "Yeah, I'm here. I'll be down in a minute." I smack my lips together and realize I have wicked cotton mouth and need water.

"Shit. Sorry," he calls. "Didn't think anyone was around."

Pushing up from the floor, I wince as the stitches at my side pull and stretch their limits. I peel back the tape and gauze to take a look at the wound. Not too bad. Neat sutures. Mostly straight. Doesn't look infected.

I'll call it a win. Lord knows I need one.

I rummage through the duffel, pull out a pair of shorts and a T-shirt, and change my clothes. I would have done it last night, but I smoked until I was so high there was nothing I wanted more than to sleep for a few solid hours. I needed that too.

With a glance in the mirror, I realize my hair is a disaster, so I shake it out and finger comb it. Rocco has never seen me any way except totally put together, but I can't bring myself to give a fuck right now.

I shove the shotgun back in the duffel, along with everything else, and do a quick wipe down to make sure I got all the blood. No need for more questions than he might already have.

That's when I remember the knife. *Shit.* I hurry to wash it clean and quickly decide it's going in the brand-new safe in the master closet.

With the duffel stowed and the knife locked away, I pick my way downstairs in the tennies from my go-bag.

Rocco looks up from nailing a piece of trim in the kitchen. The shock on his face tells me I look worse than I thought.

"You okay, Magnolia?" He doesn't usually use my first name, but his concern seems sincere.

"I'm fine. I was here late, checking everything out, and decided to crash." My voice sounds like I drank a fifth of whiskey and smoked a half ounce of weed—*because I did.*

His brows swoop together as if he's trying to figure out why I'd choose to sleep on the floor since there's no furniture. "You sure you're okay?"

"I'm perfect. The house is too." Hopefully, the compliment will cushion the blow of the bomb I'm about to drop. I need to adjust the timeline we agreed to only yesterday. "I'm moving my things into the master bedroom tonight. I need a change of scenery. Will you finish up anything you need in there so I can get someone here to clean it and the master bath?"

His eyes are as wide as saucers, but he nods. "Of course. Most of the punch list is for downstairs anyway. You don't mind being here while I'm working? It shouldn't be too loud, but it won't be exactly quiet either."

A little noise sure as hell beats getting shanked. "Do what you need to do, Rocco. I'll handle the rest."

He slaps the floor where he's crouched like it's settled. "Yes, ma'am. Whatever you like."

"Thank you." With my clutch pressed against my side, I give him a weak smile. "Well, I'm off. Check in with you later."

He waves, and I take a step toward the door leading outside to my gate. That's when I see it. On the mantel. Another fucking chess piece.

I cross the room and grab the small white horse head.

"You play pretty fast and loose with that knight of yours." Moses's voice, fifteen years in the past, echoes in my head.

Beneath the chess piece is a piece of thick white paper. It reads:

8 p.m. Arnaud's. I'll wait for you.

I crumple it into a ball.

He'll wait for me? *He'll* fucking wait for *me?*

Keep waiting, motherfucker. Because you've got a lot of catching up to do.

15
MOSES

"You think she'll show tonight?" Trey asks from behind the computer he's rarely ever separated from.

He looks up in time to catch the skeptical expression I shoot his way, but the clicking keeps coming as his fingers never stop moving.

"No way she'll fucking show tonight," Jules says with a shake of his head as he shoves a beet into the juicer for our pre-workout morning concoction. "That woman is going to be a tough nut to crack. I've got money on her putting a hole in ol' Moses before she's done."

He's not too far off. I met the business end of her sawed-off last night. Nevertheless, I throw my hand into the air and flip him off. "Fuck you, Jules. You gonna finish that shit before I turn eighty?"

Jules tosses his head back and laughs. "You're just pissed she wouldn't let you come to the rescue like some kind of white knight. Hate to break it to you, boss, but that ain't exactly you."

I ignore Jules and turn back toward Trey, who sits at the long scarred wooden table in the house we leased in the Marigny as our base of operations here in New Orleans.

We have a system, the three of us. We settle down in one place for a bit, and then travel to the jobs we decide to take. Make good money, and then move the fuck on. We've been living this way for over a decade, and I'm ready for something different.

Something slower. Something more peaceful. Something with a fiery raven-haired siren who I suspect needs peace in her life as badly as I do.

But before I could get to this phase in my life, where I was free to come back for her, there were a hell of a lot of hurdles to jump. More than I planned on, that's for damn sure.

Luckily, we cashed in big in New York and handled my long-overdue business with Gabriel Legend—the last possible blade the guillotine of life had hanging over my head. Now that my shit with him is done and over, it's time to get the girl and live happily fucking ever after. But that's easier said than done. Especially when the woman in question is Magnolia Maison.

"That woman of yours wouldn't want a white knight anyway. She can take care of herself. She needs a partner. Ride or die." Trey grins at me.

Both of my colleagues have heard about my woman for years, and since we pulled up in the Big Easy, they've been watching her as closely as I have.

"Now *that* you can do," he adds.

"Thanks for the vote of confidence," I reply as I cross the wide-open living-dining-kitchen area of the five-thousand-square-foot, modern-industrial rental, and scoop up the glass of juice Jules just poured for me.

"I don't know how the fuck you two drink that shit," Trey says, wrinkling his nose in disgust.

I peer down at the red liquid in the glass. "It doesn't look bad."

"Don't play me. I saw what the fuck he put in that. Gross."

I chug it in one swig and smack my lips for effect. "Fucking healthy. That's what it is."

Trey shakes his head. "I'll stick to my non-healthy ways. Kills the badass-motherfucker vibe to drink beet juice."

My badass-motherfucker vibe has little to do with what I drink and a lot to do with my reputation of making people disappear. My image is irrelevant. "You keep digging on that guy from last night. We're gonna catch a workout, and then we'll follow up on whatever leads you find."

"Got it, boss."

Trey salutes me as I grab my gym bag and head for the door with Jules on my heels and Magnolia on my mind.

Then again, she's always on my mind. I haven't been able to get the vision of her from last night out of my head. Sitting on the tile next to a big tub, shotgun in hand, smoking a blunt and drinking whiskey.

One hell of a woman.

As soon as we walk out the door, Jules pauses. "You think there's a real shot she'll come tonight?"

"That's one thing for sure with Magnolia. You never fucking know."

16
MAGNOLIA

I take my Honda back to my condo building and pull it into its spot in the garage.

I'm on edge when I approach the elevator bay, but my strides are purely *don't fuck with me because I've got things to do and places to go.* When I stop in front of the silver double doors, there's an OUT OF ORDER sign in front of one car, and the memory of last night flashes through my brain.

He came so fast. So fucking fast. *Goddamn it.*

"You fucking whore!"

I can still hear the words. Was it personal? My gut knows it was. Shit like that happens in New Orleans, sure. But when it happens to me, it's usually not an innocent coincidence.

Which makes what I'm doing today imperative—packing my two biggest suitcases with everything important and wheeling my way out of the building before anyone can ask me where I'm going.

That lasts until I step out on the sixth floor.

Instead of a guy coming at me with a knife this time, I spy a man in his fifties with salt-and-pepper hair standing in front of

my neighbor's door. Everything about him, down to th
suit and dusty loafers, screams *cop*.

Great.

Did someone put a gris-gris on me?

Showing zero hint of recognition or concern, I clip down the
hallway without paying him the least bit of attention.

"Excuse me. Ma'am?" he says as I walk by, but I pretend not to
hear him.

I've got my key out and about to slide it into the lock when I
sense him behind me.

He sucks his teeth and his nose whistles when he breathes.
"This is some perfect timing. I was just knocking on your door."

I glance over my shoulder, giving him as much time as I'd give a
bee buzzing around my head. "What do you want? I'm not buying
anything. Not your bibles. Not your vacuums. Not your bullshit. Not
today. This building doesn't allow soliciting, and I'm running late."

That's when I make a pivotal mistake. I meet his beady cop
eyes and there's no *aw shucks, ma'am, I didn't mean to bother you* in
them. His eyes are hard and sharp, but that's not the worst part. I
see recognition in them.

Fuck. He knows who I am.

Why am I surprised? I've spent the last fifteen years in this
city attracting the wrong kind of attention from plenty of cops,
but this guy isn't familiar.

Have I ever met him? I flip through my mental files and come
up empty.

That glint in his flat gray eyes tells me whatever is going to
come out of his mouth next is nothing I want to hear.

"Let's try this again. I'm Detective Cavender." He flips out a
badge and flashes it at me quickly, but I make out all the simple
hallmarks of a legitimate NOPD shield. Crescent on top. Star in
the middle. "I need to speak to you about last night."

"What about last night?" I ask.

His bushy brows dive together on his forehead. "You didn't hear the fire alarm?"

My eyebrows go up, and it takes no effort at all to look eminently surprised with a side of panicked. "Fire? There was a fire? Is everyone okay? Was there damage?"

His gaze narrows further. "So you weren't here last night?"

"Clearly not, if I didn't know there was a fire."

"There wasn't a fire." He sucks on his teeth again.

I blink, assuming another one of my favorite guises for dealing with cops—playing dumb. "Wait. I'm confused. You just said there was a fire." My head falls to the side, and I squint to really nail it home.

He shoves his hands in his pockets and his lips pinch. I get the sense he's frustrated with me, and inside, I smile. *I can waste your time way more effectively than you can waste mine, Detective.*

"There was a fire *alarm*. Pulled on this floor."

Again, I evince confusion. "Now you've totally lost me. You're investigating a fire alarm when there was no fire? It seems like detectives in this fine city would have better things to do."

His nostrils flare, and he looks like he's losing his patience with me. *Good.*

"No, I'm investigating the crime scene and the dead body that was discovered."

I slap a hand to my chest, thankful acting has always seemed like second nature for me. It comes with the territory when your job is to create a fantasy. "Oh my *God. Are you serious?* This building is supposed to be safe! Jesus Christ. What the hell?" I pretend to have the chills and shiver as I glance up and down the hall. "Did the cameras catch the person who did it?"

He studies me like a scientist and I'm whatever he's growing in a petri dish. "Cameras haven't worked in months, according to the building manager. You don't know anything about any of this? You weren't involved in any way, Ms. Maison?"

I jerk back in overly exaggerated surprise. "Excuse me, do I know you?"

Cavender's smile turns predatory, as if the dumbass thinks he's got an edge on me. I would shake my head if it wouldn't ruin my act, but instead I mentally roll my eyes.

"Pretty sure most everyone in the department is aware of you, Ms. Maison. You're what we like to call . . . a person of interest."

Finally, I hit my limit and drop all pretenses because I really do have shit to get done. "So, what you're saying, Detective Cavender, is that you're profiling me in connection with an ongoing investigation in hopes that somehow you'll connect me to it, even though I wasn't here and have no idea what you're talking about. Is that right? Because if it is, I'm happy to take a report of this incident to my councilperson so she knows exactly how the cops in this jurisdiction treat her constituents."

This time, when he stares at me, I get a definite impression of a snake.

"That's a lot of big words for a woman who spends most of her time on her back . . . not reading."

My shoulders go back, and I lift my chin. "I have nothing further to say to you, sir."

His gaze cuts to my door. "I need to search your condo."

"And *I* need a spa day, but we don't always get what we need."

Cavender bristles. "You're refusing to cooperate with an ongoing murder investigation now."

At this, I throw back my head and let out a burst of laughter that evaporates just as quickly as I stare daggers at him. "You know as well as I do that you don't have probable cause, and no judge is going to give you a warrant. Yes, I live in this building. No, I wasn't here last night. I don't have any idea what the hell you're investigating, nor do I want to know. Now, unless you magically produce a warrant in the next fifteen seconds, I'd like you to leave me alone before I have to report you for police harassment. Actually, if you could show me your badge again, I'd like to write that number down for my records."

He ignores my request for the badge number and continues his questioning. "Where were you last night?"

My smile is as big as my aversion to nosy, meddling law enforcement. "None of your damn business."

"So you don't have an alibi."

I tilt my head to the side and stare at him. "You think you know everything about me already. Do *you* think I was alone last night?"

"All you have to do is give me a name, and I'll leave you alone."

When I perch my hand on my hip reflexively, forgetting about my wound and stitches, it takes everything I have not to wince. "I'm afraid that's too damn bad. I pride myself on having excellent discretion, and that means I don't share the names of my *companions.*"

His whistling nostrils flare again, and I don't even want to know what the pervert is probably thinking right now. Perhaps he's trying to imagine what it would be like to be one of those companions.

Ew. Fucking gross. Not even if I were broke and starving.

"I'll be watching you, Ms. Maison. If there's a single shred of evidence that connects you to this crime, then you're going down. Mark my words."

I release a long breath and shake my head. "If only cops would investigate crimes and figure out who did it before they go around accusing people of committing them."

He backs away, his gaze steely. "That only applies to *innocent* people, madam."

With that dig, he backs away and returns to hammering on my neighbor's door.

Well, fuck. That didn't exactly go well.

Two hours later, I poke my head out of the condo and check the hallway. Detective Douchebag is gone, thankfully, but I have a feeling I haven't seen the last of him.

After a quick scan of the hall, I roll two giant suitcases through the doorway and lock up. The girls will be coming over later to take the rest of the boxes, and the furniture will be moved to Desiree's house to replace some of her old stuff.

I'm starting fresh in my new place, and I'm not coming back here again. Not fucking ever.

This building has bad juju, and my new life doesn't have room for any of that.

Thankfully, I don't see a soul as I wheel out my suitcases, and those fabulously malfunctioning cameras won't catch me leaving this time either.

I can't believe I didn't think about cameras last night. *God.* What a fucking nightmare that could have been.

Although, at least then I would have had a clear-cut case of self-defense. No way anyone could argue that the man charging into the elevator to stab me could have been *my* fault. Then again, given the attitude of Detective Cavender, maybe it wouldn't have mattered. I probably would have been in cuffs for not calling the cops myself and reporting the incident.

Well, old habits die hard, and the day I call the cops to report I stabbed someone is the day I leave this town and never look back. I load the suitcases into the back seat of the Honda and drive away, with part of me wishing I could just point my car toward the highway and do exactly that—drive away and leave it all behind.

But I love my new place. It's going to be a fresh start. No, really, it will be.

After all the time and money I've spent on the house in the Quarter, I don't have any left to skip town and live a lavish life-style on the beach. Not in a hurry, anyway. I'd have to liquidate, and that would take at least a month or longer.

But what if the attack really wasn't random? Ho-It-All asks, chiming in.

"The guy's dead, so there shouldn't be shit to worry about now," I tell the interior of the beat-up Honda and its empty car seat. "Besides, even if he weren't, no one is going to run me out of my own town over some stupid stitches."

But the unease dogs me the entire time I drive, park the car, and then wheel the suitcases to my gate.

Something doesn't feel right, but I'm not sure what it is.

That's when I decide to visit Celeste again. Maybe a reading will ease my concerns. *Or make them a million times worse.*

17
MAGNOLIA

"I had a feeling I'd be seeing you again today, *chère*."

Madame Celeste's husky voice welcomes me as I cross the threshold of her shop, the Reading Room, which is where she can be found most of the time when she's not sitting at her card table out in front of Saint Louis Cathedral.

Sunshine from the doorway highlights dust motes floating in the air, and I feel instant relief as soon as I step inside. The spicy scent of her incense. The deep colors. The quiet sounds of chimes and tabletop fountains she has around the space. They soothe me.

I pride myself on staying firmly rooted in the here and now, but after living my entire life in this city, I can't help but be drawn to forces I can't see. Especially at times like this when restless energy and uncertainty have me all twisted up in knots.

There's too much chaos in my brain, and I need to get back to being sharp and invincible. That's the only way I know how to live. Anything else makes me feel weak and powerless, and that's unacceptable.

"You always seem to know when I'll be making a pass."

She tsk-tsks at me. "Your energy is right strong. Easy to read. What happened?"

The stitches tug on my side with every step, and I consider for a moment whether I should tell her the whole truth. If there's one thing for certain, it's that Celeste didn't have a damn thing to do with the man I sent to his death in an elevator car.

"I had a rough night." The understatement of the century comes out clear and calm before I tell her what happened. Thankfully, there's not a single waver in my voice.

To her credit, Celeste doesn't react immediately, and I have incredible respect for her self-possession. Instead of launching into dozens of questions like anyone else would, she simply bobs her turban-covered head and turns to the side, indicating with one weathered hand that I should precede her into the back.

"Best go sit down. I'll lock up so we're not disturbed. This reading will be important."

A tremor shoots through me as I take a step, as if my body is bracing for the gravity of what's coming next. Like I have many times before, I make the short walk to the back room, ducking between the dangling curtain of fabric, beads, feathers, and whatever else Celeste has sewn into it.

The table is small and round, painted with a design that came from a vision she received once. She told me about it my first time back here, nearly twenty years ago.

Some people might not believe in all of this, but I can't dispute the change in my energy as I settle on the velvet cushioned chair. Probably because I *do* believe. I believe there are forces we can't see. There's wisdom and guidance waiting for us, if we only ask. I can only hope they're feeling generous today and can answer some of the questions swirling in my brain.

The front door chimes as Celeste flips the sign and locks us inside. The scent of roses and cedar grows stronger as she steps through the curtain and smooths the individual pieces of fabric before she pauses at a chest against one wall to retrieve her cards and whatever else she deems necessary for the reading. Before taking her seat, she pauses at the altar, lights a candle, and whispers a prayer. I listen carefully, but can't make out all her quick broken French.

If it were my first reading, I'd assume she was exercising showmanship, but I know Celeste better than that. This is a ritual. Serious business.

When she finally sits down, I have to remind myself to take long, slow, deep breaths.

I can handle whatever is coming next. I always do. I always will.

Celeste hands me the well-worn deck. "Knock, and then think about your question as you shuffle, child."

I do as she says while she arranges crystals on the table. I focus as I make the cards dance between my fingers, praying they're able to provide guidance.

When I hand the deck back to her, Celeste meets my gaze.

"Now we begin."

She deals the cards in the spread on the table facedown, then flips the first one over to represent me. *The Empress.*

With a smile, Celeste meets my gaze. "I think we both knew this was coming. Your power is directly related to your femininity. You know that. You feel that. Don't forget it."

Dipping my chin for her to continue, I feel a sliver of relief pass through me.

Okay. This is a promising start.

Another card represents my question, which, without me saying anything, Celeste seems to know.

The Chariot. There's a decision to be made. I can't stay caught between two choices. I have to move forward.

As I glance up at Celeste's pale blue eyes, the scent of roses coming off her is even stronger than before. "I made a decision, though. I sold the brothel, and I'm building a new business. I have a new direction. New purpose."

She tilts her head to the side. "You made that decision in the past. You have a new one to make. The winds of change cannot be denied. I felt it yesterday, girl, and I feel it even stronger today."

She flips over a couple more cards to represent my past, and they're accurate enough to tell me the reading isn't nonsense. There's something here, and I need to pay attention. When she gets to outside forces, she flips over the King of Pentacles.

"Ahhh," Celeste says with wonder underlying her tone. "And here we have a male figure. You rarely have these in your readings." She lifts her chin and tips her head to study me. "Do you know who he is?"

My first instinct is to retreat into being cagey. "Should I know?"

"Don't play games with me, Magnolia Marie. This is too important. You know exactly who he is, because he's offering you prosperity and security."

I swallow the lump rising in my throat the moment she reinforces the gravity of the situation. Softly, I admit, "I know who he is."

She sways and runs her left hand over a crystal. "There's resistance. Is it one of your former clients offering to make your life free and easy, all for the price of doing whatever he wants?" That scenario has presented itself plenty of times, but that's not what's going on now.

"No. I don't know why he's here or what he wants. At least . . ." I glance down at the card on the table, focusing on the man on his throne. "At least, I don't believe what he claims he wants is true."

"Why not?"

"Because I don't have anything left to give him." I choke on the last word, shocked to realize I'm near tears.

What the hell is going on with me?

I clear my throat and straighten my shoulders.

I do not show weakness.

But old Celeste sees right through me. "Child, you have so

much light to shine on this world, but only if you don't blow out your flame. Protect it. Nurture it. Getting burned is a risk, but being in the dark is much worse."

When she flips the next cards, the joyful, cheery reading I'd naively hoped I would receive is completely dashed.

I release a heavy sigh as I tap the Tower card. "Jesus Christ."

Celeste glances up at me as she gives me a lopsided smile. "Don't see only the bad. See the change that's coming. I sensed it yesterday, and there's no doubt in my mind it's coming and that it will manifest soon. It's time. You can't keep going on as you have been."

I tip my head back, staring at the ceiling above me, blinking at the burn behind my eyes. If Celeste were anyone else, I'd get up from the table, walk out, and dismiss the whole thing as garbage. But I can't. I feel it too.

Moses's words echo in my head. *I'm here for you, Mags. That's the only reason I'm back.*

He has the power to change everything, whether I want to admit it or not. One small part of me—the part that drew me to the damn window yesterday morning, looking for those glowing green eyes, believes he speaks the truth.

What are his motives, though?

I'm not making any decisions until I figure them out. *Trust nothing and no one.* That's been my motto for so long, I'm not sure it's possible to change.

Celeste strokes the back of the final card, still facing down. "Are you ready for the last one?"

I give her a go-ahead gesture, but if I'm being honest with myself, I'm not ready. Not at all.

As soon as she flips it, I bolt to my feet.

"Really?" I shake my head, staring down at the face of *Death.*

"Hush, girl. You know enough to know this card isn't what most people think. Sit down and breathe."

I drop into the chair and stare at the knight riding a horse, carrying a banner with a rose. "The end of something is coming," I say, almost without thought.

"That's right, *chère*. But the new beginning is going to be even brighter. Look at the patterns here. Look at what you've been through. There's no doubt you've struggled. You've survived. You've carved out a life for yourself. You're a woman of true strength and power. But you can't do this all alone. Life isn't meant to be a solitary endeavor. You've never had an equal partner who could balance you."

I choke out a laugh at that absolute truth, but Celeste continues.

"You've always been fixated on control and power, *chère*. Sometimes you have to release your grip and let the universe work in its mysterious ways."

I practically gulp down my next breath. "Release my grip? Really?"

Her turbaned head nods. "Almost as terrifying as death, isn't it?"

"Something like that," I whisper, my attention still on the mounted knight. When Celeste's bony fingers reach out to clear the cards away, I stop her with an outstretched hand. "Wait."

She meets my gaze, and I gather the courage I didn't expect I'd need sitting at her table today.

"Yes?"

"How do I know if I can trust him?"

Her thin lips curve into a secretive smile. "Let him show you."

18
MOSES

I'm sweaty as fuck, but I always feel better after a good workout. Stronger. Sharper. More determined.

I drop my gym bag on the floor next to the table where Trey's computer is set up. He's not in front of it, however, and the screen is black.

"Trey! You find him yet?" I shout to the empty space.

His disembodied voice comes from a few rooms over. "Hold on, I'm taking a shit. Give me two minutes."

"Eager to put this one to bed, man?" Jules asks from the kitchen as he tosses the remains of his protein shake into the trash. "You know it takes time."

Crossing my arms, I argue. "*Time?* If someone stabbed your woman and she had to fucking kill him to protect herself, wouldn't you want to know everything? Would you be wasting time?"

"Maybe if I knew for certain she was my woman."

Jules and I have gone toe-to-toe dozens of times over the years, but he knows damn well what my intentions are.

Narrowing my eyes, I glare at him. "You expect me to work miracles in one day?"

He grins, not at all cowed by a scowl that would make other men piss themselves. "You? Fuck yes. I know what you're capable of."

Instead of being annoyed, I laugh. "Thanks for the vote of confidence."

"Hell, I'll go one step further, boss. I might even change my vote on dinner. I think she might show."

Considering he'd said *no way in hell* before our workout, I jerk my head back in surprise. "No shit?"

Jules shrugs. "I don't know why. I've just got this feeling."

I managed to put the thoughts of dinner out of my mind during our workout, but they're back at the forefront now.

I want to believe she'll show up. I want to trust she's at least curious enough about what I might have to say and why I'm back. But Magnolia Maison has never been the predictable type. She's as Machiavellian as I am. She's got angles and motives most people would never guess—just like me. I want to clear away all the bullshit between us and lay it all out. No games. No lies. Just the truth.

"Let's hope you're right," I tell Jules as Trey opens the door of the bathroom, wiping his hands on his shorts.

"That john might need a priest."

I laugh and shake my head. "Jesus Christ, man. Really?"

He waves a hand in the air as he makes his way over. "Maybe I should try your beet juice, because that shit was pure evil. Now, let me tell you what I found out while you two meatheads were pumping iron."

I straighten. "You got a name?"

Trey shakes his head. "Nope."

"Then what do you have?"

Trey returns to his seat, taps a few keys on the laptop, and spins it around to face me. "Not a fucking thing. He's a ghost."

I bend over to look at the screen. "What am I looking at then?"

"Prints that aren't in any system. ID in his wallet was fake.

Facial rec search is still going, but I'm telling you—this guy doesn't exist."

"What the fuck," I say quietly. "You mean . . ." I glance up at Trey to find him nodding.

"Yeah. It's like *we* made him disappear and covered all our tracks like the pros we fucking are, but we didn't do this." He scratches the back of his neck and crosses his arms.

"Whoa, whoa, whoa," Jules says as he lumbers from the kitchen. "You're saying someone else erased him?"

"That's exactly what I'm saying." Trey meets my eyes, his gaze dead serious. "Whoever this guy was, he didn't want to be found. Which, in my estimation, makes him a hell of a lot more interesting than he was last night."

"Fuck," I mutter under my breath.

Of course this can't be simple. Nothing to do with Magnolia ever is.

I tap the tabletop and then point at Trey. "Keep digging. There's gotta be something. You know all the places people usually fuck up when they wipe someone. No one is as good as you, Trey. *No one.* Figure out who the fuck he is. That's the only way we're going to find out why he went after her and if there's more coming."

Jules's expression is somber, but for good reason. We all know the consequences of digging up graves, fake or not. The dead don't like being found. And the living dead will kill to prevent it.

"I don't have a good feeling about this, man. Not at all."

At least our instincts are still working on the same wavelength. "Yeah, me neither."

19
MAGNOLIA

The reading left me shaken. There's no doubt about it. I was also left with a hell of a lot more questions than answers.

And the one at the top of my mind? *Do I meet Moses tonight or not?*

Celeste's words follow me as I amble back to my new place. *"Let him show you."*

Easier said than done, because letting someone show you requires trust in its own right—and trust is one of the only luxuries my lifestyle hasn't afforded me.

"Hey, *stranger*. Fancy seeing you again. Two days in a row."

The unfamiliar voice jerks me out of my head—back to the here and now—and to the All-American blond guy from yesterday.

How did I not notice him? Jesus Christ. I'm usually a lot more aware of my surroundings, but Celeste's reading and the past twenty-four hours have me all out of sorts.

I wave at him but keep walking. But he doesn't take the hint and jogs to catch up.

"Thanks for the directions yesterday. Café Envie was great. Any other places I should try?"

I pause and stare at a guy who absolutely can't take a hint. "There's a visitor center not far from here. They can help you out."

"Nah," he says with a huff. "I don't want touristy stuff. I'm a local now. I need to find the local hot spots."

Grinding my teeth, I glance behind me. "Yep, just as I thought. I forgot my neighborhood welcome wagon. Sorry. You're going to have to find someone else to show you around town. I'm busy."

"What if I buy you dinner?"

I'd like to buy him a fucking clue. "I've got my dinner covered. Good luck."

Then I clip along down the street, but something tells me not to go to my gate until he's out of sight again. I don't want this guy knocking on my door every other day, asking for restaurant recommendations, which dry cleaner to use, or if I have a preference of florists.

"Maybe I'll run into you again next week and change your mind. Have a good one, stranger!" he calls after me.

I don't acknowledge it. I don't want to encourage the guy. I've never had a thing for Wonder bread, and that's exactly what he is.

Basic. Plain. Ordinary. No flavor. No panache.

I'll change my mind? In your dreams, you overconfident asshole.

It pisses me off all the same that he's just moved in around the corner. I pause and bend down like I'm shaking a rock out of my shoe, and he disappears from sight. *Finally.*

As I unlock my gate, I'm filled with annoyance that my new sanctuary is already tainted. First by the blood last night, and now by a guy who doesn't understand when his attention is completely unwanted. After the amount of money I've sunk into this place, it's disappointing.

Rocco is inside, working hard and singing off-key to Joan Jett.

As soon as the door shuts behind me, I debate what to do next. I could start hanging my clothes up in the closet . . . but from Rocco's belted-out notes, I can tell he's upstairs, no doubt trying to get the master bedroom finished like I asked.

He's almost done. Just be patient, Mags. It's all going to come together.

The cards from my reading shuffle through my mind. *Change is coming.* Change that's bigger than Rocco finishing the caulk work around the tub and knocking out the final items on the punch list.

I step back outside and drop into a patio chair from the set I had delivered last week.

You're stronger than this, Magnolia. You can handle whatever's coming. Have you stopped to wonder if it's you that'll be coming? That big hunk of Creole muscle is still looking mighty tasty.

I jerk my head up and look around, as if trying to figure out where the hell that thought came from. Ho-It-All, clearly. Apparently, I named my contrary inner voice well, because she's advocating for Moses now. And if he was the Devil card Celeste dealt me yesterday . . . who knows what's coming next.

Death.

It's a card that doesn't usually frighten me, but after the last twenty-four hours, I'm not myself. Maybe I should meet Moses tonight. Hear what he has to say. Do what Celeste suggested . . . *let him show me.*

As I take a minute to myself, sitting in a ray of sunshine, the damn Chariot card pops back into my head too.

Make a decision. One way or the other.

I have to choose. So I do.

Without even letting Rocco know I was here, I slip out of my gate once again.

If I'm going to face Moses, I need some shiny new armor first.

"Do my eyes deceive me, or am I really seeing Magnolia Maison step into my shop?" Yve Titan, the wife of billionaire Lucas Titan, says to me as I cross the threshold of Dirty Dog, my favorite dress shop in the Quarter. In the last couple of years, she's expanded, and her offerings have gotten even more unique and varied.

"How's it going, Yve?"

She smiles broadly. "Oh, you know, just another day in paradise." Yve moves like a dancer as she gracefully gestures to the fixtures holding scores of beautiful dresses. "To what do I owe the pleasure today? It's been a while."

Yve and I struck up a friendship of sorts over the past few years since she took over the place and turned into one of the hottest boutiques in New Orleans. She and I don't exactly come from similar backgrounds, but she's no idiot or asshole, and I respect her drive. When she married Titan, she never had to work another day in her life, but she didn't let that change her hustle. If anything, she's even more ambitious now.

"I need a dress. Something . . ." I pause, trying to decide exactly how to describe the reaction I want Moses to have. "Something to make a man *ache*."

Yve's lips purse together in an intrigued pout. "Oh, girl. Please tell me you're going to fill me in on this story while I find you *exactly* that."

"Maybe," I say as I shrug like it's no big thing. But one of Yve's perfectly shaped eyebrows rises, and I have to wonder if she can see right through me.

"I just got a shipment in from a brand-new vendor, and her pieces are to *die* for. *No one* has seen a single one yet. We're almost finished steaming them in the back, but . . ."

I sense where she's going. "But you'll let me have first dibs if I tell you who I'm wearing it for?" I ask, sure I'm on the right track.

Her guilty grin makes her even more stunning. "Damn, you're sharp. No wonder you're one of my favorite customers."

"Mm-hmm. I can smell the bullshit from here, Yve. Show me the dresses, and I'll think about telling you."

She studies me for a moment, her tongue tapping her teeth. "Fine. Only because I like you."

Yve leads me into the back, where one of her employees is adjusting a dress's skirt with one hand while gripping the steamer handle in another.

"Oh, that looks divine, Kayleigh," Yve says. "Want to take the floor so I can show Magnolia our newest beauties?"

The girl, probably in her mid-twenties, jerks her head around when Yve says my name. Her face is easily readable, and I find the proof of my infamy stamped on it. She definitely knows who I am.

I used to find it amusing that my reputation preceded me wherever I went, but now . . . it's getting old. As Kayleigh smiles my way, I can't help but wonder what it would be like to have complete anonymity again. For no one to know who I am or what I've done. It's the most indulgent thought I've had in a long time, but I don't get to dwell on it long.

"You're gorgeous. Jesus. Wow." Kayleigh blinks and lifts a hand to her mouth. "Sorry, that wasn't exactly professional. It's really nice to meet you."

She holds out her hand, and I shake it. You'd think I'm a celebrity from the awestruck look on her face.

"Nice to meet you."

The girl smiles broadly at Yve. "If you need any help, let me know. Also, not that you need my two cents, but the aubergine dress with the boning would look so bomb on her."

"Ohhh . . ." Yve makes an excited sound and claps her hands as Kayleigh disappears out of the back room to man the store. "She is *not* wrong. And I'm pretty sure we have it in your size."

The fact that Yve remembers my size when I haven't been here in a few months says a lot about the kind of shopkeeper she is.

"Purple isn't really my color—" The words coming out of my mouth die away as she pulls the most gorgeous dress off the rack and holds it out. "Damn. That's a *dress*."

Even on the hanger, it looks stunning. The deep purple pencil dress is a perfect hourglass shape, sleeveless, and instead of being a V-neck, it curves down in front to a point. The skirt looks like it'll hug my hips and thighs before stopping just above my knees. It's classy as hell, but still sexy as fuck.

I meet Yve's gaze. "Seriously? You show me one dress and it's perfect? Are you a witchy woman or something?"

She winks at me. "I gotta give Kayleigh credit for this one, although I definitely would've shown it to you too. I have another one in red . . ."

I shake my head. "No. Not red. Not for tonight. I'll look like I'm trying too hard."

Her perfectly shaped eyebrow goes up again. "You're not even going to give me a hint? Because this feels . . . different."

"It is. Moses—" I cut off what I was about to say, shocked I revealed his name to her. I haven't even told Keira about him.

And why is that, Mags? Ho-It-All chimes in, and I shut the inner voice down.

At my side, the quiet chime of a text message comes from my purse.

"Moses," Yve says with interest underlying her tone and a smile on her face. "Now that's a strong name for a man. I can't say I know anyone in this town with it. Or should I?"

She's fishing, and I don't know why I take the bait, but I do. Maybe because I just need to tell *someone* about him.

"He's not from here. We met right after Katrina. He helped me. It was . . . different. Like you said."

Her lips form a perfect *O*. "And he's in town? And you're meeting with him? Wearing this dress?"

I throw my shoulders back, feeling some of my gall return. "If I feel like it. I'm still not sure if I'll go."

"Oh, girl. You'll go. We always do. You have to let me know how it goes. I'll be dying for news if you don't."

My thumb swipes across the smooth material of the dress, and I ignore another chime from my bag. "There may not be anything to tell."

"I refuse to believe that. Any man who gets your attention is bound to be something remarkable."

I lift my gaze to her once more. "Why do you say that?"

Yve's lips press together for a beat, like she's trying to decide how to answer delicately. Finally, she does. "Because you've seen a lot. I imagine men aren't much of a mystery to you anymore. But you seem intrigued, and I have to believe that means something."

"Might be something. Might not be. I'll let you know."

Thirty minutes later, I leave with the eggplant-purple dress and new lingerie to wear beneath it.

I should have known better than to buy the lingerie, because now all I can think about is watching Moses's dick harden enough to hammer nails when he sees it.

It takes everything I have to remind myself that I don't want anything to do with his dick.

I'm also lying to myself.

Fuck.

Almost forgetting, I pull my cell from my bag, hoping it's not another problem. I silently pray my girls are okay, Norma and Bernadette don't need me, and that the sky isn't falling in the Mississippi tonight.

RHODES: I'm in town if you want to play. Let me know when would be good for you.

RHODES: Also, I plan on dominating. So be prepared.

A small smile spreads across my lips. If things fall through or go south with the sexy ghost from my past, at least I'll have a backup plan.

20
MOSES

The waiter brings me another three fingers of whiskey, and I thank him. Swirling the liquor in the glass, I check the time. *Quarter to ten.* I've been here almost two hours, sitting at the table by myself, nursing glass after glass of the best damn whiskey I've ever tasted.

Magnolia's not coming, and if I thought she might, I should have known better.

She's the most maddening woman I've ever met, but also the most fascinating. And yet . . . a smile stretches across my face because I'm a perverse motherfucker. Maybe even a masochist.

Did I really expect her to fall into my arms as soon as she saw me? *Fuck no.*

I didn't *just* come back for Magnolia. I came back for the fight that would come with winning her. Nothing worth having ever comes easy, especially a good woman.

And the best woman I've ever met is worth more than a little strife.

I take another sip of whiskey, appreciating the subtle differences in flavor of this vintage compared to the last ones, and think about my next move. Normally, I've got things planned a half dozen moves or more ahead, just like I'd play chess, but not with Mags. She's a special situation, one that requires thinking on the fly and creativity.

Maybe if I . . .

My thoughts trail off as the door opens and the most gorgeous sight of my life walks in.

I'm on my feet, but I don't even remember standing. *Christ Jesus.* My hands curl into fists to stop me from crossing the room and yanking her against me. *Holy fuck.*

Her dress doesn't show much skin, but the purple material hugs her every luscious curve and reveals just enough of her cleavage to make me hard on the spot like some kid without any control over my reactions.

And the way she walks . . . *fuck me.* One foot in front of the other, strutting toward me like she doesn't notice another soul in the room. Confident. Certain. She doesn't look like she had a single doubt about tonight, when I was thinking she must be going back and forth, trying to decide whether to come. Or maybe I'm just getting drunk on the way she's walking toward me.

Christ Almighty. Her frigging hair. It's a sleek, nearly black curtain tucked behind one ear, falling to her shoulders.

But it's her lips that nearly undo me, slicked with a sinful red that makes me think of only one thing—how fucking badly I want to hear her say she missed me.

I pull it together, because there's no fucking way I'm going to screw up this gift I've just been given. From the expression on her face and the glittering hardness of her whiskey-colored eyes, it's clear she's storming into battle.

Fine by me, Mags. Do your worst. I can handle anything you throw at me.

I force my dick to behave and find the self-possession that has served me well since I seized control of a crew in Biloxi when I was practically still a fucking kid. Power, after all, comes from within.

With easy movements, I step around the table to meet her, the corners of my mouth tugging upward in a smile just for her. "You look stunning, mama." The old nickname comes out of my mouth without thought.

Her eyes flare with heat as she shifts her weight on her heels. "Don't call me that."

I can't help but grin. "Make you remember things you'd rather keep forgotten?"

"I never said I'd forgotten a damn thing, but I just got here, so save it. Unless you want me to leave already? And why the hell are you smiling like that?"

"Because I just had a prayer answered. Guess I'm fucking thankful." And proud and relieved. "You came."

Once and for all, the winds of change are at my back and guiding me home. Guiding me to the future. Guiding me to her.

21

MAGNOLIA

He's smooth. Too fucking smooth for his own good. *Goddamn it.*

I shouldn't be reacting to Moses at all, but just seeing him in a three-piece pin-striped suit, looking like the Creole kingpin he told me was going to become, I can't help it.

I lift my chin higher, wishing I could look down my nose at him, but his tall frame seems even broader with the sleek lines of his jacket, making it impossible.

Although I'll never admit it to him, I waited outside for a good twenty minutes, watching him through the window, wondering if he'd give up and leave. True to his word, he didn't.

Too bad he wasn't true to his word when he said he'd come back for me. The memory of being forgotten comes to the forefront and hardens my heart enough for me to take control of the situation.

"I'm here. If that's an answered prayer, then you've got a fucked-up god."

His teeth flash white as he smiles again. *Damn.* I forgot how much his smile affects me. I always know how to handle men, but right now, I'm not sure, and I hate the uncertainty.

I tried to come up with a plan, but Moses Gaspard can't be planned for. Now I'm winging it.

"Maybe I just say different prayers than you do." He gestures to the seat across the white linen tablecloth from him. This restaurant has been a fixture in the French Quarter for over a hundred years, and yet I've never eaten here.

"I don't have much time for prayin' these days. What with getting stabbed in elevators and whatnot," I say with a phony bored undertone. My side still gives me twinges of pain, and the whiskey on the table looks like exactly what I need to forget about the wound—and the memories of how we once were.

"I've got some news on that front," Moses says, pulling out my chair.

I take the seat, nearly shivering when his fingertips drift across the skin of my bare upper arms. My nipples take notice too. *What the hell?* They've basically been ornamental for years, but like the ghost across from me, they've been resurrected too.

I'm not used to physically responding to men like this. Not anymore. It's been a long time since sex was anything but a basic urge to have met by someone who had no power over me. But with Moses . . . suddenly my body turns traitor.

And you're surprised because . . . ? Ho-It-All pipes up, and I shake my head to shut her up.

As Moses takes his seat, the server comes to the table.

"Sir, I see your companion has arrived. What can I get you to drink, ma'am?"

I don't bother to look at him or the menu. "Three fingers of Seven Sinners' Spirit of New Orleans. Neat."

"Excellent choice. I'll give you a few moments, and then I'll be back to take your order." The server, a middle-aged woman with a bun in stark black and white, hurries away through the tables.

I glance at the glass in front of Moses. "What are you drinking?"

"Did you really come here to shoot the shit about my beverage selection?"

My gaze cuts to his face, and I get snared by those damn green-and-gold eyes, but he asked for it. So I bite the bullet. "Fine. What the fuck do you want, Moses? Fifteen years is too damn long to assume you can come back for a woman, no matter what you said last night."

"Who says it's the first time I've been back?" He has one eyebrow with a thin scar above it, and it's lifted. I wonder how I got it. It's new, but he's too damn smug to ask.

My mouth is agape, and before it draws flies, I speak so he won't notice it's because of what he does to me and not from what he said. "The fuck does that mean?"

Sometimes my street shows, and I check myself. Diners at the tables around us turn to look at me, so I fold my hands in my lap demurely.

Instead of replying to my question, he drops another bomb on me. "You've got a ghost."

I look around, trying to find my calm, before I drill a stare into him. "What the hell are you talking about?" The only ghost I know is him, but at the moment, he's more real than anyone I've ever known.

"The guy from the elevator. He's a ghost."

I blink and lean forward with my elbows on the table. "He wasn't a ghost. He was living and breathing just like us. I know this because *ghosts don't stab people.*" I'm proud of myself for keeping my voice low enough that no one else in the restaurant can hear a damn thing I'm saying over the murmur of conversation and clinking of silverware against china.

Moses mimics my movement, leaning forward far enough that I catch a whiff of cedar with a hint of spice. That scent nearly steals me away for another trip down memory lane, but I keep my focus on his lips as they begin to move.

"He's flesh and blood, but he's not in the system. Prints were a dead end. No hits on facial recognition yet. His ID was fake."

My hair sways across my shoulders as confusion has me moving my head from side to side. "What does that mean? Is he . . . *was* he a hit man?" I ask quietly, because this isn't exactly something we should be discussing here, although I have a hell of a lot more questions, including how Moses knows all this.

Although, Moses doesn't seem to have any compunction about it. I remember he once told me the easiest way to get away with something was to do it in plain sight. Maybe that holds true for discussing murder at fancy restaurants. Hell, in this day and age, we could be simply having a chat about a true crime podcast for all anyone would know.

"Possibly," he says with a hint of skepticism. "Or he's someone who didn't want to be found by people who wanted him literally dead. We're still digging."

I picture the man's brown eyes that shined with evil intent from behind that balaclava he wore like a fucking coward.

He can't get me. Not now. He's dead.

But if he was a hit man . . .

"If he was truly after me and only me, will someone else be coming next?" I ask Moses quietly, the fear that I don't want to acknowledge giving my tone a jagged, broken edge.

"Depends," he says, his reply equally serious.

I fight a chill skating up my spine. "On what?"

"On whether someone paid him to kill you. If someone did take out a hit on you, they won't send someone else unless they really want you dead bad, and have the money to pay someone else to do the job he couldn't finish."

The way he says it, so matter-of-factly, gives me pause.

"*Fuck.*"

Moses's hand reaches out and covers my balled fist on the table. "Magnolia, I ain't gonna let no bogeyman get you. Not on my watch or while I've still got breath in my body."

Relief sweeps through me on a wave, but I don't want to trust it. I know better. Bogeymen have almost gotten me before while he's been gone. My mind flashes to a pile of corpses I was tossed on top of once. Where was he to save me then?

"I don't trust you. You could have set all this up. Things were moving toward peaceful until you wandered back into town."

His greenish-gold eyes pierce into me like he's trying to see inside my brain. "It's not me, mama. You know I wouldn't hurt you. Other people, sure. But you? Never. I'll earn your trust back. Watch and see."

I jerk my hand out from beneath his palm. "Don't be so sure about that."

"I'm not leaving without you again. That's something you and I can both be sure of."

A tiny part of me wants to cling to his words and believe them, but I brush them off instead. After all, this isn't a fucking fairy tale.

22
MOSES

Magnolia eats with gusto, just like I remember. She doesn't peck at her plate like one of those women who order salads because they care what the man across from them thinks. As far as I can tell, she doesn't give a damn what's going through my head. She's unimpressed, and it's no surprise.

But the mystery of who sliced her before he died? That's got her off-balance. I was no saint in the past, but I made it a law a long fucking time ago that no woman ever gets hurt by me or my people. But I'm also no gentleman, so I have no problem exploiting Magnolia's unsteadiness.

"You staying in your condo tonight?" I ask as she finishes half of the most expensive entrée on the menu, something that makes me smile like a damn fool.

Her tiger eyes lift to mine. "That's no business of yours."

I hold back my real answer, which is *everything you do is my business, woman.* Instead, I reply with, "What made you decide to buy a place in the Quarter?"

Her glare tells me it's another subject to add to the long list of things she doesn't want to discuss with me. Again, it's too damn bad.

"No one knows I own it, besides a couple of people who won't tell anyone. I'd prefer to keep it that way." She goes back to her meal and ignoring me, but I dissect the statement for all it's worth.

She doesn't want anyone to know where she lives. And why might that be?

I think Ms. Maison is tired of living life the way she has been. Given all the changes in the last few years, I can't say I'm surprised. It also tells me my timing may not be as bad as I thought. In fact, it might just be perfect.

"You're keeping a low profile these days. Tell me about this new business venture of yours."

It's not a question this time, but I guarantee that won't matter to Magnolia. She won't tell me anything she doesn't want to.

She looks up again. "Mount. Am I right?"

I tilt my head to the side as she nearly whispers the man's name. That's not a surprise either. He's not someone most people discuss, in polite company or otherwise. Lucky for me, he and I have an understanding—finally.

"Right about what?"

"He gave you all sorts of information on me during your little meeting, didn't he?" Her tone is threaded with annoyance, and possibly some betrayal too.

"He answered a few questions."

"Like what?" she asks, the knife stilling in her hand as if she's thinking about using it as a weapon.

I let a slow smile spread over my lips. "Like whether you have a man."

Her grip tightens on the utensil. "I don't need a man. Never have. Never will."

"Mama, you need a good fucking more than any woman I've ever seen. Whoever's been doing you over hasn't taken a strong enough hand to you. You've forgotten what it's like to scream when you come."

Those amber eyes turn to lava as her glare threatens to burn me alive. Her chest heaves, but she attempts to control her rage . . . or is that something else?

Temptation? Vengeance? Or maybe just good old-fashioned lust.

23
MAGNOLIA

I'm gonna kill him. I'm going to stab him right through the damn throat with a steak knife in the middle of the French Quarter. It'll be the second man I've killed in two days, but I think I might be fine with that.

But not because he's wrong.

Because he's right.

Motherfucker.

No one dares to talk to me like Moses. Not in a long goddamned time. And I hate that his words can have this effect on me.

"Go fuck yourself, Moses. That's the only action you're seeing tonight."

That stupid, beautiful smirk of his stretches wide across his face until the even stupider dimple pops out. He's gorgeous and he knows it.

He also knows I know it. He probably even knows I want to claw his eyes out, right after I claw up his back as he makes me scream his name. The visual bursts into my mind with the subtlety of a runaway freight train.

My panties are soaked. My nipples are hard. And I want to fuck.

Code red. Time to get the hell out of here.

I drop my knife, which is a damn shame considering how delicious the dinner is. Forcing some pride into myself because I don't know what the hell else to do right now, I set aside my napkin and rise from the candlelit table.

"I've lost my appetite." For food, but my need for sex is rampant.

He shakes his head, that piece-of-shit motherfucker. "Nah, mama. You're just getting it back."

"I hate you. All over again." Those words have never been so true as his grin widens.

"I know you do. But I don't mind. I'll give you a hate-fuckin' for dessert. *Lagniappe.*"

I can barely form words, I'm so angry. Frustration sounds like a growl in my throat, and I grab my clutch. "If I hate-fuck anyone, it'll be at the club tonight. And it sure as hell won't be you."

With that, I march out of the restaurant with steam surely rolling from my ears.

Cheers and screams from the revelers on Bourbon Street greet me as I push through the doors, but there's not a goddamned taxi at the taxi stand. I turn on my heel, dead set on walking home, yet I don't make it two steps before I find myself spun around and my back pressed up against the building.

Moses isn't grinning anymore, and through the raging inferno of my chaotic emotions, I decide to take that as a victory. If anything, I've defeated that smug smile.

"Just try it," he says quietly, challenging me. "See what happens to any man you touch. I promise you won't like it, and neither will they."

A shiver rips through me, ending directly at my clit, because clearly, I'm a wanton idiot.

I lift my chin, defiance flowing through me like it's my lifeblood. "What are you going to do? Kill him?"

The wickedly handsome grin of his is back, and this time, it's deadly. "Over you? Absolutely. Then I'll march him straight to the gates of hell myself."

This shouldn't turn me on. No. Fucking. Way. But he does. That's how fucked up I am.

I lick my lips. "You want me that bad, Moby?"

He inhales sharply when I call him that old nickname, and then bites his bottom lip as if holding back from sinking his teeth into mine.

Good. He isn't immune to me either. The scales have leveled out.

"Guess you shouldn't have left and never come back. My bed hasn't been empty in fifteen fucking years. You gonna kill them all?" It's not entirely true, but if I get into heaven, it'll be on the wings of white lies anyway.

"Only the ones who touch you now. You're mine, Magnolia. You'd best start getting used to the idea, because I ain't the kind of man who shares his woman."

If I thought my emotions were chaotic before, now they're a full-blown, tear-gassed city riot. I have to get away from him before that possessive attitude, which from anyone else would provoke me into violence, turns me on more than I can ever remember.

"No man owns me." I'm proud my voice is steady.

"I don't want to own you, mama."

My nipples harden further, loving the way he talks to me, even as I try to remain immune.

Then he continues. "That ain't why I'm here." His narrowed eyes glitter like polished emerald and topaz.

"Then why?"

"I want you to own *me*."

My heart slams into my chest at the sentiment beneath his declaration.

An unwelcome voice comes from behind Moses.

"Is there a problem here?"

I look around one of his broad shoulders to see a uniformed Louisiana state trooper standing a few feet away, no doubt stationed on Bourbon Street for the night to watch over the revelers.

Moses doesn't miss a beat. He curls one arm around my waist, and together we turn to face the cop. "No problem at all, sir. We were just debating dessert."

The cop takes in Moses's suit and my dress, and huffs good-naturedly. "Café Beignet is just up the street. Might try there if Arnaud's dessert menu wasn't to your taste."

"Thank you, sir. But I think the lady has something else in mind."

He dips his chin at us and chuckles knowingly. "Have your-selves a nice evening then."

"You too, sir."

The trooper nods, and then his eyes widen as a Rolls Royce crawls through the intersection to slow right in front of the restaurant. The *same* goddamned Rolls Royce I saw when I was leaving Mount's.

"After you," Moses says, opening the door.

"I'm only getting in this car if you tell me why the hell you went to Mount before coming to me."

Moses smiles, his eyes gleaming. "Deal. Now, get your fine ass in the car, woman."

I slide across the leather into the seat behind the driver. I swear, it smells just as good as I imagined a Rolls would, not that I ever figured I'd know for sure.

As soon as Moses closes the door with us both inside, I blurt out, "How the hell can you afford a Rolls Royce? How fucking rich are you?"

He leans forward to tap the driver's seat. "Privacy please, Jules."

"Sure thing, boss."

The divider between the front and rear seats rises, and we're the most alone we've been all night.

I stare at the man in the seat next to me. "What the hell have you been doing since you left town, Moses?"

"Which question do you want an answer to first? Because some are going to take longer than others." He shifts in the seat and crosses an ankle over his knee.

It's on the tip of my tongue to sputter out *all of them*, but I decide to go with the one most relevant. "Explain the car. Is it yours?"

Pride lifts his face an inch or two. "Bought it up in New York City, which is where I was before I came here. I had a . . ." He pauses to run his tongue along his white teeth. "Had a run of good luck up there. I made a good bet, and it turned into a windfall, you could say."

"That doesn't tell me shit, and you know it. This car may be gangster as fuck, but you sure couldn't buy it with money from running a crew of thugs like you did in Biloxi." Back in the day, he said he drove an old blue Cutlass Supreme SS. I thought he'd look fine as hell in that too, not that I got to ever see it in person.

"No. You're right about that," Moses replies, leaning back against the plush leather seat. "I haven't been a gangster in a long time. Kingpin was my goal, if you remember."

How could I forget it was more important to him than I was? Right now, that's neither here nor there.

For shits and grins, I ask, "Then what the hell are you now?"

That damn smile is back. "Remember when I told you that the guy who came at you was a ghost?"

"Yeah," I bite out.

"That's my business. Except . . . I'm the one who turns them into ghosts."

24
MOSES

"What does that mean?" Magnolia's long, dark lashes flutter as she blinks in confusion.

I didn't expect her to understand. Most people wouldn't, not that I've had many occasions to explain what I do before. People come to me through discreetly placed referrals, and they already understand the big picture.

"If someone wants a new life or needs to disappear so well that no one ever looks for them, if they know the right people, they get connected to me. My team and I make it happen . . . or at least *look* like it happened."

Her eyes are as wide and round as I've ever seen them. It's good to see something can still shock her.

"What in the hell? And it pays this well?"

That I answer with a shrug. "I'm good at what I do. Call it a niche market. And I know how to turn money into even more money. To answer your other question, I'm rich as fuck, Mags." I give her a wink before I correct myself. "No. Actually, I'm richer than fuck now."

She blinks a few more times before facing forward silently, her head barely shaking back and forth. "Jesus Christ. You were going back to Biloxi when you left me . . . but you didn't. You just *disappeared.*" Her head whips back in my direction. "*You* became a goddamned ghost."

I had no idea she'd looked for me. But the new, unexpected knowledge unleashes a surge of something deep within me. Hope, mixed with triumph. *Fuck yes.*

"You're right. I didn't go back to Biloxi. I got caught up in some shit leaving town. Turned into an opportunity I didn't expect."

Instead of prodding me more about that, she snaps out her next question. "What did you talk to Mount about?"

I know it's my chance to let everything out, put all my cards on the table, but it's the first time in so long that we're *talking* again, and I don't want to spoil it. So instead, I'm vague. "To settle a matter and declare my intentions."

"What intentions?" she asks, a guarded look crossing her face.

I lean back against the seat and stretch one arm across the back. "My intentions with regard to one Ms. Magnolia Marie Maison."

Her jaw slackens, letting her lower lip drop again before she catches herself. "What the fuck does that mean? And explain it to me like I'm a toddler. No more riddles."

I move toward her and give her the truth. "I'm forty fucking years old, mama. I haven't had a home in fifteen years—hell, even before that, I didn't have one I'd want to go back to—and I want one something powerful now. I want to settle down. Put down some roots. I want a wife, and I want her to give me a houseful of babies who'll have me wrapped around their fingers just like their mother."

Magnolia can't school her reactions quick enough. She's floored. Emotions dash across her face like shooting stars, one after another. Hope. Denial. Curiosity. Doubt.

"Wh-what does that have to do with me?" she sputters.

"You've always been the one, Mags. I haven't gone an hour without thinking about you since the night I left."

The soft glow of the streetlights glints off the sheen of tears gathering in her eyes. Tears I'm sure she'd rather kill me for than admit to. She blinks them back.

"It's too late, Moses. Too fucking late."

I shake my head. "No. I refuse to believe that. And Mount clearly doesn't believe it either."

The sheen is gone in an instant, traded out for another glare. "What the hell does that mean?"

This time, my cheeks stretch wide with a grin. "He gave me his blessing when I told him I'd come back to put a ring on your finger. Said he and his wife would be happy to stand up for us when we say our vows."

The beautiful brat beside me chokes.

Pure shock. That's the only way to describe her expression.

After a minute, she schools her features. "You don't even know me anymore. That girl you came back for? She's long gone."

"Good," I tell her. "I'm a grown-ass man. I'm not some john looking for a high-value suck-and-fuck. I came back for a woman, not a girl. I know who you are, and I want everything you bring to the table."

She shakes her head. "You've lost your fucking Mississippi-mud-filled mind."

I chuckle. "Scared?"

Her expression turns mulish. "Of you? Not a chance in hell."

"Good. Because Jules is taking us back to your new place. You're not sleeping alone tonight."

25
MAGNOLIA

I stare at the man sitting beside me in this silent car that reeks of all the changes he's made in his life.

A man who came back for *me.*

A man who told Mount he's going to *marry me.*

The *only* man I've never forgotten for a single damn day in fifteen years, no matter how much I wished I could wake up with amnesia just to erase those two fucking weeks we shared.

Two weeks. That's all the time we had together.

Right after Katrina turned the city I'd lived in my whole life into something completely unrecognizable, he saved me. And . . . I fell hard for him, but when it was time for him to go, choices were made.

I couldn't leave, and he wouldn't stay.

Two weeks shouldn't change you forever, but in the wake of tragedy and chaos, things are different. Unbreakable bonds are formed faster than you can imagine.

But I don't want to think about that now. No way in hell. If I do, I won't be able to find the strength to tell him to walk away again.

Moses might have carved out a new life for himself, but so

have I. I have a new home and a business that's still finding its feet, and he doesn't have to tell me he has no plans to stay here. Just like he refused to before.

The problem we faced fifteen years ago isn't any different now. I won't go with him, and I can't imagine he'll stick around. Which means I need to watch myself. The heartbreak that comes from falling for Moses Gaspard isn't something I can experience twice.

Not that I'd ever admit to him exactly how badly it destroyed me.

I stay quiet the entire short ride to my place, completely ignoring the mention of us getting married. It's simply not based in reality.

When we pull up in front of my gate, pride straightens my spine once more. This place is all mine, something no one, not even Moses, can take away.

The reunion wasn't bad, but this is where I get off the fantasy bus before someone—like me—gets hurt.

"No need to get out. I'll see myself inside," I tell Moses, ignoring his dictate from earlier that I wasn't sleeping alone tonight.

I reach for the door handle, but it opens without me touching it. His driver, a tall, light-skinned black man with close-cropped black hair, stands there with a smile.

"You aren't staying anywhere by yourself, Mags. Not until we find out exactly what kind of situation you've tied yourself up in."

I look at Moses, feeling like the glare I've been sporting all evening is going to become the permanent expression on my face. If I need Botox after this, I'm sending Mr. Baller Rolls Royce the bill.

"You aren't staying here."

One of his thick shoulders rises and his bottom lip juts out. "That's fine. Then you're coming home with us."

Anger at being maneuvered and ordered around lights me up

with a streak of contrariness. No one tells me what to do. Not in a long damn time. But Moses doesn't seem to understand, and neither does my body, based on the moment we had against the wall after dinner.

I form a new plan. Leaning back in the seat, I cross my arms. "With both of you?" I look from Moses to the attractive man holding my door open. "A ménage with this guy? Now you have my attention."

The man who was lazily leaning back against the seat beside me swells with anger, seeming to double in size. "Shut the fucking door, Jules."

Jules doesn't reply, but the door closes before I can get the fuck out. Now I'm trapped inside with a seething Moses.

A sexy, seething Moses. I can feel the territorial masculinity rolling off of him like steam from a hot sidewalk after a sprinkle of rain.

He turns in his seat, crowding me against the door. "You want a reaction out of me, woman? You'll get one. I meant what I said. Ain't no other fucking man touching you until we've settled what's between us. Damn it, you owe me that."

My lower lip drops, which seems to be another new habit I've acquired against my will this evening.

"I don't owe you *shit*, Moses."

His face turns to stone. Thin lipped. Chiseled, hard-set jaw. No easy grin now. "You sure as fuck do. You wouldn't even think about coming with me. You're part of the reason we lost fifteen fucking years together too."

I gasp. "You motherfucking asshole." I surge forward in my seat and shove him with both hands. "You left me! You wouldn't stay!"

"I couldn't! Not without putting you in danger. You think that's the kind of man I am? One who would put his woman at risk? No fucking way, Magnolia."

I shake my head, fury causing unshed tears to burn like acid in my eyes. "Let me out of this fucking car. I'm done with this little reunion of yours. Whatever you came for, you won't find it. Go, Moses. There's nothing for you here now."

He reaches out and yanks me across the center seat, pulling me against him. "Bull fucking shit, Magnolia."

His mouth crashes down on mine, and I declare temporary insanity.

His scent. His taste. His touch.

I desperately want to push him away, but I can't. The one thing I never thought I'd have again . . . I allow my body to take over, and I fucking maul him. My nails dig into his shoulder and the back of his neck as I cling to his rigid muscles, my tongue demanding entrance into his mouth.

God, I need more. More. More.

I don't even know how it happened, but his hands grip my waist, bringing me down on his lap as my knees dig into the leather on either side of his hips. I grind hard against one heavy thigh, not caring that my dress is riding up.

Moses shifts his grip, spearing a hand into my hair and pinning me against him.

Fuck. It feels too good. Too right. Too perfect.

"Inside," he says into my mouth as he shifts me to drive his hips up and the hard ridge of his cock against my clit. "Inside. Now."

His voice brings me to my senses.

What the fuck am I doing? Letting a man waltz into my life and tell me what to do after he bailed for fifteen years, whatever the reason? No. Not tonight I'm not.

I try to move away, but Moses keeps my forehead pressed against his.

"For fifteen goddamned years I've wanted to be able to fuck and not think of you. Do you have any idea what that's like?"

More than I'll ever admit to him.

I freeze in his arms. "Let me go. Now."

Shockingly, he does, and I scramble to the other side. "I'm not doing this again. I can't do this."

"What the hell does that mean?" Moses stares at me with disbelief on his face.

"I'm not fucking you *until* you understand you get no say-so about what I do or who I touch. You don't get to walk into town and pretend like you own me. I've busted my ass and done things I never want to think about ever again, all to get me where I am. *Free.* I'm not handing that over to anyone. Not even you."

He nearly growls as he rubs his palms over his clean-shaven face. "Stubborn fucking woman. You know this is what you want. You can't lie to me, Magnolia."

"How the hell do you know what I want, Moses? Because *I* don't even know what the fuck I want anymore." My heart is hammering behind this dark purple dress, hard enough to bust it at the seams.

His lips close, and the anger that was rolling off him dies instantly. His chest rises and falls with a few deep, steadying breaths.

"You need time to get used to the idea. I can respect that. But you can't ask me to leave you unprotected. That's not something I'm capable of anymore. You want to stay here tonight, then I'll take a guest room." He relents, and something like surrender flashes in his color-shifting eyes.

Even though I would have sworn it was impossible, a chuckle spills from my lips. "Sure thing, big man. You want the guest room? You've got the guest room."

26
MOSES

Magnolia opens her door and climbs out of the Rolls onto the sidewalk. I have only a few seconds to get back my hard-won self-possession.

I've spent years mastering my emotions so no one else could control me. But Magnolia seems to defy all the rules I've put in place to keep myself levelheaded. Not surprising, I suppose, considering Magnolia doesn't follow anyone's rules but her own. Something I fucking love about her, even if it's driving me crazy right now.

I get out of the car and hustle to the gate just before it closes, leaving me and Jules outside. I stop with one hand holding it open and turn back to him.

"I'll call you."

He gives me a thumbs-up, and I head inside.

A thin layer of construction dust coats every surface, but it also shows me exactly where Magnolia went. *Upstairs.*

When I was here last night, I noticed there was no furniture on the first level, but I didn't think anything of it because I was too busy worrying about Magnolia and the blood from the door handle of her condo. It didn't even occur to me to ask if she had a damn bed in the place. Obviously, I should have, because when I step into the master bedroom, I see a deflated air mattress rolled out on the floor.

No wonder she gave in so easily when I said I'd take the guest room. If the master doesn't have a bed, the guest room won't either. That joke's on me.

She turns around in the white-on-white-on-white room so we're face to beautifully smug face. "You still wanna stay?"

The triumphant smile on her lips should piss me off, but it does the opposite. I want to peel that dress off her, lay her down on that cheap-ass air mattress, and make short work of popping the damn thing. If she thinks this will scare me off, she has another think coming.

"No way in hell I'm leaving now that I'm inside with your permission."

She glances down at the air mattress. "I've only got one, and I'm not sharing. You can take a floor. Doesn't even have to be the guest room. Any floor you want is fine by me, so long as it's not in this room."

The corners of my mouth tug at my lips, and I try to hold back my smile. It's a losing battle.

"Mighty generous offer, mama. I'll take it."

She pretends she's tired, stretches and yawns, tapping her fingers against her sexy open mouth. "I'm going to shower. Do whatever you want." She marches toward the doorway I'm blocking.

I move to the side, giving her just enough space to squeeze by me, but I put my arm out to halt her. "You trying to wash the taste and feel of me away?"

Magnolia tilts her head to the side. "I don't need a shower to put you out of my mind. I'm a professional at that now."

"Then what?"

She slowly bats her long black lashes and stares me dead in

the eye. "I'm going to make myself come so hard that I'll sleep like a baby tonight, with or without you in my house."

My dick fights against my suit pants. "No need for you to do that yourself, mama. I'm ready, willing, able, and right fucking here."

She pouts at me like I'm a poor gutter puppy. "Not interested, Moby. Now, get out of my doorway."

My smile can't be held back now. "You're a real piece of work. One hell of a woman, Magnolia."

She rolls her eyes and turns her rosy cheek to break our eye contact. "Whatever."

She tramps into the bathroom as I stand there, watching her as she closes the door. Surprisingly, she pauses when there's an inch remaining and calls out, "You want to make yourself useful, blow up the air mattress. Blowing shit ain't my thing."

The bathroom door closes, and a burst of laughter leaves my lungs.

I told her the truth. She's one hell of a woman.

My woman.

I just have to remind her, and then make sure she never forgets again.

27
MAGNOLIA

I don't know where Moses sleeps in my house, but he doesn't push to sleep on the mattress he inflated. True to my word, I went to bed sated and slept like the dead. I refuse to admit my sleep was undisturbed because I knew he was watching over me.

When I rise from the air mattress, there's a crick in my neck, but I don't have time to think about it because I hear something coming from downstairs.

Voices. As in plural.

I quickly throw on some loose shorts, a bra, and a tank top before heading down to see what the hell is going on.

I stop short in my kitchen when I see Moses at the counter, wearing his slacks and a white undershirt, going over my punch list with Rocco.

"You'll have it all done today?"

"Yes, sir. Absolutely. The cleaning crew can come tomorrow, and then she can have furniture delivered—" Rocco cuts off his statement when he sees me.

Hands on my hips, I glower at the pair of men at my new marble island. "What the hell is going on?"

Moses answers as if he's been here all along, every day, throughout this renovation. "Rocco was just telling me he'll be done this evening with the punch list and out of your hair."

I face Rocco, who is studying me and my casual look. "Already?"

He glances down at the sheet of paper we made the list on, and then back up at me. "Yes, ma'am. Just give me today to have a few more guys come in, and we'll be out of here for good."

"A few more guys?" I repeat the phrase because I know Rocco didn't plan on using more help due to the labor expense. "Is that going to cost me more?"

He shakes his head, catching Moses's eyes, which are firmly drilled at him to answer the way he's been instructed. "No. Not a penny more." The look tells me there's something I'm missing here, but Rocco excuses himself before I can ask more questions.

Left alone in the kitchen with Moses, I cross my arms over my chest. "What did you say to him?"

"What needed to be said to get you a house that's livable." He stretches his neck to one side and then the other. "Because I'm not sleeping across your doorway again. I'm too old for that shit, Mags." He holds up an index finger to hammer home his point. "One long, miserable night was enough."

Scowling, I remind him, "No one asked you to."

I try to breeze through the kitchen, but Moses snags me around the waist with an arm and brings me to stand between his legs. Body heat radiates off him, soaking through my clothes and creating a flush up my chest.

"You sleep okay?"

As I smile up at him with all the sweetness I can manage, I pretend I'm not feeling a bit affected by his presence. Plus, since he slept like shit, I'm inclined to rub my semi-restful night in a little. A girl's got to have her fun when she can. "Like a baby."

Heat flashes in his hypnotic eyes. "You enjoyed making me listen to you come in the shower, didn't you?"

My smile widens as I recall how I used the handheld sprayer I specifically had installed for that very purpose. I turned it to a pulsating setting, and all it took was a few thoughts about Moses to have me screaming—not that I'd ever admit to him what or who I was thinking about.

"More than you'll ever know."

"You've got a mean streak in you, woman."

I can't help but laugh. "Damn right I do. Now, I'm going to get coffee."

"Perfect. I could use some."

When he releases me from his hold, I hate that I miss the warmth of his body almost instantly. I've never been at war with myself like this before.

I want him. There's no doubt about that. But I'm not ready to confess it. That would be handing him way too much power over me, and I'm not willing to do it.

As I step toward the door, the chime on the gate rings, and I pause.

"Who the hell could that be?" I mumble to myself, but my gaze collides with Moses's. "One of your people?"

He shakes his head. "No. Let me look."

He strides to the front of the house and looks through the shutters. I'm right behind him, because it's my damn house.

As soon as I peek, I wish I hadn't.

"*Motherfucker*," I whisper, gritting my teeth when I see Detective Cavender standing on the sidewalk. "What the fuck is he doing here?"

Moses shifts, his bulky shoulder brushing against my bare skin. "Who is it?"

I gaze up into his green-gold eyes and fill him in. "A fucking cop. Detective Cavender. He's investigating the elevator murder and already decided he likes me for it. I told him I wasn't at my condo the night it happened. Wouldn't give him an alibi.

Wouldn't let him search my place. I told him to come back with a warrant. He knows who I am and what I used to do."

Moses's stare narrows on me. "How does he know about this place?"

"I don't know," I tell him with my palms pressed against my temples. "He shouldn't. No one should. Fuck. This isn't supposed to happen like this. *Fuck*."

"You trust me?" Moses asks.

I jerk my head back, totally uncertain of what he's getting at. "Why?"

"Because I know you didn't buy this place in your name, and there's no way a run-of-the-mill NOPD detective should know you own it with how well you've covered your tracks."

I want to ask him how the hell *he* knows all that, but I don't. The chime rings again, and I hear Rocco coming down the stairs.

"You need me to answer?"

"No, we got this. Thanks, man," Moses replies before the contractor gets too far down the steps.

I'm starting to panic. Having him around does nothing for my focus, and time is running out. "Make your point, Moses."

"I'll handle it, mama. Trust me."

I want to tell him I don't trust him at all, but I can't. What other option do I have? "Then fucking handle it, Moby. Get rid of him."

A grin lights up Moses's features at my use of his old nickname again. "My pleasure." He leans down and presses a hard kiss to my lips and heads for the door before I have a chance to say another word or take it back.

That man . . . He's already got me falling back into old habits before I've even decided if it's what I want.

What the hell am I going to do about him now?

28
MOSES

I open the gate to face a man I would have pegged as a cop, regardless of whether Magnolia had told me he was one. His wrinkled suit, the way he stands, and the air of confidence that comes only from carrying a badge gives him away.

"Good morning. Can I help you?" I ask as I open the gate.

He tries to hide the surprise on his face when he sees me. He wasn't expecting a man like me. Six-three, light-skinned, but definitely black somewhere in my Creole lineage, muscles with enough bulk to show I hit the gym regularly. Unlike the cop, I've got confidence ingrained in me that comes from knowing I *will* handle any fucking situation that might crop up. Including a detective making a house call to an address he shouldn't know shit about.

He measures me up and down. "Who are you?"

"Shouldn't I be asking you that, considering you're ringing my bell?"

"Your bell?" He breaks eye contact, looking up and down the street before his narrowed gaze lands on my face again.

"You were expecting someone else, I take it?"

I have to give the cop some credit, he recovers from the

surprise of me in a hurry. "Yes, actually. Sorry to disturb you. What did you say your name was again?"

Grinning, I catch the old trick. "I didn't. Just like you didn't. But feel free to introduce yourself anytime. And if you want to tell me who you were looking for here, you can do that too."

The cop rocks back on the heels of his beat-up dress shoes that haven't seen a shine in way too long. After a moment's deliberation, he pulls his shield from the inner breast pocket of his suit and flashes it at me.

"Detective Cavender. I'm looking for Magnolia Maison. You know her?"

Yeah, I know her, man. I listened to her come last night, wishing I was buried inside that sweet pussy.

I ignore his question and reply with one of my own. "And why are you looking for the woman here?"

Cavender's lips press into a hard line. "Can't disclose that information. Police business."

This time, I chuckle. "Ahh . . . I get you. Well, either way, you won't be talking to Ms. Maison today or anytime in the future."

The cop jerks his head back. "So you do know her."

"Sure do. She's my woman." I reach into my pocket and pull out my billfold. One flick of my thumb pulls out what I need. "And if you have any questions for her, you can call this gentleman right here. He'll make sure you get the appropriate responses."

I hold out my lawyer's business card to the cop, and he snatches it from my hand, looking down at it before staring back at me.

"Who the hell are you?" He rocks from foot to foot, entitled and waiting.

"Moses Buford Gaspard, and I'd appreciate you not bothering me at my residence again. Have a good day, Detective."

I shut the gate in his face.

29
MAGNOLIA

I shouldn't be turned on, but I am. *Damn it*. I overheard every word Moses said to the cop, and I was floored by how he dealt with the situation. He had my back. Protected me and shielded me. Handled Cavender like a boss.

Goddamn it, why does Moses have to be so fucking capable?

All my life, I've had to cope with shit alone. Every step of the way. If I wanted something to happen, I had to make it happen. If I had a problem, I had to solve it. Not since those two weeks fifteen years ago have I had someone I could lean on to share my burdens.

And Moses didn't think twice about it.

First with Rocco, and now with Cavender. He's stepping up without even being asked.

Goddamn it all.

Moses stands in the doorway, practically blocking out the sunlight because he's a big bastard. I just stare at him, wondering how I'm supposed to feel right now, because I sure as hell don't know.

He claps his hands together as if dusting them off. "Done and done. What's next?"

"You gave him your name," I blurt. "Why would you do that?"

"So he'll spend his time running me rather than trying to dig deeper into who really owns this house."

My eyes feel like they're about to shoot from their sockets. "Isn't that even worse?"

That lazy grin stretches across his face. "Nah. I'm squeaky clean."

"But what about Biloxi?" He told me all those years ago about his many petty—and not so petty—crimes.

"Mama. I told you what I do. You don't think I'd handle my own shit first and clear out my history? I'm covered."

"And the lawyer? What's he going to say?"

Moses's shoulders shake with unconcerned laughter. "He'll tell Cavender to go fuck himself in the politest way a thousand-dollar-an-hour New York lawyer can. If they want more, they can get a fucking warrant, which no judge is going to give them based on only you living in a building where someone died. Especially since there's nothing to tie it to you."

The massive man plucks a fallen eyelash off of my cheek and holds it in front of my lips to blow. When I don't, he does, and then moves on like what happened outside was no big deal.

"Now, how about that coffee? I could use a beignet."

30

Somewhere else in New Orleans

I hate this dirty city, full of people who'd rather party than work.

As I let myself into my brother's apartment, I crack my neck, fully expecting to find him passed out with a hooker or two in his bed. That is how I found him last time he didn't answer my texts or calls for two days.

But that's not what I find this time.

I check every room. It's a pigsty, not that I'm surprised. Pizza boxes, beer cans, and empty daiquiri cups litter the coffee table. The expensive TV sits silent in the corner, and there's an inch of dust on the stereo system. It might be the housekeeper's year off, but Ricky has no problem blowing money on anything he wants. That's always been his problem. *Mi hermano* goes through money like water. He's always asking for his deposit early, which is the other reason I'm here.

He hasn't asked, which tells me something's not right.

"Where are you, Ricardo?"

Silence is the only answer, and it is not one I'm willing to accept.

Ten minutes later, I have even more questions. Starting with how he has twenty-five thousand dollars in his safe. *Idiot* used his own fucking birthday as a combination too. Not that anyone else alive would be able to match him with that date.

"Ricky . . . Ricky . . . Ricky . . . What the fuck have you been doing?"

To prove a point, I take the cash and start for the door. Except one thing stops me—a piece of paper on the counter with a phone number written in Ricky's sloppy handwriting. Next to it is a prepaid cell phone.

I flip it open. The battery is dead, so I plug it into the charger attached to the wall and wait a few minutes to power it on. After it comes back to life, I scroll down to check the last dialed number. It's the one on the sheet.

Dumb fuck. Throw the fucking paper away then, imbécil. If Ricky's dealing with some shady shit, I'm going to have to get involved. He's the worst criminal I've ever known.

I tap the number and wait for the call to connect. A woman answers on the third ring.

"Jesus. I've been waiting a week. Is it done? Are they dead?"

I am not a bad criminal. In fact, I am a very fucking good one.

I take a single guess at exactly what my little brother has gotten himself into and reply to her. "Yes. I want the rest of the money."

"I want proof before I wire it." The woman on the other end sounds like she's got balls of brass and no respect, but then again, she was dealing with Ricky and not me.

"Then you'll have to meet me. Change of plans . . . no wire. Bring cash. I'll text you a time and address. Don't be late unless you want to end up like them."

"Hey," she says, starting to protest, but I hang up.

Fucking Ricky . . . trying to be a hit man like I used to be. I shake my head. Now I must find him, because something is not right.

31
MAGNOLIA

I must be living in an alternate reality, because Moses is sitting across from me at a café. He looks comfortable as hell in his fitted undershirt with a steaming double shot of espresso in front of him and an empty plate that used to hold a mound of beignets that I never thought a man who looks like he's carved from stone would eat. But he sure as hell didn't waste any time putting them away.

How is this even happening right now? I swear to God, I will never understand how the universe works.

"What?" he asks as I stare at his mouth, which has a smudge of powdered sugar smeared across it.

I point to my own mouth to show him where it is.

"You want me to kiss you? Right here? I can do that."

His chair slides across the tile floor as he leans over the table to come toward me. I throw my hands out to stop him, because I don't need his candied lips adding even more confusion to my messed-up head.

"Powdered sugar," I blurt instead, but force myself to remove the panic from my voice. "Your mouth. Wipe it," I say more calmly, picking up a napkin from the table and holding it out to him.

His eyes sparkle like he's amused as hell at how flustered I am at the thought of him kissing me. *Asshole.*

I'm *never* flustered. And yet here we are, on this ass-backward day when the thought of a man kissing me has the power to make me act like a goddamned virgin and prize idiot.

"Why don't you come over here and get it for me, mama. After making me listen to what you did to yourself in the shower last night, it's the least you could do."

If I still had the capability of blushing, I might, but I don't because that part of me is long dead. I search for some of the sassiness I felt last night when I decided to torture him so I can kick this out-of-control sensation.

Thankfully, it doesn't take long at all.

I reach out, dab my finger into the powdered sugar, and bring it to my lips, sucking the sweetness off and letting it melt in my mouth. I'm making a show of it for my sake, but just as much for his.

Glancing up at Moses, I find his hooded, slowly blinking eyes on my lips, and I lick the smile off my sugary lips.

That's right. I'm in control here.

I tilt my head to the side. "You deserved it for how you acted last night."

Mimicking my motion, he tilts his head in the opposite direc-tion. "You brought up a threesome with my employee." His voice is even and calm, but he's quick to respond.

My right shoulder rises because a three-way isn't really all that wild in my world. Well, in my old world. "You know I like variety."

I expect thunderclouds to gather in Moses's eyes, showing me he's lost his patience, but they don't come. His easy smile returns.

"No. You don't. You'll be happy with one cock for the rest of your life—as long as it's mine."

I scrunch my face in annoyance. How am I supposed to deal with this man? I truly don't know. So I snap back. "Just because you say it doesn't make it the truth. Eventually, you'll realize that."

The shake of his head is almost enough to drive me crazy. He always had a way of playing and teasing that made me come unglued. Almost like he wound me up just to see me spin out like a toy car.

"Nothing to say with that big mouth of yours now?" Big . . . and incredibly talented from what I remember.

He relaxes in the chair and crosses one muscular leg over the other. People pass and it's loud in the café, but all I see and hear is him.

"Think what you want, but I know you, Mags. You're scared as shit. You want me, but you won't admit it. That's okay, for now. Eventually, *you'll* realize what I've got to offer you is exactly what you want."

I hate how he cuts to the heart of the matter. It's just so out of nowhere, nearly impossible to believe, and probably too good to be true.

"You're scared as shit." How the fuck does he know? He doesn't know me anymore. He shouldn't be able to read me so easily.

Frustration and doubt rise inside me. "You're full of yourself, Moses."

"I'd rather you be full of me, but that'll come soon enough. And I'll hear those cries in my ear instead of through the door and walls." He winks, and I could strangle him. "You're a hell of a woman, Magnolia. I've learned a lot in fifteen years. There's no one else like you anywhere. You're everything I want."

Every time he says something like that, it throws me for a loop. I'm not used to it, and I sure as hell have no idea what to do with it. "That's not a compliment. You want me by default? No one else was better, so I'll do now? Stop saying shit like that. I don't want to hear it."

His brow pinches, and finally I've landed a blow. Maybe now he gets it. I wanted him more than any other man on the planet, and he wanted to see if he could find something better.

Am I supposed to feel lucky that he didn't?

Probably not, but that doesn't erase the fact that I do, and I hate it.

He tries to reach for my hand, but I dodge him. His gaze says he's sorry, but his lips don't. Instead, he says, "Fine, then we'll change the subject. Tell me about your man who died."

Now I'm the one catching blows. Anger, humiliation, and hurt ignite through me like a blast furnace set to high. They do every single time someone mentions *him,* but normally I'm way more emotionally stable and can mask it without so much as a blip.

But not with Moses. Not right now.

I suck in a breath to steady myself and jerk my gaze upward to stare at the stamped tin ceiling, wishing there was whiskey in my cup instead of chicory.

Just breathe. That part of your life is over. Pull it together, Mags. "Fucking Mount," I whisper, knowing exactly who provided Moses with the information.

He doesn't confirm or deny his source.

I swallow a lump in my throat and meet his warm gaze once more. "I'm not talking about it."

He drags his bottom lip through his teeth and then asks, "You still in love with him? Still grieving him?"

If Moses is in for a penny, he's in for a pound, and he's not holding anything back. But I do. I have too many cards on the table already, and he's not shown any that I'm willing to believe are real yet.

My entire body tenses, and my jaw sets into stone. "That's none of your damn business."

"He fucked you over pretty bad," Moses says, pausing to take another sip. "I'm guessing that's a *no* on you still being in love or grieving."

The breath is crushed out of my chest by the weight of the topic. "I said *I'm not talking about it.*"

Moses finally gets it. I'm not fucking around. He holds his hands up between us. "Fine. Then what do you want to talk about?"

I'm pissed and emotional, and so I lash out. "When you're leaving. That sounds like a right fine subject."

He casually gathers our trash and piles it onto his plate. "When you tell me you're coming with me."

I squeeze my eyes shut, wanting to disappear. "You're fucking impossible."

He grins. "Be glad I'm on your side."

My phone buzzes on the table, and I snatch it up like a life raft sent to save me from drowning.

Just being around Moses has me on edge, and the fortress around my heart is taking a thrashing. Damn near every word out of his mouth is like a battering ram. Any distraction or interruption I can get will help me pull myself together.

When I look down at the screen, a rush of relief washes over me.

Keira. Thank God.

I tap the screen and lift the phone to my ear. "Hey, Ke-ke. What's happening?" My voice sounds as close to normal as I can manage under the circumstances.

"Oh no, you don't. You're not going to *hey, Ke-ke* me, Mags. What in the hell is going on? My husband just told me I need to be ready to stand up with you at your *wedding.*"

Oh. Fuck.

So much for a life raft. This will be more like the Spanish Inquisition. While part of me says I've got no one but myself to blame for the fact this conversation is happening right now, the rest of me knows I *do,* in fact, have someone else to blame. *Moby.*

My scowl focuses on Moses, and it's fueled with so much frustration, I'm surprised the skin doesn't melt off his face.

His grin just widens, and I can feel the vein throbbing in my temple.

I pop out of my chair, mouthing, *"I'm going to kill you,"* and stride for the door because I won't spend another second watching him stare at me with a silly smile on his face while life as I know it changes completely without my consent.

When Keira speaks again, her tone is shrill, but in an excited and wildly curious way that only best friends take with each other. *"Mags?* I can hear you breathing, damn it. You can't dodge the question. What in the hell is going on?"

Through my grinding teeth, I reply, "Hold on. I'm going outside. I don't want to talk about this in front of him."

"He's there? Right now?"

The squeal in Keira's voice threatens to blow my eardrum clear out of my spinning head, and I hold the phone out a few extra inches as I step into a meager patch of shade.

"He's inside. We just had coffee."

"You had coffee with him?"

Spinning around, I face the street and sigh. "If you're just going to repeat everything I say, this conversation can be cut a whole hell of a lot shorter."

"Oh, shut up. I'm the one who just had to hear from my husband that my best friend has some long-lost love who's back to claim her, and this blast from the past wants to *marry her.* What in the actual fuck is going on?"

I clear my throat as I form an answer that will be brief enough to wrap this up quickly, and sufficient enough that she doesn't feel slighted by me. *"One.* He's not my long-lost love." I roll my neck as I speak, not liking the flutter in my chest when she called him that. *"Two.* He's . . . fuck, I don't know what he is. A mistake. The sort I thought was never coming back. If I had, I would've told you."

She's calmer now. "When did this start?"

I pace a few steps and then back to the cover of shade. "Katrina. You were away. It wasn't something I was bothering you with back then. Just like your husband shouldn't have bothered you with it now."

"Uh. No, bitch. Back up right there," she says, attitude clipping her words. *So much for defusing the situation.* I can practically feel Keira get pissy again at my statement. "He absolutely should've bothered me with it, because I hear you right now. I hear that tremor in your voice. You're freaking the fuck out, and you didn't even think to call me for help? Or does that only apply to me? I call you with my problems, but you don't share yours with me?"

Keira hits me hard where it hurts, because . . . in a way, she's right.

She's my best friend. The girl who refused to snub me, no matter what people had to say about my reputation. She even defied her own mother when she told her she wasn't allowed to speak to me again. Keira Kilgore Mount is one of those good humans you count yourself lucky to know, and I've always wondered why she stuck by me. I sure didn't always deserve it.

"Magnolia." Her voice sounds less self-righteous when she says my full first name to break the silence hanging between us.

"I can't ask you to carry my burdens, Ke-ke. It's just different. You know that. There's no way in hell I could've laid it on you. I wouldn't."

She's quiet for another moment, and when she speaks, her irritation is gone just as quickly as it came. "You don't have to protect me anymore, Mags. You know that as well as I do. You could've told me about him. That's all I want you to know."

These damn emotions of mine are all swirled up again. "Jesus Christ, you're gonna make me fuckin' cry on the damn sidewalk. You'd think I'm a fourteen-year-old girl with how fucking mixed up I am right now. I don't know which end is up or what the fuck to do about this man. I just . . . fuck me, Ke-ke. I never saw this coming. Not after all this time."

"Oh, honey. I'm so sorry. I should've started with—*how are you?*"

I chuckle at Keira and her manners. "To tell you the truth, I'm not sure how to answer that question." I lean against the building and release a long breath. "He's got me so damn confused. I don't like how I fucking feel."

"How's that?"

"Like I'm losing my grip on control, and I can't have that."

A few beats of silence pass before she replies. "I hate to tell you this, Mags . . . but if you're falling for the guy again, the grip on control you're trying to keep hold of is only going to give you rope burn."

Fear shoots through me. "Don't say that. I'm not falling for him. I'm not. That shit is in the past."

"Whatever you say." And then she chokes on a laugh.

"What the fuck?" I roll my eyes, even though she can't see me, and then scold her. "Are you seriously laughing at me right now? Bitch. If you weren't my best friend, I'd hang up on you. Like, right fucking now, Ke-ke."

"I'm sorry. I'm so sorry. I really shouldn't be laughing. But, *oh my God*, I never thought I'd see the day."

When she starts chuckling again, I go quiet, really contemplating hanging up on her, but she catches her breath a few seconds later.

"I'm so glad you find it amusing that I'm confused as hell and don't know what the fuck to do about this man. Jesus Christ. You should see him. And hear him. I don't know what the hell to believe." I'm pacing in circles again, trying to keep my voice down, but inside, I'm wigging the fuck out.

"What do you want to do, Mags? What will make you happy?"

Her question stops me mid-step, and I stare at the plaster-work of the building like I've never seen white paint before.

What will make me happy? A lump forms in my throat because I can't let myself think about the answer.

"That's not helping. I gotta get rid of him. It's the only choice I have. I've worked too long and hard, building my life to where it is, to allow someone to sweep in and change everything on a whim. I can't trust it. I can't put my faith in it. It doesn't work like that."

"Mags, calm down. You're freaking out for real now. It's okay. I didn't mean to get you riled up. Just take a deep breath."

The concern in Keira's tone cuts through the cloud of panic threatening to choke me. I take a deep breath and slowly exhale. Then again.

"Good girl. It's going to be okay. I promise," Keira says, and for the first time in our over twenty-year-long friendship, she sounds like the one who has her shit together and knows all the answers. That's the role I've always played.

How the mighty have fallen, Ho-It-All says, piping up. *Where's your self-respect, Magnolia? Losing it right out in the open? When did you let yourself become so weak? And over a* man. *Yes, how the mighty have fallen . . .*

It's the reminder I need to pull my shit together.

"You're right. It'll be fine. It's a shock, is all," I tell Keira, straightening my shoulders and trying to shake it off. "I just need a bit of time to think. How about we talk later?"

"Are you sure you're good? Because I can—"

Knowing she's going to offer to send someone to get me, or to stay on the line until I've actually pulled it together instead of just pretending I'm okay, I say, "I'm just fine, girl. You know that nothing fazes me for long. Especially not a man."

"If you're sure . . ."

Clearly, I'm not doing the best job at selling this. "I'll text you tomorrow. Give Rory my love. Gotta go." Before she can protest, I hang up the call.

That's when I catch sight of Moses, watching me from the corner.

Instantly, my spine goes ramrod straight. "You taking up eavesdropping now too? Can't a person get some damn privacy?"

His face is completely devoid of his normal easy grin. "I didn't come back to ruin your life, mama."

My stomach sinks when I think of what he could have overheard to say something like that.

Then he adds, "And you're no second-rate backup plan either."

"I don't know what you're talking about," I say as I sweep a hand over my ass to brush off any plaster that might have stuck when I leaned on the building.

"I'll let you play it like that if you want, but only if you answer one more question for me."

"I don't have to answer any of your questions," I say with attitude that makes me feel more like myself.

I paste a smile on my face that the Cheshire cat would be proud of, and start marching down the sidewalk in the direction of my place. As I expected, Moses falls into step beside me.

"If she's your best friend, why didn't you tell her about me?"

His question scrapes off some of the veneer I've just regained. I walk faster, but his long legs easily keep pace no matter the speed.

"I want an answer, Magnolia. You ain't running away from me until I get one."

Finally, I stop in front of a shuttered building and face him, my hands on my hips. "Why do you care?"

Moses's eerie green eyes scan my face, and it's like he sees through the strong facade I'm trying desperately to keep intact. "Because I want to know if I'm right."

"Right about what?" My tone warns him to tread carefully.

"Whether or not you loved me."

I flinch as if I've been slapped.

Jerking my head to the left, I glance at him sideways after his whispered declaration. I take a step, intending to run away from this whole conversation, but I lose my footing on the solid ground beneath me. My world's been shaken and my entire body flies forward, but instead of landing sprawled on the sidewalk, I'm surprised when Moses catches me.

He lifts me off my feet and brings me flush against his body, chest to chest. As he lowers me to my feet, every fiber of my being begs me to relax against him.

To let him hold me.

Keep me safe.

Protect me.

God, it's so tempting. But I can't.

I shove out of his hold and put space between us. If it's the truth he wants, I'll give it to him. Straight, no chaser.

"It doesn't matter anymore what I felt for you *then*, Moses, because I don't trust you *now*. You can say whatever you want, be all smooth and slick, but if it's an act, I'm not gonna fall for it. I don't need a man to rescue me. I've done fine all by myself."

"I hurt you, mama."

He reaches out to take my hand, but I yank it back because if I let him touch me . . . *No.*

His eyes narrow at my movement, and it's the first time I've seen him annoyed since he's been back. *Good.* I want to see the real him. Not this sugarcoated version trying to wine and dine me into driving off into the sunset.

So I decide to give him another bitter sip of *my truth.*

"Yeah. You did hurt me. *Then.* But you're not going to hurt me now. I won't let you." If my words are bullets, then they find their mark, because his gaze darkens.

I lift my chin, determined not to let it make me pull my punches. He can't think I'm going to cave for him easily, no matter what I felt back then or how much it hurt when he left and never came back.

With newfound power, I continue. "I've learned a lot in the last fifteen years too. Lesson number one: Magnolia takes care of

Magnolia. I don't need anyone else. I appreciate your help with the cop this morning, but I've got it from here. You can go on ahead with your day."

His palms land on the sides of his forehead and his jaw rocks. "Just like that? You expect me to walk away just like that? Go on about my fucking day?"

"Shouldn't be too hard. It's what you've been doing since you left."

"You know what I've been doing since I left?"

Moses takes two steps toward me, and I step back instinctively. A wrought-iron gate clangs when my shoulder blades bump into it. He stands in front of me, his features carved from granite.

"I've been trying to find my way back to you without putting you in fucking danger. It took me a while. I did a lot of shit I'll never tell you about. But I'm finally free and clear, and so are you. That's why I'm here now, after all this fucking time. Because life doesn't always work out the way you hope, when you hope. But if you're lucky, sometimes you get a second fucking shot at the one thing you want more than anything else. This is me taking my shot, mama. And I don't fucking miss."

His eyes are dilated, and his breathing is labored as he speaks.

"Fight me all you want, but I see through the tough-broad exterior you're so used to wearing. I see *you*, Magnolia. That's who I came back for."

A myriad of emotions roll off Moses in waves, until I swear I can feel every single thing he's feeling. Frustration, heartache, devastation, determination . . .

The man's just as close to the edge right now as I am. He's ready to lay it all out on the line, and it fucking terrifies me.

I take a few moments to knit the edges of my pride and self-possession together, and then meet his burning green eyes.

"Well, I'm glad you know exactly why you're here. But you don't get to tell me how I should feel about it. You're gonna have to give me some goddamned space and time. I will not be manipulated. Not by you. Not by Mount. Not by anyone. You hear me?"

I hate the vulnerability that's crept into my voice, even as I battle to keep it steady. The fortress around my heart is crumbling, and I have to fucking retreat before he gets inside.

"Mama—"

The pain in his voice pulverizes another chunk of my protective wall. My traitorous eyes burn, threatening to cry. *No. No. No.* I'm not going to do this here. Not now. I refuse.

"Leave me alone, Moses. Just leave me the hell alone!"

I turn and run for home like the coward I am, because I'd rather avoid every bit of this than relive the devastation I felt the day I realized he was never coming back for me.

32
MOSES

Well, hell. That didn't go as planned. Not even a fucking little bit.

Magnolia disappears around the corner like the hounds of hell are on her heels. The strongest woman I've ever met, and she's fucking running *from me.*

I scrub my hand over my face and mouth, feeling the scratch of stubble there. Christ *Jesus.* I fucked this up so goddamned bad, I don't even know how we got here.

The spooked look on Magnolia's face was one I've witnessed before. I saw what the call with Keira did to her. It was as if the rug had been pulled out from beneath her feet. Her nature and former profession have made Magnolia an incredibly private woman. This morning, she was getting railroaded from all sides.

I thought, like a fucking asshole, I could use it to my advantage. To get through to her. To make her understand just how fucking serious I am about why I'm here.

Instead, I fucked it all up beyond recognition. I should have known better.

I lean against the building and drop my head back against the plaster. Pushing off a moment later with a sigh, I crack my neck to the left, then right.

Magnolia isn't like any other woman. She won't fall to pieces. But in this state she's fragile—like TNT. Handle with fucking care, or she'll detonate and blow your plans to smithereens.

Lesson learned. Time for a new plan anyway.

I pull out my phone and call Jules. He picks up on the second ring. "Yeah, boss?"

"Take the SUV and keep tabs on Magnolia. She's headed home now. Follow her wherever she goes and don't let her out of your sight. Keep her safe."

"Okay . . ." he says slowly. "Obviously, I'm happy to take care of this for you, but . . . wasn't the plan for you to hang with her all day?"

I kick at a stone on the broken concrete as I march forward. It's not too bad of a walk back to our place, but I've got plenty to think about on the way. "Plans changed."

"Is that a good thing?"

Jules keeps fishing for information, so I decide to just tell him what the fuck he wants to know.

"I fucked up. Miscalculated. I gotta give her some space."

There's a beat of silence, and I can practically hear what Jules isn't saying. *How the fuck did you, the man who always knows how to get people to do what you want, fuck up so badly with something this important?*

"Okay. I'll get the SUV and watch her. It'll work out, boss. There's more than one way to catch a rabbit. You just have to keep trying until you find one that works. Get yourself another way and try again."

Jules is right. Hell, Mags is right. I'm just not willing to lose her twice. Once was hell enough.

33
MAGNOLIA

I lock myself in the bathroom and drop onto the closed toilet seat while the water for the shower heats up. *Goddamn it*, if I'm going to cry, it's going to be where I can deny those tears ever fell.

Then after I'm done, I'm going to put myself back together one piece at a time—armor and war paint included—so I remember exactly who I am.

Magnolia Marie Maison.

No man owns me. No man controls me.

I do what the hell I want, when I want. Things work the way *I* want them to work.

And what if that's exactly what Moses wants? Ho-It-All pops into my head for another ill-timed thought.

"Shut the fuck up," I tell the empty room. "It doesn't matter what the man wants. He can't just show up and decide I belong to him. I belong to *me*."

And he wants to belong to you too.

"Ugh!" I let out a screech of frustration and strip before climbing into the shower, where hopefully the spray can drive out the stupid voice that has suddenly decided it's a fan of Moses Gaspard. Well, too fucking bad.

However, the voice has helped steer me away from enough trouble over the years that I don't want to discount it completely, but it also needs a reality check.

Moses is crazy. All the shit he said might sound pretty, but nothing can take away the fact that he waited fifteen damn years to come back and say any of it.

Fifteen. Years. He left me *alone.*

He doesn't get a pass because he's the most beautiful man I've ever seen, and what we had in those two weeks so long ago was close to a perfect fantasy. It doesn't matter.

I've got a life I've worked my ass off to build, and even if it doesn't always go according to plan, it's *mine.* I'm supposed to just magically trust him and whatever he has planned?

I don't think so.

Then how do you explain how you feel? Ho-It-All asks in a silky tone. *You really think you can resist him? It's not like you're going to the club to play with Rhodes.*

I freeze for a beat, water spraying me in the face as I push open the door of the shower and reach for my phone on the counter.

Screw Ho-It-All. She doesn't know everything. Because maybe I *am* going to play with Rhodes.

Leaving puddles everywhere, I blink the water out of my eyes and type out a quick message.

MAGNOLIA: *Are you still in town? I might want to play tonight.*

Dropping my phone on the counter, I seal myself back in the shower, hoping the spray drumming against my head will somehow provide answers, or at least a little fucking relief.

I can stay here and sit on my pitiful air mattress all night thinking about Moses, or I can go to the club and put him out of my mind for a few hours.

It's easy to lose myself with Rhodes. And there's a bonus to visiting the club tonight.

I tap my fingers along the side of my naked thigh as I consider it. A feline smile tugs at the corners of my mouth. If I go . . . there's no way in hell Moses won't find out. Maybe it'll drive him crazy for a while, and he'll know what it's like to wonder what I'm doing, the same as I've done for years thinking about him.

Don't do it, Mags. You know better than to play with fire . . .

But I don't listen to Ho-It-All. I'm too busy thinking about how brilliant I am. If I wanted one easy way to show Moses he doesn't control me, this is it.

And he'll never know what happened, because he can't get inside.

Ten hours later, Ho-It-All has me almost reconsidering my plan. *Now isn't the time to play games. Just shoot straight with Moses. Tell him how you feel.*

But I can't do that. I can't take the risk. Not with him. Not after all this time. Because if I let my guard down, and then if he leaves again after seeing the real me, I'll fall apart. So it's better to test him now. Trial by fire. Can he take it—take me and my life—or will he walk away?

From my bedroom, I stare down at the street as Rocco and his crew drive away from my place for the last time. I start to turn, eager to walk through my house now that it's completely finished, but I notice the SUV parked across the street didn't move. It's still exactly where it's been since I got out of the shower.

Fuck. A cop? A Fed?

I squint, trying to see if it looks like Cavender's face. But as soon as I get a look at the man in the driver's seat, I know it's not a cop or a Fed. It's Moses's man, Jules. The guy who drove us home last night in the Rolls.

My mind drifts to what happened after the restaurant, back to when I could have gotten myself off on Moses's lap. All those damn emotions I've managed to keep locked away all day bubble up to the surface again.

Fucking hell. I need to put him out of my mind or I'm going to flip the fuck out.

Why would he have someone watch me after I told him to leave me alone? To protect me?

My heart starts to tingle at the thought, but I fight it. *Don't let him sneak in there, Mags. You'll fall for him so damn fast. And remember what happened last time. He could be gone tomorrow. You don't know.*

No. No. No. I'm not *falling for him again.* I refuse to put my heart on the line like I did before.

If I was wavering about going to the club tonight, the decision has officially been made.

I reach for my dress and find lingerie to wear beneath it.

Fuck this nonsense. It's time for Moses to sweat.

34
MOSES

"She just got into a black car. She's wearing a dress. You want me to follow her, right?"

My hand aches from being so tightly balled up in a fist. "Of course I want you to fucking follow her. Wherever she goes, you go."

"Just making sure, boss. I'll let you know where we end up."

Jules ends the call, and Trey stares at me from across the room. "You didn't think this was going to be easy, did you?"

The man might be a wizard when you hand him a computer, but human behavior isn't usually his forte. It's mine. *Usually.*

"Your strengths are ones and zeros, but if you've got some relationship wisdom to impart, go right ahead."

Trey chuckles. "You know I'm shit with women, but even I could've told you that you can't leave someone with a promise you'll come back, and not expect her to be pissed when you don't make good on it for over a decade. I'm pretty sure that's not what she thought you meant."

"You know why I couldn't."

He pulls his glasses off and cleans the lenses with his shirttail.

"*I* know, but *she* doesn't. When are you going to tell her the truth? All of it. Not just the shit you want her to know."

Trey's question brings the conversation I had with Mount back to the forefront of my mind—and the promise he extracted from me. At this rate, I may not get the chance to keep my word, and the consequences of not making good on a deal with him aren't pretty. But, fuck. He's right. I need to tell Magnolia the truth—and not just because I gave my word that I would.

I force myself back to Trey's comment as I drop onto the couch and let my head fall back against the cushion. "When she's ready for the truth, I'll tell her. And since she'll barely have a conversation with me, I don't know when that's gonna be."

Trey starts to say something else, but when his computer dings, he forgets about the conversation immediately and his fingers fly across the keyboard. I know better than to ask him what he's doing, because he wouldn't stop and ignore me like this if it wasn't important. I wait a solid five minutes while his brows knit together and he types so fast, you'd think the keyboard would be smoking.

Finally, he looks up. "I knew I was right!" He pops out of his seat and pumps his fist in the air.

"About what?"

He taps on the table in front of him with his index finger. "That someone erased our wannabe killer, and I was fucking right!"

I push off the couch and stride over. "I thought we already established that. Why are you getting so excited about it now?" I'm not taking any chances with this shit. I need to know for sure that Magnolia is safe and no one else is coming after her. It's the least I can fucking do.

Trey spins his computer around on the long kitchen table. "Because I got a name." He points to the screen. "Almost everyone forgets about high school yearbooks saved on micro-film—and I just got a facial recognition match to the picture we took of the body to a member of the class of 2010 in Brownsville, Texas. It's him. Thankfully, whoever wiped him wasn't as good as I am." He grins. "And now we have ourselves a *name*, and that means I can keep digging and see what else they missed."

"Who was he?"

"Ricardo Ortiz."

"Keep digging. Find everything you can. And I mean fucking *everything*, Trey."

"On it, boss," he says, turning his computer back around and cracking his knuckles. "He should've paid the big bucks, because if we'd been the ones to erase him, there wouldn't be a damn thing to find."

I snatch up my phone when I see Jules's number flash across the display. *Finally.* I've been waiting for an update on Magnolia. I tap the screen to answer and lift it to my ear.

"What's going on?"

"Got a problem, boss."

I set down the pieces of the gun I've been cleaning to keep my mind off things I've got no control over. Waiting has never been my strong suit, and being so close to Magnolia and still having to keep my distance today is even worse than being two thousand miles away. But at least our entire arsenal is cleaned and oiled.

"What kind of problem?" I brace, waiting for him to tell me she busted him near her house and told him to fuck off.

"Remember that club Magnolia used to manage?"

Instantly, I recall the *sex club* she used to manage a couple of years back. "I don't like where this is going, Jules," I tell him as my jaw tenses and my palm wraps around a suppressor like I need help holding on to my sanity.

"Sorry, boss. But . . . she's in there, and I can't get past the gate.

Would've called sooner when I figured out where she was going, but I didn't have service."

I drop the suppressor on the rubber mat I laid out on the living room coffee table as static fills my ears.

"Are you fucking kidding me?" My roar fills the room, and Trey practically jumps out of his seat as a burst of anger shoots through me. "She's at the fucking *sex club right now?*"

"What do you want me to do?"

That woman . . . I could throttle her.

I force myself to wrestle the anger into submission before I speak. "Wait there. I'm on my way."

"Got it. I'll be up the road from the gate."

As soon as I hang up, I look at Trey, who has a big shit-eating grin on his face. "Don't say a motherfucking word."

Trey's laughter follows me as I storm out of the room. Lightning fast, I wash the grease and oil off my hands, put on some decent clothes, and head for the garage.

As I slide into the driver's seat of the Rolls, I dial the one number I swore I wouldn't need.

"I told you not to call me."

"I need a favor," I tell the king of New Orleans as I haul ass out of the driveway. I already know I won't be able to get inside the club without Mount pulling strings, and I'm *getting inside* that fucking club.

"And you think your best choice was to call me? I thought I was clear when you sat in my office. You're here for one reason, and one reason only. You're on borrowed time, Moses."

"Get me into the club. The one outside town. You know what I'm talking about."

The other end of the call is silent for moments. I have a feeling Mount would shoot me on the spot for giving him orders, but I don't give a fuck. I'm a man on a mission, and nothing is standing in my way.

"Did you tell her yet?"

As soon as he asks the question, my shoulders go back, and I grip the steering wheel of the Rolls tighter. "I'm working on it. I need in that club. Can you help me?"

Another long pause follows. "It's not whether I can help you. It's whether I want to. You haven't held up your end of the bargain yet. So, no. You're on your own, Moses."

The call ends, and the interior of the Rolls goes silent.

That motherfucker.

Fine. I'll handle this shit myself.

Seething with anger the whole drive, I pull up behind where Jules is parked on the left side of the road, about fifty yards from the gate. Jules is out of the SUV and at my window before I can throw the Rolls into park. I roll the window down as he leans closer.

"You got us a way in?"

I shake my head. "No. Mount told me to fuck off."

Jules's eyebrows shoot up to his hairline like he can't believe someone would talk to me that way. And most wouldn't dare. But Mount . . . he's a different story. This is his town, and as much as it grates, I'm only here because he allows it.

We made a deal, and he's right—I haven't held up my end yet. But I will. I glance at the gate up ahead that's keeping me away from what I want.

"So . . . we going home then?"

My gaze cuts to Jules. "Not a fucking chance."

He drums his fingers against the roof. "Not saying you haven't already thought of this, boss, but maybe you should just call her? See if she'll have them let you in?"

I glare at him. "You keep your phone on you when you're fucking in a sex club?" My expression could make a lesser man piss himself, but Jules has known me a hell of a long time. I slam my forearm on the wheel. "That woman. When I get my hands on her . . ."

"We got a car coming, boss." Jules steps away from the door, and I'm out of the Rolls in a second.

A car means an opportunity to get to Mags, and I'm not fucking wasting a goddamned second. I'm getting inside the fucking club if I have to rip the gate off its hinges with my bare hands and go in guns blazing.

The car, a sporty red Audi TT, slows when it approaches our two parked vehicles, and the window rolls down to reveal an attractive woman with blond hair falling straight to her shoulders.

"You boys lost?" By the time she finishes surveying me and Jules from head to toe, I've put a name to the face from the digging I did on Magnolia before we made it to New Orleans.

Desiree Harding. The madam who took over managing Magnolia's house when she stepped aside. The glint in her eye tells me she probably has a gun and isn't afraid to shoot us if we make a wrong move.

Don't worry, you won't have to shoot us, I think. *You're going to help us.*

"Not lost, ma'am, but we sure could use a little assistance." I gesture to the gate up ahead. "We seem to have lost our invitations."

She practically devours us with her eyes even as she shakes her head. "Private club. No invitation, no entry. No matter how big a shame it is that you won't get to play tonight."

I take a step toward her car, but only one. I don't want to spook her before I gain her cooperation. "We've got a mutual friend inside waiting for me."

Her expression changes, suspicion creasing the corners of her eyes. "Who is that, exactly? And how the fuck do you know it's a mutual friend? I don't know you, and trust me when I say I would remember if we'd ever met."

Giving her one of my most charming smiles, I say, "Magnolia Maison."

Desiree's eyes widen with surprise for a beat before she wipes her reaction away, leaving cool suspicion on her features. "We're done here. Best move on, because I'm gonna tell security you're here, and you don't want them to come out and make you leave."

Her window smoothly inches upward, and I've only got one last shot before tonight takes a bad turn, because I'm not leaving this place without Magnolia. Not a fucking chance.

"Give me five minutes to tell you a story. If you aren't convinced, you can tell me to fuck off. If you are, you get me inside to Mags."

For a moment, I think she's going to tell me to fuck off without hearing me out, but the window pauses.

"If I don't like the story, I'll fucking shoot you and save *Mags* the trouble. Because that's what you clearly are. I don't care how big or sexy a motherfucker you might be. Deal?"

The corners of my mouth tug upward. "Deal."

35
MAGNOLIA

I adjust my mask and try not to think about the SUV I'm pretty damn certain followed my driver all the way to the club gates. Which means Jules has probably told his boss exactly where I am by now.

The mercenary part of me is responsible for the blood-red smile curving my lips.

I hope he thinks I'm here to fuck anyone and everyone who isn't him. Even though I'm only really here to see one man.

It's cruel and it makes me a bitch, but I don't care. I'm grasping onto whatever I can to make myself feel in control. I won't let Moses take that from me too.

I'm almost twenty minutes late when I finally open the door to the private room.

I step inside, expecting a teasing greeting to come from Rhodes's deep, rough voice, but all I get is silence. My first thought is that *he* must be late too, but I realize my error as I take in the entire room and find him on the bed. He's fully clothed, laid out on his back, his arms overhead with his hands beneath thick locks of wild brown hair.

Asleep.

"Really, Rhodes?"

"You're late, and I haven't slept in three days," he replies with his eyes still closed, but the corners of his mouth turn up. "I gotta take opportunities when I find them."

I push the door shut behind me. "You didn't have to come."

At this, he peeks at me with one blue eye. "And miss playing with you? Never." He pushes himself off of the bed and comes toward me with the easy grace of a man comfortable in his own skin. "I'm going to make you work tonight, Mags. You'll wish you had a nap too."

"Pssh." I shake my head, glancing toward the chessboard set up on the table at the side of the room. Just the sight of it shakes my self-possession because it makes me think of *him*.

No. I'm putting Moses out of my head for tonight. I can worry about him in the morning.

I gather myself and cross to the table, grasping for normalcy with each step. "You win *once* and suddenly you think you can take me. Not a chance, rookie."

"Hope springs eternal," he says with a yawn. "Damn, I'm getting too old for this up-for-days-at-a-time shit."

"Whatever. You still love running around, catching all the bad guys, and collecting your big fat checks." Rhodes is a fugitive recovery agent, which is basically a high-class bounty hunter.

His lips quirk as he walks toward the two decanters on the sideboard that we always request. "Yeah, you're right. I'll do this shit until I'm dead. I fucking love it."

I trail a finger along the edge of the chessboard, stopping right next to the knight, and a lump rises in my throat. I have two chess pieces in my purse, but they don't belong to this set.

God, Moses is going to kill me when he figures out where I am.

Thankfully, Rhodes interrupts my runaway train of thought, one that's leading me nowhere good, by lifting the whiskey. "Your usual, I presume?"

I glance at the board one more time. "Make it a double."

"Rough day?" Rhodes's sharp-eyed gaze cuts to me.

Slowly, I inhale a breath. "You could say that. Lot of shit going on."

He pours both glasses and carries them to the table. "You want to talk about it?" he asks as he offers the lowball with the most liquor in it to me.

Under normal circumstances, I'd say *no way in hell*, but tonight . . . well, nothing's normal anymore.

"I don't know." I sip the whiskey.

He sets his glass beside the game board. "You can tell me about it as we play."

I give him a good, long, squinted side-eye. I'm on to him. "So you can distract me and try to win? Nah. I know your game."

"Really, Mags? We're friends, not fuck buddies. How many times have you come in here and listened to me unload all my shit on you?"

He's speaking the truth. Rhodes is . . . well, he's a friend. Probably the only male friend I have, other than Mount, who I don't really count because he's not exactly *friendly*. But Rhodes and I go back a ways, and he's never done anything but shoot straight with me. He's also never tried to fuck me. He gets big points for that.

I remember asking him the third night we played, *"You never make a move on me. You're not into women?"*

He looked me in the eye and told me, *"I can find a woman to fuck anywhere. But a worthy opponent at chess who I actually enjoy playing . . . I'm not gonna fuck that up. Not for anything in the world."*

That's when our friendship really started, and Rhodes hasn't given me a single reason not to trust him since.

"My shit's different," I say.

Part of me wants to tell him my life is spiraling out of control, and I don't know what the fuck is going on, but I'm terrified. That's not the kind of thing Magnolia Marie Maison admits to anyone. *Ever.*

Rhodes shakes his head. "You're still human, Mags. In case you forgot. Now, let's play."

"You're playing like shit," Rhodes says as he puts me in check *way* too soon after we start. "Not that I don't like to beat your ass, but —no offense—what the hell is wrong with you, Mags?"

I shake my head, like somehow it's going to help me regain my sanity. *Only Moses leaving will do that. Or . . . hell, that might just put me over the edge once and for all.*

"Nothing. Besides, if there was something wrong with me, you'd just try to fix it because you're a man. Some shit can't be fixed." I make my move, nullifying his position, and nod to him. "See? You're not going to beat me this time. Everything's fine."

Rhodes leans back in his chair, his arms crossed over his chest. "I never thought I'd see the day."

My eyes dart from the board to him and back. "What are you talking about?"

"You've got *man problems.*" He announces it as if it's a bona fide diagnosis.

I deny it like the liar I am. "What? No, I fucking don't."

Rhodes wags his index finger between us and tsk-tsks. "You're fucking lying to me right now. I see it. The legendary Magnolia Maison, *former* chess prodigy and madam extraordinaire, is tied up in knots over a man."

"Go fuck yourself, Rhodes. Or play the goddamned game. I'm not talking about it."

He waits in silence, and I refuse to meet his scrutinizing blue stare.

Instead, I reach for my glass and drain the rest of the whiskey. "Fine. Sit there and wait as long as you want. I'll get shit-faced and still beat your ass." I pop out of my chair and march to the sideboard.

"Let the good times roll." He laughs and shakes his head. "You go right on ahead and get shit-faced. It ain't going to change the fact that you've got someone willing to listen to whatever the fuck is bothering you, and that someone also happens to have a dick, so I just might be able to help you with your problem. Maybe offer some male perspective on the subject."

I splash a good four fingers of whiskey into the glass and take a swig before I even set the decanter down. Instead, I bring it back to the table with me and set it beside the board.

"You can't help. It's impossible."

"Everything's impossible until it's done. Or at least that's what the poster in my brother's AA meeting says."

I know exactly why he says that. It's a reminder he's shared some painful shit with me, and I helped him work through it. Because Rhodes and I are friends, even if we only see each other once a month, at most.

"Goddamn it, Rhodes. Why do you have to be so fucking stubborn?"

He lifts his gaze to mine. "Because I care. Now talk."

"Fine. Play and I'll tell you."

He nods and makes his move. It's a good one, but I'm still going to beat him. That is, if I don't lose it when I tell him about Moses.

"There was a guy, once upon a time. He was a gangster. Wanted to be a kingpin. I was young and stupid, and I fell hard." I slide my rook across the board.

"No shit." Rhodes sits up in his seat, worrying his bottom lip as he studies the game, and then makes his next move. "What happened?"

I go with the CliffsNotes version to spare myself. "He couldn't stay. I couldn't leave. He promised he'd come back. He didn't."

"When was this?"

I clear my thick throat. "Fifteen years ago."

Rhodes's eyes widen. "And you're just *now* getting pissed about it?"

My arms cross over my chest. "No. Damn motherfucking man just showed back up, and now he wants to make it right and fucking marry me or some shit. Like that's gonna happen—"

"Whoa. Hold up." Rhodes leans an elbow on the table and rubs his chin. "He came back after fifteen years with no word and now he wants to marry you?"

"Yeah. Fucking ridiculous. He even put a man on my house. Pretty sure he tailed me here." I shake my head, and the sheer fuckery of all of it rattles around inside. "What kind of man shows back up after fifteen years of *no word* and then just drops shit like this on a person?"

Rhodes is on his feet before I realize he's even moving. "His man tailed you here? Fuck, Magnolia."

"So what?" My hand slices dismissively through the air. "He can't get past the gate. It's not like I give a fuck if the guy sits there all night. I'm sure I'll fucking hear about it tomorrow, though. The man is impossible."

I might be buzzed, because my opinions are shifting around like a load in the back of a U-Haul. Actually, saying all this shit makes me wonder if I should believe Moses, but how the fuck do I believe someone who said they'd come back for me and *never did*?

"Goddamn it, woman." Rhodes stalks to the table where his bag sits and pulls out a gun.

"What the fuck is that for?" I push back my chair and bolt to my feet, luckily without swaying too much.

"You just told me some kingpin motherfucker came back to town to *marry you*, and now you're at a sex club with another man. If you really think a gate is going to keep him out . . . Fucking hell, Magnolia. You know men better than that. You think he's *not* gonna find a way in?"

There's a light knock on the door. Both Rhodes and I turn just in time to see it burst open, and Moses's big body fills the doorway.

Shit. I picked a bad day to be wrong.

36
MOSES

W hat was I expecting to find when I stepped around Desiree and shoved the door open? Fuck, I don't even want to think about it, but this sure as shit wasn't it.

It might have been easier to walk in on Magnolia fucking someone, because then I would have just killed him. But this . . . this is a complete goddamned shock. The kidney-punch kind where you piss blood for a week.

"I take it this is the guy?" The question comes from the man standing a few feet from Magnolia—*and the motherfucking chess game they were clearly playing together.*

The anger I felt before morphs into something totally different. Something I did *not* expect to feel tonight. But, goddamn it, seeing a chessboard set up between them is like a knife through my fucking ribs.

That was ours. And she gave it to someone else.

I force the feeling down and bring the anger back to the forefront, because that I can defuse and turn into ice-cold rage.

Stepping forward, I reach for Magnolia, but the dude moves

too, putting himself between us. That's when I spot the Glock in his hand.

"So it's like that," I say, staring him down.

He shrugs. "Depends on your next move, brother."

"Rhodes! What the hell are you doing?" Magnolia says *his fucking name* as she tries to come around him, but he throws an arm out to block her.

My hands ball into fists. Desiree made me promise I'd leave my heat in the car, so I don't have a gun. But I will beat him to death, no matter how many bullets he puts in me, if he won't get out of the fucking way and let her come to me.

"Making sure you're fucking safe," Rhodes says.

His gaze is sharp and flinty blue, and from the confident way he holds the gun, I'm guessing he'd have no problem pulling the trigger. We stare hard at each other, and I take a step forward.

He raises the gun a few inches, ready to point it directly at my chest, no doubt. "Not another move until you calm the fuck down, man. It's not what you think. She's just here playing chess. Not shit else. All we ever do is play chess."

His words are meant to defuse my temper, but they stoke it higher and hotter instead. *All they ever do is play chess?* Betrayal slashes through me, and I step toward him, silently daring him to make a move. He doesn't disappoint. The Glock comes up, out of instinct, I'm guessing from the way he moves. But I don't stop. I walk straight up to the barrel until the metal presses against my shirt.

"Goddamn it. Both of you need to back the fuck off," Magnolia says, but we ignore her.

I bare my teeth and speak with a clenched jaw. "I don't give a fuck why you're here. You're between me and my woman, and I've got no problem going through you to get to her." I level my unblinking stare on him. "So you'd best decide right the fuck now. You willing to die for her? Because I am."

I hear a sharp indrawn breath from behind him, but I don't

look at her face. Not yet. Because I've got a point to prove, and clearly, so does he.

"Not moving if you're gonna hurt her."

I squint and my jaw rocks. "I'd cut off my own fucking arm first."

He studies my face for a beat, and Magnolia steps around him.

"If he hurts me, I'll cut off his fucking balls." She crosses her arms over her chest and pops her hip to the side. "You've made your point, Moses. You got in. Now, what do you want?"

"We're leaving." I hold out a hand, keeping everything I'm feeling locked down.

"But I'm in the middle of a game."

Bull-fucking-shit you are. I take a step to the table, scan the board, and move a piece I assume is Magnolia's. Then I pivot to look at both of them.

"Check-fucking-mate, mama."

37
MAGNOLIA

Moses moves so fast.

Rhodes doesn't have a chance to react before I'm lifted into the air, landing over Moses's shoulder.

"Moses!" My screech fills the room, and Rhodes steps toward us, his gun at his side. "No. Rhodes, back off. Don't fucking shoot him. That's something only *I* get to do. Now, put me down!"

Rhodes stills, but Moses doesn't listen to a word I say. He turns for the door and stalks out of it.

From my upside-down vantage point, I see Desiree with her jaw practically on the floor, and Moses's man, Jules, with a big smile on his face.

Assholes. Because the only way Moses could have gotten into the club was if someone let him in. I just never expected one of my own people would betray me like that. Then again, I'm well aware of how persuasive that Creole Casanova can be. It's those fucking eyes and his silver tongue.

And his voice.

And his scent.

And his smile too, if I'm being honest.

Okay, Desiree didn't have a chance.

Moses stomps out of the club with me bouncing on his shoulder as we pass curious onlookers. Not one person does a single thing to stop him.

I want to scream and rage and cuss them all out, but that would be beneath me.

Instead, I wait until we're outside, and then I let it rip.

"What in the fuck do you think you're doing? You don't own me. You don't get to just come back after fifteen years and storm into my life and carry me out of somewhere *I want to be*. Do you hear me, Moses? This is not gonna fucking fly. I'm in charge of my own goddamned life, and I won't be—" He yanks open the back door, and my words cut off when he flips me around to dump me inside. "Didn't you listen to a single thing I just said?"

His greenish-gold eyes burn so intensely, they practically sear me as he slams the door.

My mouth drops open. *Again.* "Oh no. No, you did not just fucking do that."

I wait for him to open the other door and slide inside the back with me so I can keep tearing strips off his hide and tell him exactly how he *does not* get to treat me, when the engine growls to life and we start moving.

"What the fuck?" The divider is up between the front and back seats, and I can't see Moses, but I have to assume he's driving. "Hey! I know you're up there."

When he doesn't roll the divider down, I slap at the thing.

A moment later, it moves down several inches, until I can see his face in the rearview mirror.

"Give me five fucking minutes to calm down before I lose my goddamned mind over what I just walked in on." Moses's deep voice is so low, it's barely audible. It's more of a growl.

"What the fuck are you pissed about? It's not like I was doing anything wrong."

He brakes hard as we approach the rising gate he shouldn't have been able to get past to get into the club in the first place, and I put up a hand to brace myself. Then he turns around and stares me dead in the eye.

"If you think you weren't doing anything I'd be pissed about, maybe I don't know you like I thought I did. And you sure as fuck don't know me."

The divider slides back up, leaving me alone in the back of a Rolls Royce, wondering what in the fuck just happened.

38
MOSES

"**W**hat the fuck are you pissed about? It's not like I was doing anything wrong."

Magnolia's words repeat in my head as I drive back to the city.

Not doing anything wrong? Maybe not to anyone else's way of thinking, but *Jesus Christ.*

Chess was ours.

I still remember the exact moment I knew she was unlike any other woman I'd ever met.

Fifteen years ago

"You wanna play again? Really? Don't you know I'm just gonna keep beating you?" Magnolia flashed me a megawatt smile as she settled onto the chair opposite from me and crossed her legs.

God, this woman was something else. The face of a siren, the body of a goddess, and the chess skills of a master. She was the whole damn package.

She didn't care who I was or what I did. She was just grateful not to be alone, trying to protect her house from looters who might decide they wanted something more. Like the last ones . . .

I thought of the men I killed. Their bodies were long gone, so at least I didn't have to worry about anyone pinning that shit on me. The only thing I wished was that I could have made them suffer longer.

Maybe it was hypocritical, but I didn't care. What they planned to do to her . . . no real man ever did that shit to a woman. I thought of the orders I'd given right before I left Biloxi, and regret, something I'd never much felt before, trickled through me.

It didn't make sense, but this woman . . . she was changing me. I didn't know how, especially this fast, but I guessed that was how shit worked sometimes.

I smiled at her across the table. "I'll keep playing you until I win."

She laughed, and it wasn't one of those nervous giggles I was used to hearing from women. It was loud and throaty as Magnolia threw her head back.

Goddamn. That's a beautiful sight.

"Then you'll be playing me for a long damn time, Moby. Because I'm that good." She winked as she used the nickname she'd given me.

In that moment, I wanted to see her laugh for a hell of a lot longer than I'd be staying in New Orleans. I had a ticking time bomb on my hands, and I wouldn't be able to stick around much longer. Hell, I shouldn't have stuck around this long. But as I took my seat across from Magnolia, I was certain I'd stay as long as I fucking could.

God, I should just take her with me.

The thought came out of nowhere, but I couldn't say it was altogether crazy. Hell, it was the only good option, because I sure as shit didn't want to walk away from New Orleans and leave her here.

"You're one of a kind, mama. Never met a woman like you before."

Her laughter died away as her whiskey-colored eyes met mine. "I find that hard to believe. Besides, you're already getting laid. No need to flatter me for it."

She couldn't see what I saw in her, and that was a goddamned tragedy.

"It ain't flattery when it's the truth," I told her. "Now, let's play. You gotta admit I'm getting better. A few more days, and I'm gonna give you a run for your money."

Her hand froze as she reached for the chess piece. "You're staying a few more days?" she asked quietly.

I nodded slowly. "Damn right, unless you want me out of here."

That brilliant smile of hers came back, and it was even brighter than before. The world was going to hell outside her doors, but inside that rickety old house, it was paradise. "I'll let you stay. You're good entertainment." She winked again, and my dick went rock hard.

I rose from the chair. "Game can wait. I've got something else to keep you entertained right now." One step brought me next to her, and I scooped her out of her chair and bounced her against my chest. "Unless you've got a problem with that."

She was laughing as she kissed me, and it was the best fucking kiss of my life. It was the first time I realized Magnolia tasted exactly like happiness. Like forever.

"Does it feel like I have a problem with that? I already know how the game's gonna go. This way, at least you might surprise me."

This woman. *One of a kind.* "You're asking for it now." I carried her to her bed and held her a few feet above it.

"You'd best believe I'm asking for it," she said with a cocky, playful grin.

So I dropped her.

Her laughter came even harder when she bounced twice, and then I was on her.

"Laughing at my chess skills. Laughing at me as I take you to bed. You just can't stop laughing," I said as I pulled her against me and rolled so I was beneath her. The stitches in my shoulder smarted at the movement, but I hid it. At least, I thought I did.

She sat up on top of me, her face flashing to serious in an instant. "I saw that. You've gotta take it easy. Leave the manhandling for later."

I reached out to grip her around the waist. "I'll manhandle you every chance I get, stitches or not."

"Stubborn fucking man." She shook her head, and her thick, dark hair swayed between us. "You're lucky I like you."

"Is that right?" I asked, feeling my lips lift at her admission. My hands skimmed down to the curves of her peach-shaped ass.

"That you're lucky? Fuck yes, because I'm about to do all the work." She pressed her palm against the center of my chest, and I settled back onto the mattress.

I was talking about the part about her liking me, but I decided not to press her too hard on it yet. There'd be more time for that later. More time to see if she'd leave with me. Walk away from this life and figure out a new one together.

Who the fuck am I right now? Thinking like this?

It didn't matter how fucking crazy it sounded—it was the only answer that worked for me. You didn't find a woman like Magnolia without thinking shit like that.

Later.

Because the second her hand closed around my dick, the only thing I cared about was how many times I'd be able to get her off before I lost my mind inside that tight cunt of hers.

She squeezed hard and jacked me until she saw pre-cum bead at the tip.

"Maybe I should just suck your dick until you shoot your load all over my tits," she murmured, those whiskey eyes turning greedy as they locked on my dick. "Because, goddamn, do you have a perfect cock. You and your Moby Dick."

"And you've got the perfect tits." I reached for her shirt and pulled it up to get it off her, but she slapped my hands away.

"Mind your stitches," she said as she released my dick to strip her shirt off herself.

"Okay, mama."

That got a smile out of her, right before her mouth covered the head of my cock, and I forgot everything except how fucking glad I was that I'd taken the call that brought me to New Orleans . . . no matter the consequences.

Present day

I drag myself out of the memory, hating the choices I had to make, because they took me away from Magnolia. If it wasn't for the path I took, I could have been the guy she played chess with all these years. We could have had a *life* together.

But we didn't get that.

Because of me.

39
MAGNOLIA

I f that man thinks that he can just put me in the back of a car and shut me in here until he's ready to deal with me, he's dead wrong. And if he thinks a woman scorned has fury, he's not seen me mad yet.

I am *not* the kind of woman who does what she's told, or is seen and not heard.

Fuck that.

With every mile we drive, I get more and more pissed off. I mentally rehearse exactly what I'll say to him the second he opens that damn door.

If you came back to win me back, you're doing it the wrong fucking way. Because I'm not the kind of woman who will let you steamroll me. I don't care if you drive a Rolls Royce, you don't just put a person in the back and ignore them the whole way home. You could at least talk to me about why you're so damn pissed off.

Finally, I realize we're *not* going back to my house like I thought we were. We're in the Marigny when we slow and turn into a driveway. There's a pause before we move forward again.

The hell?

I'm determined to get some goddamned answers, do some yelling, and then march my ass home if I have to.

When the engine shuts off, I reach for the door handle and yank on it. But it won't open. With a growl, I start pushing buttons, but none of them unlock the door from the inside.

What the hell? He did not *lock me inside here. No fucking way.*

I hear the driver's door open and shut, and I expect Moses to let me out immediately.

Boy, am I ready.

But he doesn't come open my door.

What in the actual fuck?

I crane my neck to see outside the window, but it's pitch black, and I can't make out anything.

"You'd best not fucking leave me in here! Let me out!" I yell, and my words echo in the tightly sealed cabin of the Rolls. Suddenly, the door pops open, and I open my mouth to unleash hell on Moses—but it's not his face I see.

It's Jules.

"Right this way, Ms. Maison. I'll show you inside." He doesn't even wait before starting for the door.

"Where the hell is Moses?"

"He had other business to attend to. He's unavailable at the moment. But I have your purse."

My mouth drops open as I take it from him. "What? He was just here. Driving the car. He—" I cut off my words, because clearly Moses *left me.* "Never mind. I'll walk my ass home."

Jules turns and faces me again. "You're staying here tonight, Ms. Maison."

"Give me one good reason," I tell him as my hands go to my hips. "You've got ten seconds."

"Do you want to live to see tomorrow?" he asks, and the grave question takes me by surprise.

I fall back on my heels and stop in my tracks. "What?"

His hands rise as he explains. "You're safe here. At home, you may not be. Plus, I hear you don't have any furniture, and the beds here are damn comfy."

It's on the tip of my tongue to tell him to fuck off, but . . . that whole *do you want to live to see tomorrow* question has my sense of self-preservation kicking in.

"Fine. But only because I don't have a bed yet." Silently, I add, *And because I really fucking like the idea of being safe.* It's not something I've had enough of in my life to take for granted.

He tilts his head and raises his brows. "And because you want to ream Moses?"

I glare at him. "That's not part of the reason."

With a shrug, he replies, "Whatever you say. Follow me."

He takes me through a courtyard with a pool, and then a sliding glass door that leads into a wide-open living space. There's a long table in the middle, and a young-looking guy with short brown hair and glasses sits in front of it, typing away.

He gives me a chin lift as I follow Jules. "Hi, Magnolia, heard a lot about you. Go easy on the boss. By the way, I'm Trey. Nice to meet you."

My reputation precedes me, even here. "Hi."

"You want something to eat?" Jules asks, pointing to the fridge. "We have food, or we can order in for you. Just say the word, and we'll make it happen."

I shake my head. "No. I'm good. Just . . . show me to the dungeon, I guess."

Trey chokes out a laugh. "Damn. Shit really must've gone wrong tonight. Between that comment and how Moses stomped through here and disappeared . . ."

Jules shoots his friend a look that shuts him up.

"I don't care what Moses is doing," I tell both of them. "He can go fuck himself for all I care." I turn to Jules. "You mentioned there's a bed?"

"Through here." He takes me down a hall and shows me to a bedroom. I shut the door in his face as soon as I'm inside, but I don't do it out of spite. I do it because I realize where I'm sleeping as soon as he opened the door.

Moses's room.

How did I know? There's a chessboard set up on a small table near the window. I cross the room to look at it and immediately notice the missing pieces.

Pawn and knight.

I set my purse on the table and dig them out. I've been carrying them with me, feeling sentimental as hell every time I touch them.

Who has time for sentiment, anyway?

I place them in their respective spots and turn away from the board. But Ho-It-All rears her ugly head.

How would you feel if you walked into this room and saw Moses playing chess with another woman? Would you be okay with it? Or would you want to rip her goddamned eyes out of her head for knowing how sexy he looks across a chessboard? You know, admiring the way he rocks his jaw back and forth when he considers his next move. How he reaches up and grips the back of his neck when he's watching you win— trying to hold back a grin all the while? Yeah, I guess you wouldn't have a problem with that. No big deal. Right?

That fucking bitch of a conscience. She just had to go there.

I turn back around and drop into one of the chairs.

Fuck.

I wait for hours, but Moses doesn't show. Finally, I curl up on the bed and pass out. He can see a miracle occur in broad daylight then—me apologizing.

40
MOSES

I don't go back to the house until I've exhausted myself with a punishing workout and spent a couple of hours walking the French Quarter, just for good measure, to calm my temper.

Magnolia fires me up the way no one else can, that's for damn sure. When I get inside, Trey is still working at the table, but Jules is nowhere to be found.

Trey's head swivels when he hears the sliding door. "I wondered if you were ever coming back."

"I'm back. What of it?" Guess my mood still isn't all that great.

"Nothing. Didn't hear any breaking glass or anything after Jules put her in your room. I figure that's a good sign, considering how pissed off she was when he brought her inside."

Of course Jules would put her in my room. I don't know whether to shake his hand or ask him if he's fucking crazy when I find him.

"She eat?"

Trey shakes his head. "Not hungry, or so she said. I think she was feeding on the fires of her rage, if you want to know the truth."

His sense of humor usually makes me laugh, but tonight, I'm not in the mood.

"Thanks, man. I'm crashing."

His eyes widen. "In your room with the fire-breathing beauty?"

I think about it for a second. "Yeah, that's exactly where I'm heading."

"God bless and Godspeed, my man. I hope I see you alive in the morning."

"If I'm dead, Jules gets the Rolls," I tell him as I cross the kitchen to head for the bedroom.

"That's not fucking fair," Trey says as I disappear around the corner to the hallway.

I take a long shower in another bathroom before I finally head to bed with a towel wrapped around my waist. I listen outside the door for a few moments, and when I don't hear anything inside, I open it. Part of me expects her to be breathing fire and smoldering from the ears, just like Trey said, but that's not what I find at all.

No, inside there's a gorgeous raven-haired beauty with golden skin curled up on top of the covers, her chest rising and falling rhythmically.

She's asleep.

I'm not sure if I'm disappointed or relieved.

Silently, I cross the room and slide under the sheets, careful not to disturb Magnolia. But I'm clearly not as silent as I think I am, because her sleep-roughened voice comes out of the darkness.

"I only played chess with him because it reminded me of you, Moby. It's the only time I ever let myself remember us."

I couldn't have known how good it would feel to hear her say those words, because I never thought she would.

A lump rises in my throat. "Sleep, mama. We'll talk about it in the morning."

She reaches out, finds my fingers, and I squeeze hers back. It doesn't take but another minute before she's breathing deep and even again.

I lie awake for as long as I can, savoring the moment. Until eventually, I succumb to a deep sleep, where my dreams are filled with laughter and sunshine, and dark-haired babies calling me Daddy and asking for their mama.

It's a good sleep. A real fucking good sleep.

41

Somewhere else in New Orleans

"Please, just let me go. I gave you the money. I've got jewelry too. You can have it. *All of it.* Just take whatever you want and go. Please, just leave me alone."

She hasn't stopped crying since I put her in her own trunk, drove back to her house, and tied her up to an ugly chair in the living room. I smile to myself because the blood that's going to stain it won't make it any uglier. It might even be an improvement.

I sit down on the coffee table in front of her and watch her cringe as I knock off a vase. It shatters on the floor and her gaze follows it. If she wasn't tied up, she would have jumped out of her seat to save it.

She doesn't realize her problems are just starting. *Perra estúpida.*

"You are going to tell me what I want to know."

Wide-eyed, she jerks her head around to look at me. "What do you want to know?"

I pull out the only picture of Ricky I have and hold it in front of her face. "You know him?"

She squirms against the duct tape trapping her in the chair. "Why?"

I pull a knife from my boot and test the sharpness on my thumb. Blood wells as the blade slices into it. I smear a red streak across her cheek. "I am the one asking the questions here. Another one out of you, and this will be your blood. Understand?"

Tears stream down her face as she trembles, nodding her head so fast her teeth clack together.

I hold the photo up again. "You know him?"

"I don't know him. I just saw him once. At a bar. When you called, I thought you were him."

I nod slowly. "Good. Who did you pay him to kill?"

She goes sheet white. "How—" Correcting herself, she shuts her mouth and takes a deep breath. "Three people."

"Who?"

She snuffles and nods. "My husband. His whore. And the madam."

I shake my head at her. I was right. *Estúpida perra.*

"Names."

"Alberto Brandon. That's my husband. His phone said the whore's name was Naya."

"And the madam?"

"Magnolia Maison. She owns the house they fuck in. I looked her up on the property tax records." There's snot rolling out of her sniveling nose. So pathetic.

"And did this man," I tap the picture, "call you to tell you that he had completed any of the kills?"

She shakes her head. "No. I told you, I thought . . . I thought he might be dead because the police found a body—a man—in the madam's condo building. I thought . . . maybe it was him. I thought maybe that bitch killed him."

Ice-cold rage fills my veins, but I don't let it show. I learned long ago how to mask my feelings. That's what working with the cartel teaches you. Never let them see your emotions on your face.

I smile at her instead, hoping her blood runs just as cold as my rage. "Where is your husband?"

She shakes her head. "I don't know. I haven't seen him in over a week."

"Good."

She looks hopeful all of a sudden. *Puta perra.*

"Are you . . . are you going to cut me loose now?"

"I told you not to ask questions."

My blade flashes, and she gurgles as I slit her throat. She's dead in less than a minute. I wipe the blade on the chair and slide it back into my boot.

Now I'm going to go find the woman who killed my brother. And she will not die so quickly. No, I will make that last a long, long time.

42
MAGNOLIA

I wake up alone, but I know Moses slept next to me. I remember the heat from his body last night. The pillow still shows the indent from his head.

I can't believe I slept in the same bed with him for the first time in fifteen years, and we just . . . slept. That's not happening again, I decide.

Despite my anger last night, the words he spoke to Rhodes in that room at the club come rushing back into my head.

"You willing to die for her? Because I am."

I was too pissed to really think about them until now. And one thing I know for certain—a man doesn't say that about a woman he doesn't care about. He doesn't say it if he's not all in.

But why did he wait so damn long to come back? As soon as I ask the silent question, Ho-It-All is ready with an answer.

Have you given him a chance to tell you? No, you've been throwing everything back in his face and shutting him down. Maybe try talking to the man. Like, an actual fucking conversation.

I'm tempted to flip my inner voice the bird, but she's right.

Even though the old us only existed for a flicker of time—two weeks—it was the most real thing I've ever had in my life. Even my relationship with Rafe didn't feel as real as those two weeks I spent with Moses.

Maybe it's because all Moses and I had to rely on during that crazy time was each other. Two perfect strangers, riding out the aftermath of an insane storm, bonding over a shared experience. I don't care what anyone says. Until they've experienced what we went through, they can't say dick about what we had together.

And, God, I remember how we *talked*. Over the chessboard, especially. It was easy then, even if most of what I said was naive as hell when I think back on it now.

I distinctly remember telling him about the empire I was going to build. How it was the most important thing in the world. I'd just inherited the house from the old madam who got me off the streets and took me under her wing, and I wasn't walking away and letting that go. Not when I just got my hands on it. Not for anyone.

That was the other naive part. Thinking a house meant more than spending my life with someone who I *knew*, even after that short span of time, was unlike anyone else I'd ever met in my life. We were drawn together like magnets. It's the only explanation I have.

What would it have been like to wake up next to Moses every day for the last fifteen years? How different would life have been if I'd gone with him?

I stop myself there.

Doesn't matter now. It's all coulda, woulda, shoulda, and those thoughts are a waste of time and energy.

What I have is *right now*, and I'm getting my ass out of bed to take advantage of it.

With a final glance at Moses's pillow, I roll off the comfortable mattress, take care of business in the bathroom, not even pausing to look in the mirror, and automatically grab my phone from where I left it on the nightstand before I go in search of him.

My first stop is the kitchen because that's where the long hallway leads, but instead of finding Moses there, I find Jules.

I'm proud of myself for not losing my temper last night any more than I did, because facing him this morning would make me feel like an asshole. It's a good reminder not to be a dick to people I'm going to have to see more than once. Which could literally be anyone.

"Morning, Ms. Maison," Jules says from where he stands near the center island of the open-concept kitchen and living room area.

"Magnolia's fine. Ms. Maison makes me sound like I'm fancier than I really am."

He pauses chopping whatever he's got on the cutting board and takes me in. "You look pretty fancy to me. Everything he's said about you over the years is starting to make sense."

Instantly, I want to ask what Moses could have possibly said about me over the years, but I don't. I'm stunned by the fact he talked about me at all, truthfully.

Sensing my shock, Jules smiles, and there's a kindness to it that's undeniable. "Moses is out in the courtyard. You want coffee?"

Coffee. My entire body practically moans at the thought. "I would love some."

He puts his knife down and wipes his hands as he gives me that easy smile. "I'll bring some out to you. How do you take it?"

"Black." My standard retort, *like my heart,* is on the tip of my tongue, but I don't say it. Even in lightheartedness, the words seem wrong now somehow.

Maybe because my heart isn't what I thought it was. It's changing. Coming to life again. Beating with anticipation about the thought of walking out the big glass doors to find the man who slept next to me, even after he was so mad he didn't want to face me.

I swallow, not knowing how this will go. But to Jules, I offer a quiet, "Thank you. I appreciate that."

"My pleasure, Magnolia. And, by the way, it's really good to finally meet you."

His statement makes me smile. I'm not used to men just being friendly and polite without wanting something in return. It's refreshing.

My entire body vibrates as I walk through the doors and out into the morning sunshine. The golden rays reflect off the crystal blue waters of the pool, but my attention goes directly to the man sitting at the table with his back to me.

As I step onto the paver path through the grass, I see the newspaper in front of him and watch as he lifts a steaming cup of coffee to his lips.

He's wearing black basketball shorts and a ribbed tank top. And, *good Lord*, does he look good. He was a beautiful man before, and time has done nothing but hone his perfection.

I haven't given myself much of a chance to compare this new version of Moses to the old, but in the bright light of day, I can't help but do exactly that. His muscles are bigger, and he's definitely more built than before.

There's a maturity to him he didn't have back then. The Moses of old wouldn't have walked away from me last night to let his temper cool rather than going at it and saying things we didn't mean. He's still not willing to take shit from anyone, though, if how he handled Rhodes was any indication. Comfortable in his own skin and sexy as hell, that's Moses.

For a single moment, I let myself imagine what it would be like if this was our life. Like, our *real life*. Moses up early while I sleep in. I come outside to him drinking coffee and reading the paper. I imagine coming up behind him and leaning over to press a kiss against one of those big, beautiful shoulders and saying, *"Morning, Moby. Thanks for the extra shut-eye. I needed it after last night."* Because, of course, in our fantasy life, he'd work me over good every night, making sure I get what I need—and not just because he loves it when I scream his name when I come. But also because I do the same for him.

God, with that vision in my head, I wish it were true.

I wish I felt well-used this morning. I wish with every step I took, I could feel him between my legs. *I miss him.* All of him.

"You okay?"

Moses's deep voice pulls me from my daydream, where I'm standing ten feet away, creeping like a pro. He turns his head, and I catch his sharply handsome profile.

I still my shaky, sweaty hands by running them down my sides. "Yeah . . . uh, sorry. I was just thinking."

"Thinking about joining me?" He motions to the chair across from him. "Because you're more than welcome."

"Thank you," I say, pulling my shit together and crossing the remaining distance between me and the chair, but I pause with my hand on the back of it first. "I'm sorry about last night."

Before I can say more, Moses shakes his head. "You don't have shit to be sorry for. You didn't ask for this. You didn't ask me to come back after fifteen years and barge into your life. I should apologize, but I can't be sorry for it either." He leans back and gazes up at me. "Hell, Mags. We're both stubborn and hotheaded. We're bound to fight."

He's giving me an out, but deep down, I'm sure I can't take it. I need to say what's on my mind.

"Still, I need you to know I took a walk in your shoes, when you didn't come to bed last night. I get it. Chess is special. It's been special since the first game we played. I'd be pissed as hell if I walked in on what you did. I get it." I trace the iron edge of the table. "I've always done what I had to do to survive. And sometimes, playing chess was the only thing getting me through. It made me feel good because it made me feel closer to you."

It should be easy, but I have to fight to look directly at Moses. His green eyes linger on my face, and there's no anger or sharpness in them. There's something else, something that fills me with warmth, even more than the heat of the sun on my skin.

"Ah, mama. I get that. More than you probably imagine. We all do what we gotta do to survive, including me. I've been doing the same thing. Missing you like crazy." He nods at the seat I'm standing beside. "Sit. Join me."

I lower myself into the chair, and his confession knocks loose more words I never expected I'd have the chance to say.

"I've missed the hell out of you too, Moby. It didn't even seem real sometimes, you know? Two weeks is nothing in the grand scheme of things, but you left a mark on me I couldn't erase, no matter how hard I tried sometimes."

He reaches out to cover my hands with his. "I know. I didn't want to wait fifteen years to come back to you either. Trust me, that was never the plan. But . . . sometimes, shit doesn't work out the way we expect."

The air is sweeter this morning, and somehow it's easier to breathe. Easier to let things go too. "Coulda, woulda, shouldas will haunt us if we let them. I'm not down with that." I meet those expressive eyes of his again and ask him point-blank what's on my mind. "So, what the hell do we do now?"

He squeezes my fingers. "You tell me, Mags. What do *you* want?"

"That's the million-dollar question, isn't it?" I ask, taking another deep breath to think about how I want to answer it. I don't want to rush or make a mistake. I want to treat this like it's special and fragile, because it's new and means everything to me.

Before I can speak, my phone buzzes on my lap, and I jump.

"What?"

I lift it with my free hand and show it to him. "My condo building manager. Sorry, wasn't expecting any calls. It can wait."

He shakes his head. "Answer it. Could be important. You never know."

Even though I don't want to, I tap the screen and accept the call. "Hello?"

"Magnolia?"

"Yeah, Carl. What do you need?" The condo isn't home anymore, but it was a good steppingstone for me, and Carl was always helpful when I could get ahold of him.

"I hate to interrupt your morning with bad news, but . . ."

I sit up straighter in my chair, and Moses leans in to listen. I lower the cell and tap the button to put it on speakerphone so we can both hear whatever bad news Carl is about to deliver.

Moses reaches out, snags my free hand, and squeezes.

"But what?" I ask, giving the guy across from me a squeeze back.

"Someone broke into your condo last night. Neighbor across the hall noticed the door open when she was leaving for work. She went to close it and saw some fucked-up shit, so she called me."

I can picture the older woman, mid-fifties, who lived across the hall, but she never made eye contact with me or said hello.

"What kind of fucked-up shit?" Maybe a sex toy fell out of a box when the movers were there. Hell, they could have left the door open too. Shit happens.

"Well, first, it's basically empty—so I hope you already knew that."

Jules places a cup of coffee on the table for me, and Moses quietly thanks him before he goes back inside.

"Yeah, I'm moving. I told you that. The sale is closing soon."

"Okay, good." Carl sounds a bit more relieved. "Well, you should be able to get it all cleaned up before that."

"Cleaned up?" My tone jumps an octave, and Moses grips my hand tighter.

"There is . . . something written on the wall. At first, I thought it was spray paint when I went up there . . . but I don't think it's spray paint." He hesitates for a minute and then hacks, almost like he's gagging. "Excuse me. I . . . I think it's blood."

A chill tears through me, but somehow I manage to say, "I'll be right there."

"That'd be good. Cops should be here any minute. I called them when I saw it."

"Thanks, Carl." The hits just keep coming, and more than ever, I'm tired of always having to *survive* every day. Will there ever be a time when things are easy, and I don't have to be on guard every second of every day?

"Sorry, Magnolia. I wish this was a better call."

"Not your fault," I say and hang up.

As soon as the call ends, Moses is on his feet, pulling me out of my chair and against him. He wraps me in those strong arms and holds me as I shake.

"It's gonna be okay, mama. We'll handle whatever comes together. You're not alone in this. Not for a single fucking bit of it."

Hearing those words washes away the dread building inside me with a flood of relief. The twisting in the pit of my stomach calms enough that I don't feel like I'm going to vomit on the table at the visual my head keeps creating. That's when the answer to the question Moses asked before we were interrupted by the phone call hits me. I pull back a few inches so I can see his face.

"*That.* That's what I want, Moby. I want a partner. I want someone to stand by me while we weather the storms. Because my life seems to be filled with fucking storms."

He lowers his chin to press a kiss to my forehead. "That's exactly what you got, mama. Whatever comes, we'll take it together. Now, let's go handle this shit. It could be hours before the cops come. If there's anything left you want from your place, we're getting it now."

Tension drains from my body at his statement. I'm not alone. I don't have to figure this all out by myself. I *could*, if I needed to. But, *damn*, it's nice to know that I don't have to.

"Thank you."

"No thanks necessary. Let's get going."

43
MOSES

W hen we get to Magnolia's old building, the cops are already there. I don't take it as a good sign. With Cavender sniffing around yesterday, I would put money on the fact that he's on alert for anything that relates to Magnolia, because he's trying to pin the dead body on her.

When we step off the elevator onto her floor, I spot him walking out of her condo.

He locks onto me and Magnolia immediately, and the expression on his face clues me in to the fact that the man is *pissed*.

Magnolia stiffens when she sees him, and I pull her tighter against my side and squeeze. She's a badass, but even the toughest people need to lean on somebody every now and again. I'm happy to be that someone for her. If she wants a partner, she's got the right man, because there's no way in hell I'd let her face this ever-growing mountain of shit alone. Never.

What happens to her happens to me. That's how it's going to be, from today until the last breaths leave our bodies.

The cop coming our way wastes no time. "Mr. Gaspard. Ms. Maison."

"Detective Cavender." I give him a nod as I say his name, but he just stands there, staring at both of us for almost a minute. "You got something to say to us, or can we go see what the fuck happened to my woman's condo?"

"It's a crime scene," he says. "Techs are on their way. You're not allowed inside until they've finished their job."

He's being rude and it pisses me off, considering we're talking about Magnolia's former home being violated.

"It's my damn condo. I want to see what the hell happened to it," Magnolia says, ready to pick a fight with the cop.

Instead of letting us inside, the detective pulls out his phone and taps the screen a few times before holding it up in front of us. "You know who would do this to your condo?"

A tremor rips through Magnolia's entire body, and I have to lock down the fury bursting into my system at the sight of the picture.

On the wall, written in smears of red, it reads:

I'M COMING FOR YOU NEXT

Jesus fucking Christ.

I hold Magnolia closer, rubbing up and down her arm because goose bumps just rose beneath my hand.

"Oh my God," she whispers with another tremor racking her body. "Carl said it didn't look like spray paint." She looks up at me, and we lock eyes. "That doesn't look like spray paint to me either."

"It's not, Ms. Maison. It's blood."

"Hey, man." I pitch my voice low as I take a step toward Cavender. "You wanna take some goddamned care with your words when you're delivering news like that? Because I got no fucking problem going to your superior to tell him what a fucking dick you're being with a victim of a fucked-up crime."

Something flashes across the cop's face, and it looks a hell of a lot like embarrassment. He steps back, puts his hands on his hips and shifts on his feet, staring at the floor. "Sorry. I could've delivered that better."

Magnolia straightens her shoulders under my arm. "Thank you. I accept your apology. Because whatever you think of me and the life I've lived, I've *never* had someone write *anything* on *any wall of mine* in *fucking blood.*" Her eyes are the size of the Rolls' rims and full of raw fear. Her voice wobbles as she adds, "I don't know who the fuck would do something like this. I literally can't think of anyone."

Cavender clears his throat. "You don't have any idea what it means? Or why someone might be coming for you next?"

Magnolia shakes her head. "I don't know who the fuck they got first, so I sure as shit don't know what being next means."

The detective shoves his phone and hands into his pockets and rocks back on the heels of his cheap shoes. "You don't think it has anything to do with the murder committed in your building?"

"I have absolutely no idea, Detective. That's really more your area of expertise."

I give her another squeeze to communicate that she's doing a great fucking job with the cop.

"In order for me to do my job," Cavender says, "I'm going to need some information from you. Starting with a list of possible enemies. Old colleagues. Old *companions*. Anyone you can think of who may want to hurt you physically, financially, or otherwise."

Magnolia laughs sardonically. "I'm sure you'd love that list, but honestly, I don't know a single person who would be on it that would pull some shit like this. They wouldn't dare."

Mount, I think. *Everyone knows Magnolia is under Mount's protection. She's right. No one who knew that would chance making a move against her.*

The cop latches onto her statement. "What do you mean— they wouldn't dare? Because they know you'd retaliate? Or is there another reason?"

Magnolia stares him down. "Look, Cavender. I have no idea why the fuck it happened. I don't have anything I can give you that would be a good lead, but I'm gonna think really fucking hard about it. If I come up with anyone who might've been inclined to do something like this . . . I'll let you know."

That's my girl. A boss in her own right.

"You heard her, Detective. She doesn't know anything. Now, if you won't let us inside, then there's really no reason for us to be here right now. Let the building manager know when the techs are done so we can arrange cleanup. We'll be in touch if we think of anything that could be relevant to your investigation."

I spin us, as a unit, away from Cavender, but he stops me with his next question.

"Ms. Maison. I couldn't help but notice your place was almost totally cleaned out. Manager says you're selling it soon. Where are you headed if that house in the Quarter isn't yours?"

Magnolia turns her head just enough to look at the detective. "None of your goddamned business, Detective. If you've got something to report on this *crime*, you can get my number from Carl or call Moses's attorney. I'll be waiting for answers *from you* about who the fuck did this . . . *to me*."

44
MAGNOLIA

As Moses and I walk out of my former condo building, I'm grateful for the strength he offers. He's not holding me up, but he is helping me hold it together.

Before this morning, I thought I'd seen it all. Because, *goddamn*, I've been through some fucked-up shit. I've been raped. I've been shot and left for dead in the worst way imaginable. I've even been in a fucking coma.

I'm a fighter.

But seeing those words—*I'm coming for you next*—written in blood on my fucking wall? Well, it sent a chill down my spine. I know evil when I see it, because I've seen plenty.

Now it's looking for me.

I think of the card Celeste dealt me the first day I knew Moses was back in town. *The Devil.*

It's not supposed to be literal. It's supposed to be symbolic. But leave it to me to have someone literally coming to drag me into hell.

Maybe it's because I'm no innocent. I've done so many things I regret. *Fuck*, I killed a man in the damn elevator only three days ago. Sure, that was self-defense, but can God forgive all that? I'd like to think so, but he and I haven't exactly been on speaking terms in a long while.

"You okay?" Moses asks as we leave the building I never want to return to. There's nothing left for me here.

I suck in a long, deep breath of fresh air, trying to get the picture Cavender shoved in my face out of my head.

My first instinct is to say, *Yes, I'm fine. Takes a lot more than that to rattle me.* But I find his sympathetic green eyes and admit the truth. "I don't know what I am right now, but that's some fucked-up shit."

Moses's expression softens as he stops on the sidewalk to cup my cheek. "You didn't need to see it. And whatever you do, you do *not* need to be thinking about it for longer than it takes for us to get in the car, but you probably will."

As soon as he says *car*, I remember the Lexus I left in the parking garage, and I grasp onto that thought because it's better than anything else running through my head.

"I have a car in the garage. I don't want to come back, but I need to get it out of here before I close on the condo."

Moses presses a finger to my lips to shush me. "I'll have Jules and Trey get it. You don't have to come back here again. I'll take care of it."

It's strange having someone have my back so completely and help me deal with shit, but like I told Moses, *this* is exactly what I want.

No, at this point in my life, it's what I *need*.

"Thank you. Then I'm never coming back. Let's get the hell out of here."

45

Somewhere close by

I see them. Rage floods my system. I want to carve her up like I did in my dreams last night. That fucking *puta* killed my brother. Her every single breath is an insult to me.

If she were alone, I would take her right now. Make her fucking wish she'd never been born.

But him . . . he is a problem.

A problem I have to eliminate. Soon.

As they climb in the SUV, I write down the plate number and get ready to follow them.

I hope you got my message, puta. Because I am coming for you next.

46
MOSES

My blood is fucking boiling. Whoever painted that shit on Magnolia's wall might think he's coming for her next, but he's going to find me instead.

I won't let that sick fuck anywhere near her. Now that I've got her cooperation, she'll be guarded like the Hope Diamond because she's fucking priceless and deserves to shine in peace.

As we pull away from the building, I hold Magnolia's hand, but my attention is on the road and my rearview mirror. With a threat like that, details matter, and I'm not going to miss a single one.

If I were sick and twisted—which I'm fucking not—and I was expecting to find my prey in her place but found it empty instead, I'd want to know where the fuck she went. Which means I'd expect her to come assess the damage, and I'd be waiting to follow her home. That's exactly what's *not* going to happen.

"We're gonna take the long way back, mama. Just to be safe."

Magnolia looks over at me from the passenger seat of the SUV. "You think whoever did that will follow us?"

"It's a real possibility, and I'm not taking any chances. Not with you. Not ever again."

A ghost of a smile crosses her lips. "Thank you."

I press a few buttons on my phone, and Jules answers on the first ring.

"Hey, boss. Get any answers?"

I wish we had. "No, but we got a fuck of a lot more questions. Trey with you?"

"Yeah."

"Put me on speaker."

"You got us both now," Jules says.

"All right, listen up. Trey—I need you to dig faster and harder. Whoever the asshole was who bled out in the elevator, Ricardo What's-his-fucking-name? There's a damn good chance that someone's looking to avenge his death. And somehow, I don't fucking know how, that someone has figured out Mags was responsible."

"Fuck," Trey and Jules whisper in tandem.

"Exactly. We need friends, family, associates, everything you can possibly find so we can figure out who it is and stop him. Or, if I'm wrong and this is unrelated, we need to figure out who the hell else could be targeting her and why."

"I'm on it," Trey says with absolute confidence in his tone.

"Good. We also gotta take into account the possibility that if the elevator dude was erased, his family might've been too." I don't have to go into detail; they know the drill. "You know where to look."

"Yeah, I'll dig in every direction. If there's someone out there who wants vengeance—for any reason—I'll find them."

"Perfect. Jules—Mags has a car at the condo building. We're going to get you her keys, and you're going to get over there and move it. Stash it somewhere else. Make sure you're not followed."

"You think whoever broke into the condo is following you?" Jules asks.

"He didn't just break in. I'll give you the details later," I say, not wanting to bring it up again in front of Magnolia.

But I should have known she was stronger than that.

"He wrote *I'm coming for you next* on my wall. In blood," she says, her voice steady. "He's definitely looking for me."

"Fuck," Trey whispers again. "That is so fucked up. Okay, I'll dig deep. You need me, you holler."

"Thank you both. We'll be back once I'm sure we don't have a tail."

"What if you do?" Jules asks, his concern clear. "You want me ready to intercept?"

I glance over at Magnolia sitting next to me. I want this asshole dead before the sun sets, but I'm not willing to do it in any way that puts her in danger.

Could Jules handle it by himself? Depends on who the guy is and what he's packing. Revenge is a hell of a motivator, and I don't want to send Jules into a fight until we know what—or who —we're dealing with. That's not shit you do to family if you can avoid it.

"If he's following us, then I'll get the make, model, and plate. We'll go after him and take him out when he doesn't expect it." It's the best I can do on the fly with so many unknowns looming, and trying to keep everyone who matters to me breathing.

"Got it, boss. Call if you have any trouble. I'm ready."

"We'll see you soon, and then it's time to lock shit down and get our strategy together."

I hang up the call and glance at Magnolia again.

"This is serious, isn't it?" she asks.

"Because you're involved, it's serious as a motherfucking heart attack. But for now, we're just going for a drive to see how smart this asshole is."

❦

As we ride past the World War II Museum, I spot a black Ford Fusion staying three or four cars behind us. He's followed me through a few turns, and now I've got a lock on him. With Magnolia beside me scanning every alley and side street, I've got a choice to make.

Do I tell her or not?

I recall what she said to me this morning. *"That's what I want, Moby. I want a partner."*

What the hell kind of partner am I if I don't trust her too? Not the kind I want to be.

Gripping the wheel, I say, "I'm pretty sure we've got ourselves a tail."

Her head swivels to me and then right back to the sideview mirror. "Which car?"

"Black Ford Fusion. Three cars back."

She nods when she notices it. "I see him. How do we find out for sure?"

The *we* in her sentence makes me smile despite the situation.

"I'm gonna whip a U-turn at the next intersection, and try to get a look at him and see if we can catch his plate going the other way."

Magnolia reaches into her purse and pulls out a pen. "I'm fucking ready. This bastard's going down."

"That's my girl. All right. Hold on. Here we go."

Even as I change lanes, I know this is a long shot, but it's as much as I'm willing to do with Magnolia in the car. Keeping her safe is priority number one, and that means not taking too many risks. Just a few.

At the next green light, I whip the car around and punch it.

"Sunglasses. Hat. He's ducking. Doesn't want to be seen," Magnolia says as we drive by him.

"Good girl. Get ready for the plate." I cut off a car that slams on the horn.

"JQ2009. I got it," she says with a note of triumph in her voice as she scribbles down the tag number.

"Fuck yeah." I turn at the next corner, peeling off to the right and then turning again and again until I don't even know where the fuck we are anymore.

Magnolia's gaze is glued to the sideview mirror. "He's not following us. He knows we spotted him. Fucker." She faces me. "Should we call Trey with the plate?"

I can't help but smile as we pass tree-lined streets and people on the sidewalks. This isn't what I pictured for us when I came back, but even a shitty day with Magnolia is better than a good day without her. Still, she's beside me now, so things could be much worse. It doesn't hurt that at least I know nothing's happening to her on my watch.

"Yeah, mama. Let's do that. And maybe, just maybe, we'll get lucky today after all."

She reaches across the center console of the SUV and threads her fingers through mine. "Feels like we already did."

I totally fucking agree.

47
MAGNOLIA

"Y ou ready to go home?" Moses asks, and my heart does a squeezing thing it hasn't done in a long, long time.

Home. With Moses.

Damn, that sounds good.

Then I remember I don't have anything at all there to wear, or my makeup, or my face shit.

"Yeah, but now that we've lost the tail, can we go get my stuff? If I'm staying with you, I'm gonna need it."

"Shit. Yeah. Of course. I should've thought of that." Moses glances over, heat in his eyes. "But then again, the idea of you wearing only my clothes has a real strong appeal to it."

"You're such a man."

He looks down at the vicinity of his dick and nods. "Damn right I am. Bona fide."

"Well, maybe if we weren't sharing a house with two *other* men, that'd work. But my days of parading around in lingerie in front of a crowd are long over." The smile on his face dies at my words, and I want to bring it back. "Hey. Don't look like that. It's the past. Don't let it take what we have today from us too. Okay?"

Moses makes a turn toward the French Quarter, and I see him half grinning. "When'd you get all wise, woman?"

I knock my shoulder into his. "I don't know if I'd say I'm wise, but I'm . . . learning. Just makes sense that you can't hold on to yesterday if you want to live every bit of today. Also, you just missed our turn."

His full smile is back, and he laughs full out. "I should've let you drive. You know this city a hell of a lot better than I do."

I grimace, all too sure my driving skills aren't up to par with his, given the way he whipped that U-turn and drifted the rear end of the car perfectly before bringing it back into line. "I don't know if I could've done what you did back there. I imagine you've got some stories if you know how to drive like that."

He winks, making me melt into the leather beneath me. "I have a few. And all three of us—me, Jules, and Trey—took a lot of tactical driving classes. Partly because we needed to, but mostly because they were fun as hell. Saved our asses more than once, though."

"Then I'm glad you did. Turn here, Earnhardt."

A few minutes later, we pull up in front of my cheery yellow house.

"It won't take me long," I tell him as I reach for the door handle.

"I'll help. We're a team, after all. Where you go, I go."

Moses shoots me a winning smile, and it's in that moment that I realize I'm falling in love with him all over again. Not with the man I knew fifteen years ago, but with the man he is today.

Despite everything, today is a lucky day, I decide. Now, here's hoping it keeps on going.

48
MOSES

When we get back to the house in the Marigny, my gaze lands on Trey as I carry in Magnolia's twin suitcases. "Any luck? We could use some good news right about now."

His attention darts from us to his keyboard as he speaks. "I got a hit on the plates, but it doesn't match the description you gave of the driver, unless he's secretly a seventy-four-year-old black woman and his disguise was damn good."

"Damn it," Magnolia says from behind me. "Does that mean he stole it?"

Trey's head bobs from his seat at the kitchen table. "Most likely, or he stole the plate of another black Fusion."

Jules leans against the kitchen island. "What's our next move? Because we gotta do something."

Part of me wishes I'd taken Jules's advice and had him intercept the guy, but there's no way in hell I was going to let him take this on alone. I also wasn't risking a confrontation, one that would most likely end in blood being spilled, with Magnolia at my side.

She might be tough as hell, but she doesn't need to be in any more danger. Visions of her getting ready to stitch up the slice in her own side are still all too recent in my brain, and I refuse to let it happen again.

Across the table that Trey has turned into central command, complete with notebooks littered by scribblings and a slew of empty coffee cups, I ask, "You find anything else on the dead guy?"

"Nothing helpful yet. I'm still looking." He scratches the back of his neck, and then his fingers are flying again.

I don't need to tell him to hurry or look harder, because Trey's already doing everything he can. The man is a beast on a computer, and I trust him to do the job better than anyone else could. Plus, he doesn't know the word *quit*, which is exactly why we work well together.

"Okay, so we keep running that down, and we're on high alert everywhere. No driving without checking for tails. Mama, you're with me. Like glue. We're taking *no* chances."

She worries her bottom lip and crosses her arms over her stomach, feeling whatever is going through her head. "What about my girls? And Desiree's? Is there a chance he could go after them? I still own the house. Because I was young and dumb, it was in my real name from the beginning." Magnolia's weary tone is filled with concern. "If this guy is looking for me and tracked me to my condo, would he try to find me through them? I mean, the bond for deed between me and Desiree is filed, but technically, my name is still on the house, so I'm connected."

"Shit, yeah. She's got a point, man," Trey says with a nod. "We don't know what the hell this guy will do."

"He looked for you at the condo and not the house first, so this guy clearly has some intel of his own on you."

"Just like the guy who tried to kill me in the elevator," Magnolia says, and the reminder burns a hole in my gut.

Not letting that shit happen ever again.

I reach an arm around her shoulders and pull her near. "Yeah. Going to the same place as the attempted hit makes sense."

"*Attempted hit?* You really think someone paid the guy in the elevator to kill me?" Magnolia asks, fear causing her voice to rise.

"It's a strong possibility. Too many things have happened since. It all adds up to none of this being random, including Ricardo." I press a kiss into her hair, hating that she has to deal with any of this. "We'll clear the girls out of the house. If it's empty, there won't be anyone he can hurt there. Is there somewhere they can go? Friends? Families?"

Magnolia presses her lips together, but not once does she falter or lose her grip on the situation or her emotions. *Strong as hell.*

After a minute, she says, "They'll all find somewhere to go. It's just the money part. Some of them will have to leave town completely, and if they can't work where they're safe and protected, they can't pay their bills. I don't like doing that to any of them—my girls or Desiree's." She groans, looking skyward as if searching for an answer from above. "I don't like putting them in a position where they might have to make choices that could put their safety at risk. It's too dangerous."

The decision is easy to make. "I'll cover them. Whatever they would've made in an average week, I'll cover it. Travel too. Whatever it takes."

Magnolia's eyes practically bug out of her head. "What? That's . . . are you . . . You can't . . . how?" It's the first time I've ever heard her sputter and trip over her words.

I turn her to face me and stare deep into her caramel eyes. I want it to hit home that I'm serious about being here for her. I have lost time to make up for, and money isn't an issue. Her safety and happiness are priceless.

"If they're important to you, then they're important to me. It's just money, and we've got it to spare. And if they don't have a place to go, I've got a buddy with a couple of houses over in Gulf

Shores he never uses. Not too bad of a drive. They can take a vacation. Get in some beach time."

Magnolia's lower lip wobbles and drops. "You'd do that . . . for women you've never met?"

"I'm doing it for *you*, Mags. And if you care about them, then I do too."

With no thought to Trey or Jules, she reaches up to wrap a hand around my neck and yanks my face down to hers. She kisses me hard. When she finally releases me, her gaze is soft and warm on my face.

"Thank you, Moby. It means a hell of a lot to me."

I lift my hand and run the back of my knuckles across her jaw. "Whatever you need, mama. I got you."

She squeezes her eyes shut, and when she opens them again, they're shining. "I'll call Desiree and get that moving."

"I'll have Jules make the arrangements and run cash over today."

Magnolia sighs, and to see her relax is lifegiving. "Thank you. Desiree's girls are already on high alert because of the Feds."

"The Feds?" Trey, Jules, and I all blurt out the same thing at the same time.

Magnolia's head swivels between the three of us before her attention comes back to me. "You didn't know about the FBI?"

"No, but you have our attention now."

Magnolia's brows pinch together as she explains. "The day you came into Mount's office, just when I was leaving, I saw you as the fireplace spun."

"He planned that," I say quietly with a shake of my head. "Fucking devious bastard."

"Takes one to know one," Jules mumbles, and I shoot him a *don't-fucking-start-bro* stare.

He doesn't even pretend I worry him and shrugs, grinning like a dickhead.

Magnolia continues. "He called me in to tell me the Feds were watching the house, because he knows I'm still connected to it until Desiree pays it totally off. Mount warned me to be careful. So I had Desiree put her girls on hotel mode. No sex work in the house while the Feds were babysitting."

"Did he say why they were zeroed in on the house?" I ask her.

She nods. "They were watching for a client. Alberto Brandon. Older guy. Mid-fifties. I guess he was into some shady business or something. I don't know. Anyway, to hear it from Mount, the Feds have been looking for him and can't find him. So they must've gotten desperate and decided to watch my old house too, because he had a regular thing with one of Desiree's girls, Naya."

I point at Trey. "Add this guy to your list. Dig around and see what you can find, but he's a second priority."

Trey's already writing the guy's name down on one of the only blank areas left on his notepad. "Got it."

I put my hands on Mags's shoulders and work her tense muscles in my palms. "All right, mama. Call your girls. Get things moving. Then we'll get money and arrangements settled. One thing at a time."

Over her shoulder, she gazes up at me. Nothing and no one can ever get to her. Come hell or high water, she'll know I'm her partner from here on out. That's the vow I'm making with every single one of our moves right fucking now.

I already lost fifteen years with her because of my own choices. But that was the past, and all we have now is forever.

Still, a heavy feeling in my gut reminds me that I still have a bomb to drop on her. But, *goddamn it*, she's got enough on her plate right now. I swear, as soon as everything is settled, I'll come clean.

I just hope it's not too late.

49
MAGNOLIA

My clothes are in the closet next to Moses's, my shoes lined up beside his much bigger ones. I even have an entire side of the bathroom counter. This living-together situation feels so . . . domestic. It's also something completely new to me.

Other than the two weeks Moses and I spent together after Katrina, I've never lived with a man. Not even when I was dating Rafe. He had his space, I had mine, and that's how we both liked it. But with Moses . . . it just feels right.

Except last time, he didn't exactly have any clothes with him. We had to scrounge up shorts and shirts from the men's clothes stashed in the other girls' rooms. Since Moses was a big bastard even then, most of them didn't fit right, but he made do. It wasn't like either of us were trying to impress the other when we had no power and were just doing what we had to do to make it through until life went back to normal.

Except, as soon as signs of life restarting showed up in the neighborhoods around us, I knew Moses was going to move on. We'd met under fucked-up circumstances, and I was never under any illusion it was going to last forever. I just didn't expect it to end quite so suddenly.

I still remember like it was yesterday.

Fifteen years ago

With every person who came back, Moses looked more and more tense. I saw him leaning against the window, watching the house across the street as a big truck drove through standing water in the road.

"Everything okay?" I asked him, coming up from behind to rub a palm over his shirtless back.

He turned and looked at me, his quick smile subdued. "People are coming back. I wondered how long it would take for the city to come to life again."

For the eleven days since Katrina, the world had been unrecognizable. We were an island, the water coming up to the front stoop of the house and completely flooding everything down two streets. I'd lost count of how many times I'd sent up a prayer, thanking God that this house was on a little patch of high ground. Another foot of floodwater, and we'd be standing in it, but at least only the basement was full.

There wasn't shit I could do about that right now, except be thankful I had flood insurance. The previous owner, Linnie, had it when she died, and I made sure to do the same. This was New Orleans, a town that sat mostly below sea level. I knew not everyone got it, but it just made sense to cover my ass on that front, because I wasn't about to take chances with the one thing of value I owned. So the basement would be fine, eventually.

But right now, I was more worried about the man in front of me. I wasn't stupid. I knew he couldn't stay forever, but I hated to think about how fucking bad it was going to hurt when he left.

He'd brought up me going with him, but we didn't talk much about it because I couldn't leave. Not when I'd just gotten my hands on something worth a damn. The house was all I had, and the memory of being out on the street corner with no protection, at the mercy of a pimp, was still all too fresh in my mind.

This rickety house was my only security.

No matter how I felt about Moses, I'd only known him for *eleven days.* But then again, going through an experience like this with someone went far beyond the connection you'd make under normal circumstances. From the moment he stormed into the house . . . we had something I'd never had with anyone else, and I didn't want to let it go. But I was even more terrified to take a chance and leave.

For all I knew, he'd grow tired of me in a few months. Where would I be then?

"It's good people are coming back," I replied. "Maybe it means we'll get power eventually. God, I miss hot water."

He turned away from the window, his green-gold eyes locking on my face as if he was memorizing it.

I knew then the faster life went back to normal, the faster I'd lose him.

"Don't worry about what's going on out there. We've got plenty going on in here," I said as I pulled him away from the glass. "Besides, you haven't beat me at chess yet. I'll give you another shot tonight."

Moses laughed. "I'm gonna need a hell of a distraction to beat you." A grin split his face right before he scooped me up into his arms. "And I've got an idea I think you're gonna like. A *lot.*"

"If it involves your mouth on my pussy and me screaming your name when I come, then I'm all for it."

Present day

The memory of Moses fades away as I hear him call my name.

He pokes his head into the room, catching me with my hand on the dresser, staring at the wall. "You hungry?"

I cut my unfocused gaze to his face, shaking free of the dreamlike memories. "Yeah. I could eat."

"Good deal. I sent Jules out to handle the girls, and Trey moved his shit out to the pool house so he can blast music to help his searching." Moses's smile charms me when his head falls to the side and he adds, "So we've got the house to ourselves for the rest of the night."

"Just like old times," I say, excited and still nostalgic. "Except, you know . . . no flooding, and we have power and hot water."

Moses comes into the room, wraps his thick arms around my waist, and pulls me against his body. It's like no time has passed at all between this moment and the memory I was reliving. I curl into his heat and breathe in his unique spicy scent.

"We made it work, didn't we?" he asks.

"Yeah, we did. Those should've been the worst days of my life, and instead, because you were there with me, they were some of the best."

His body tenses for a beat before he pulls back to look down at me. "I'm glad I was there. So fucking glad."

It's like he shows up when I need him most in my life.

We both know what would have happened to me if he hadn't been there after the storm, so I don't have to say a thing. Instead, I lift my lips to his and sweep them across his warm skin.

After kissing him earlier, I need more.

This time, Moses takes over, one hand burying in my hair as he tilts my head to the side. My mouth opens and his tongue steals inside, and all I taste is Moses. After going *years* without kissing anyone, I want to live in this kiss. There's something so perfect about the feel of his lips on mine, and the way he holds me like he's never letting me go.

I love it.

My thought from earlier comes back. *I'm falling in love with him all over again, and I'm not doing a damn thing to stop it.*

Finally, Moses pulls back. I meet his gaze, and the flames in those green-gold eyes are so hot, they could blister me.

"I want you bad, mama. I told myself I'd wait. I told myself I'd make you dinner. Remind you who we are together. Then . . . then I'd bring you in here and lay you down and show you exactly how fucking much I've missed you."

"I don't want to wait. I need you. God, I've fucking missed you, Moby."

I reach up again, dragging his mouth down to mine. I want everything from him, even if I don't know what the hell is going to happen tomorrow or the next day. Tonight, I'm giving myself this. I'm giving myself permission to let go with a man, and that isn't something I've done in a long damn time.

But with Moses, all my barriers drop away. He must feel it in my kiss. Must feel the longing and desperation I've had pent up for years. His hands find my ass and grip, lifting me off my feet. I wrap my legs around his waist and kiss him with everything I'm feeling. I devour his mouth, loving the battle of lips, tongues, and teeth. I feel us moving through the room, but I don't worry about where he's going to put me or whether he'll drop me.

Not with Moses.

Never with Moses.

I trusted him from the beginning—*me*, the woman who doesn't trust anyone or anything until it's been proven beyond a reasonable doubt with me sitting as judge and jury. But with Moses, it was second nature to trust him. I guess that happens when someone saves you and then appoints himself your protector so nothing can happen to you as long as he's on watch.

That's what Moses did for me, and tonight, all I want is everything I've missed for the last fifteen years. We can't get the lost time back, but we can start this very second by not taking *now* for granted.

When he lowers me to the bed, I pull him down with me, wanting the heavy weight of his body pressing me into the mattress. I've always loved the weight of him. So strong and capable. And as a woman who's had to watch out for herself and couldn't rely on anyone, being able to give him that part of me is like finding freedom I didn't know existed.

Our lips don't separate as he rolls, pulling me on top. I'm laid out above him, and I feel his touch everywhere. One hand coasts up my back, threading through my hair, and the other anchors my hips against the hard ridge of his cock. I buck against him, my body already going soft and wet for the only man who's ever made me feel like a real woman. With Moses, I'm not an object, a toy, or a tool whose sole purpose is to get a man off.

With him, I'm my *real* self. I matter. My emotions, my thoughts, and my soul.

It took me years to be able to enjoy sex, because to me, it started out as a business transaction. But with Moses, it was never anything but exactly what it was meant to be—perfection in its own way.

He groans into my mouth, and I finally pull away.

Looking down at this gorgeous man, I say, "I need you. You probably want to take this slow and sweet, but I'm hard up, Moby. Fuck, it's been forever, and I want you so fucking bad that I don't have time for slow and sweet. I need this to happen *now*."

"You're gonna let me give it to you slow and sweet next, then. Because I want to savor you, mama. You deserve that."

"Later," I say, going for his shirt and dragging it up his muscular body.

He pushes up on his hands, allowing me to tug it from beneath him and yank it over his head. All that's left is smooth, golden skin that speaks of his Creole heritage. I've never seen skin as beautiful as this man's. My palms glide over his chest and the hard blocks of his abs.

"God, I love a man who takes care of himself," I whisper.

"Pshhh," he says as he reaches for the hem of my shirt. "I'm nothing. You, on the other hand, are a work of fucking art." He slides the shirt over my head, and his eyes practically glow with appreciation of what's beneath it. "These tits . . . Fuck, woman. Fucking perfect."

I snort a laugh at that. "You can thank my surgeon for those. He's the artist."

Moses shakes his head. "Well, he ain't here, so you're just gonna have to listen to me tell you how fucking perfect you are." His hands bracket my waist. "I can tell you put in the work too. You're fit as fuck, mama."

"Fit for fucking you," I say, rocking against his hard cock as I tease him. "And, goddamn it, I need it."

He lets me grind on him for a few more seconds before he flips us again. "Then you get what you need."

My shorts are gone in a split second, and so are his. As soon as we're both naked, it's like someone has unleashed pure decadence.

We're on each other, and our sole purpose is to *feast*. My lips skim over his pecs, sucking a nipple into my mouth and scraping it with my teeth. He moves me up, so he can do the same, sucking one into his mouth at a time. Wetness slicks between my legs, and I throw one over his hip to put his cock between my lower lips. As soon as I find friction against the rock-hard shaft, my body ignites.

"Oh, fuck yes. Oh God."

"You gonna come just from bucking against my cock, mama? Because that's hot as fucking hell."

I'm already too far gone to answer him. My orgasm is right there, waiting for me to take it.

I grind harder until the pressure is too much, and I throw my head back and let out a scream. "Yes, yes, yes."

"Fuck, mama. *Fuck*." Moses reaches between us and readjusts his cock, and I scream again.

"Hurry. Hurry. Now."

With one hand gripping my hip, he slams home, filling me full with a single thrust. My body welcomes him, despite being out of practice, and my inner muscles clamp down hard.

"Holy fuck, woman. Goddamn." Moses sucks in a breath before he pulls back and pounds home again. Stroke after stroke, he unleashes more pleasure than I can handle.

I start coming, and I swear to Christ, I never stop.

Every thrust has me screaming unintelligible sounds, and all I know is that if this is what kills me, I'll die a happy woman.

I lose track of time, space, earth, and everything else. All that exists is Moses and the insane waves of pleasure swamping me. My head thrashes from side to side, until one of his hands cups my cheek and he plants his mouth on mine.

"Never letting you go. Ever."

My pussy clamps down so hard, surely it'll strangle his cock. Moses's mouth crushes against mine before he throws his head back with a roar I feel to the very marrow of my bones.

My body goes limp, and I let go, allowing the pleasure to drag me under one final time.

He's even better than my memories, and here in the flesh, it's *bliss*.

50
MOSES

My heart thunders in my chest, pounding so hard it might explode. My lungs burn like I've sprinted for a gold medal, and my lungs heave in breath after breath.

I don't know what the fuck just happened in this bed, but it goes so far beyond sex, I can't even explain it. It's . . . like coming alive after being asleep for most of my life.

Energy buzzes across my skin and through my veins. I feel fucking invincible.

Beside me, Magnolia goes limp, and I pull her against my chest, not wanting any space between us. Her heart hammers in nearly perfect rhythm with mine as she fights to catch her breath.

I press my palm to her chest. "Slow and steady, mama. Slow and steady."

She doesn't open her eyes, but she follows my command, slowing her breathing from its frenetic pace.

"You killed me," she whispers, letting her head loll to the side. "I . . . goddamn . . . what happened?"

A chuckle falls from my lips. "You happened. Jesus Christ. You're . . . I don't even know." I need more oxygen before I can form coherent sentences. "Almost killed me too. But what a way to go."

She snorts, and my lips twitch at the sound.

"Did you just snort?"

She does it again, and suddenly, we're both laughing our asses off. That's when I remember what it feels like to be *happy*.

We lie on top of the covers for a long time until the sweat on our skin begins to cool and Magnolia shivers.

"Here, I got you." I tug the blanket out from beneath us and pull it over her body, curling mine around her to share my heat.

"You said something about food earlier, but . . ." She pauses to cover her mouth and yawn. "I'm gonna need a nap after that. Just a few minutes. I'll be ready in just a few minutes." And with that, her entire body relaxes, and she drifts off to sleep.

I hold her for two hours, never letting myself doze off, because I want to savor every moment of her in my arms. She's the piece that's been missing my whole life.

51
MAGNOLIA

It's dark outside by the time we make it into the kitchen. I sit on a bar stool with a glass of wine in front of me, wearing Moses's shirt and my shorts, watching as he chops onions, celery, and bell peppers—the holy trinity of Creole food.

"You sure you don't want help? Because I'm a pretty damn good cook these days. I finally learned."

He glances at me from across the island, his expression skeptical, but because he's a smart man, he doesn't say a word. I can, however, guess exactly what he's thinking.

"One time. I burned rice *one time on a camp stove* when the city was underwater, but I really have learned since then."

Moses's smile tells me he was remembering the exact same thing.

"And, yes, I admit, I would've probably starved after the hurricane if you hadn't kept me fed, but really . . . I'm better now."

Moses pauses with the knife still in hand. "You want to make dinner tomorrow, you go right on ahead. Tonight, I'm cooking for my woman. You deserve it after nearly ending me in bed."

I snort out a laugh again, something I haven't done in . . . well, fifteen years. Apparently, it's something brought on only by Moses.

"All right. Tomorrow then. Dinner's on me. So, what are you making? Gumbo?" I guess the obvious choice given the ingredients he has assembled.

"Shrimp Creole. My grand-mère's recipe."

As soon as he mentions his grandmother, I recall him telling me about her all those years ago. "She raised you?"

He nods, continuing to chop. "Most important woman in my life, God rest her soul."

"What was she like?"

He glances up at me as I take a sip of the wine. "She would've liked you. She would've gotten a kick out of your fire. Your determination. She didn't hold with people who expected everything to be handed to them. Which was apparently why she didn't care for my ma much. I don't have anything independent to go off, so I gotta assume Grand-mère was right about her."

Moses never mentioned either of his parents before, so this revelation feels big. I won't pry, but I want to understand the man in front of me more than anyone in my life.

"You didn't know your mom either?" I ask the question quietly and add the last word so he knows he's not alone.

The rhythm of the knife slows to a stop.

"Sounds like you know about that too?"

I nod. "Complications with my birth. I made it. She didn't."

Moses's entire body seems to soften where he stands. "I hate that for you."

My shoulders rise and fall. "I struggled with the guilt of it— thinking I'd killed her—for a long time. But . . . I know now it wasn't my fault. How could it have been? I was a baby. I didn't ask to be born."

"Yeah . . . that's the truth. You sure as hell aren't to blame." He goes back to chopping, his gaze focused on the remaining chunk of onion. "My ma wasn't good people. She got pregnant to trap my dad, or so Grand-mère said. My dad died when she was carrying me. Never lived to see me born either."

My heart cracks for the pain in his voice. "I'm so sorry," I whisper.

He gathers the vegetables with his massive hands and tosses them into a pot. "Yeah, well, it turned out for the best, because after I was born, she dropped me on Grand-mère and split. No point in keeping me around since my dad was gone, and that's what she wanted."

"Some people shouldn't be allowed to have kids, but I'm glad she had you and that you ended up with your grand-mère, because she was who you needed."

A smile replaces the sorrow gracing his features for a moment. "Likewise, mama. Likewise. And Grand-mère, well, at least she was happy. Most grandparents wouldn't be thrilled about raising another baby, but Grand-mère saw my dad in me, and she loved him like crazy."

"You were lucky then."

His chin dips. "Damn lucky, at least until I was fifteen. She got sick. Cancer. It was nasty. I dropped out of school when she had to quit working, because there wasn't enough money to pay the bills and get her well. And I wasn't about to let her fade away and not do a damn thing about it."

I can hear the sadness in his voice, but also a sense of pride. He did the right thing.

"She was lucky to have you too."

"Maybe. Maybe not. I learned right quick the jobs I could get with no diploma weren't gonna pay me enough to make a dent in the money we needed."

I know all too well where the story is headed, but I say nothing, just waiting to hear Moses tell it.

"I got involved with other things that could make the money we needed, and goddamn, did I piss her off. She told me sacrificing my future wasn't worth it, but there was nothing I wouldn't have done to save her."

I fold a leg underneath myself. Regardless of how deep this conversation is, it's also easy in a surprising way. "I'm willing to guess she understood the choices you made, even if she wished you would've made other ones."

"Maybe. But realizing I had a talent for stealing other people's shit and selling it for a solid profit wasn't exactly the work of God she always hoped I'd do."

He gathers other ingredients from the pantry and refrigerator, and I could literally watch him move around a kitchen forever. The food already smells divine, and watching him cook is one of the sexiest, most satisfying sights I've ever seen.

"You were a kid, trapped in circumstances beyond your control. What you did was out of necessity."

"I know. But that's where necessity ended. Because when she died . . . I went crazy. Hated the world. Hated myself. Hated God. How could he take such a good woman and end her life so soon?"

He stirs the vegetables, turns the burner down a bit before adding stock and more spices, and then continues.

"I didn't give a fuck about my soul after that. I got deep into shit, decided I was gonna be a kingpin, and climbed my way to the top of the toughest crew in Biloxi. I had no fucking limits. There was nothing I wouldn't do. Rage dictated my every move. I wanted everyone to hurt the way I did. I didn't care about anyone or anything."

Moses's throat works as he swallows, and I stay silent. *He needs to get this out.* He finally looks up and makes eye contact again. This time, his green eyes are glowing.

"I did some fucked-up shit, Mags. Real fucked up. And then . . . I met you. And that's when shit changed." He snaps his fingers. "In the blink of an eye, I knew I couldn't keep doing what I was. If I would've kept running that crew, I'd have been dead by thirty —if I even made it that long. So I couldn't go back to Biloxi after

Katrina. It would've been the end of me. Everything shifted for me after you."

This time, I swallow a lump in my throat, because I had no idea meeting me was a turning point in his life. I thought it had been just me who'd changed. "You wanted to live? That's why you didn't want to go back?"

He shakes his head slowly and takes a swig of beer from his neglected bottle of Abita. "It wasn't that I didn't want to go back, it was that I couldn't. Sometimes you just *know*, to the marrow of your bones, when something is gonna kill you sooner rather than later."

"I get that." I bite at the corner of my mouth, debating whether I should say what I'm thinking.

Moses notices. "What?"

What's the worst that could happen? I think, then open up to him.

"I get it, is all. If I hadn't inherited that house, I was sure I'd end up back out on the streets. Eventually, I would've been just another dead hooker someone found in an alley. That house saved me."

Moses locks eyes with me. "That's why I didn't beg you to leave with me. I couldn't expect you to take a chance on me and give up everything you knew. Not then. Not when I had no idea where my path was going to take me. Not when there was a good chance you or me or both of us could end up dead."

We're both quiet for a few moments, and he opens a can of tomatoes to add to his delicious-smelling pan.

"I'm glad you didn't push for me to go with you. Even though I wanted to stay with you bad, I knew I needed to be where I was." A bead of condensation rolls down my glass of chilled white wine. "You know I never fucked another regular john after you left?"

He freezes and stares at me like a deer in headlights. "What do you mean by that?"

"I couldn't do it. So I became someone else—a legendary

madam who everyone would want and almost no one would get to have. I don't know if I would've done it if I hadn't met you. I might've just kept on the way I was. But I couldn't. I made myself exclusive and expensive, and from that day forward, I never fucked anyone for money who I wouldn't have fucked for free."

Most men wouldn't smile when their woman, a former sex worker, told them something like that, but Moses's face lights up like a Mardi Gras float.

"I'm glad you finally realized your value, mama. I could see it back then, but I didn't think you did."

I take another sip of the wine and feel it flushing my cheeks. It has to be the wine because I don't blush. Right?

Staring at my glass, I say, "It all worked out the way it was supposed to, I guess. I was no saint, so don't go thinking that. But . . . I found a way to get what I wanted from that life without it eating me alive. Well, until now. I wouldn't call the past few days ideal . . . except for spending them with this cocky motherfucker who likes curling my toes."

His grin widens, and his teeth show when he laughs out loud. "You deserved the best." He quiets for a beat, and then adds, "I only hate that I wasn't here for you the whole time. To give you everything you needed."

I shake my head. "I didn't want you to give it to me. I needed to earn it myself. And I did. I made my own choices. Had control over my life. Found power in myself I never would have if you'd been around to do all the heavy lifting."

His brows rise as he pours dry rice into boiling water. "We're a pair, aren't we? A former gangster-thief and a madam, who both made a life worth living despite the odds stacked against us."

I lift my wineglass and salute him. "I'll drink to that."

52
MOSES

We're nearly through with dinner, outside on the patio, when the sky cracks open and rain comes pouring down. Magnolia and I grab our plates and rush inside, both soaked by the time we slip through the slider.

"Where the hell did that come from?" Magnolia asks, shaking her wet hair, but all I can see is the white T-shirt sticking to her tawny skin.

"I don't know. You're the expert on New Orleans weather, not me. Here," I say as I grab her plate. "Let me get you set up at the table. I'd hate for you to miss a bite of my cooking. Mainly because I like the way you moan when you chew."

She laughs. "I guess that means I'm going back out to save the wine."

"Oh no you don't. Because as much as I'd love seeing you look like you're in a wet T-shirt contest, you need to go dry off. And if I follow you, I'm just gonna fuck you again."

Her smile turns into temptation made manifest, and in three steps, she's back outside in the rain, and the shirt is completely transparent.

"Is this what you mean? You don't like it?" she calls from outside as thunder rumbles.

"Get your ass in here, woman. You can't get struck by lightning on our first dinner date when you're not spitting fire at me."

"Come and get me then!" Magnolia spins in a circle, her arms wide, as rain falls from the sky. Her hair sticks to her face and the soaked shirt, and I wish I could capture the moment and keep it forever.

She looks . . . free. And happy as hell.

Come and get her? Damn right I will. Always.

I drop the plates on the counter and run outside, wrapping my arm around her waist and scooping her up into my arms. "You're crazy, mama."

With water rolling down her cheeks, she grins. "Crazy about you, Moby Dick."

"The feeling's mutual." I take her mouth and kiss her, standing in the rain while it drenches us both, as if we didn't have a single care in the world.

At least, until the next rumble of thunder cracks and reminds me that us getting fried means that there's no more sex.

I carry her inside, not giving a shit about the water running off us all over the floor. I don't stop until I reach the bathroom attached to our bedroom and flip the faucet to start the shower.

I lower her to her feet, running my hands over the wet T-shirt, cupping her generous tits and bringing them to my mouth. I suck her nipples through the fabric, rolling them between my teeth. Magnolia's hands grip my head, pulling my mouth tighter against her.

Her whimper in my ear is the ultimate turn-on.

Heat from the steam of the shower hits my skin, and I finally pull back. "Strip, mama. I want you wet *and naked* for me."

Magnolia's lips curve up as soon as she steps back, following my order to a T. She shoves the shorts down her legs and then reaches for the hem of the shirt. Little by little, she draws it up, revealing all that smooth, *smooth* skin. The tee gets caught on her tits, and my cock is rock hard by the time her nipples pop free.

My groan sounds twice as loud in the bathroom, and I'm a man faced with a feast when the shirt hits the floor with a slap. I prowl toward her and she steps back into the shower, tempting me with a roll of her hips.

There's only one thing for a man to do when faced with that kind of temptation.

Devour.

53
MAGNOLIA

Moses follows me into the shower, and instead of taking my mouth or going for my tits again, he shocks me by dropping to his knees. The spray bounces off his back and head as he wraps those big hands around my hips and goes straight to my pussy.

Oh, hell yes. That's my only thought as he sucks my clit into his mouth and tongues it, damn near sending me into an orgasm before I realize I'm even close.

Who am I fooling? I've been turned on since he fucked the hell out of me earlier. Round two? *Bring it.*

Moses doesn't disappoint, and never has when it comes to this.

He slides a finger inside me, pumping in and out, curling it forward to hit my G-spot. That, combined with the suction on my clit, has me grasping his shoulders to stay upright as my knees go weak.

"How do you do this to me? Christ, Moby."

Moses glances up, his lips shiny with my juices, and smiles. "We're just getting started, mama. Best hold on."

And hold on I do. Because Moses makes me come again

before he finally stands, and I cling to him for support. My lungs heave like I just put myself through a punishing workout.

"Good God. The government should force you to register your tongue as a lethal weapon, because you damn near slayed me again."

His grin couldn't get any bigger, but his cock bounces between us like it's dead set on growing another inch at the praise—and it's already a monster. I reach down to jack him and return the favor, but he shakes his head.

"Later. Right now, I'm fucking you. And I apologize in advance. Slow and sweet is gonna have to be round three."

I can't stop laughing, and I realize sex with Moses is the most fun I've had in a long, long time. Maybe ever.

"Give it to me any way you want, Moby. I'm ready."

He lifts me up as he turns us so my back is against the wall once more. "Legs around my waist."

When I comply, he swipes a kiss across my mouth, and I taste myself on his lips. Wetness gushes between my legs, soaking his cock.

"Put my cock in that tight, little cunt, woman. I want to fuck."

The guttural command turns me on more than I knew was possible. I'm not about taking orders, but Moses's make me hotter and needier.

I grip his cock, giving it a hard stroke because I can't resist. He releases a harsh breath.

"Don't tease me, mama. I need that pussy. Bad. I'm a man on the edge."

I line his shaft up with my entrance and meet his gaze. "Then you'd best take what you need."

Instead of slamming home, he lowers me inch by inch, fucking himself with my body, and it might be the sexiest thing I've ever witnessed. The heavy muscles of his shoulders bunch and flex as he lifts me up and brings me down. Over and over, until I can't watch anymore, because my head is thrashing from side to side as pleasure threatens to drown me.

The bathroom echoes with our screams as we both come, and the only thought left in my head is . . . *Moses is mine, and I'm not letting him go. Never again.*

54
MAGNOLIA

When my cell phone rings the next morning, I'm having the best dream and don't want to wake up. But I do, because the stupid thing is loud as hell.

"Why did I turn my ringer on?" I murmur, reaching for the nightstand. It's at this same moment that I realize I wasn't dreaming. Moses is wrapped around me like a kudzu vine, and the heat I was curling into while I was asleep is all from him.

"What's going on?" he mumbles with a sleep-roughened voice.

"Sorry. I didn't know my phone was on. I'll shut it off." I grab it off the nightstand, intending to decline the call, no matter who it is, but I see Norma's name on the display. She doesn't usually call unless it's important. "Shit. I'd better get this."

"Okay, mama. You do that." He yawns and rolls to his back, throwing one arm over his head.

I slip out from under the covers and tap the screen. "Hey, Norma. What's up?"

"I hope I didn't wake you. I was trying to wait to call, but . . . ."

"But what? What's wrong? Bernie okay?"

At the concern in my voice, Moses opens his eyes and sits up.

"I don't know. She keeps knocking things over when she

reaches for them, like they aren't where she thinks they are, and it's freaking me out. We're on her third glass this morning already, and she swears she's fine and refuses to go to a doctor."

"What do you think it could be?" I ask. Hell, for all I know, Bernadette could just be bored and winding Norma up for entertainment.

"I don't know. I keep watching for signs of a stroke, because that's all I can think of."

When she says *stroke*, a heavy knot forms in my gut. "Shit. Okay. I'll be right there. We can bully her into going to the hospital together."

She sighs. "Thank you, Mags. You know how she is. She'll kill me if I call an ambulance without her say-so."

"Don't you worry, Norma. She can kill me instead."

When I hang up and turn around, Moses is already out of bed and reaching for his clothes.

"Where we heading?" he asks as he pulls on a pair of shorts.

Could this man be any more perfect?

It takes me a second to remember he asked me a question, and that I'm standing here naked while he's already half-dressed.

"My great-aunt's house. That was Norma. She used to be Bernie's maid. Now I pay her to take care of the old bat, because she's one of the few people who can handle her battle-ax attitude."

He tosses a gray T-shirt over his head and tugs it down over his chest and stomach. "She okay?"

"I don't know. Norma thinks she might be having a stroke. Even if she is, Bernie will never admit it."

I go to the drawer and pull out a bra and underwear, and then grab a simple dress from the closet. We're both fully clothed and ready to leave in under ten minutes.

"This the great-aunt that kicked you out when you were sixteen?" he asks as we slide into the Rolls.

"Yeah. That's Bernie, all right. She, unlike your grand-mère, wasn't thrilled to be raising someone else's kid. My mom was a whore, and Bernie told me I'd end up just like her. Guess I proved her right. She's never let me live it down."

"Hey," Moses says, grabbing my hand across the center console. "That's the last time I hear you say something sorry like that about yourself. Hear me?"

There's a flutter in my stomach, and I'm so damn thankful he came back.

"I hear you. But you'd best brace yourself. Bernie is . . . well, she's not a cheerful woman, and I don't think she's ever been accused of being remotely friendly. I, however, get great delight from pissing her off. So . . . yeah. Do what you will with that."

He smiles and squeezes my hand. "It'll be fine. I can handle a little old lady."

I laugh, knowing better. "Just so you know. She's gonna hate your fucking guts."

The laughter that fills the car is borderline deafening. Moses shoots me a grin. "Challenge accepted."

55
MOSES

The well-kept white row house with black shutters where Magnolia's great-aunt lives is in a decent neighborhood. Thanks to Trey's skills, I'm aware Magnolia pays for it and any of her great-aunt's upkeep that isn't covered by the woman's Social Security check.

That says something about Magnolia, that she takes care of the old woman, even when her great-aunt didn't take care of her.

I'm already predisposed to dislike the woman for throwing Magnolia out when she was still a kid, but I'll keep that to myself and do everything I can to charm her. Not only because I'm sure Magnolia will get a kick out of it, but because my grand-mère was a big fan of killing people with kindness. While I'm better at just plain killing people, I'm willing to go the extra mile for my woman.

I park, and she climbs out of the car and opens the wrought-iron gate in the fence blocking off the tiny patch of yard from the sidewalk. We walk up hand in hand, and I give her a squeeze before she leads me up the stairs to the front door.

"Brace yourself," she warns me as she knocks on the door

instead of going right in. That tells me a lot. She doesn't feel at home here, but she keeps coming back all the same.

Yeah, this whole situation says a hell of a lot about Magnolia's character, even if she doesn't realize it.

An old black woman with a worried expression on her face answers the door. "Thank you for coming so quickly. I think she needs to go to the hospital. I just told her so and she fired me." The lady's eyes widen as they study me.

Magnolia rolls her eyes. "Bernie can't fire you because she doesn't pay you. I do. You're not fired."

The woman, who I presume is Norma, nods. "That's what I told her, but she didn't listen." Her gaze cuts to me again. "Who is . . . *all* this?"

Magnolia huffs out a short laugh. "*All* this," she waves a hand along the length of my torso, "is Moses. He's my . . . friend. A very good friend."

"Nice to meet you, Moses. I hope you know what the hell you're doing bringing him here, Mags. Because she's on a tear today."

A voice calls from inside, "I don't care what you two say! I'm not going to the hospital. You can't make me."

"I'd best get in there and talk some sense into her," Magnolia says.

Norma steps out of the way, and Magnolia drops my hand before we head inside.

I pause in front of Norma. "It's nice to meet you too, ma'am. I'll stay out of the way, unless I can help."

She takes me in with a sweeping glance, starting from my head and going to my toes. "Well, worse comes to worst, you can just pick Bernie up and put her in the car. My old bones can't do that anymore. We have to take the van, and with the fit she's been pitching today, she'd roll her wheelchair right off the platform and kill herself just to be spiteful."

"Like I said, whatever I can do to help. I'm at your disposal, ma'am."

"What the hell did you call her for?" Magnolia's great-aunt Bernadette yells from the next room. "I told you not to tell her anything!"

I smile at Norma. "I'd best go in after her and give Bernie someone else to yell at."

"God bless you, boy. If only it were that easy."

56
MAGNOLIA

Bernadette is spitting mad when I walk into the room, but I don't care.

I don't pull any punches and start right in. "What the hell is your problem, old woman? If there's something wrong with you, you've gotta go to the hospital."

"All I did was knock over a couple of glasses. Sue me for being human and a little clumsy once in a while. I'm not having a damn stroke, no matter what Norma thinks. See—I can still talk just fine."

She's right about that. Her speech doesn't sound impaired at all, and her face isn't droopy or anything. Still, Norma wouldn't panic if there was no reason for concern.

Then Bernadette's entire face changes and her eyes go wide. "Who are *you*?"

I don't have to turn around to know Moses just stepped into the living room.

"Moses Gaspard, ma'am."

Bernadette's jaw drops, and I expect her to light into Moses just like she does me, but a transformation comes over her demeanor. She sits back in her chair, folds her hands over her lap, and stares at him like she's never seen a man before.

I can't blame her. He's quite something to look at.

"You're a big one, aren't you?"

I turn around now to see what she's seeing. Sure enough, Moses fills the entire doorway to the living room, blocking Norma completely behind him with his body.

He clears his throat, I suspect to choke back a laugh. "Big enough, I reckon. I hear you're having an interesting morning."

"Hmph. Nothing exciting here." She waves a scrawny hand through the air like she's swatting a horsefly. "They're making too much of it, just like always. I'm fine. I've always been fine. I will be fine until the night I kick the bucket in my sleep. The good Lord and I have got a deal, and that's how I'm going out."

Moses isn't afraid of her, and I'm eating it up.

"Far be it from me to interfere with your bargain with the man upstairs," he says, "but don't you think it might be worth it to get checked out? You know, to make sure you can keep your end of the deal?"

She pats her hair, her vanity still as strong as ever. "Who'd you say you were again?"

"Moses. I'm Magnolia's man."

Bernadette's gaze lands on me as she speaks. "You pay her?"

I pray for patience, because I really don't want to go to prison for murdering my great-aunt in the next three minutes.

"No, ma'am. Your great-niece is priceless, if you didn't know."

My heart melts at his words, even though he's just digging his grave with Bernadette.

"You've got a quicksilver tongue, boy. She bring you along to try to talk me into going to the doctor? Thinking a handsome man would change my mind?"

He steps forward, and I feel his hand on the small of my back. *Partners.*

"No, ma'am. She brought me along because I wanted to meet you. You're important to Magnolia, and she's important to me."

Bernadette turns to scowl at me again. "Where'd you find this one? The street corner?"

"No, he saved me fifteen years ago. He's the reason you didn't have to decide whether or not to attend my funeral." It's raw, but it's true.

Bernadette's lips press together in a thin line, and a heavy silence blankets the room while she decides how to reply. "Then I guess I ought to thank the boy." She holds out a hand. "Come over here. I want to see you up close. My vision isn't what it used to be, and there's no way you can be as handsome as you look from over there."

I don't know whether to gasp at her response, laugh, or roll my eyes, but Moses does as she asks, coming toward her chair and crouching in front of her. He takes her hand and lifts it to kiss the back.

"It's a pleasure to meet you, Ms. Maison. How are you feeling today? We got any cause for concern? Because both of these ladies have a right powerful need to make sure you keep on thriving." Moses's Creole accent thickens as he talks to Bernadette, and she eats it up.

"I'm as well as can be expected, given I'm stuck in this chair and can't stretch my legs anymore."

"You seeing double?" Moses asks.

She clamps her mouth shut for a beat before replying. "I was. But it passed. Nothing to write the president about."

"Now, I've never been to medical school, so I don't know much about this kind of thing, ma'am, but it might be worth making an appointment to follow up with your doctor, just to make sure."

I think Norma and I both hold our breath as we wait for her reply.

Bernadette narrows her eyes on Moses. "Where are you from, boy? Who are your people? With that name and your accent, I'd say you're Creole, aren't you?"

He inclines his chin. "I am. My family started out in New Orleans, but I was born in Biloxi and raised by my grand-mère. She was a woman with strong opinions like you."

Bernadette harrumphs. "You've got that right. There's nothing wrong with a matriarch having a strong moral compass. No one knows how hard it is overseeing a family that doesn't want to take direction." At this, Bernadette looks at me. "This one was impossible to control."

Moses rises and puts an arm around my shoulders. "She's got spirit, all right, and that's my favorite thing about her. You raised a hell of a woman . . . pardon my French, Ms. Maison."

Bernadette looks from Moses to me and back again. "Maybe you can finally straighten her out. She's taken the wrong path."

I open my mouth to snap out something, but Moses speaks first.

"I beg to differ. She took a path that led her straight back to me, and I wouldn't change a thing. I'm sure you wouldn't either."

Bernadette doesn't know what to say. Moses put her on the spot, and she's struggling. I can see she wants to contradict him, but she can't get it out.

"She's done right by me. *I guess* I can't argue that."

I can't believe Bernadette doesn't expire on the spot after making the admission, but something I never realized was tangled in my chest suddenly unknots. "And I'll keep doing right by you, Bernie. You took me in when you didn't have to. I'd like to keep you around a while."

Bernadette's gaze cuts to me, and I see something there I haven't seen before . . . maybe ever. *Affection.*

"I'll be around as long as the good Lord bids. Now, I suppose I could make an appointment with the doctor, just to make sure."

"All right. I'll have Norma give him a call," I say, watching Norma nod in the reflection of a mirror across the room.

"Now it's time for my stories. Thank y'all for stopping by."

Moses crouches back down in front of her. "It was a pleasure, Ms. Maison. I look forward to seeing you again."

57
MAGNOLIA

"You worked a goddamned miracle," I tell Moses as Norma shuts the door behind us and we walk down the steps. "I don't know how you did it, but you did." I shake my head, still shocked that Bernadette didn't slice him to ribbons with her sharp tongue.

"What can I say? I've got a way with the . . . what the hell?"

I turn to follow Moses's gaze, which is caught on a fancy stretched black car parked behind his Rolls Royce. As the window rolls down, I see a familiar face.

Mount.

"Get in," he orders before rolling the window up again.

"Fuck," Moses whispers under his breath.

"What the hell does he want?" I ask him, but Moses just shakes his head.

My heart picks up, thudding harder as we walk toward the car, and I don't know why. I calmed my fears about Mount after he and Keira got together, and I know he won't hurt me because she'd kill him.

But still . . . something about this is unsettling.

Moses's posture is rigid as V comes around to open the back door for us. I thank him and slide in first, taking the seat closest to the other side of the vehicle, opposite Mount. Moses takes the seat directly across from him.

"Is Keira okay?" I ask as soon as the door shuts. "Rory?"

"They're fine," Mount replies, and my pulse calms a little. "But Alberto Brandon's wife was found murdered in their home yesterday. Her throat was slit."

Goose bumps rise on my arms. "Jesus Christ." I turn to Moses. "He's the one the FBI was watching the house for."

"I remember." Moses is stiff and still where he sits across from Mount. "Who did it?"

Mount shakes his head. "I don't know, but I heard the police determined that human blood was used to write on Magnolia's condo wall later that same night. Makes a person wonder whose blood it was, and if the same person committed both crimes."

Moses's tone is clipped when he asks, "You having whoever you got inside the department running that down?"

"I've made the suggestion."

Suggestion. Right. He gave an order.

"That means Cavender is going to come knocking again. And he'll try to tie this to me too somehow."

Mount nods. "He's determined to take you out for that murder in your building. You kill the guy?"

"It was self-defense. He tried to stab me, but only sliced my side. Took me by surprise. I was trapped in the elevator. It was me or him, and I picked me." Hearing myself say it out loud, I realize it's the absolute truth. Life is like that sometimes. Kill or be killed.

"As one does." Mount is quiet for a long moment. "Brandon's in the wind. Know any reason why his wife might want you dead bad enough to pay someone to do it?"

My mouth drops open. "You think . . . you think *she* paid a hit man to kill me? I don't even know the woman. I barely know who her husband is."

"A woman scorned is dangerous and unpredictable," Mount says.

"It's not on me if her husband was fucking one of the girls. I don't have shit to do with it anymore."

The king crosses his legs. "Yet you still own the house. Maybe she assumed."

I glance at Moses, who is being uncharacteristically quiet. I ask him, "You think that's possible?"

Moses shrugs. "I don't know. Anything's possible. But we can't ask either of them now. We just gotta find the motherfucker who killed her."

"Good plan." Mount's attention goes back to Moses. "Now, have you told Magnolia everything yet?"

Moses's face goes blank and he exhales, filling the cabin with this strange, thick pressure.

"Told me what?" I ask, something twisting in the pit of my stomach.

Mount shakes his head. "We made a deal, Gaspard. And just like last time . . . you're too damn slow to hold up your end of the bargain."

"I'm working on it," Moses says, and the words sound like he's speaking through gritted teeth. "Let me do this my way, Mount. It's not your concern."

Mount taps his index finger against his lips, moving his gaze between us. "You forget, this is *my city,* and Magnolia's under *my protection.* You don't give me orders. You never did seem to understand that very well."

"What the hell are you two talking about? Tell me what?" I look from Mount to Moses and back again.

Mount stares long and hard at Moses before turning to face me head-on. "That he's been lying to you since the moment you met him, and it's about fucking time he tells you the truth about why he was in your house fifteen years ago to begin with. Because it sure as hell wasn't to save you."

Moses and Magnolia's story continues in *Madam Temptress*, the second book of the Magnolia Duet.

ALSO BY MEGHAN MARCH

MAGNOLIA DUET
Creole Kingpin
Madam Temptress

LEGEND TRILOGY
The Fall of Legend
House of Scarlett
The Fight for Forever

DIRTY MAFIA DUET:
Black Sheep
White Knight

FORGE TRILOGY:
Deal with the Devil
Luck of the Devil
Heart of the Devil

SIN TRILOGY:
Richer Than Sin
Guilty as Sin
Reveling in Sin

MOUNT TRILOGY:
Ruthless King
Defiant Queen

Real Sexy

FLASH BANG SERIES:
Flash Bang
Hard Charger

STANDALONES:
Take Me Back
Bad Judgment

ABOUT THE AUTHOR

Making the jump from corporate lawyer to romance author was a leap of faith that *New York Times*, #1 *Wall Street Journal*, and *USA Today* bestselling author Meghan March will never regret. With over thirty titles published, she has sold millions of books in nearly a dozen languages to fellow romance-lovers around the world. A nomad at heart, she can currently be found in the woods of the Pacific Northwest, living her happily ever after with her real-life alpha hero.

She'd love to hear from you. Connect with her at:

Website:
www.meghanmarch.com
Facebook:
www.facebook.com/MeghanMarchAuthor
Twitter:
www.twitter.com/meghan_march
Instagram:
www.instagram.com/meghanmarch

Made in the USA
Monee, IL
19 July 2020

36757543R00156